MATERIALITY

MATER

IALITY

EDITED BY DANIEL MILLER

DUKE   DURHAM
UNIVERSITY   AND LONDON
PRESS   2005

© 2005 DUKE UNIVERSITY PRESS ALL RIGHTS RESERVED
PRINTED IN THE UNITED STATES OF AMERICA ON ACID-FREE PAPER ∞
DESIGNED BY REBECCA GIMÉNEZ
TYPESET IN MINION AND FUTURA BY KEYSTONE TYPESETTING
LIBRARY OF CONGRESS CATALOGING-IN-PUBLICATION DATA APPEAR
ON THE LAST PRINTED PAGE OF THIS BOOK.

CONTENTS

DANIEL MILLER

Materiality: An Introduction

here is an underlying principle to be found in most of the religions that dominate recorded history. Wisdom has been accredited to those who claim that materiality represents the merely apparent, behind which lies that which is real. Perhaps the most systematic development of this belief arose over two millennia within South Asia. For religions such as Buddhism and Hinduism, theology has been centered upon the critique of materiality. At its simplest Hinduism, for example, rests upon the concept of *maya*, which proclaims the illusory nature of the material world. The aim of life is to transcend the apparently obvious: the stone we stub our toe against, or the body as the core of our sensuous existence. Truth comes from our apprehension that this is mere illusion. Nevertheless, paradoxically, material culture has been of considerable consequence as the means of expressing this conviction. The merely vestigial forms at the center of a temple may be contrasted with the massive gates at the periphery. The faded pastels of an elderly woman are in stark contrast with the bright and sensual colors of the bride precisely in order to express in material form the goal of transcending our attachment to material life.[1]

But the history of South Asia is not just the history of its religions. There is a parallel history, which tells of the endless struggle of cosmology with practice. This is the history of accumulation, taxation, wars and looting, empire and excess. It culminates in the integration of this region within a global political economy in which politics is increasingly subservient to an economics whose premise with respect to materiality could hardly be more different. In economic thought the accumulation of material commodities is itself the source of our extended capacity as humanity.[2] Poverty is defined as the critical limit to our ability to realize ourselves as persons, consequent upon a lack of commodities. The focus upon materiality, though here in the form of accumulation, is therefore just as strong in economics as it is in Hinduism. For a discipline, such as anthropology, that is concerned with what it is to be human, we need to therefore start our discussion of this issue with an acknowledgment that the definition of humanity has often become almost synonymous with the position taken on the question of materiality. Furthermore, this has been a highly normative quest, closely linked to the question of what morality is, in the society or period in question.

Even within the most secular and self-consciously modern systems of belief the issue of materiality remains foundational to most people's stance to the world. The first major secular theory of humanity that seemed capable of dominating the world, Marxism, rested upon a philosophy of praxis, whose foundation also lies in its stance to materiality. Humanity is viewed as the product of its capacity to transform the material world in production, in the mirror of which we create ourselves. Capitalism is condemned above all for interrupting this virtuous cycle by which we create the objects that in turn create our understanding of who we can be. Instead commodities are fetishized and come to oppress those who made them. Contemporary critiques, such as Naomi Klein's (2001) *No Logo*, whether expressed as environmentalism or anti-globalism, may be cruder in their philosophical underpinnings, but seem to be just as focused upon the issue of materiality—for instance a loss of humanity in the face of commodities and brands—as is the neoclassical economics they confront. The centrality of materiality to the way we understand ourselves may equally well emerge from topics as diverse as love[3] or science[4] and associated beliefs such as the epistemology of positivism.

This constant return to the same issue demonstrates why we need to engage with the issue of materiality as far more than a mere footnote or esoteric extra to the study of anthropology. The stance to materiality also remains the driving force behind humanity's attempts to transform the world in order to make it accord with beliefs as to how the world should be.

Hinduism and economics are not just beliefs about the world, but vast institutional forces that try to ensure that people live according to their tenets through priesthoods or through structural adjustment programs. In this respect capitalism and religion are equal and analogous. Chapters in this volume will attest to this foundational relationship between the stance toward materiality and the stance toward humanity through case studies ranging from ancient to contemporary practices and based around topics as diverse as theology, technology, finance, politics, and art.

This introduction will begin with two attempts to theorize materiality: the first, a vulgar theory of mere things as artifacts; the second, a theory that claims to entirely transcend the dualism of subjects and objects. It will then engage with theories associated with Bruno Latour and Alfred Gell that seek to follow a similar path, but with a greater emphasis upon the nature of agency. This is followed by a consideration of materiality and power, including claims to transcend materiality, and a consideration of the relativity of materiality where some things and some people are seen as more material than others, leading finally to an exploration of the plurality of forms of materiality. In turn, three case studies of finance and religion are used to explore the plurality of immateriality and the relationship between materiality and immateriality.

Throughout these discussions two issues emerge which are then considered in their own right. The first is the tendency to reduce all such concerns with materiality through a reification of ourselves, defined variously as the subject, as social relations or as society. In opposition to this social anthropology several chapters critique definitions of humanity as purely social, or indeed as *Homo sapiens*, and critique approaches which view material culture as merely the semiotic representation of some bedrock of social relations. This culminates in a section on the "tyranny of the subject" which seeks to bury society and the subject as the privileged premise for a discipline called Anthropology. Finally in the conclusion we return to a metacommentary upon the whole. It will become evident that we can indeed resolve the dualism of subjects and objects through philosophy. But these "resolutions" are so dependent upon the abstract nature of philosophy that in and of themselves they may be of only limited benefit to anthropology. What anthropology offers, by contrast, is not just philosophical solutions or definitions, but a means to employ these understandings within forms of engagement that yield analytical insight, but which must be realized again and again with respect to each situation, because we live in a changing and varied world of practice.

WHAT IS MATERIALITY?

A volume that spans topics as diverse as cosmology and finance cannot afford to rest upon any simplistic definition of what we mean by the word *material*. It needs to encompass both colloquial and philosophical uses of this term. We may want to refute the very possibility of calling anything immaterial. We may want to refuse a vulgar reduction of materialism to simply the quantity of objects. But we cannot deny that such colloquial uses of the term *materiality* are common. The standard critiques of materialism found in newspapers and everyday discussions take their stand against the apparently endless proliferation of artifacts, what Georg Simmel (1978: 448) termed the "increase in material culture." An anthropological volume devoted to materiality should not ignore this colloquial usage, and I will for this reason, start this investigation with a theory of the most obvious and most mundane expression of what the term *material* might convey—artifacts. But this definition soon breaks down as we move on to consider the large compass of materiality, the ephemeral, the imaginary, the biological, and the theoretical; all that which would have been external to the simple definition of an artifact. So the second theory of materiality to be introduced here will be the most encompassing and will situate material culture within a larger conceptualization of culture.

CAN WE HAVE A THEORY OF THINGS?

Can one have a theory of things where "things" stand for the most evident category of artifacts as both tangible and lasting? Certainly I confess that when I first took up a post as a professional academic in the field of material culture studies in 1981, this seemed to be the limit to the ambition of those studies. At that time I employed two sources in this quest. The first was the book *Frame Analysis*, in which the sociologist Erving Goffman (1975) argued that much of our behavior is cued by expectations which are determined by the frames that constitute the context of action. We don't charge up on stage to rescue an actress in apparent distress, since there are many elements of theater which proclaim this as "enacted" as against "real" violence. We look for signs by which people distance themselves from the social roles they are playing. Are they being ironic, or wanting to be taken "at face value"? We take note, usually unconsciously, of the place in which the action is set, or the clothes they wear, to give us clues. If a lecturer suddenly started a private conversation with a student in the middle of a lecture, everyone would become acutely aware of the underlying norms of lectures as a genre.

My second source was *The Sense of Order* by the art historian E. H. Gombrich (1979). Unlike all his other books, this focused not upon the artwork, but the frame in which the artwork was set. Gombrich argued that when a frame is appropriate we simply don't see it, because it seamlessly conveys to us the appropriate mode by which we should encounter that which it frames. It is mainly when it is inappropriate (a Titian framed in Perspex, a Picasso in baroque gilt) that we are suddenly aware that there is indeed a frame. A more radical version of Gombrich's thesis could argue that art exists only inasmuch as frames such as art galleries or the category of "art" itself ensure that we pay particular respect, or pay particular money, for that which is contained within such frames. It is the frame, rather than any quality independently manifested by the artwork, that elicits the special response we give it as art. Between them, these ideas of Goffman and Gombrich constituted an argument for what I called "the humility of things" (Miller 1987: 85–108). The surprising conclusion is that objects are important not because they are evident and physically constrain or enable, but often precisely because we do not "see" them. The less we are aware of them, the more powerfully they can determine our expectations by setting the scene and ensuring normative behavior, without being open to challenge. They determine what takes place to the extent that we are unconscious of their capacity to do so.

Such a perspective seems properly described as "material culture," since it implies that much of what we are exists not through our consciousness or body, but as an exterior environment that habituates and prompts us. This somewhat unexpected capacity of objects to fade out of focus and remain peripheral to our vision and yet determinant of our behavior and identity had another important result. It helped explain why so many anthropologists looked down upon material culture studies as somehow either trivial or missing the point. The objects had managed to obscure their role and appear inconsequential. At a time when material culture studies had an extremely low status within the discipline, it seemed that objects had been very success-ful in achieving this humility, at least within anthropology.

The work that had established such ideas as foundational to anthropol-ogy, and to my mind still one of the premier publications within anthro-pology, was *Outline of a Theory of Practice*, by Pierre Bourdieu (1977). In this book Bourdieu showed how the same ability of objects to implicitly condi-tion human actors becomes the primary means by which people are so-cialized as social beings. The foundation of these ideas came from Claude Lévi-Strauss, who played Hegel to Bourdieu's Marx, in the sense that Lévi-Strauss demonstrated at an intellectual level how anthropologists needed to abandon the study of entities and consider things only as defined by the relationships that constituted them. But while for Lévi-Strauss this became a rather grand ordering implying, if not a cognitive, at least a largely intellec-tual foundation, with myth as philosophy, Bourdieu turned this into a much more contextualized theory of practice. Structuralism was turned into both a material, and a much more fluid and less deterministic engagement with the world. We are brought up with the expectations characteristic of our particular social group largely through what we learn in our engagement with the relationships found between everyday things. Bourdieu emphasized the categories, orders, and placements of objects—for example, spatial op-positions in the home, or the relationship between agricultural implements and the seasons. Each order was argued to be homologous with other orders such as gender, or social hierarchy, and thus the less tangible was grounded in the more tangible. These became habitual ways of being in the world and in their underlying order emerged as second nature or habitus. This com-bined Marx's emphasis on material practice with the phenomenological insights of figures such as Maurice Merleau-Ponty (1989) into our funda-mental "orientation" to the world.

For Bourdieu, who wore another cap as a theorist of education, it was these practical taxonomies, these orders of everyday life, that stored up the power of social reproduction, since they in effect educated people into the normative orders and expectations of their society. What we now attempt to inculcate in children through explicit pedagogic teaching, based largely in language, had previously been inculcated largely through material culture.

As habitus this became the social equivalent to Kant's system of categories. On analogy with space, time, or mathematics, there exist for each social group certain underlying parameters by which children come to apprehend the world, an order they come to assume and expect in any new set of objects they encounter. So this was a theory of objects, but not as lame, sole, artifacts. Material Culture as a network of homologous orders emerged as the powerful foundation for more or less everything that constitutes a given society. This theory also helps account for the initial observation that even within a religion such as Hinduism, a belief in the ultimate truth as a form of immateriality is still commonly expressed through material forms and practices, such as temple architecture or yogic control over bodies.

What this example hopefully demonstrates is that, yes, it is entirely possible to have a theory of objects as artifacts. Indeed, there are likely to be many of these. A particularly influential example in anthropology was that created by Arjun Appadurai's (1986) book *The Social Life of Things*, in which the editor's introduction in combination with the chapter by Igor Kopytoff (1986) reconsidered objects in respect to a core anthropological dualism between the gift and the commodity. It plotted a trajectory for things in their ability to move in and out of different conditions of identification and alienation. Just as Bourdieu softened and made more applicable the harder structuralism of Lévi-Strauss, Appadurai's work had the virtue of softening the dualistic frame into which this debate about gifts and commodities had become lodged and helping to ease its application to the analysis of exchange and indeed the larger social life of things.

OBJECTIFICATION

As already noted, while it is possible to have theories of things, any such theory seems to ignore the evident lack of any defensible definition of thingness. All may be condemned as "vulgar" because they adopt a commonsense rather than academic presupposition of what we mean by the word *thing*. Is an ephemeral image, a moment in a streaming video, a thing? Or if the image is frozen as a still, is it now a thing? Is a dream, a city, a sensation, a derivative, an ideology, a landscape, a decay, a kiss? I haven't the least idea. But the questions that are left begging indicate that in practice a theory of material culture will tend to stand as a subset of some more general theory of culture. But the term *culture* when put into the spotlight may be at least as problematic as the term *material culture*. Indeed, it is probably the single most criticized concept within contemporary anthropology. It too seems to be best understood as a pragmatic limitation upon some still larger understanding of the world. So the temptation is to start instead from the top, from the most encompassing definition of our object of understanding, and then to work downward.

I would argue that this philosophical encompassment was first achieved through the work of Hegel, and that some of his presumption in seeing his own contribution as constituting "the end of philosophy" was warranted. The system of thought he developed does, at the highest level, resolve many of the major issues of philosophy, including that of materiality. In his *Phenomenology of Spirit*, Hegel (1977) suggests that there can be no fundamental separation between humanity and materiality—that everything that we are and do arises out of the reflection upon ourselves given by the mirror image of the process by which we create form and are created by this same process. Take Bourdieu's (1970) best-known example, the Kabyle house. The house is not some natural emanation. It is created by artisans of greater or lesser skill to become the cultural object within which these same artisans see their own identity as Kabyle reflected and understood. We cannot comprehend anything, including ourselves, except as a form, a body, a category, even a dream. As such forms develop in their sophistication we are able to see more complex possibilities for ourselves in them. As we create law, we understand ourselves as people with rights and limitations. As we create art we may see ourselves as a genius, or as unsophisticated. We cannot know who we are, or become what we are, except by looking in a material mirror, which is the historical world created by those who lived before us. This world confronts us as material culture and continues to evolve through us.

For Hegel this circular process had a particular sequential form: the fundamental process of objectification (Miller 1987: 19–33). Everything that we create has, by virtue of that act, the potential both to appear, and to become, alien to us. We may not recognize our creations as those of history or ourselves. They may take on their own interest and trajectory. A social order, such as a hierarchy, may come to us as immutable and one that situates us as oppressed. It does not appear to have been created by people; it is experienced as sui generis. Even a dream may be attributed to some other agency and literally "haunt" us. But once we appreciate that these things are created in history or in imaginations, we can start to understand the very process which accounts for our own specificity, and this understanding changes us into a new kind of person, one who can potentially act upon that understanding. As Rowlands notes in his contribution, the critical point about a dialectical theory such as objectification is that this is *not* a theory of the mutual constitution of prior forms, such as subjects and objects. It is entirely distinct from any theory of representation. In objectification all we have is a process in time by which the very act of creating form creates consciousness or capacity such as skill and thereby transforms both form and the self-consciousness of that which has consciousness, or the capacity of that which now has skill.

A society may gradually develop a system of education. By going to school a member of that society gains the ability to reproduce accumulated understandings from the generations. As such education may correspond to an element of our "reason," and in *The Philosophy of Right* Hegel (1967) argues that such an educational system corresponds to what may be called "real" education: that is, one that fulfils the reason behind the idea of education, which is to enhance the capacities of those who are educated. A person is created through such a process. It is not that education *happened* to them; we can't separate out the bit of them that is constituted as educated from some other bit that is not (Miller 2001: 176–183).

But every form we produce will tend to its own self-aggrandizement and interests. Education may become institutionalized as a system increasingly geared to its own interests. It may become an oppressive single-sex boarding school whose sadistic staff cripple rather than build the capacity of its pupils. As such it detracts from, rather than expands, who we may be. For Hegel this would no longer be "real" education; rather, it would be a form of alienation. A similar argument may be made for law, religion, art, or indeed any human practice. Law may be the instrument of the justice it is supposed to represent, or it can become merely the self-aggrandizement and income generation of lawyers. Dialectically we both produce and are the products of these historical processes. On the one hand, we produce religion or finance; on the other, the existence of religion and finance produces our specificity as a priest in ancient Egypt, or as a Japanese derivatives trader. So our humanity is not prior to what it creates. What is prior is the process of objectification that gives form and that produces in its wake what appear to us as both autonomous subjects and autonomous objects, which leads us to think in terms of a person using an object or an institution.

So there is a level of philosophy at which it is wrong to talk about subjects and objects. These are merely appearances that we see emerging in the wake of the process of objectification as it proceeds as a historical process. All that can properly be privileged at this philosophical level is the process of objectification itself. As anthropologists, however, we will have at some point to descend from this place of ultimate revelation at the mountain's peak. We will have to return to the mass populations who consider themselves to be, in fact, people using objects. It is important therefore to explicitly map the downward path back to ethnography. I prefer to see this as a series of steps leading to the particular place of material culture that I would wish to reside in. In the philosophy of objectification Hegel provides much more than a theory of culture. His primary concern was with the nature of logic and reason. But a subset of this theory may indeed be used as a theory of culture; those forms that are of interest because they produce the capacities of particular peoples in particular space and time. Simmel and Marx in their different ways strive for a dialectical theory of culture, as indeed have others, such as Jean-Paul Sartre (1976) or, to take a recent example, the human geographer David Harvey (1996). In turn, a theory of material culture may be formulated as a vulgarized subset of such a theory of culture. This brings us back down, with a bump, to a site not far from Bourdieu, who took a parallel but recognizable route. In coming down the mountain we need not jettison that which has been given us. There was a reason for going up there in the first place. We now appreciate that whether we are dealing with mundane artifacts such as clothes or statues, or with more complex images and institutions such as dreams or law, there is nothing without objectification. There are no pre-objectified forms, and any romantic claims by, for example, art, primitivism, psychoanalysis, evolutionary psychology, or others that imply such a possibility can be safely rejected. But dialectical theory is by no means the only source of this experience of transcendence. There are plenty of other people who claim to have invented the wheel that rescues anthropology from the simplistic duality of subjects and objects.

The two most recent influential additions to a potential theory of material culture and materiality come from the work of Bruno Latour and Alfred Gell, and conveniently both focus upon the term *agency*. As several chapters in this volume make clear, Latour is equally concerned with lifting anthropology to a height above that of the conventional distinctions of society and its objects. His primary critique has been aimed at the way this dualism has been expressed in the apparently absolute distinction between science and society. By means of a scholarly investigation into the practice of science, he has been able to demonstrate that it actually bears little relation to its own dominant representation—that the reality of the world consists almost entirely of a hybridity within which it is impossible to disaggregate that which is natural and lawlike and unchangeable and that which is human, interpretive, and at times capricious.[5]

Latour regards us as engaged in a constant and somewhat deluded practice of "purification." In our society science routinely ignores the evidence for the hybrid character of practice, and strives to enhance its own status, by a form of self-representation that renders it unequivocally objective and determined. The corollary of this theorem lies in the degree to which the status of our humanity is enhanced by rendering us cleansed of any such deterministic or mechanistic quality. One of his most influential strategies in the war against purification has been to take the concept of agency, once sacralized as the essential and defining property of persons, and apply this concept to the nonhuman world, whether this be organisms such as bacteria or putative transport systems for Paris. Where material forms have consequences for people that are autonomous from human agency, they may be said to possess the agency that causes these effects. A computer that crashes, and thereby prevents a form from being submitted in time, an illness that kills us, a plant that "refuses" to grow the way we meant it to when we planted it, are the agents behind what subsequently happens. In a partial throwback to structuralism, what matters may often not be the entities themselves, human or otherwise, but rather the network of agents and the relationships between them. "The prime mover of an action becomes a new, distributed, and nested set of practices whose sum may be possible to add up but only if we respect the mediating role of all the actants mobilized in the series" (Latour 1999: 181). People do not fly, nor does a B52 bomber, but the U.S. Air Force does.

To make this point Latour needs to be as firm in his critique of "social" anthropology as in his critique of science. His comments on Émile Durkheim are always to the effect that social science privileges society and regards objects largely as projected representations of society, bracketing culture in opposition to nature. The hybridity that social anthropology recognizes as central to premodern societies is not applied to the analysis of modern societies such as our own, defined as those which fetishize science, nature, and society. He chastises this Durkheimian tradition for missing the profusion of nonhumans and the effects of their agency. By contrast, he emphasizes the agency of this nonhuman world, such as microbes or machines, which cannot be reduced to a mere epiphenomenon of the social.

Latour would never describe himself as a dialectical thinker, perhaps (I am guessing) because of the strident critique of dialectics as "grand narrative" by postmodern French philosophy, or the association of agency with personhood in the existentialism of Jean-Paul Sartre, who viewed himself as a dialectical thinker. So "the Hegelian dialectic, according to Latour, expands the abyss between the poles of subject and object that it aims to fill" (Dosse 1999: 99). This is more or less the exact opposite of what I have just suggested. But I see no merit in a dispute where academics influenced by Latour accuse dialectical thinkers of retaining the dualism of subjects and objects they claim to have transcended, and dialectical thinkers make the same accusation of the followers of Latour. In either case we benefit most from those who have used these philosophical ideals to produce ethnography that demonstrates the gains made by a refusal to reduce to subjects and objects. Much of the beauty of Latour's writing comes when he is carefully tracing through the stages of mediation between these two (e.g., Latour 1999: 24–79). Nevertheless, by placing the emphasis on objects of science, rather than on artifacts, we do lose something of that quality of the artifact redolent with prior historical creativity. It is the artifact which is the focus of habitus and indeed much of recent material culture studies.

Artifacts are also very much to the fore within the other major contribution in recent years to a theory of object agency, that of Gell (1998) in his book *Art and Agency.* Essentially Gell's book is a refutation of an aesthetic theory of art, which is replaced by a theory of the effects that art has achieved as the distributed agency of some subjects upon other subjects. Central to this is a theory of abduction. This is not a theory of causal inference, but rather a theory of inferred intentionality. In short he argues that we naturally tend to imagine there must have been some kind of social agency whenever we encounter an effect. We seem to have a love of imputing agency to other persons and to things. For example, we happily anthropomorphize objects as agents: we may accuse a car of treachery if it breaks down when we need it. Webb Keane (1997) has contributed an entire ethnography based on much the same argument. In Keane's book a cloth does not "tear" merely by accident; someone must have caused this. So we need to attribute the agency that is assumed to lie behind the event. This strikes me as remarkably close to the logic expressed in the newspapers I read everyday. No matter how complex our institutions, no news occurs without the assumption that there must be blame attached, in the form of intentional action. The only difference is that in contemporary journalism we insist the blame must be attached to persons, while other societies would be prepared to blame evil spirits of some kind. So Gell's is a theory of natural anthropomorphism, where our primary reference point is to people and their intentionality behind the world of artifacts. In his final chapter he argues that this provides a theory of the work of art. In effect the creative products of a person or people become their "distributed mind" which turns their agency into their effects, as influences upon the minds of others. I like to think of his book as a prime example of his theory. Tragically, Alfred Gell died before it was published, but the book as an artifact or artwork remains as his distributed mind and continues to create effects that we properly in this case attribute to his wisdom and often his wit.

Gell (1998: 20–21) and Latour (1999: 176–180) have similar discussions of the agency of guns and land mines as against those that fire or plant them, in order to make their points about the centrality of agency. But while Latour is looking for the nonhumans below the level of human agency, Gell is looking through objects to the embedded human agency we infer that they contain. In this sense Gell is closer to the core of recent British social anthropology, which seems to have gravitated around an axis that leads from Durkheim to Marcel Mauss. For Marilyn Strathern (1988) the form of objectification that dominates in Melanesia is that of personification, where it is a person that becomes the object through which people read the prior agency that created them.

To conclude this discussion of the philosophical resolution of materiality I want to suggest its limitations. It seems as though all theorists of materiality are doomed to reinvent a particular philosophical wheel. This wheel consists of the circular process at which level we cannot differentiate either subjects per se or objects per se. There exists therefore in philosophy a "solution" to the problem of materiality, which consists of the dissolution of our "commonsense" dualism in which objects and subjects are viewed as separate and in relationship to each other. This was evidently the conclusion of dialectical theory and was also found in the work of Bruno Latour. An alternative which I have not chosen to discuss here might have been phenomenology. Obviously such philosophical debates never really end, and many of the contributions to this volume may be seen as trying to put various spokes into this philosophical wheel or remove various spokes from that one.

While it is possible to thereby transcend the vulgarity of our dualistic apprehension of the world through engaging with it only at the heightened and abstract levels given us in philosophy, I would argue that this can never fully constitute an anthropological approach to materiality. Anthropology always incorporates an engagement that starts from the opposite position to that of philosophy—a position taken from its empathetic encounter with the least abstracted and most fully engaged practices of the various peoples of the world. In this encounter we come down from the philosophical heights and strive for the very vulgarity that philosophy necessarily eschews. We may often find ourselves conducting research among people for whom "common sense" consists of a clear distinction between subjects and objects, defined by their opposition. They may regard any attempt to transcend this distinction as mystificatory and obfuscating. As part of our own engagement we will necessarily attempt to empathize with these views. Furthermore, we will strive to include within our analysis the social consequences of conceptualizing the world as divided in this way. For example, we might find that those who strive for more abstract resolutions, as in philosophy, tend to denigrate others as deluded, vulgar, or simplistic in their preference for more pragmatic and less abstract perspectives. Philosophy can become simply a tool for describing others as false or stupid.

So our role is one of mediators. First we take these commonsense apprehensions and draw analytical and theoretical conclusions from the particular places they hold in particular worlds. We try to recognize that in a given time and place there will be a link between the practical engagement with materiality and the beliefs or philosophy that emerged at that time. A wonderful example comes from James Davidson's (1998) success in linking the modes of consumption, such as the eating of fish, in fifth-century B.C. Athens, with the rise of certain political and philosophical systems of thought. So having acknowledged this linkage, we mediate between the poles of philosophy and practice. At the same time that we have shown it is possible in philosophy to transcend the dualism of subjects and objects, as anthropologists we need to be aware of whose interests are served by making this claim. As Jürgen Habermas (1972) argued in *Knowledge and Human Interests*, we cannot, in anthropology, separate our stance on the veracity of such representations from our study of the consequences of those representations. Having shown that we can be philosophers, we need the courage to refuse this ambition and return to ethnographic empathy and ordinary language.[6] I will return to this theme at the end of the chapter.

MATERIALITY AND POWER

I began with the observation that the search for immateriality has dominated the engagement between cosmology and materiality. This is demonstrated in the first chapter of this volume. Our continued fascination with ancient Egypt rests in no small measure upon its monumentality. These people were so successful in their obsessive concern with preserving themselves for the afterlife that their remains permeate our own lives. We remain entranced by the trilogy of mummies, statues, and pyramids. What Lynn Meskell forces us to acknowledge is that this encounter immediately implicates two stances toward the nature of materiality itself: that of the people who created these forms, and that of our apprehension of these forms. Through her investigation of the sources Meskell reveals how each of this trilogy of fascinating objects was founded upon a set of beliefs about materiality, including particular philosophical assumptions about preservation, scale, and mimesis. They required an imagination of what precise material form is appropriate for a deity, or for the soul in its afterlife. For the gods, the correct form of statue was actually life-giving. For the living, much of their time on earth could be spent in trying to secure their subsequent preservation through constructing the materiality of the afterlife as mummies. Sheer materiality expressed as one of the great pyramids gave the very sense of "being" a precise shape and form.

Along with Hinduism or Christianity, this cosmology rested upon a belief in the inherent superiority of the immaterial world. But it was the ancient Egyptians' faith in the potential of monumentality to express immateriality that has created their legacy as a material presence in our own world. We continue to be enthralled by statues, mummies, and pyramids because of the very exuberant faith that the Egyptians put into the process of materialization as a means for securing their own immortal transubstantiation. They thereby created among the first monuments to humanity's search for a means to transcend our own materiality. The very scale and temporality of ancient Egypt seems to diminish us as mere individuals in much the same way it was intended to diminish the population that built it. The central paradox continues within modern consumerism, where the pyramid stands both as a symbol of massive consumerism (the pyramid of a Las Vegas casino) and as a key sign (or, as often, key ring) of that New Age spirituality which imagines itself in opposition to this consumerism.

Central to Meskell's analysis is the evidence that through monumentality the divine could be apprehended and both society and nature controlled. The issue of monumentality thereby foregrounds humanity's attempt to control the degrees of materiality. With monuments some things seem more material than others, and their very massivity and gravity becomes their source of power. This point can be generalized well beyond the case of monuments, as demonstrated in the next chapter by Michael Rowlands, for whom the key distinction in materialism must be not between "ready-made" subjects but between relative materiality. That is the degree to which some persons and things may be seen as more material than others. Appropriate metaphors abound: some persons and objects are seen as weighty with gravitas, others are superficial and slight. Some people loom large, even

relative
materiality

when we had rather they didn't. Others, however hard they try to gain our attention, we manage to leave at the periphery of our vision

In his key example, one particular person, the Fon (a chief in Cameroon), and all those objects that are understood to emanate from his presence, have considerable density. Materiality is gained by substances through the process of circulating through his body and presence, so, for example, his spit is itself efficacious in changing the order of things. By contrast, his subjects strive to have a presence as persons, but they simply do not possess the reality granted to the body of the Fon. All other bodies are mere shadows of the one real body. While Meskell indicates the extraordinary gulf between the godlike and ordinary in death, Rowlands draws our attention to the assertion of such distinctions in life.

Rowlands uses the example of the Fon to indicate why, for Marx, the stance to materiality was central to both his philosophy and his politics. Here we are trying to recognize persons' materiality in order to prevent their reification into a subject, a thing purified of objects. But under the lens provided us by Marx this takes on a particular nuance. For Marx, the proletariat under capitalism was reduced to a mere thing, stripped of its personhood. But this was *not* based on a dualist separation—subjects with personhood and objects with materiality. Quite the contrary. For Marx, the dialectical philosopher, the workers lost their humanity precisely because what was denied them was their material being as people who made themselves through their own labor, in their transformation of nature. Under capitalism nature itself was alienated as private property. So in dialectical thought, proper materialism is one that recognizes the irreducible relation of culture, which through production (I would add consumption) creates persons in and through their materiality. Capitalism splits culture and person apart into commodities separated from their intrinsic person-making capacities, and the illusion of pure humanism outside of materiality. For Marx, materialism is an acknowledgment of the consequences of materiality. Owners of private property could, like the Fon, have greater consequences as a result of their extended presence in the material world; those who do not possess property are by comparison rendered insubstantial. Colonialism, for Rowlands, becomes the larger instance of this same point. The colonial powers took upon themselves the ownership of most of the world as property, such that persons and things now existed differentially. Substance re-sided in those or that which possesses what colonialism recognized as form, or quite often literally as "forms" that had to be filled out for one to be "recognized." Some people had access to this acknowledged materiality and thus to themselves; others were alienated from both. They were estranged from their own materiality and thus rendered insubstantial. The implication of Rowland's chapter is that we need to have much greater sensitivity to relative materiality.

This in turn leads us to the central point in the chapter by Fred Myers, which takes us from an insistence upon relative materiality to an emphasis on plural materialities. In Myers's chapter there are at least three different ideological dimensions, each of which would contest this attribution of substance to persons and things. First, there are the ideological under-pinnings of what has become the conventional conceptualization of art. Art is founded in the Kantian aesthetic, which attributes greater material pres-ence to some images than others. While our consciousness (or indeed un-consciousness) can quickly assimilate and dismiss mere ordinary objects, a work of art is said to resist any such easy or quick apprehension. It forces itself upon our attention. This is seen as universal, a property of the image, irrespective of who produced it. An artwork is defined by its density, an opacity we cannot simply gaze through without seeing. Art is the image that returns the investment of our gaze with interest.

But Myers then introduces a second ideology, that which generates the law of private property, which is invoked by concerns over copyright and the rights over images created by Aboriginal artists. Private property introduces a distinct legalistic form which insists that if an object has a relationship to a particular person or corporation, that relationship gives it fixity and solidity. It gives that person or corporation the right to claim the image as an instru-ment in its own self-creation and may deny that right to others. These laws can be used to protect the rights of creators, but only to the degree that the authority and principles that lie behind such a law are accepted. The prob-lem faced by Myers is not that the Aboriginal people do not have a system of aesthetics and law, but precisely—as evident in all Myers's previous work (1986, 2003)—that they do. So the first two ideologies interact with a third. For these painters, some things have always been more material than others. Some have considerable solidity, power, ritual authority, and identity as collective property, while others do not. Among the Aboriginals as in any society, some things matter more than others. So at the heart of Myers's chapter is the potential for conflict between three systems, each of which would hierarchize some images as more material than others. The universality of art, the universality of property law, and the universality of Aboriginal cosmology (what Myers calls the "revelatory system of value"), are all contending for the same field of practice. Power relations may cause a movement from one register, which determines how solid a thing is, to another.

Many approaches to power acknowledge the ways in which certain forms are privileged as categories, or indeed discourses, while others are neglected as detritus. Not for nothing did Foucault choose titles such as *The Order of Things* (2001) and *Archaeology of Knowledge* (2002) for books which documented historical shifts in the way people have thought about materiality and allocated certain orders and objects this or that way accordingly. These juxtapositions are often fortuitous rather than deliberate. Often what anthropologists such as Myers encounter is simply the struggle to make sense of, and establish some kind of consistency between, these different registers of materiality within particular conditions of power. The responsibility of the ethnographer is to document the way these seem to pan out in practice. So the study of material culture often becomes an effective way to understand power, not as some abstraction, but as the mode by which certain forms or people become realized, often at the expense of others. While Rowland's chapter demonstrates how materiality, in general, is relative to power, Myers's chapter complements this by showing how materiality is relative to specific regimes, each of which attempts to command our apprehension of this relative materiality.

At the beginning of this introduction two primary linkages between materiality and humanity were noted. The first is associated with the religious repudiation of mere materiality as a facade that masks reality, and the second with an economics that sees humanity as a capacity that is developed by its possession of commodities. The former leads to the concerns in Rowlands's and Myers's chapters with the plural forms of materiality and their relative degree. But anthropology has also been deeply engaged with the implications of the latter for the study of power. This has arisen partly from its critique of an increase in possessions per se being used as a sufficient measure of welfare. At least since Marshall Sahlins's (1974) essay "The

Original Affluent Society," anthropologists have insisted upon a more rela-
tivistic notion of human welfare. Typically anthropologists insist that it is
not merely the possession of objects that determines well-being but the
capacity for self-creation by a society or individual that is created through
objects' appropriation.[7] A focus upon persons and their capacities could
easily have led from a crude materialism to a crude humanism. Instead
anthropologists and some economists work with a wider sense of capacity.

This perspective can be reincorporated within the more general concern
for power found in the chapters of Rowlands and Myers. It is ethnographic
encounters in Central Australia and the Cameroonian grasslands that demonstrate just why we need to replace simplistic "measures" of welfare. It is
also often when dealing with such development organizations and other
bureaucracies that the contradictions of materiality emerge more clearly.
The ethnographer sees how the agency of persons becomes mostly an expression, rather than a source, of the aesthetics and structures of those
institutions. People in institutions such as bureaucracy appear mostly as the
product of the sheer density and authority constituted by institutionalized
materiality—that is, as subjected to forms, regulations, conventions, and
procedures (e.g., Riles 2001, Miller 2003, but also Rose 1990 and others
influenced by Foucault). It is at this institutional level that the general point
becomes remarkably clear: that power is, among other things, a property of
materiality.

IMMATERIALITY

Kaori O'Connor, a recently completed PhD student of mine, wrote her
thesis (2003) on immaterial culture. Many studies within material culture
reveal the way groups come to understand themselves and become what they
are through their appropriation of goods—for example, the use by sub-
cultures of motorscooters and clothing styles. She argued that the cohort of
baby boomers might have been similarly transformed into a more appropriate identity than merely that of "faded youth" if there had been goods
through which such a self-transformation could have been conducted. But
the appropriate goods do not exist, and therefore they remain baby boomers. Her question was why these goods do not exist. In contrast to most
historical research, her perspective is that of a counterfactual history to

explore immateriality as the absence of material culture. It is not simply a
case of market failure to produce the goods that this group wanted; it is,
rather, the absence of a coming into being of both producers and consumers
through a failure in objectification, which becomes evident only when we
trace through what otherwise might have happened. This is one of several
ways in which immaterial culture as the other side of the coin to materiality
can be productive. Victor Buchli and Gavin Lucas (2001), for example,
consider the premises of archaeology as based on speculation on what materials have not survived and what objects have not been left behind.

A theory of objectification leaves very little space to a concept of the
immaterial, since even to conceptualize is to give form and to create consciousness. At the most we can recognize that people regard some things as
less tangible or more abstract. Nevertheless, as we come down from that
philosophical peak we meet many different dualisms which oppose the
material to the immaterial. To return to my initial example, in Hinduism the
route to immateriality takes many "forms." In India we find a hierarchy from
the mass of small and disparate images of regional spirits and divinities who
have been incorporated into the larger pantheon of Hindu deities. These
deities are in turn often viewed as "avatars," expressive manifestations of the
major deities such as Siva and Vishnu. The major deities in turn are seen by
some as aspects of the one supreme deity. At higher philosophical levels the
idea of a deity is seen as itself a vulgar rendition of a more transcendent sense
of enlightenment for those whose consciousness can achieve such heights.
So one can correctly label Hinduism as polytheistic, monotheistic, and even
atheistic, partly because each is seen as appropriate to the capacity of certain
kinds of people to apprehend the "reality" behind mere materiality. In turn
these different understandings of immateriality become expressed through
material forms. Consider how in Buddhism enlightenment is indicated by
icons ranging from aspects of the Buddha to the impression of his feet. As a
primary example of what Latour (2002) calls Iconoclash, the Taliban destroyed the Buddhas of Bamiyan, but as Jean-Michel Frodon (2002: 221–223)
notes, they thereby in a sense betrayed themselves, because thereby they too
"did politics with images." For this reason Latour (2002) argues for a greater
acknowledgment of the materiality implicit in the technology by which
images are created and destroyed.

If there is an inherent cultural trajectory toward immateriality implicated in most religious belief and practice, then it is not surprising that from time to time we see this trajectory break free to become a dominant imperative of particular religious groups. The chapter by Matthew Engelke concerns a population that seems to exist in large part in order to clarify the logic of this position. The original break between Protestantism and Catholicism contained some fascinating debates about the materiality of religion. Ever since then there have been movements within Protestantism that have tended toward iconoclasm and asceticism as attempts to foreground the importance of immateriality to spirituality. The Masowe apostolics studied by Engelke take this to its logical conclusion in several respects. In Engelke (2004) the importance of repudiating the Bible as a material book is found to be central to this mission toward immateriality. In his chapter we see this extended to their repudiation of the church as a building, and to their preference for objects whose mundane form, such as unexceptional stones picked from the ground, are selected in order to repudiate the symbolic legacy of specific material objects within pre-Christian religious life. Most anthropological analyses seeks to link such communities, even instances of rupture (Sahlins 1985), with the rich or dense symbolic contexts given by their history and cosmology. But this is exactly what these people systematically attempt to repudiate.

Once again the very clarity within this mission toward immateriality brings out the inherent contradiction that follows from the impossibility of ever transcending the process of objectification itself. Just as there is no pre-objectified culture, there is no post-objectified transcendence. So the passion for immateriality puts even greater pressure upon the precise symbolic and efficacious potential of whatever material form remains as the expression of spiritual power. Thus Engelke notes the ambiguity surrounding honey and the temptation to use this lapse of immaterialism as a conduit that as it were brings spiritual power back down to our instrumental earth. The temptation is to turn the honey into something more like the amulets studied by Stanley Tambiah (1984) in Buddhist Thailand, where again asceticism and immaterialism become a resource for capturing spiritual power that can then be transmuted through material forms such as amulets into temporal efficacy.

There is, however, more than one cultural logic leading to immateriality in religion. In Meskell's chapter we have seen monumentality employed as a resource in this regard. In Islam and Judaism there seems to be a sense that the transmateriality of the deity is such that the superficiality of mere human reproduction would be a slight upon them, a failure to properly grasp what they are, reducing them to mere idol as fetish. This produces a radical immateriality which in turn informs Bill Maurer's chapter: Maurer seems to me to be embarking upon an important project which could be termed the study of comparative immateriality. His starting point is that there is more than one reason why form itself might be refused, avoided, or transcended. Set alongside his other recent articles, which focus upon equivalence and upon rhetorical aspects of finance (Maurer 2002, 2003), this chapter, which lays stress on substitutability rather than abstraction and representation, has combined with them to set out an array of such processes. Abstraction, substitutability, equivalence, and rhetoric are all processes that are employed within the larger project of relating the material to the immaterial.

The premise of Maurer's chapter is that we almost always respond to money as a project of abstraction in which the key question is whether money as material form is adequate to its task in representation. We hierarchize the relationship such that money as the more abstract and immaterial seems to look down upon the mere material assets it represents. He argues that this perspective misses the critical point of Islamic finance, where the issue is not one of what he calls adequation, but rather of forms of substitution whose ultimate aim is sometimes theological, not pragmatic. Some were (and are) ultimately much more concerned with ways of objectifying and thus coming to understand the oneness of creation, here reflected in the substitutability of its various elements. Others have far less of a problem with abstraction. As such their theological arguments reflect our current academic arguments, which may turn toward abstraction, or toward alternative logics of immateriality, or toward ways of avoiding such debates altogether.

In the early caliphate a consequence of the replacement of the caliph's head, on coins, by Qur'anic inscriptions is the subordination of the issue of representation in coinage to that of the technologies for the imagination of the divine. The way a coin faces both sides, upwards to the transcendent and downward to functionalism, is utilized to give words themselves (as in calligraphy) a role in objectification. The coin helps the believer to conceive of this Janus-faced relationship, through giving a form to the process of the emptying out of form itself—(compare Coleman 2000 and Keane 1997, 1998 on the word in Protestantism). We are no longer concerned just with whether coins are adequate to their role in representing assets. Rather, if there is an issue of what he calls adequation, it is whether they are capable of capturing the subtlety of these theological debates. Maurer argues that the effect of the new coinage is to bring down the issue of how one understands the deity to the somewhat safer question of how one understands the coinage. At the same time this secures the authority of coinage, since in their attempt to do what Maurer calls "hedging" this issue of divine representation, they thereby "leveraged" their coinage as value by giving it divine authority. Through the removal of the face, the coin is actually "countenanced" by the word.[8]

The implication of this becomes clearer in Maurer's second example of the securitization of Islam. Once again, securitization would seem to us a problem of increasing abstraction. In securitization some lower form of asset, such as the medical fees for hospitals, or the future profit stream from household mortgages, or the risk involved in currency transactions, are reconceptualized as a financial instrument. A trader turns this future profit stream into a "package" that can be traded. At least this is how I would have understood such processes. As such one can see how this could become a problem within Islamic theology, since it might be viewed as representing an entry point for forbidden principles of increase. These higher-level packages might appear to facilitate illicit forms of increase by coming "over the top" of simpler financial instruments, which can more easily be controlled. But for Maurer this is once again to focus upon the wrong end of this particular stick, since for some the concern is not to find theological justifications for secular practice, but to use financial practice as a means to objectify and thus come to understand theology. So securitization is here used as a means to think through analytical issues of substitutability, and its virtue as practice is that it shows how this comes to be done. In both these case studies Maurer reveals how what we reduce to a single trajectory leading to immateriality can be the product of alternative logics or debates about their relative probity. With this chapter and his other publications he has opened up to this pluralism the issue of immateriality. So in the previous section the chapters by Meskell, Rowlands, and Myers demonstrated the variety of different forms of materiality, each with their own consequences for power. In this section Maurer's research on finance acclimatizes us to the idea of plural immaterialities, again each with its own consequences not only for power but also for analysis. By showing how the internal debate within Islamic banking itself questions the logic of representational adequacy for analysis, Maurer also begins a critique that will be taken up later by Keane.

Although Maurer is concerned with the theological concerns that lead to a quite different logic and imagination of immateriality, when considered in terms of the consequences of these logics, these various routes toward immateriality still end up having to contend with the issues raised by their specific materiality. As was the case for Engelke, the greater the emphasis upon immateriality, the more finessed becomes the exploitation of the specificities of the form of materiality by which that immateriality is expressed. The significance of this observation has been clarified by a series of recent ethnographic studies of finance in practice. Caitlin Zaloom (2003) shows that while we talk in terms of a rather general concept of "economic rationality," financial practice may be conditioned by a very immediate set of objects. By comparing screen-based trading to the "pit" of human traders, we find that it is the very specific aspects of these particular materialities, by which numbers appear and are expressed, that actually dominates activity. It is the precise nuance of voice and call in the pit, and the way screens appear and can be read, that becomes the relevant skills. Within global financial trading (see Hasselström 2003) we find a triangle made up of the propensities of the new technologies, the ways people find to exploit their strengths and weaknesses, and the social relations that thereby arise. Several other chapters within Garsten and Wulff (2003) reveal a fourth factor: the discrepancies between the practice of technology and the ideals it was intended to express.

An examination of the precise relationship between materiality and immateriality leads us to Hirokazu Miyazaki's contribution to this volume: a focus upon the material effects of theory. More specifically, he shows how finance seeks out ways of making the materialization of theory productive. Money is made by exploiting a critical relationship between the increasingly immaterial conceptualization of what's being traded and the quasi-material forms by which this is expressed. So, for example, a common contemporary financial practice is arbitrage. This is a technique whereby traders exploit any discrepancy they can identify between an actual price and what a price "should" be. The normative implication of the word *should* is a property of theories about how perfect markets determine proper price. These are theories which, as Maurer (2002), MacKenzie (2001), and others have shown, try to reach up to the highest abstractions of theoretical physics, and which appeal because of their purity. In the unsullied world of pure probability is found the "real" market, which is the source of their models. As in all attempts to adhere to the project of immateriality, the real is equated with that which transcends the merely actual. For these traders the real market is not the sullied version they trade in, but the pure version they model. They import mathematicians and engineers in order to learn finance theory. All of this is fundamental to arbitrage trading, which operates in the momentary discrepancy between the theoretical price given by these models and the actual price. But by identifying and exploiting such discrepancies, it also removes them from the financial system. So it is also a corrective mechanism that makes money at the same time that it makes the market appear to fulfill this ideal about itself: "The act of arbitrage reduces arbitrage opportunities" (Miyazaki 2003: 256). It brings the mere reality of financial practice closer to the perfection of the "real" market, in which there could be no arbitrage because there would be no imperfections to exploit.

Miyazaki stresses the utopianism to these beliefs. Everything in the world ought to accord with this virtualist (as in Miller 1998b) conception arising out of theory. In one respect what Miyazaki describes is instantly recognizable because it is so quintessentially academic. And like most academics, traders hold a strong belief in their disciplinary legitimacy and underlying epistemology. So after the financial crash in Japan, these traders wrote papers defending arbitrage as legitimate market activity. Clearly they did not see themselves as only exploiting the weakness, that is, the materiality of trade. Rather, they saw themselves as exposing that weakness and making it accord with its "real" form, which is its higher immaterial theoretical form. This is why for them the discovery of a discrepancy is just that—a scientific discovery—and their utilization of this discovery ought properly to be "risk free." What the public see as theory or as immaterial for them is the site of reality, the holy grail of the true market. These Japanese traders actually work on fixed salaries; their delight is in the refinement of economic theory backed by the belief that, like science, this work brings the world closer to a higher truth.

What Miyazaki sees as utopianism is no doubt for the traders simply evident in the fabulous productivity of applied financial theory. Finance is a dialectical process of imagination followed by its realization. Key processes in contemporary finance, such as securitization and leverage, start with reconceptualization. Once the initial stage of securitization is secured, the next stage becomes the creation of derivatives. If securitization turns a potential future profit stream into something that can be traded, then a derivative may be formed by trading the risk involved in speculating on what that profit stream will be. A new way of conceiving something as tradable becomes a new form of value. Similarly, in leverage a smaller financial asset is used as a kind of collateral to bring to bear much larger sums, as in buying out a company. In both cases theory can be incredibly productive. In securitization and leverage, trading on them "as though they existed" is sufficient to make them exist. A million units can thereby be traded as a billion units. Well, more, actually. "By June 2000 the total notional amounts of derivatives contracts outstanding worldwide was $108 trillion, the equivalent of $18,000 for every human being on earth" (MacKenzie and Millo 2003). Pryke and Allen (2000) suggest that derivatives may be thought of as a new form of money based on a new conception of incredibly fast space-time, which as Miyazaki argues elsewhere makes arbitrage essentially a sensitivity to a particular form of temporality (2003). Anthropologists should not really have a hard time in understanding such activities, because this dialectic between the development of the immaterial and its dependence upon materiality may be viewed as an expansion of what we have already learned about the potential expansion of space-time in Munn's (1986) analysis of fame or Simmel's (1978) *Philosophy of Money*. Theory here is an example of culture as process, something that expands our space-time. Theory/cosmology creates a kind of super-fame/money that now has materiality, at least sufficient materiality, to be traded. We don't need to understand the more exoteric modeling that produces this effect. We need only see that it can be realized as something we certainly do recognize—loads of money. The subsequent lifestyle of financiers thereby confirms another side to this dialectic: the material productivity of this expanded immaterial or theoretical work.

Maurer's and Miyazaki's observations show why the world of finance is such an integral part of this volume as a whole. Finance is the contemporary version of the same phenomenon that is being tackled by other chapters using mainly historical and religious examples; indeed, Maurer's chapter combines the two. Humanity constantly returns to vast projects devoted to immateriality, whether as religion, as philosophy, or, for Miyazaki, theory as the practice of finance. But all of these rest upon the same paradox: that immateriality can only be expressed through materiality. In each case its theologians, or theorists as financial experts, become intensely skilled in the finessing of this relationship. For them immateriality is power. In arbitrage the theories have the authority of the belief in the market and so the legitimacy to punish/make money out of those who fail to accord with market principles. This is analogous to the way that, during the Protestant Reformation, populations were slaughtered because of debates over whether the bread and wine in communion was actually the body and blood of the Christian messiah. In both cases the assumption was that material practice should always accord with the proper vision of the immaterial, the market/ the divine, which was its source of authority. The reason it is useful to bracket the chapter by Engelke with those on finance is that both attest to what happens when groups such as Masowe apostolics or institutions such as derivatives traders are committed to following through this logic of immateriality with its consequences for residual materiality.

So we approach a kind of general rule: the more humanity reaches toward the conceptualization of the immaterial, the more important the specific form of its materialization. This is appropriate to a wide range of other areas. Modern art depends on a very similar strategy. The more esoteric the conceptualized, the more value its performance. The more we come to believe that art is actually transcendent, the more its material form is worth in dollars. Similarly in the field of religion, the more we feel the deity is beyond our comprehension and representation, the more valuable the medium of our objectification, whether sacrifice or prayer. Religions such as Islam and Judaism, which are stridently resistant to representation, become stridently legalistic about practice. In all such cases, what makes materiality so important is very often the systematic cultivation of immateriality.[9] Humanity proceeds as though the most effective means to create value is that of immateriality.

This conclusion begs (at least) three further questions. The first is that since these are dialectical processes they are always subject to potential reification, what I would call "virtualism" (see Miller 1998b).[10] Indeed, for the skeptic they amount to nothing more than evidence for actual reification. They claim to reveal reality, but actually mask it. This is the way the secular sees all religion; the way the "philistine" regards the cult of modern art; and the way most of us regard, not just stock market bubbles such as the dot.com fiasco (Cassidy 2002), but quite possibly (following Marx and to an extent Keynes) the whole phenomenon of the stock market. The second issue, which is the subject of the next section, is the relationship between these levels of representation as theorized in semiotics. The third issue, which is the subject of the final section of this introduction, focuses upon the single most privileged moment in this allocation of relative materiality: the assumption that objects represent people, or what I will refer to as the *tyranny of the subject*.

WHY THE CLOTHES HAVE NO EMPEROR

Having debated the pluralism of materiality and the pluralism of immateriality, we find, not surprisingly, that there is also a plurality to their relationship. One example of the relationship between materiality and immateriality is evident in a common technique of representation: we often assume that a material form makes manifest some underlying presence which accounts for that which is apparent. The classic anthropological portrait is of the shaman, an individual who, faced with a body suffering from illness or witchcraft, finds an object such as a stone and draws it out, thereby making the cause of the affliction manifest. The appearance of the object demonstrates that which must have been responsible for its existence. There are echoes of this in Strathern's (1988) analysis of Melanesian society. Strathern argued that in Melanesia persons are the manifestation of a prior cause, their presence gives account of what must have taken place for them to be the consequence. As objects they make manifest what otherwise might be hidden or obscure.

Not surprisingly, there are equivalents within our own society. Psychoanalysts often take a problematic symptom, such as a debilitating or compulsive habit, to be evidence for some underlying cause that has so far remained hidden. The process of analysis brings forth language as a complementary manifestation. This has the merit, when revealed by the analyst, of providing a fuller account of the hidden cause. So a "proper" manifestation replaces an improper one. In what is probably the fastest-growing religion of our time, Pentecostalism, the externalization of "The Word" is the evidence for the proper and prior internalization of God's word (Coleman 2000: 171). So for a wide spectrum of cultural practices, from shamanistic healing and psychoanalysis to Melanesian religion and Pentecostalism, making manifest is itself the practice of explanation which becomes tantamount to cure or to being saved.

Another cultural logic that connects materiality and immateriality has emerged in recent work on the concept of fetishism. This explores how societies try to police the boundaries between where and when materiality should be manifest (see Spyer 1998). As Keane (1998) noted, colonial authorities saw fetishism as implicit in tribal people's respect for the autonomy of things, analogous to a sense of objects having "agency" in the contemporary theories of Gell and Latour. But to call indigenous peoples fetishists was to claim that these were misunderstandings, certainly not to regard them as philosophers blessed by a better appreciation of the agency of things. Foster (1998) notes the colonial authorities' desire to represent the use of money as body decoration by New Guinea highlanders as a kind of naive misunderstanding of what money properly "is." Similarly, there is our own sense of threat when derivatives traders seem too far removed from recognizable assets, or when we read how Islam creates banks with different principles of interest and accumulation. These all seem to threaten accepted conventions about what is the sign and what is the signified. We want to regard other people's delineation of the materiality and capacity of money, not as different, but as wrong (Maurer 2003). This leads us in turn to a more general consideration of semiotics, and also to a greater concern with the moral dimension that seems to constantly permeate these assumptions about what is sign and what is signified. We can discern a consistency in these discussions, a desire to protect one particular signified, which is ourselves. It is as though the proper hierarchy of representation needs to be maintained as a semiotic dualism: on the one hand, the material sign that gains autonomy as mere representation; on the other, the human signified that gains authenticity to the degree that it transcends the paltry attempts by objects to signify it.

These issues are brought out with particular clarity by the contributions of Webb Keane and Susanne Küchler. Both of them recognize the underlying problem within semiotics itself and the assumptions behind continuing to privilege ourselves as the subject. Fortunately both of them discuss this issue with respect to the same intimate relationship: the one between ourselves and our clothing. Without Keane's contribution the edifice of argument being constructed by this volume could not be maintained, because he speaks directly to this issue of implied systems and levels of representation. We cannot escape the dominant relationship between immateriality and materiality being understood as one of representation, where we tend to speak of coins and statues as signs or tokens. But if our very understanding of the nature of representation is such that it privileges the immaterial, it is that much harder to give respect to the nature of human action and history as merely material culture. Fortunately, Maurer's chapter has already demonstrated the parochial nature of our treatment of representation, by showing how in Islamic finance there are very different ways in which this relationship is seen—not as a hierarchy based upon abstraction but more as an alliance between the material and immaterial as means to conceptualize the divine. In a very different but parallel argument Keane suggests it is entirely possible to construct a theory of signification in which materiality is integral, not subservient. Following Charles Sanders Peirce he constructs an approach to the sign that takes the tangible and sensual aspect of our engagement with the world and respects its evident centrality to the way we think and practice in the world. He acknowledges the role of materiality in causation whether or not we notice its effects. Often this consists of the copresence of qualities, that happen to go together in a particular object, like lightness and wood in a canoe, or of what is taken to be a significant resemblance between things. We subsequently have to come to terms with convention, which orients us toward some things and some resemblances and not others, constraining and inviting possible ways of acting. Finally his chapter speaks to the essential historicity of interpretation, which takes its orientation from the past and creates a propensity toward the future, often acting through expectation and modes of acceptance. Within this it is what Keane calls the openness of things, which makes them so proficient to guiding our futures. So signs cannot be considered immaterial representations of a lower material presence. Rather, they are themselves what he calls the semiotic ideologies that guide practice.

To appreciate the significance of these rather abstract ideas, it is worth reflecting upon that common story about the emperor who has no clothes, because in many respects the gist of Keane's argument is that we also need to finally acknowledge that the clothes have no emperor. We assume that to study texture and cloth is by default to study symbols, representations, and surfaces of society and subjects. In an older social anthropology, clothes are commonly signs of social relations. Anything else would be a fetishism of them as objects. But as he shows, if you strip away the clothing, you find no such "thing" as society or social relations lurking inside. The clothing did not stand for the person; rather, there was an integral phenomenon which was the clothing/person. This same point is then generalized into a critique of what he sees as a misguided rendition of semiotics itself. Just as clothes are not a cover for subjects or society, the "sign" is not necessarily a vicarious representative of society. In one blow we eliminate not just the emperor but also our status as mere "subjects." The reason is simple. These material forms constituted and were not just superficial cover for that which they created, in part through their enclosing and giving shape. The subject is the product of the same act of objectification that creates the clothing. A woman who habitually wears saris as compared to one who wears Western clothing or a *shalwar kamiz* is not just a person wearing a sari, because the dynamism and demands of the sari may transform everything from the manner in which she encounters other people to her sense of what it is to be modern or rational (Banerjee and Miller 2003). Social relations exist in and through our material worlds that often act in entirely unexpected ways that cannot be traced back to some clear sense of will or intention.

Different people have an extraordinary power to delineate surface and substance differently. I was brought up with a concept of superficiality that denigrates surfaces as against a greater reality. I was taught that "the real person" was supposed to lie deep within oneself. It is a very common mode of denigration to call something or someone "superficial" (though see Wigley 1995). But as Strathern (1979) argued for Mount Hagen (see also O'Hanlon 1989) and I have argued for Trinidad (1995), other people simply don't see the world this way. They may regard the reality of the person as on the surface where it can be seen and kept "honest" because it is where the person is revealed. By contrast, our depth ontology is viewed as false, since for them it is obvious that deep inside is the place of deception. There are many versions of this cosmology of depth and surface. The Aztecs (Moctezume and Olguin 2002) removed the surfaces of bodies by flaying their victims and gave priests these skins to wear as clothing. One person's skin became another person's . . . skin, expressing mutability in what we deem immutable.

The power of Küchler's contribution lies in the depth of the wound that she strikes against the apparent unassailability of conventional humanism. Her target is not the superficial materiality of the body and person, but that which is usually held as transcending this—that is, thought itself. She strikes at the self-definition of *Homo sapiens* as sentient, as the thinking being. It is not surprising, therefore, that having made her strike deep inside the head, she claims to have landed a mortal blow. Like Keane, she shows that once the emperor humanity lays slain, we can welcome a more modest, but more genuine representation of our humanity—one that respects rather than denies the materiality of thought. She argues that the significance of new intelligent fabrics, ones that appear in some sense to be able to "think" for themselves and start to take responsibility for their actions and responses, is that in their light we can see how many precursors already existed with these attributes. Küchler examines clothing that has inscribed upon its surface forms that are simultaneously the sign of what they can do and the means to do it. As such she confirms precisely Keane's point about transcending any simple representational form of semiotic.

More than this, Küchler forces us to confront not just ordinary thinking of the kind we might undertake in day-to-day calculations but also the pretensions of the most esoteric forms of thinking: the previously introduced mutual relationship between high art and high mathematics. In, for example, drawing or modeling a Klein bottle we can give form and give mathematical substance to an idea that is otherwise quite difficult to conceive of—something that has neither an end nor a beginning. Not even mathematics can ever transcend the process of objectification which allows it, quite literally, to think and thereby to be. So for Küchler mathematics is as much a product of art as art is the product of mathematics. Both are forms of thought in their concrete aspects, which is essential to all forms of thought. Once again their quest for immateriality exacerbates the importance of their materiality. Curiously, in her chapter, clarity of mind turns out to derive from being tied up in knots, knots which speak to the tactile nature of connection and relation, as well as their necessarily formulaic propensities. For Küchler it thereby makes sense to think in terms of the sapient tool as well as *Homo sapiens*. Between them, Keane and Küchler—through their emphasis on clothing, in particular—make sure that we do not allow a proper consideration of the body and the mind to become a return to the privileging of the purified subject. On the contrary, both body and mind are seen are routes that lead us to the same conclusions as these other studies, because among other things our concern with their materiality both internally, as with mind, and externally, as with the clothed body, forces us to acknowledge the centrality of materiality itself to the constitution of humanity.

Keane and Küchler prepare us for the larger realization of the extent to which, as Nigel Thrift puts it, we have accepted approaches that are falsely "predicated on stable conceptions of what it is to be human and material." We need to recognize not only the significance of new developments that Thrift then documents in the very possibilities of what it is to be material in the future; equally, as Mauss helped us to understand, we need to be reminded of the very different understandings other peoples may have of this centrality of materiality to the sense of what it is to be human in the past. Having dethroned the emperors, we are in a position to give credence to the increasing impact of sapient materiality (while acknowledging that objects are as plebeian as we are—they are not alternative emperors). This is precisely the purpose of Thrift's chapter. His chapter follows neatly upon that of Küchler in helping us think through the very concept of sapient objects. He indicates this through a return to a forgotten contribution by the psychophysicists. Their theories as to the impact of screens brings us back to a time when it was regarded as much more obvious and pertinent that both consciousness and cognition were bound to the specifics of materiality rather than defined by their opposition to the material world. The specifics of screens matter—a point we have met earlier in the consideration of finance (Zaloom 2003). If psychophysics was concerned with the anticipatory nature of consciousness, then Thrift's next example, that of software, is concerned with the anticipatory nature of materiality. For software to work properly it has, in effect, to become the material anticipation of its users. Software, for Thrift, is important, as are clothes for Küchler and Keane, in that it does not mesh with our dominant academic concerns over representation. Material forms such as screens and software are best understood as mediating in our lives through becoming a kind of personal infrastructure. This is quite different from the more simplistic ideas of representation that Keane has also just critiqued. This is why, as Thrift shows, they are often apprehended with analogies and metaphors that are more fundamental and increasingly taken from biology.

Thrift weaves back and forth between the present and the philosophical discussions that generally accompany the first appearance of some new surface as people try to envisage its future consequences. There seems to be an almost standard sequence. First the material innovation is subject to heated debate, which often makes wild claims of technological determinism and how our essential humanity has now changed forever. Then typically there seems to be a long period of relative lack of regard and theory as the new forms become naturalized into the taken-for-granted background to our lived experience. Only later do we seem able to once again detach ourselves from our own acceptance of this new world to reinvent these explicit discussions about the consequences of technologies, as more modest acknowledgments of what this subject or object has subsequently become. Perhaps this is consistent with Thrift's emphasis upon a phenomenological concern with the sensuous nature of these material mediations, their visceral character as becoming ingrained into our feel of the world both as the world and as our apprehension of it, all of which creates what he calls the lyrical and wondrous form of intelligibility today. Thrift shows how phenomenology needs to look forward as much as backward. A twenty-year-old Londoner with a devotion to makeup, techno music, and multiple orgasms is probably rather more in touch with the world through her body than was your average Scandinavian peasant chopping logs. We gain nothing from that form of phenomenology that continues to romanticize a diluted conception of *Heimat* as the only authentic relationship to the world (Ingold 2000, see also Gell 1995).

Thrift ends on larger issues that speak to our capacity to envisage futures. His theme, starting with psychophysics, concerns our ability to predict and apprehend changes in stimuli. His chapter can be read as an attempt to do the same thing intellectually. For example, I believe the fact that I had to read *Brave New World* at school could be seen as a kind of "inoculation" that helps prepare me for the possible advent of what Thrift predicts as a brave new body of the future. Ideally his chapter help us to steer a course for that future politics of the sensory which Thrift regards as essential.

The chapters by Keane, Küchler, and Thrift have cut down the pretensions of both the somatic and the cognitive as constituting a humanity defined in opposition to materiality. They have thereby hammered in what should be the last nails in the coffin whose contents I now propose to consider. Who or what is it exactly that we propose to inter? It is perhaps the most fundamental burial that a discipline called Anthropology could ever contemplate, and one that has considerable implications for our understanding of what the discipline has been and could be. Although I concede that things never were quite this simple, for a moment let us reduce the foundations of contemporary social science to one particular set of ideas: Durkheim's *Elementary Forms of Religious Life*.[11] The possibility of modern anthropology was at the least secured with the radical secularism that viewed religion as the emanation of the social collective. At the same moment that Durkheim desacralized religion, he sacralized the social. The social sciences become devoted to the study of all phenomena that stand for what we now call society, social relations, or indeed simply the subject. By whichever name, these are the terms that describe the contents of the coffin we are about to bury.

In a recent volume Adam Kuper (1999) castigated American anthropology for its reification of the term *culture*. What he entirely missed was the degree to which a parallel tendency to reification exists within British social anthropology, but around the twin terms *society* and *social relations*, which are just as subject to reification as is the term *culture* in the United States. Even in the heydey of 1970s structuralist and Marxist approaches to anthropology, writers such as Mary Douglas (1978) insisted that structural analysis must always return to its vicarious role as the order of signs that stand for social relations, and even Althusserian modes of production were seen as only properly grounded in these same "social relations." This may well explain why, as discussed earlier on, Gell (1998), working within this tradition, permits agency for objects only as a matter of inference not as an inherent property of objects themselves.[12] It is not surprising, then, that Durkheim stands as the bête noire of Latourian science studies, a bastion of the dualism he wants to confront, or that Strathern excavates the reification of both society and culture implicit in the concept of "context" (see also Dilley 1999), or that Ian Hacking (1999) targets its philosophical foundations in his recent *The Social Construction of What?* In this volume we are concerned with the rites of burial of the subject, and its consequences, but plenty of others have already had a hand in the death. Indeed, the term *culture*, where this means the anthropological study of the normative (rather than a classification of people), could be said to be less naturalized or apparently neutral. We are rather more readily aware that we have constructed culture than that we are dealing with a constructed subject or society.

We can hardly be surprised that a discipline called anthropology for so long encouraged the social subject to retain a reified position to which all else should be reduced. Behind this may lie an assumption that our ethical stance to the world depends upon retaining some fundamental allegiance to ourselves and our essential humanism. Yet just as the secular believe that the dethronement of the previous essential guarantor of morality—that is, the deity—released, rather than suppressed, the development of a modern ethical sensibility, so also it could be argued that the dethronement of humanity, or "social relations," can be the premise for the further development of modern ethics, not its dissolution.[13] So if the first revolution consisted of Durkheim enthroning society in the stead of religion, we now look to gain maturity by burying the corpse of our imperial majesty: society. In both cases revolutionary action is premised on a refusal to have our morality gilt-edged by an emperor.

But then who or what climbs up upon the now empty pedestal? It is essential that the pedestal remains empty. As Keane shows, the clothes should have no emperor—no emperor society, no emperor culture, no emperor identity, no emperor the subject, and certainly no emperor the object. There could be candidates who would like to seize this throne. For example, some postfeminist vision of a New Age "Gaia," even less sullied by materialism, a vision of earth mother as "super(ior)-man," that heals without conventional medicine, cures poverty without industrial agriculture, and communicates pure thoughts of caring motherhood. But the future is no more the female subject than the male subject: the future lies in human modesty about being human. Upon abdication of this throne we can lower our sights and face up to that which created us—that is, the processes of objectification that create our sense of ourselves as subjects and the institutions that constitute society but which are always appropriations of the materiality by which they are constituted. Ultimately, as argued at the beginning of this chapter, the concepts of subject and object are always failures to acknowledge this process of objectification.

The idea is not to swing the pendulum too far toward materiality either. It would be easy to conflate Thrift's discussion of screens and software into a return to some kind of technological determinacy, but only by ignoring the much larger picture. Rather, I think what Thrift documents is a return to the centrality of materiality that anthropologists have encountered in most societies, but in the form of canoes, landscapes, or cultivation. Technology does have an impact, Thrift is indeed asserting that new materialities such as screens and software have consequences, sometimes unprecedented consequences, because they are unprecedented materials, but these consequences are as much a product of our history of self-regard, now viewed as part of the history of our materiality. Thrift's discussion of software can be compared with Strathern (1990) on artifacts. *Unprecedented* does not mean *unanticipated*, and software in many respects merely makes explicit a common property of artifacts as forming our anticipatory infrastructure. Having dethroned the emperor's culture, society, and representation, there is no virtue in enthroning objects and materialism in their place. The goal of this revolution is to promote equality, a dialectical republic in which persons and things exist in mutual self-construction and respect for their mutual origin and mutual dependency.

Sociology and anthropology have usually been strongest and most effective when the emphasis has been on what makes people rather than what people make: on the frames rather than what's inside them. Consider Goffman's various essays on how roles as the identity of persons are constituted by institutions or Bourdieu on socialization through the practical taxonomies of everyday things. One of the reasons anthropology still needs to return to writings such as Bourdieu to make this point rather than only to, for example, Latour's is that we need our ethnographies to focus upon how precisely our sense of ourselves as subjects is created. Bourdieu's sensitivity to the process of socialization becomes a vital piece in this jigsaw. It is not just that objects can be agents; it is that practices and their relationships create the appearance of both subjects and objects through the dialectics of objectification, and we need to be able to document how people internalize and then externalize the normative. In short, we need to show how the things that people make, make people.

It is perhaps worth ending this section with an illustration that can help address the obvious question. What does an anthropology that does not privilege social relations as the core to our own authenticity actually look like? In my previous work on modernity in Trinidad (Miller 1994), I argued that the best way to understand kinship in Trinidad was through seeing the way kinship was used to express certain key systems of value that had emerged through a historical process that started with slavery and was now increasingly directed toward the issue of being modern. But I then argued that after the oil boom Trinidadians started to put increasing emphasis upon the more flexible possibilities of mass consumption goods such as cars and clothing, rather than kinship, as a means to express these contradictions in value. So, for example, the kinds of freedom that were previously expressed by an antipathy to marriage, which was seen as leading to relationships being "taken for granted," were now being expressed through a very intense relationship to cars as vehicles for achieving freedom.

Now the obvious reaction to such a trajectory is to see people as losing their authentic sociality as they become more obsessed with material things. But this is to miss certain major advantages of such a shift. It was not just kinship that was used to express values in the absence of consumer goods; ethnicity, class, and age were used too. As a result, individual persons had previously been very commonly judged as tokens that embodied those particular values. There was abundant discussion on how "Indians" are mean, or engage in violent disputes over inheritance, or how "men" tend to be feckless and unreliable. All such stereotyping derives from the use of social relations and distinctions as a medium for expressing values. As consumer goods started to take over more of the burden for objectifying and thus creating the way values were visualized and understood, there was less of a tendency to use people as, in effect, the objects for objectifying such values. To indicate transience one referred to the unreliability of car parts rather than the unreliability of women. In short, anthropologists tend to forget what might be called the downside of the Maussian equation: that in a society where objects are reduced to their personlike qualities, people also tend to be reduced to their objectlike qualities, as vehicles for the expression of values.[14] The work of ethnography is to reveal these reductive processes.

All of this argument for a resolution, or republic of mutual respect, between what colloquially are thought of as objects and subjects may appear rather too neat —which is precisely the point of the final chapter in this collection, that by Christopher Pinney. It seems to me to entirely befit a dialectical perspective that we end with a chapter, part of whose purpose is to negate this introduction through critique. It is a critique whose principal contention is that this introduction simply does not go far enough. It is clear that Pinney agrees very strongly with the importance of removing the tyranny of the subject. His chapter is in part an assault on what he sees as a continuing tendency to reduce objects to their "social lives," or the contexts of social relations. Pinney gives full blessing to the Latourian refusal of purification in terms of subjects and objects. He strengthens the case by his excavation of the implicit contextualizations found in the form of temporality that underlies most narrative history. History, he argues, makes assumptions that mere contemporaneity is enough to reduce materiality to its position as a representation of its time and, by extension, its social context. His critique of temporality is analogous to Keane's critique of semiotics. Both materiality and immateriality do more than simply stand as representations of the social. While the focus of this volume has been on the implications of this observation for anthropology, it may well be, as Pinney suggests, that this critique is even more pertinent when directed against the tradition of historical studies, with its reliance upon a simple notion of events in sequence. Pinney is trying to move us away from our assumption that images simply exist within a given sequence of time, to a sense that images by their very materiality, for example recursive nature, may contain within them their own relative temporality (compare Gell 1992).

Where he parts company from my arguments is the conclusion that he draws from this intransigent aspect of the image, which is argued to derive from its multiple temporalities. I suspect we are trading here in implied accusations of romanticism. Pinney sees my emphasis upon resolution and the smoothly turning wheel as a reflection of the romanticism that comes out of the German romantic tradition that strongly influenced Hegel. I would throw this accusation straight back into Pinney's court. Pinney wants to see more jolts and dislocations in the wheel, but I suspect that the philosophers and cultural theorists he cites want to read into images their own romantic ideal of the image or art object as a work of resistance. What is termed figural excess or "radical exteriority" becomes celebrated, precisely as radical. Such theorists as Theodor Adorno and Georges Bataille and Jean-

François Lyotard had an abiding horror of the merely mundane, and they project a radical potential upon the significant image. They celebrate, as does Pinney, the disruptive quality that can put spokes into smoothly turning wheels. But what fascinates me is quite the opposite. I am drawn to the ethnographic experience of the mundane, to the constant encounter with juxtapositions in people's lives which, for cultural theorists, ought to be incommensurable and contradictory, yet appear to be lived with and through, accompanied by little more than a shrug of the shoulders. Perhaps things "shouldn't" be this smooth. Most ethnography no doubt appears as terribly irritating or even infuriating for such cultural theorists and their attendant artists, but notwithstanding their protests, I contend that for the most part, from the perspective of ethnographic observation, that old wheel just keeps on turning.

CONCLUSION

This volume is intended to contribute to three interrelated projects. The first is to acknowledge the central role played in history by the desire to transcend and repudiate materiality. The second is to consider the consequence of acknowledging this fact and subsequently accepting materiality and to go on to explore the nuances, relativism, and plural nature of both materiality and immateriality. The third is to follow through the most radical of these implications, which leads us to repudiate the privilege accorded to a humanity defined by its opposition to materiality as pure subject or social relations. In addition to these three projects, this introduction has proposed a kind of meta-commentary upon them all. It has been suggested that in order to carry out these projects we are likely to embrace various forms of philosophical resolution to the problematic dualism between persons and things. While this resort to philosophy is essential to our academic purpose, the integrity of anthropology demands another commitment: a promise to betray such philosophical resolutions and return us to the messy terrain of ethnography.

Meskell has provided this volume with its ideal first chapter. Her case study establishes some basic parameters for the whole. The remains of ancient Egypt present us in spectacular form with the initial paradox that the whole volume must contend with: that throughout history there have arisen systems of belief that are founded upon a fundamental desire to define humanity through the transcendence of the merely material and to relocate us within a divine realm which alone is understood as "real." Yet in many cases the way this sense of immateriality has had to be expressed is precisely through the efflorescence of the material. Her sensitive analysis of the theologies of practice implicit in these remains are then linked to the degree to which we still today use "pyramids" both to express the monumentality of commodification in Las Vegas and our increasingly desperate appeals to some transcendent New Age spirituality that defines us against the material.

The chapters that follow reveal increasingly complex and nuanced logics by which these contradictions have played themselves out. Rowlands and Myers start to construct an anthropology of the relativism and then the plurality of materiality. A case study in the field of finance by Maurer and Miyazaki, in conjunction with Engelke on apostolic repudiations, constitutes an anthropology of the relativism and pluralism of immateriality. Together they present some of the cultural logics that arise from these pluralisms and also the relationship between materiality and immateriality. Whether we are considering Aboriginal artworks or financial instruments such as arbitrage, it is extraordinary to observe just how much of what actually takes place is based on the creative exploitation of the material expressions of the immaterial ideal.

By exposing the necessity of the material, these chapters lead us to some of the fundamental issues at stake in confronting the underlying contradictions of materiality and immateriality. Above all they reveal a core, or kernel, to these entanglements. As Keane, Küchler, and Thrift reveal, we are not just clothed; rather, we are constituted by our clothing. Getting tied up in knots by the very idea of intelligent fabrics, or Peircian semiotics, or an anticipatory carapace, is precisely where we should seek to be: at the place where we confront the materiality of our own intelligence. At this stage we are doing precisely what has been so uncharacteristic of the approaches to materiality documented here. Our aim is to consider materiality directly, not vicariously through the quest for immateriality. But as these chapters have shown, this has important consequences, since it forces us to face up to the very reason why this quest for the immaterial is so driven. To acknowledge materiality amounts to a refusal to retain that reification of ourselves which has sustained anthropology since its inception as the very point (both purpose and pinnacle) of this discipline.

The intention is to create conditions for a mature anthropology that will also provide the impetus to tackle areas where these issues of materiality continue to dominate. If historically it was religion that constituted the most consequential arena of debate, today it is probably economics. As the chapters by Maurer and Miyazaki reveal (and in a different way also that of Myers), anthropology lies in pole position to lead an assault upon an economics where, as Miyazaki suggests, its practice is its precept. Lévi-Strauss stressed the materiality of philosophy for "tribal" peoples; his heirs today recognize that finance is equally "tribal" in that it does philosophy through the construction of its own mythic realm, which is its own field of practice. Such an anthropology can freely reengage with a world dominated by mass consumption, poverty, and economics without seeing these merely as the forms of diminished sociality.

This is precisely why we cannot follow this trajectory without also taking into account a final project, a meta-commentary upon the others. We recognize that we can indeed resolve many of the issues at stake here, but at some cost. As was stated early on, all approaches to the problem of materiality are to some extent inventing and reinventing the same wheel. One can follow the writings of Latour, or one can take up a dialectical position, or one can translate the legacy of phenomenology. All of these will make claims to have finally and fully transcended the dualism of subjects and objects. At the level of philosophical discourse this claim seems tenable. Instead of a dualism, we have an endlessly turning process that spins off what, at a lower level, takes on the appearance of more vulgar forms—that is, things and persons. So it should now be apparent what was meant by characterizing these chapters as busily putting spokes into (e.g., Pinney) and taking spokes out of (e.g., Küchler) this philosophical wheel.

But a wheel, however finely crafted, is not in and of itself a vehicle. To take us anywhere, a wheel must be hitched to some mechanism that does more than just turn in circles. We achieve a philosophical resolution only if we forget the vehicle and its journey and contemplate the turning wheel as an autonomous force. To conduct anthropology we need to hitch the wheel back to a vehicle that returns us to the muddy paths of diverse humanity. Philosophy is therefore not (I hope) what anthropologists want to do; rather, it is our insurance policy against doing badly what we do want to do. A focus on the particular in ethnography sometimes obscures the larger horizons which help us assess wider reasons and consequences of that ethnographic experience. Anthropology in its own practice returns us to the practice of others, to an ethnographic engagement with people who generally think of themselves these days as subjects, living in societies, having culture(s), and employing a variety of objects whose unproblematic materiality is taken for granted. Not always. Every chapter in this volume has documented instances where the issue of materiality is problematic for those being studied as much as for those writing about them. In almost every case we have encountered philosophical engagements with this issue as something practiced or implicit in the ideas and actions of those being studied. But many of these cases also have their own equivalents of the vulgar or colloquial arena, so evident in our own largely secular society, where a dualism of subjects and objects is merely presumed.

So there are times when we directly employ a philosophical argument to prevent the reification of either subjects or objects. While early uses of objectification (as in Marx) concentrated upon production, I would argue that today consumption is at least as important as the practice through which people potentially make themselves. For example, in the intensely nationalistic and normative environment of contemporary Trinidad, individuals' sense of themselves is saturated with the self-consciousness of being "Trini." But ethnographic research (Miller and Slater 2000) made clear that "being Trini" had manifestly changed as a result of the way "being Trini" could be performed on the Internet, a technology Trinidadians took to with particular alacrity. So this could not be a study of the "Trinidadian appropriation of the Internet," as though it was an encounter between two separate entities, the Trinidadian and the Internet. The very concept of "the Internet" dissolved from being a given thing into the specificity of its local consumption. There is no such thing as the Internet, it becomes what it is only through its local appropriations. So what we studied was not for us "the Internet," nor "Trinidadians"—it was the process of objectification that created what subsequently came to be understood as both contemporary "Trinidadians" and "the Internet" in its wake.

It is therefore entirely possible to hitch the philosophical wheel that transcends dualism to an analytical vehicle in order to interpret an ethnographic study. But while this becomes an insurance against reductionism or reification, the point, once made, would quickly become tedious if claimed to be the sole point of philosophically informed anthropology. The term *mutually constituted* is much overused in contemporary anthropology. Furthermore, the abstractions required to attach ourselves to this wheel also limit the ability of anthropology to engage with colloquial and empathetic understandings and language. Terms such as *culture* and *society*—or, indeed, *cultures* and *societies*—can all become entirely justifiable shorthands for our necessary generalizations. But we need to bear in mind that ultimately they are heuristic terms anthropology needs to use, or terms used by those we study. They are not ultimate foundations to which all else can be reduced. Once all such terms are recognized as merely our subjects, and no longer our emperors, they become quite useful vehicles that, with the proper wheels attached, will safely take us somewhere. So in my current research project on poverty and communications in Jamaica, I imagine that my analysis will commonly use terms such as *social relations*, *subjects*, and *objects*. Partly because I want to reflect the way the people I work with think and talk, but also because I will want to find ways to convey my research both to the people I am working among and very likely to policy-related institutions working on issues of poverty and development. Where philosophy and theory makes anthropology too "precious" or "pure," it changes from something facilitating understanding to a force preventing engagement. This should not detract from the intellectual agenda of this introduction. To expose the "tyranny of the subject" is still important as a bulwark against reification within academic discussion.

An essential part of anthropology, then, is a commitment to betrayal—a promise to betray the philosophical understandings we strive for in gaining our intellectual purchase, as we return to the vulgarity of our relativism and our empathy with the world. Philosophy is useful, but necessarily obfuscating and abstract when brought down as tablets of stone to people whose philosophy emerges essentially as a practice. We may want to bake our philosophical cake, but we hope for a much wider commensality than merely with those few others who would wish to consume it. As long as it is clear that the usage is heuristic or intended to reflect colloquial language, we all need to talk and write in terms of subjects, objects, and social relations. But none of this, I believe, gainsays the importance of what the contributors to this volume have tried to do singularly and collectively. At the end of the day we still think we have invented a better wheel.

NOTES

1. See, for example, Banerjee and Miller 2003: 137–147.

2. Such levels of generalization hugely simplify this opposition. Indeed, although theology and economics may be in direct opposition as abstractions, in the world of practice, and even within theology itself, each may become the vehicles for the expression of the other—for example, in Parry 1994.

3. See, for example, Miller 1998a.

4. See later discussion of Latour.

5. See in particular Latour 1993, 1999, and for a case study relevant to this volume, Latour 1996.

6. There are, of course, as many variants of philosophy as of anthropology. Furthermore, my working definition is to a degree tautologous, given the point I am making. I take as philosophical that which is both more universal and more abstract, and as anthropological as that which is more ethnographically based and specifically engaged. Clearly there are variants of both philosophy and of anthropology for which such assumptions are quite unwarranted.

7. Compare Sen 1987, 1999, but also Nussbaum's "neo-Aristotelian" position (2000; Nussbaum and Sen 1993).

8. For other contradictions based on the two sides of coins see Hart 1986, 2000: 235–256.

9. Many other examples come to mind: for instance, Zelizer's (1987) work *Pricing the Priceless Child* is based on a very similar logic, as is Campbell's (1986) historical study of why it was that the ethos of Puritans and later Californian hippies became the necessary foundation for what we see today as the most elaborated versions of contemporary commodity materialism. Many times in the history of Christianity it was these same beliefs in the greater reward of asceticism through Christ that allowed the leaders of the church to amass considerable wealth from family inheritance (Goody 1983).

10. In the theory of virtualism (Miller 1998b) I have tried to produce a more general theory as to the effects of these tendencies to reification, but I have also tried to show why these are extremely important for understanding the particular moment of history we are living through. I don't have space to reiterate those points here.

11. This is not intended to be so serious a claim as could be subject to argument. If someone would rather latch on to Kant's universalism, or British ethnography, or Boas, or Vico, that's just fine. Durkheim is simply a representation of the trend I am concerned with excavating.

12. A tendency to use the term *social relations* in a reified or reductionist manner is not to imply that all uses of the term lead in this direction. Indeed, one of the bastions of British social anthropology, the study of kinship, has perhaps been one of the least reductionist, as kinship became progressively understood as an idiom or homology of other cultural genres (e.g., Strathern 1992).

13. This doesn't happen to be my own view. I suspect that both humanism and religion itself can thrive on the ethics that is set free by this kind of radical or material doubt—but that, as they say, is another story.

14. That is, before one comes to Mauss's discussion of the Maori *hau* and *taonga* in *The Gift* (1954: 8–10), there is a section on the Samoan *tonga*, the giving of a child as a piece of property (ibid.: 6–8).

REFERENCES

Appadurai, A., ed. 1986. *The Social Life of Things: Commodities in Cultural Perspective.* Cambridge: Cambridge University Press.

Banerjee, M., and D. Miller. 2003. *The Sari*. Oxford: Berg.

Baudrillard, J. 1981. *For a Critique of the Political Economy of the Sign*. St. Louis: Telos Press.

Bourdieu, P. 1970. "The Berber House, or the World Reversed." *Social Science Information* 9:151–170.

———. 1977. *Outline of a Theory of Practice*. Cambridge: Cambridge University Press.

Buchli, V., and G. Lucas. 2001. *Archaeologies of the Contemporary Past*. London: Routledge.

Campbell, C. 1986. *The Romantic Ethic and the Spirit of Modern Consumerism*. Oxford: Blackwell.

Cassidy, J. 2002. *Dot.con*. London: Allen Lane, Penguin.

Coleman, S. 2000. *The Globalisation of Charismatic Christianity*. Cambridge: Cambridge University Press.

Davidson, J. 1998. *Courtesans and Fishcakes*. London: Fontana Press.

Dilley, M., ed. 1999. *The Problem of Context: Perspectives from Social Anthropology and Elsewhere*. London: Berghahn Books.

Dosse, F. 1999. *Empire of Meaning: The Humanization of the Social Sciences*. University of Minnesota Press.

Douglas, M. 1978. *Implicit Meanings: Essays in Anthropology*. London: Routledge.

Durkheim, E. 2001. *The Elementary Forms of Religious Life*. Oxford: Oxford University Press.

Engelke, M. 2004. "Text and Performance in an African Church: The Book, 'Live and Direct.' " *American Ethnologist* 31.1:76–91.

Foster, R. 1998. "Your Money, Our Money, the Government's Money: Finance and Fetishism in Melanesia." In P. Spyer, ed., *Border Fetishisms*. London: Routledge.

Foucault, M. 2001. *The Order of Things*. London: Routledge.

———. 2002. *Archaeology of Knowledge*. London: Routledge.

Frodon, J.-M. 2002. "The War of Images, or the Bamiyan Paradox." In B. Latour and P. Weisbel, eds., *Iconoclash*, 221–23. Cambridge: MIT Press.

Garsten, C., and F. Wulff, eds. 2003. *New Technologies at Work*. Oxford: Berg.

Gell, A. 1992. *The Anthropology of Time*. Oxford: Berg.

———. 1995. "The Language of the Forest: Landscape and Phonological Iconism in Umeda." In E. Hirsch and M. O'Hanlon, eds., *The Anthropology of Landscape: Perspectives on Place and Space*, 232–254. Oxford: Clarendon Press.

———. 1998. *Art and Agency: An Anthropological Theory*. Oxford: Oxford University Press.

Goffman, E. 1975. *Frame Analysis*. Harmondsworth: Penguin.

Gombrich, E. 1979. *The Sense of Order*. London: Phaidon Press.

Goody, J. 1983. *The Development of the Family and Marriage in Europe*. Cambridge: Cambridge University Press.

Habermas, J. 1972. *Knowledge and Human Interests*. London: Heinemann.

Hacking, I. 1999. *The Social Construction of What?*. Cambridge: Harvard University Press.

Hart, K. 1986. "Heads or Tails? Two Sides of the Same Coin." *Man* 21.4:637–656.

———. 2000. *The Memory Bank*. London: Profile Books.

Harvey, D. 1996. *Justice, Nature and the Geography of Difference*. Oxford: Blackwell.

Hasselström, A. 2003. "Real-Time, Real-Place Market: Transational Connections and Disconnections in Financial Markets." In C. Garsten and H. Wulff, eds., *New Technologies at Work*, 69–90. Oxford: Berg.

Hegel, G. 1967. *The Philosophy of Right*. Trans. T. Knox. Oxford: Oxford University Press.

———. 1977. *Phenomenology of Spirit*. Oxford: Oxford University Press.

Ingold, T. 2000. *The Perception of the Environment*. London: Routledge.

Keane, W. 1997. *Signs of Recognition*. Berkeley: University of California Press.

———. 1998. "Calvin in the Tropics. Objects and Subjects at the Religious Frontier." In P. Spyer, ed., *Border Fetishisms: Material Objects in Unstable Places*. London: Routledge.

Klein, N. 2001. *No Logo*. Flamingo.

Kopytoff, I. 1986. "The Cultural Biography of Things: Commoditization as Process." In A. Appadurai, ed., *The Social Life of Things*. Cambridge: Cambridge University Press.

Kuper, A. 1999. *Culture: The Anthropologist's Account*. Cambridge: Harvard University Press.

Latour, B. 1993. *We Have Never Been Modern*. Hemel Hempstead: Harvester Wheatsheaf.

———. 1996. *Aramis, or the Love of Technology*. Cambridge: Harvard University Press.

———. 1999. *Pandora's Hope: An Essay on the Reality of Science Studies*. Cambridge: Harvard University Press.

———. 2002. "What Is Iconoclash? Or Is There a World beyond the Image Wars?" In B. Latour and P. Weisbel, eds., *Iconoclash*, 14–37. Cambridge: MIT Press.

MacKenzie, D. 2001. "Physics and Finance: S-Terms and Modern Finance as a Topic for Science Studies." *Science, Technology, and Human Values* 26.2:115–144.

MacKenzie, D., and Y. Millo. 2003. "Constructing a Market, Performing Theory: The Historical Sociology of a Financial Derivatives Exchange." *American Journal of Sociology*:107–145.

Maurer, B. 2002. "Repressed Futures: Functional Derivatives' Theological Unconscious." *Economy and Society* 31:15–36.

———. 2003. "Uncanny Exchanges: The Possibilities and Failures of 'Making Change' with Alternative Monetary Forms." *Society and Space* 21:317–340.

Mauss, M. 1954. *The Gift*. London: Cohen and West.

Merleau-Ponty, M. 1989. *Phenomenology of Perception*. London: Routledge.

Miller, D. 1987. *Material Culture and Mass Consumption*. Oxford: Blackwell.

———. 1994. *Modernity: An Ethnographic Approach*. Oxford: Berg.

——. 1995. "Style and Ontology in Trinidad." In J. Friedman, ed., *Consumption and Identity*. Chur: Harcourt.

——. 1998a. *A Theory of Shopping*. Cambridge: Polity/Cornell: Cornell University Press.

——. 1998b. "A Theory of Virtualism." In J. Carrier and D. Miller, eds., *Virtualism: A New Political Economy*. Oxford: Berg.

——. 2001. *The Dialectics of Shopping*. Chicago: Chicago University Press.

——. 2003. "The Virtual Moment." *Journal of the Royal Anthropological Institute* 14:57–75.

Miller, D., and D. Slater. 2000. *The Internet: An Ethnographic Approach*. Oxford: Berg.

Miyazaki, H. 2003. The Temporalities of the Market. *American Anthropologist* 105:255–265.

Moctezume, E. M., and F. S. Olguin. 2002. *Aztecs*. London: Royal Academy of Arts.

Munn, N. 1986. *The Fame of Gawa*. Cambridge: Cambridge University Press.

Myers, F. 1986. *Pintupi Country, Pintupi Self*. Washington: Smithsonian Institution Press.

——. 2003. *Painting Culture*. Durham, N.C.: Duke University Press.

Nussbaum, M. 2000. *Women and Human Development: The Capabilities Approach*. Cambridge: Cambridge University Press.

Nussbaum, M., and A. Sen, eds. 1993. *The Quality of Life*. Oxford: Clarendon Press.

O'Connor, K. 2003. "Lycra, Babyboomers and the Immaterial Culture of the New Midlife." PhD thesis, University of London.

O'Hanlon, M. 1989. *Reading the Skin: Adornment, Display and Society among the Wahgi*. London: British Museum Publications.

Parry, J. 1994. *Death in Banares*. Cambridge: Cambridge University Press.

Pryke, M., and J. Allen. 2000. "Monetized Time-Space: Derivatives—Money's 'New Imaginary'?" *Economy and Society* 29.2:264–284.

Riles, A. 2001. *The Network Inside Out*. Ann Arbor: University of Michigan Press.

Rose, N. 1990. *Governing the Soul: The Shaping of the Private Self*. London: Routledge.

Sahlins, M. 1974. "The Original Affluent Society." In *Stone Age Economics*, 1–39. London: Tavistock.

——. 1985. *Islands of History*. Chicago: University of Chicago Press.

Sartre, J.-P. 1976. *Critique of Dialectical Reason*. London: New Left Books.

Sen, A. 1982. *Poverty and Famines: An Essay on Entitlement and Deprivation*. Oxford: Oxford University Press.

——. 1987. *The Tanner Lectures in Human Values: The Standard of Living*. Cambridge: Cambridge University Press.

——. 1999. *Commodities and Capabilities*. Oxford: Oxford University Press.

Simmel, G. 1968. *The Conflict in Modern Culture and Other Essays*. New York: New York Teachers College Press.

——. 1978. *The Philosophy of Money*. London: Routledge.

Spyer, P. 1998. *Border Fetishisms: Material Objects in Unstable Places*. London: Routledge.

Strathern, M. 1979. "The Self in Self-Decoration." *Oceania* 44:241–257.

——. 1988. *The Gender of the Gift*. Berkeley: University of California Press.

——. 1990. "Artifacts of History: Events and the Interpretation of Images." In J. Siikala, ed.,

"Culture and History in the Pacific." *Transactions of the Finnish Anthropological Society* no. 27:25–44.

——. 1992. *After Nature: English Kinship in the Late Twentieth Century.* Cambridge: Cambridge University Press.

Tambiah, S. 1984. *The Buddhist Saints of the Forest and the Cult of Amulets: A Study in Charisma, Hagiography, Sectarianism, and Millennial Buddhism.* Cambridge: Cambridge University Press.

Thrift, N. 1998. "Virtual Capitalism: The Globalisation of Reflexive Business Knowledge." In J. Carrier and D. Miller, eds., *Virtualism: A New Political Economy*, 161–186. Oxford: Berg.

Wigley, M. 1995. *White Walls, Designer Dresses: The Fashioning of Modern Architecture.* Cambridge: MIT Press.

Zaloom, C. 2003. "Ambiguous Numbers: Trading Technologies and Interpretation in Financial Markets." *American Ethnologist* 30:258–272.

Zelizer, V. 1987. *Pricing the Priceless Child: The Changing Social Value of Children.* New York: Basic Books.

LYNN MESKELL

Objects in the Mirror Appear
Closer Than They Are

For many people, to reflect on a culture such as ancient Egypt is to invariably conjure up three of the most distinct arenas of Egyptian materiality: pyramids, statues, and mummies. Their evocative and concrete images have a great deal to do with their "affecting presence" (Armstrong 1981) for contemporary culture. In turn each also implicates a particular theory of materiality as held by their creators. In this chapter I explore these philosophies of the material in an ancient context and try to reflect forward to contemporary culture to assess the linkages and legacies of ancient materiality. This is part of a larger project (Meskell 2004) that seeks to map the constitution of the object world, the exploration of the situated experiences of material life, and concomitantly its shaping of human experience. Through this triad we might challenge our own understandings of subject-object relations as discrete and essential entities that inhabit particular, impermeable worlds. Recent writing on the specific contours of agentic objects or fetishes, as interlocutors between persons, things, and worlds, undermines the fixity of our imposed boundaries. Materiality represents a presence of power in realizing the world, crafting things from nothing, subjects from nonsubjects. This affecting presence is shaped through enactment with the physical world, projecting or imprinting ourselves onto the world (Armstrong 1981: 19). Such originary crafting acknowledges that there are no a priori objects. They can never be simply inferred as axiomatic;

rather, they must be sensed, experienced, and believed (Simmel 1979: 61). Reciprocally it is this same material world within which human beings are constituted as cultural agents. This inherent tension is very much part of the current project.

Within archaeology these issues are generally seen as of concern only with respect to our own apprehension of ancient artifacts. We have lacked, because we have not tried to create, substantive and compelling accounts of materiality in ancient contexts. Empirically, archaeology has been devoted to precise object analyses; but form, materials, and manufacture do not automatically engage with social relations. Theoretical trends focus more directly on broader interpretive connotations around and beyond the object (Attfield 2000: 40–41), on the unstable terrain of interrelationships between sociality and materiality and the neglected area of the cultural constitution of objects. What is missing has been the sense that our own engagement with the theory and nature of materiality must always also infer a parallel theory and engagement on behalf of the populations that created these objects in the first place. Bodies of artifacts (or for that matter artifacts made from bodies) implicate particular cosmologies where the role of materiality may have been central to peoples' relationships to each other and to the deities. Fortunately, in the case of Egyptian materials it is possible to coherently interrogate the specific moments of crafting, forging, exchanging, installing, using, and discarding objects. From this evidence we can start to include the ancient Egyptians, not just as the objects of our study, but as a comparative population to our own, contributing their own theory and practice of materiality. These can in turn be compared with the assumptions about materiality that are implicated in our own contemporary practices, where Egyptian things are reified and commodified (Meskell 2004). Not all ancient objects have rich and illustrious histories. But the categories of object that have come to stand for ancient Egypt largely have magical, ritual, religious, or commemorative inflections rather than mundane utilities. Things that have the status of "work" are defined by virtue of their lack, since they are not accorded the deference or assigned the rights and personae reserved for *powerful* things, people, or divinities (Armstrong 1981: 7).

Things have always existed which may assume the status of ordinary objects in our contemporary eyes but are in fact treated very differently and are accorded an altogether other status for their creators. Peoples often confer enormous respect upon fabricated things. They materialize our engagement with the world, our understandings, and our desires to shape its physicality. Egyptian culture placed enormous emphasis upon material rendering and representation as an instantiation of individual permanence, cultural longevity, and the endurance of powerful socioreligious concepts. For a society obsessed and to some degree constituted by cultural institutions of doubling and pairing, the act of mimesis was the perfect expression of Egypt's organizing core. The processes of fabrication and copying, imbuing doubles with the potency of the original, were central to the examples that follow. Egyptian culture had its own understanding of materiality and its significations, its sense of ontology and religion, that may in turn impinge upon our own contemporary and profound debates about subjects and objects. Statues, figurines, and carved or painted images of the individual were all doubles for the self that could extend the biography and trajectory of the individual. The images were the bearers of the owner's identity, personality, and visual likeness and could be called upon as active referents in the afterlife. These material renderings also had the power to improve upon reality, such as portraying a person as youthful, beautiful, and free from imperfections. The physical reality of the depiction was thought to have such efficacy as to bestow that desired corporeality upon the person at death as they entered a new domain of existence. If any harm were to befall the deceased's body, those doubles would also physically substitute for his person and guarantee a successful embodied afterlife. The mummified body as a material instantiation for, and carapace of, the person; personalized coffins and cartonnage representations; numerous substitutes in statue and figurine form; wall paintings depicting the deceased and so on, were each physical doubles considered to have long-term vitality and power. At a meta-level one could see the construction of the tomb, and tomb culture in general, as the most salient evocation of the specific configuration of Egyptian materiality and its potency (see below). In the New Kingdom (1539–1070 B.C.) a man could devote much of his adult life and his wages to constructing a tomb for himself and, in many cases, his family. One could think of the tomb as a time machine that housed all the materials necessary for eternal life: bodies, coffins, statues, paintings of the deceased and his family, ritual paraphernalia, furniture, clothing and jewelry, household goods, food, wine, and so on—"every good thing," as the Egyptians would proclaim. It was clearly not enough to simply aspire to having it all next time around; it was necessary to provide that material world in the context of the tomb, so as to secure it for the future. This buried object geography provided the mimetic basis for this next life.

As it happens, the three material forms that most people today immediately associate with ancient Egypt also provide three densely connected classes of material culture that form the case studies for this chapter: the statue, the mummy, and the pyramid. By investigating the theories and concepts of materiality that are implicit in the practices as known to us we can see how they were just as excised as we with issues that transcend any simple notions of subject-object divisions and embodiments.

DIVINE STATUES IN ANCIENT EGYPT

The Egyptian term for sculptor was "he who keeps alive," which underscores the significance of the image as a living materiality. In a reconfiguration of the fabrication act, the Egyptians considered divine statues to be born, not made. Inscriptions employ the term *to bear* for the practical and technical manufacture of a cult statue. Similarly, artisans claim that in the act of making, they "bore" the statues of deities and even the deities themselves. As Jan Assmann (2001: 46) suggests, "The statue is not the image of the deity's body, but the body itself. It does not represent his form but rather gives him form. The deity takes form in the statue, just as in a sacred animal or a natural phenomenon." This enforces the notion of the fetish and its concomitant power as a *power of*, not simply *power in*. The Egyptians may have recognized that while the transcendent nature of the gods was not to be reducible to any form that they could be easily conceived—material or otherwise—there was also a sense that it was only through the act of objectification that they were empowered for humanity. Objectification imbued them with agency. The gods did not dwell on earth or experience the terrestrial as ordinary mortals did. Rather, they installed themselves within their images, not in a singular, originary embodiment but through a series of events and forms that occurred regularly. In one account known as the Memphite theology, the creator god Ptah was said to have made the bodies of the gods, to have established their divine images, and to oversee their indwelling. Ptah proclaims (Morenz 1973: 154): "He made their bodies according to their wishes. So the gods entered their bodies, of all kinds of wood, all kinds of minerals, all kinds of clay . . . in which they took form." The collaboration of humankind through ritual practice and invocation was necessary, and this suite of actions formed the basis of the cult.

As part of cultic devotion and reflection of their subject status, divine statues were provided with clean clothes each day, in addition to food and drink offerings, in an ongoing daily routine of verbal and material sustenance. The complex stages of daily cultic ritual are made evident in clothing rites that alone consisted of some forty-five individual acts. These in turn were increasingly complicated by a necessary adherence to the smallest constituent elements of the rites. According to Assmann (2001: 48), the first acts of the morning clothing ritual in the New Kingdom consisted of (1) lighting the flame, (2) taking up the arm-shaped censer, (3) placing incense in the flame, (4) going to the sanctuary, (5) breaking the cord, (6) breaking the seal, (7) sliding the door bolt, and finally, (8) *revealing the god* or opening the door-leaves of the shrine. Their purpose was to awaken the god and to wash, dress, and feed the deity at the start of each new day in a cycle similar to that of human subjects. Altars piled high with provisions were set up, incense burned, and libations poured. The Egyptian word for incense also meant "to make divine" (Robins 2001: 7), adding another layer upon the dense stratigraphy of ritual devotion. Among incense and the recitation of hymns, officiating priests approached the sanctuary. The body of the god was then uncovered, he was presented with myrrh, anointed, and purified with water; then the sanctuary was sealed, accompanied by spells and hymns. It should be remembered that statues were placed in the inner sanctuary of the temple, within a shrine, and not on public view. Cult statues traditionally dwelt within their shrines inside a small, dark room in the heart of the temple as the focus of cosmic order (Shafer 1997: 6). Daily cult ritual formed a temporal cycle as well as a performative one. There were three elaborate services—at dawn, at midday, and in the evening—and the morning ritual was the most significant. A scaled-down set of rituals were performed twice more throughout the day. Through ritualized speech and action, priests accomplished the transposition of the cultic events into the divine realm. The cult was essentially performative on the part of humans whose actions invoked the gods and goddesses' benevolent participation.

For the Egyptian populace it was largely impossible to see the gods, even if one experienced such visions in a dream, as in the literary tale *The Shipwrecked Sailor* (Hornung 1982: 128). However, during great festivals the deity could leave the dark recesses of the sanctuary when a portable image was taken out into the world. It was not sufficient that pharaoh might travel as a substitute for the gods at festival time; the conditions of possibility deemed that the person of the god was required. Yet since access to the gods in statue form was so restricted, many individuals sought material intermediaries, also in the form of statues—physical conduits that facilitated communication with the gods and supplication from individual petitioners. Two such inscribed statues of Amenhotep, son of Hapu, were installed within the Karnak temple complex. Inscriptional evidence makes it clear that all that was spoken to Amenhotep, as messenger, would be passed on to Amun so long as people performed the offering spell, invoked his name twice daily, and so on. This is an apt example of the enmeshed spheres of material and immaterial, of concretized and performative memory. One inscribed statue reads: "I am the messenger of the mistress of the sky, I belong to her outer court. Tell me your petitions so that I can report them to the mistress of the Two Lands, for she hears my supplications" (Morenz 1973: 102). The centrality of the material image and its agentic force in these rituals has several implications. First, individuals rendered in statue form had themselves represented and invoked in perpetuity, so that memory of them was constantly brought into the sphere of the living, long after their bodily death. Thus they were actively sustained in the next life through the actions of the living. Second, the role of mediators is underscored: they could be living individuals such as priests or material embodiments of individuals (alive or dead) such as Amenhotep, son of Hapu. Here the materialization of memory may indeed be inseparable from the power of the mediating statue, and hence conjoined for maximum efficacy. Did the Egyptians consider the distinction important, and was there a hierarchy of service, that is, was a priest preferable and perceived as more efficacious? To my knowledge we cannot comment on these fine-grained distinctions, if indeed they were salient categorical differences for an Egyptian audience. But clearly the statue as a supra-object was considered an effective and legitimate agentic intermediary. Ritual practice concerned with petitioning the gods was intimately woven around the statue as if it were the person; they were spoken to, prayed too, invoked, and so on. Collapsing the contemporary boundaries of subject and object in this context seems inevitable.

From an anthropological perspective, a statue in a temple was believed to be both the body of the divinity and a spirit-medium that likewise provided the divinity with a temporary body. These two aspects of body and spirit were treated as theoretically on a par, although the former is an artifact and the latter a living deity (Gell 1998: 7). Once the mouth and eyes of an image had been touched, that image could house the spiritual elements, thus providing the material entity for eternal life (Forman and Quirke 1996: 32). Images were thus called upon to play active roles and to fill gaps in the social fabric of daily life. As Belting (1994: 45) contends, "Many religions are concerned to make visible an object of veneration, to protect it and to approach it with the same piety that they would lavish on the higher being; symbolic acts toward the image thus reveal one's inner attitude." One could see the active statue agents as following the tropic operations of projection, reprojection, ventriloquism, subject making, object making, belief, and knowledge (Latour 1996). What we classify as statues could be refigured to accord with an emic view: that these are not simply contained essences of the divine, but come to be divine in their own right. Thus from an Egyptian perspective, what we perceive as statues were not simply vehicles, but the materialization of the gods themselves. This morphing or crossing of boundaries extends the embodiment of objects and subjects alike in an inevitable fabricating of the world. The fetish is a social fact, one that deserves its own taxonomy, coined by Bruno Latour as *faitich,* a parallel blurring of fact and fetish. In English, his neologism *factishes* reminds us that the dichotomy of "facts" and "social constructions" is nearly useless (2000: 113). "And if religion, arts or styles are necessary to 'reflect,' 'reify,' 'materialize,' 'embody' society—to use some of the social theorists' favorite verbs—then are objects not, in the end, its co-producers? Is society not built literally—not metaphorically—of gods, machines, sciences, arts and styles?" (Latour 1991: 54). Whether one thinks of Amenhotep as oracle, the divine embodiments of the gods, or simply the polymorphous images of deceased ancestors, we can see how mutually constitutive subjects and objects are and how object worlds impinge on the fate of individuals.

What matters most is the embedding of the thing in a social and material network, in specific moments and particular places. Statues perform intelligibly, and since Egyptian representation was highly iconic, the realistic element was devised to capture and enthrall, to render the object more divine and more interiorized, and to open up other routes of access. At each level, humans as agents are required within these social networks to facilitate and anchor the efficacy of objects. They provide a concrete locus of engagement between persons and divinities. Gell suggests that we are all natural dualists with a propensity for believing the ghost in the machine. Yet people can imbue things with humanlike qualities without mixing their categorical understandings: this entails a fine-tuning of the notion of agency and a local contextualization (Gell 1998: 123). Gell specifically draws upon the example of the Egyptian statue in its temple setting, albeit using some rather outmoded scholarship. He concludes that the daily routines, outlined above, entailed the imposition of human agency in a social setting where statues could be rendered both objects and subjects, passive and active. Rightly, he asserts that actions were neither make-believe nor purely emblematic; rather, these were "life-endowing rituals and thus literal transpositions of the means in which we induce agency in social others, in human form" (134). They were symbolic actions rendered meaningful, deriving from the real or causal outcome of physical interactions. Whether in feeding or clothing the god, the efficacy of the divine was interpolated into the relational texture of social praxis, social relations, language, and understanding. Here the indexical object could be seen to exert agency and engage in a double session of representation, for it both portrays and stands in for its prototype (98). Egyptian statues were indeed the gods in material form.

MUMMIFYING DESIRE

Thomas Mann famously said of Egypt, "Your dead are gods and your gods dead" (1978: 510). The mummy is perhaps the most iconic image of Egypt, one that has haunted Western culture long after the demise of pharaonic civilization. The signifier of the mummy, oscillating between human and object status, has long captured the imagination of cultural theorists. The body is not reducible to a system of signs; its materiality in the mortuary sphere was a source for the extension of individual being and potential biography and ensured that it reclaimed the position of a privileged subject. For Jean Baudrillard (1993: 180), the decayed body was an abject sign of mortality in this world, and subsequently the afterlife, and of the nondivine status of the individual. Numerous cultures find it necessary to ward off death, to smother it in artificiality in order to evade the unbearable moment when flesh returns to dust and ceases to be a sign. And for Jacques Derrida (1987: 43), while the mummy bore the trace of the individual, and the identity was made visible and material, it was scarcely readable. It was a matter not of continuing the lifelike body of the original subject, but of radically transforming it into another sort of object. It was eternally self-referential and yet only a trace, a trace soon to be lost, residing at the interstices of subject and object. More negatively, Andy Warhol believed that being embalmed, with one's organs separately wrapped, and then interred in a pyramid was the worst of fates: "I want my machinery to disappear" (quoted in Taylor 1997: 234). There is something about the dead or nondead status of the mummy, its powerful physical presence and powers for animation, that troubles us and lies at the nexus of our fantasies. In many respects, the mummy is also the first cyborg (see Meskell 1999). Egyptian technologies of the body were complex and sophisticated, suggesting that while knowledge changes, our contemporary desires are not necessarily unique: transcending bodily death is a cogent example of this desire for a cyborg future. Egyptian material strategies surrounding death were well developed and have ultimately influenced some of our own Western cyborg techniques for the body in death, such as cryogenics and other means of bodily suspension.

From the perspective of materiality, many Egyptian images and objects operated as personal biographies for the deceased individual through mimetic and iterative processes. Deceased individuals could be represented or doubled through statuary, images, and wall paintings. Mimesis can be read here as the nature that culture uses to create second nature, in this case the living body. This second nature is foundering and highly unstable, spiraling between nature and culture, essentialism and constructionism, forging new identities and offering dramatic new possibilities (Taussig 1993: 252). We see this creatively concretized in Egypt, where the dead individual represented an Osiris—a dead but deified being capable of being reborn in the next world. In corporeal terms the body of the living subject, through a series of bodily processes, becomes an object—at the nexus between the living world and the next, a type of artifact in and of itself (Meskell and Joyce 2003). The body of the dead individual was more than a human carapace; in its mummified state it existed as the physical remains of a human being albeit transformed by technology into another, or an other, sort of product. The body in death and its inherent partibility formed a major cultural focus— explicitly, the bodily organs performed metonymically for the entire person. In death, the body was a plastic entity that had to be manipulated before its successful entry into the next world, since the unique characteristics of the individual and his or her narrative biography also persisted beyond death. The integrity of the bodily self, its material representation in statue or visual form, and the existence of the person were inseparably tied together.

Central to Egyptian funerary ideology was an obsession with preserving the living body through and beyond the zone of death, coupled with an attendant dread of physical decay. Decomposition of the corpse is a source of anxiety that lies at the heart of many cultures, requiring the materiality of the dead to be manipulated and made perfect in appearance. In Egyptian language bodily decay was referred to as transitoriness: to decay was to consume, to dry up, to perish, to become maggoty, to go bad, to flow away, and to smell (Zandee 1960: 56–60). Decomposition and decay voids the corpse of its signs and its social force of signification. It depersonifies the individual, leaving it as nothing more than a substance. For the community who countenance that decay, the process reinforces the fragility of life and the existential terror of its own symbolic decomposition. One interpretation posits that the Egyptians sought to abjure or defeat death through artificiality: specifically, via elaborate bodily rituals and preparations the elite sought to evade the unbearable moment when flesh becomes nothing but flesh and ceases to be part of the embodied whole. At the point of death, the motionless body becomes a thing, now deprived of the capabilities of living individuals. Magical spells were required to explicitly bring those functions back to the corpse, to make the dead body akin to its living counterpart. A series of opposition spells in the Book of the Dead were needed to stave off the process of perishing, to confer physical perfection and activate bodily facilities (Faulkner 1985: 153): "I have not decayed, there is no destruction in my viscera, I have not been injured, my eye has not rotted, my skull has not been crushed, my ears are not deaf, my head has not removed itself from my neck, my tongue has not been taken away, my hair has not been cut off, my eyebrows have not been stripped, no injury has happened to me. My corpse is permanent, it will not perish nor be destroyed in this land forever." Mummies continue to prove powerfully ambiguous entities; they are things and beyond things, subjects and objects, physical and cognitive categories, perceptible and apperceptible (Armstrong 1981: 43). Through time-consuming practices of enculturation, the "natural" body with its biological realities had to be transcended through mummification and sarcophagic practices, resulting in a very specific form of transubstantiation.

Death and its attendant rituals were anchored in this commitment to materiality. Extended or distributed selfhood (Gell 1998) was not simply contingent upon arcane ritual practices that inhabited the ethereal; it was also reliant on the physicality of the body and its propensity for fabrication and prosthesis. Bodies and body parts in Egyptian mortuary culture could be apprehended as prostheses, replacing the frailties of the body, and thought of as supplementing the body and coextensive to it, thereby extending the self through material means. Mummification was tantamount to preservation of the body through its violation: one had to attack the physical fabric of the body before a new permanence could be imparted. The human body was never considered naturally immutably divine and thus required substantive modification or construction. In some myths even the gods were not considered immutable, reflected, for example, in the dismemberment of Osiris, and thus they too required transformative rituals. Egyptian mummies aspired to a perfectly preserved and often embellished image of the deceased, transmuting the body into a simulacrum of itself. The transubstantiated body was the person, the self, and yet only a remnant of its earthly being. The final product was a newly crafted corporeality, hermetically sealed, free from imperfections, orifices, openings, or fissures that might allow demonic forces to seep into the body and, thus, the self. This new body must bear no trace of its nature in the realm of death; it must be clean, proper, and impenetrable in order to be fully symbolic (Kristeva 1982: 102). In this new guise of perfection it should be presented as free from earthly disfigurement; even the mark of the embalmer is masked. Although many cultural practices were deployed to deflect the force of death, the difficulty lay in reconciling the abhorrence of bodily intervention with the explicit requirements of fabricating a new type of body through artificial means. In sum, Egyptian notions of death operated simultaneously within monistic and dualistic ideologies: the monist perspective regarded death as a necessary condition for eternal existence, whereas the dualistic one recognized death as the enemy of life and something to be feared. The first is based on religious reflection, the second grounded in the materiality of death and personal experience of the natural world.

PYRAMIDAL FANTASIES

Pyramid: Greek *puramis*, pure – funeral pyre. Latin *pyramis*, pyra – funeral pyre. Just as the mummy has occupied a privileged position in the Western imaginary, the massive materiality of the pyramid has been captivating for some five millennia. The Great Pyramid of Khufu is the lone survivor of the seven wonders of the ancient world and possibly the most comprehensively studied building in the world. Khufu came to power around 2551 B.C., and while pharaohs before him had previously erected pyramids, nothing before nor since rivaled this masterpiece. It has been estimated that the pyramid comprises 2,300,000 blocks of stone; on average each block weighs 2.5 tons. The pyramid's exterior was originally encased in another layer of fine white limestone (Lehner 1997: 108). Stretching 147 meters into the sky, it dwarfs the Statue of Liberty in New York, which stands only 93 meters: the ancient empire of Egypt is still a point of comparison to modern achievements. It is only by comparing the pyramids with the achievements of modernity that we can make sense of their ancient accomplishment, as if they were intensely and already modern themselves. By bringing them closer in this manner we make redundant any pretense to modernity. Pyramids can alternatively operate as distancing devises for onlookers, ancient and modern. They are remote objects and for moderns their original interest and value is long forgotten, thus ensuring that we gain purer aesthetic satisfaction from their form and appearance (Simmel 1979: 75). For the ancients, the pyramid tomb was beyond the scope of mere mortals, reserved in the main for the great living god, pharaoh. It was, moreover, part of a larger complex that included temples, endowments of land, people, and produce, that resulted in an "economic machine" in service of the state as well as pharaoh. Its multifaceted role can be encapsulated in the following terms: a "massive labour

1. British troops enacting the battle of the pyramids after the occupation of Cairo in 1882.
Copyright The Illustrated London News Picture Library.

2. Pyramid at Giza. Photo by the author.

project, baker and brewer for hundreds of consumers; colonizer of the Egyptian provinces; employer of farmers, herdsmen and craftsmen of all kinds; temple and ritual centre at the core of the Egyptian state; reliquary of the king; embodiment of light and shadow; and the union of heaven and earth, encapsulating the mystery of death and rebirth" (Lehner 1997: 9). Distance enhanced that experience of the royal pyramid, and for ordinary Egyptians either working on its construction or revering it in subsequent epochs, that distance spoke to hierarchy, power, and life eternal. The being of such radiating objects cannot be inferred logically, but must be apprehended by the senses, both experienced and believed. Derrida (quoted in Taylor 1997: 219) put it this way: "The erection of the pyramid guards life— the dead—in order to give rise to the form—(it)self of adoration. . . . The sacrifice they offer, the gifts do not destroy the all-burning that destroys itself in them; they make it reach the form—(it)self, they monumentalize it." The Great Pyramid at Giza is one of the earliest and most concrete attempts to overcome the limitations of the human condition: it is an objectification of that desire.

Being there and not there, monumentalizing the destruction of life and ultimately civilization, lies at the heart of Derrida's concerns. This tension between the immateriality of existence on one hand, and the materiality of the trace on the other, has been central in much philosophical writing. As he hints here, specific objects exercise a form of irradiation and fascination (Baudrillard 1997: 15). They are reborn as material evidence, as fetishes exuding maximal intensity. The pyramid is also a material sign of labor and time, and the sacrifice of both to the larger project of memorialization. The longing, effort, and sacrifice that separate us from the objects are the very things that draw us to them (Simmel 1979: 75). Writing specifically on sacrifice, and presaging Derrida, Georges Bataille (1993: 223) encapsulated the particularly Egyptian vision of death, memory, and materiality:

> In the eyes of the Egyptians, the pyramid was an image of solar radiation. In the person of the dead king, death was changed into a radiance, changed into an indefinite being. The pyramid is not only the most lasting monument, it is also the equivalency of the monument and absence of a monument, of passage and obliterated traces, of being and the *absence* of being. There death is no longer anything but death's inability to maintain an icy little horror, which is the projected shadow of individual anguish. Horror is the limit of the individual. What it proclaims is man's reduction into thinghood. It announces the world of practice. The intent of the world of practice is to banish, once and for all, the horror that cannot be separated from it by any means. But at the foot of the pyramid, the world of practice has disappeared; its limit is no longer perceptible.

Like the mummy, the being/nonbeing aspects objectified in the pyramid are portentous: they herald the fragility of the human experience and summon a more robust materiality to instantiate our worldly presence. But while the physical body is susceptible to the corrosive forces of natural decay, the pyramid's robust materiality effectively survives those forces. Following Georg Simmel, nature often destroys objects that, in terms of value, should be preserved (the body), and keeps in existence the object that assumes its place (the pyramid). This is particularly true for Egypt, where the tomb and its grandest expression, the pyramid, are but material edifices marking the passing of the fragile corporeality that frames human subjectivity. Only the trace remains in the form of the mummy, which must be safeguarded at all costs by the physical obduracy of the tomb. Pharaonic mortuary practices could be described as constituting a "mausoleum culture" (Baines and Laco-vara 2002); given the powerful associations of the pyramid, this would seem a particularly apt description. However, such expensive constructions as stone-hewn pyramids were possible only for the pharaoh, and for a rela-tively short moment in the vast span of Egyptian history, although smaller pyramidal constructions were created after the Old Kingdom. The super-structure of the pyramid serves as a visible and tangible reminder of one's death and the hereafter. In principle, the tomb formed a material, yet limi-nal, installation for maintaining the deceased in life, where the world of the living and dead could overlap. The preservation of the deceased's mum-mified body, the grave goods, and the integrity of the tomb itself were fundamental. Monumental tombs fulfilled the double function of hiding the body of the deceased and leaving a sign of the deceased within the world of the living. In the tomb culture of the Egyptians, both these foci are widely extended (Assmann 1996: 61). The pyramid tomb operated as visualized memory. In addition, the associated chapel was the locus for the offering cult, which was crucial to the maintenance of the deceased and memory of them. But despite a well-developed ideology concerning death and the here-after, some literary texts reveal a profound skepticism about mortuary pro-vision, the survival of monuments, and bodily destruction. And there was good reason to be skeptical: successive violations, robberies, and desecra-tions all attest to the porosity of burial. Mortuary practices extended beyond the physicality of interment: commemoration and memorialization were fundamental both for a successful afterlife for the dead and for a prosperous earthly existence for the living through venerating one's ancestors. In Egypt the dead were sustained through ongoing reflexive practices conducted by the living. These took place in the mortuary sphere, usually in chapels or in the vicinity of the burial site. The necropolis was the most potent locale—there the dead held the greatest, most obvious influence—and the optimum zone for contact between the two worlds. The pyramid and the tomb were a material testament to the deceased, his life history and his achievements.

Because of its monumental material mass, the pyramid entraps and en-gages its observers. It brings history closer while diminishing us as individ-uals in the overall scheme of that history. Things bigger than ourselves are infused with the lived reality of past lives and speak to an immensity most of us find difficult to grasp, although we recognize our small part in it (Trouillot

3. Pyramid at Luxor. Photo by the author.

1995). The Great Pyramid on the Giza plateau is surely the grandest evocation of that precarious balance between presence and absence. Pyramids
raise historically grounded issues today around monumentality, materiality,
and immateriality. Their multivalency conveys to us everything from a notion of gross materialism and despotism to the notion of pure spirituality
and eternal essence. In this manner they refract ideas about the material and
the immaterial, which continue to be critical to both their production and
continued consumption. This enduring fascination can be traced from ancient Rome and the Renaissance, to the seventeenth and eighteenth centuries, to works of Giambattista Piranesi and Johann Gottfried von Herder
(Lehner 1997: 241). One example of contemporary consumption, thought by
many to be a signifier of modern materialism, is the Luxor Casino and Hotel,
Las Vegas. The Luxor designers have exhibited a consummate dedication to
Egyptian art, architecture, and cultural custom at every level, from the
cutlery and carpeting to the enormous statuary, wall paintings, and architecture itself (Meskell 2004). Egyptian ritual objects of veneration, in their
original ancient settings—the pyramid, divine statues, mummies—have been

transposed to the modern sphere; only the understandings and inherent religiosity has changed. As a heterotopic space where time and space have collapsed, people pose for photographs with Egyptian statues just as they do in Egypt. It is the perfect site for the flip-side analysis of the reification of Egyptian objects and their potent materialities.

The Luxor consists of a thirty-story black glass pyramid and replica Sphinx that sits in its geometrical splendor on the desert, not unlike the original Great Pyramid (Schull 2001). When it was built, the 4,455-room casino cost $700 million; it is the second largest hotel in the world, employing 4,000 people, and receives between 15,000 and 20,000 visitors daily. Despite the rigorous theming and dedication to authentic reproduction by designers who copied from Egyptology books, two huge Mayan pyramids have surreptitiously crept into the construction; one in the pool area, another on the entertainment level. On one level a pyramid is a pyramid is a pyramid, and somehow it is all redolent of Egypt. This is what Kant referred to as aesthetic indifference: historicity does not matter so much as the form and visibility. Inside the casino is the largest atrium in the world, some 29 million cubic feet; there one would be able to encase not merely a dead pharaoh but the gigantic mass of nine 747 airplanes (Gottdiener, Collins, and Dickens 1999: 39). Reproductions and simulations at this staggering scale reinforce the fantasy environment, and the close proximity of this tightly knit urban texture proffers a phantasmagoric landscape. Robust theming of exteriors (and, in the Luxor's case, interiors) results in a hyper-real spectacle that in turn belies the real logic of commodity production. Some 30 million visitors come each year for the sex, glitter, fantasy, entertainment, and risk. Vegas underscores Guy Debord's notion of spectacle as the defining attribute of industrial society (Gottdiener, Collins, and Dickens 1999: 93). In that sense Las Vegas is not atypical—it is simply an extreme signifier of symbolic capital, of fantasy and leisure and amusing ourselves to death.

Luxor Casino's pyramid is a vehicle that transforms and transports visitors to another time and place, past and future (Schull 2001: 395). This plays on the trope of the pyramid as time machine, popular in many films and other media. As Bernard Tschumi encapsulates it (cited in Taylor 1997), the pyramid is a figure of longing for transcendence and permanence. The pyramid, as a shape, supposedly exudes its own force, offering visitors weird and wonderful experiences of alterity and perhaps luck. Guests claim to experience odd sensations from sleeping in the pyramid. As one masseuse at the Oasis Spa told me, "Lots of people come in needing a massage because they think the pyramid has negative energy." When I suggested that pyramid power was once thought to exert positive energy, she replied, "Some people say the pyramid makes them feel worse, others better."

Egyptian death also becomes a source of edutainment. Collapsing education and entertainment, the Luxor also boasts a replica of the tomb of Tutankhamun. However, nothing but the semblance of the king's body was ever present. The secret of the Luxor pyramid is that there is no tomb (Taylor 1997: 248), and certainly no entombed pharaoh and his accompanying treasure, although the specter of treasure pervades the casino. Since the opening of Tutankhamun's tomb, people have not been able to get enough of Egypt, to consume its luxuries and bask in its iconography. In fact, since the nineteenth century ancient Egypt has been a recurrent motif in art, film, clothing, décor and design. Tutankhamun is a constant presence throughout much of the casino, from restaurant props, to decorative statues, to replicas, to children's toys. The Luxor's stock in trade is pyramids, obelisks, statues of gods and pharaohs, Tutankhamun replicas, mummies, and so on, iterating a clear focus on ritual and religion, specifically around the domain of death. Educational books and videos jostle for space alongside T-shirts, clothing, bags, replicas, prints, jewelry, glasses, homewares, toys, magnets, key rings, pens, and stationery. It is therefore somehow apt that all these ancient representations of death and ritual be housed in a modern pyramid which iterates that compelling materiality.

In sum, ancient Egypt possessed perhaps the earliest and best-known culture to fetishize material objects in ways moderns can apprehend: to adorn the body, replicate the self, immortalize and memorialize the individual, magically intervene into otherworldly spheres, improve upon nature, and accumulate a wide array of things during life, and subsequently take them to the grave. Egypt's legacy of embodied materiality and its specific cultural inheritance clearly demand our attention. Its particularities should be studied contextually, yet these object lessons have the interpretative power to contrast with our own culture and make us reflect on our practices of materiality. The highly charged nature of visualizing and materializing in ancient Egyptian society can be explored in relation to human agency, power, and the desire to control fate and technologies of enchantment. From life to death the material world instantiated, reflected, and shaped social life, and concomitantly, potential existence in the afterworld. Those same evocative Egyptian materials are still potent signifiers in Western culture, and one can readily trace their appreciation in the modern world. The Luxor Casino may be an extreme example of Egypt and the saturation of its signifiers but is in itself a monumental testament to the desire and longing that coalesces around the materiality of Egypt today. Thousands of years after the demise of pharaonic Egypt as a coherent cultural sphere, so many laypeople as well as scholars remain fascinated with Egypt's tangible and spiritual achievements. What we must not forget is that ultimately it was the Egyptians' own belief in the power and process of materiality that created the overpowering physicality which now serves as the bedrock for our fantasies and fascinations.

NOTE

My greatest debt is to Daniel Miller, who extended this invitation and has worked tirelessly with me on this chapter and the larger book project of which it is part. His insights and suggestions have greatly influenced and improved my work, for which I am extremely grateful. A number of other people were also kind enough to read and comment upon related versions of this text: Emma Blake, Ian Hodder, Nan Rothschild, Natasha Schull, and Norm Yoffee.

REFERENCES

Armstrong, R. P. 1981. *The Powers of Presence: Consciousness, Myth and Affecting Presence.* Philadelphia: University of Pennsylvania Press.

Assmann, J. 1996. "Preservation and Presentation of Self in Ancient Egyptian Portraiture." In P. D. Manuelian, ed., *Studies in Honor of William Kelly Simpson*, vol. 1, 55–81. Boston: Museum of Fine Arts.

——. 2001. *The Search for God in Ancient Egypt.* Ithaca, N.Y.: Cornell University Press.

Attfield, J. 2000. *Wild Things: Material Culture of Everyday Life.* New York: Berg.

Baines, J., and P. Lacovara. 2002. "Burial and the Dead in Ancient Egyptian Society: Respect, Formalism, Neglect." *Journal of Social Archaeology* 2:5–36.

Bataille, G. 1993. *The Accursed Share.* Vols. 2 and 3. New York: Zone Books.

Baudrillard, J. 1993. *Symbolic Exchange and Death.* London: Sage.

——. 1997. *Art and Artifact.* London: Sage.

Belting, H. 1994. *Likeness and Presence: A History of the Image before the Era of Art.* Chicago: University of Chicago Press.

Derrida, J. 1987. *Cinders.* Lincoln: University of Nebraska Press.

Faulkner, R. O. 1985. *The Ancient Egyptian Book of the Dead*. London: British Museum Press.

Forman, W., and S. Quirke. 1996. *Hieroglyphs and the Afterlife in Ancient Egypt*. London: British Museum Press.

Gell, A. 1998. *Art and Agency: An Anthropological Theory*. Oxford: Oxford University Press.

Gottdiener, M., C. C. Collins, and D. R. Dickens. 1999. *Las Vegas: The Social Production of an All-American City*. Oxford: Blackwell.

Hornung, E. 1982. *Conceptions of God in Ancient Egypt: The One and the Many*. Ithaca, N.Y.: Cornell University Press.

Kristeva, J. 1982. *Powers of Horror: An Essay on Abjection*. New York: Columbia University Press.

Latour, B. 1991. *We Have Never Been Modern*. Cambridge: Harvard University Press.

——. 1996. *Petite réflexion sur le culture moderne des dieux faitiches*. Paris: Collection, Les Empecheurs de Penser en Rond.

——. 2000. "When Things Strike Back: A Possible Contribution of 'Science Studies' to the Social Sciences." *British Journal of Sociology* 51:107–123.

Lehner, M. 1997. *The Complete Pyramids*. New York: Thames and Hudson.

Mann, T. 1978. *Joseph and His Brothers*. Harmondsworth: Penguin.

Meskell, L. M. 1999. *Archaeologies of Social Life: Age, Sex, Class Etc. in Ancient Egypt*. Oxford: Blackwell.

——. 2004. *Material Biographies: Object Worlds from Ancient Egypt and Beyond*. Oxford: Berg.

Meskell, L. M., and R. A. Joyce. 2003. *Embodied Lives: Figuring Ancient Maya and Egyptian Experience*. London: Routledge.

Morenz, S. 1973. *Egyptian Religion*. Ithaca, N.Y.: Cornell University Press.

Robins, G. 2001. *Egyptian Statues*. Buckinghamshire: Shire Publications.

Schull, N. D. 2001. "Oasis/Mirage: Fantasies of Nature in Las Vegas." In B. Herzogenrath, ed., *From Virgin Land to Disney World: Nature and Its Discontents in the USA of Yesterday and Today*, 377–402. Amsterdam: Rodopi.

Shafer, B. E. 1997. "Temples, Priests, and Rituals: An Overview." In B. E. Shafer, ed., *Temples in Ancient Egypt*, 1–30. Ithaca, N.Y.: Cornell University Press.

Simmel, G. 1979. *The Philosophy of Money*. Boston: Routledge and Kegan Paul.

Taussig, M. 1993. *Mimesis and Alterity: A Particular History of the Senses*. New York: Routledge.

Taylor, M. C. 1997. *Hiding*. Chicago: University of Chicago Press.

Trouillot, M.-R. 1995. *Silencing the Past: Power and the Production of History*. Boston: Beacon Press.

Zandee, J. 1960. *Death as an Enemy According to Ancient Egyptian Conceptions*. Leiden: E. J. Brill.

MICHAEL ROWLANDS

A Materialist Approach to Materiality

Materialism and materiality sound like they could be almost interchangeable in meaning. But there is a significant difference. In the well-known phrase from the "Theses on Feuerbach" that the chief defect of all previous materialisms is "that the thing, reality, sensuousness is conceived only in the form of the object or of contemplation and not as human, sensuous activity, as practice," Marx claimed that perceiving the object-in-itself is to reduce it to an image or thing, as the product of a contemplative, theoretical attitude (Marx and Engels 1975: 5, 3–5). The issue this raises for a materialist is the recognition of a radical separation of subject from object or thought from material existence due to their separate dependence on the practical activity of producing a way of life. Hence the materialist claim that it is impossible to merge subject and object (e.g., by making the object social, as Arjun Appadurai [1986] does) is based on the argument that they are radically different in their nature (cf. Elster 1985). The materialist argument contains the intriguing suggestion that if self-realization is a product of practical activity, then we will experience this as inequalities in a materiality of being. This is not so far from the general psychoanalytic point that consciousness expands in relation to others and to significant objects that exist independently both inside and outside the person. We can therefore not only be more or less material in our being, either more or less ephemeral or massive and condensed in material presence, but these are also potentials, and we judge their realizability by our capacity to understand what blocks this process. The issue of praxis as against the mutual constitution of subject and object as "ready-mades" will turn out to have major consequences for this chapter. It will emerge that under a proper materialist perspective we have to be deeply engaged in questions of power not as abstract but as intrinsic. In turn this leads to a critical understanding of materiality as a process of materialization such that some people and things are perceived to be more material than others, the consequences of which are the main concern of this chapter.

MATERIALIZING MATERIALITY

While I do not think we need to go back to turning Hegel on his head, a corrective is needed to the imputing of agency and materiality to persons and things as "ready-mades," as existing constituents of thought. I include here all those approaches that see persons and things as mutually constitutive in some way and yet start from the premise that things as "social objects" have some a priori existence but do not constitute "a world out there." Essentially I take these positions to depend upon some notion of separation of person and thing in relational terms in order to argue that identity is constructed through their mediation in a socially constructed field. By contrast, materialism poses the question of identity in terms of formation and how the actions of making and doing constitute both consciousness and things as a process and the positing of "a world out there" or, as Marx endlessly states, on the existence of a materiality separate from being. To say instead that nature conceived abstractly, in and of itself, means nothing unless socially constituted and appropriated is therefore a product of a reading of being that can assert material sense only to the agency of "social objects." Materialism must therefore be committed to a correspondence or realist epistemology, but for Marx it did not mean that materiality is abstract—rather, that it forms part of a theory of praxis which on the one hand asserts that while there must be an independence of nature from praxis, the latter is inevitably part of the former (Marx 1973: 360). The idea that things must be both inside and outside the body, that they must have a separate existence, is also highlighted by Latour's view of materialization. In his discussion of Pasteur's lactic acid fermentation process he argues that microbes exist only as and when they become visible (Latour 1998: 199). If microbes existed before 1864, the date of Pasteur's discovery, they did so as a substrate unknown to anybody. But in a vital sense of whether we really do control our worlds, the materialist position, which asserts that objects do exist separate from our realization of them, would study the archaeology of the substrate and the extent to which it has been substantiated or materialized by Pasteur and at what costs. After all, it has been our unwillingness or hubris in not recognizing this possibility that continues to invite environmental and social catastrophes.

That Marx in order to construct his critique of capitalism ended up putting so much of his emphasis upon production in his working out of materialism as a political philosophy meant that a reduction of praxis to either technology or ecology was an almost inevitable outcome of these debates. But some alternative guides exist. There is a large body of writing on cultural technology that basically caters to the idea that making and doing constitutes both persons and things (Ingold 2000; Lemonnier 1993; Leroi-Gourhan 1993). Mauss, in his less well known article on techniques of the body, describes how in the First World War, the shovels for digging trenches had to be completely replaced when British troops replaced the French on a battlefield (Mauss 1950). He accounted for this and other examples (e.g., the Kabyle slipper) as a cultural product of socialization, but this skirts the issue that both bodily habits and prosthetic objects are the products of actions of making and doing (and therefore part of the nature of corporeality) and not their determinants. Criticizing phenomenology for treating the body as a blank schemata for meaning to be inscribed upon, Warnier (2001) has recently claimed that a praxeological approach forms a synthesis of techniques of the body and instrumental techniques to incorporate objects and skilled practices internalized subjectively through action and movement. The focus on movement as a material action in Warnier's argument is intriguing because it has only really been considered before in the context of technology—weaving a basket or making a pot—and not in the wider context of the formation of personhood. He uses the later Foucault writings on technologies of the self to make the link between praxeology, subjectivation, and a power system or governmentality to consider how materialities are "the standard forms of mediating between acting and moving subjects" (Warnier 2001: 19). Latour, on the other hand, uses the "guns kill people" slogan to illustrate the fact that the gun, as object, acts by virtue of its material components that are irreducible to the social qualities of the person holding the gun (Latour 1998: 176). In this case, we have an example of an independent material practice that transforms the otherwise latent dangers of a citizen into lunacy. But that is not the limit of studying the gun as an object; one can also consider how it is available to be used because of a global trade in weapons, because of links between the trade in guns and drugs, because of the collapse of communism in eastern Europe freeing control over gun production, or because of the technology of warfare miniaturizing weapon power into easily disguisable forms. None of these considerations is reducible to the gun either as a role player or as a passive vehicle in human interaction. Latour's argument, which serves to reduce materialism to intriguing suggestions about how the qualities of subjects depends on what they hold in their hands, leaves out political economy, an understanding of which would allow some control to be imposed on such a chaotic and disastrous situation for the world. As Slavoj Žižek remarks, "This feeling for inert materiality has a special significance for our age, in which the obverse of the capitalist drive to produce ever more new objects is a growing mountain of useless waste, used cars, out of date computers etc. . . . in these piles of stuff, one can perceive the capitalist drive at rest" (Žižek 2003: 13).

MATERIALITY AND SELF-REALIZATION

This reading of the contrasts between materiality and materialism has one particular advantage: it suitably raises questions of power and, specifically, whether the attainment of personhood, consciousness, or thing-ness is a process that can be achieved, controlled, or diminished. Marx is quite clear that while he wishes to make an epistemological point about the contrast between abstract and concrete thought, his principal concern is to describe the changes in human beings that will come with the advent of communism (Marx 1967: 99–101). Emancipatory knowledge is distinctive not only in an epistemological sense but because it will lead to freedom of the human senses and attributes that under capitalism had been subverted to the satisfaction of false needs. In particular, since self-understanding is what a group or individual needs in order to change their situation, it is also a change in consciousness, that is, a form of cognition "in which the act of knowing alters what it contemplates." Moreover, if such knowledge moves people to alter their material conditions in a practical way, it also becomes a kind of social and political force (cf. Eagleton 1997: 4). By arguing for the close linkage between the form taken by consciousness and material conditions, Marx saw emancipation both as the result of an increase in economic surplus over material necessity, thus releasing people to develop to the limits of their own potential, and as inhibited by alienation from the conditions of self-realization, which could be resolved only in a future where consciousness, as a force of production, was no longer dehumanized. A vital measure of self-realization would be the understanding that subjects have of this context and how their actions can have the capacity to make a difference (i.e., to make history).

Take the example of a young man who at the turn of the twentieth century in the Cameroon Grassfields may have had the opportunity to realize several emerging opportunities. As a young unmarried male who had not been fortunate to inherit a lineage or chiefly title, he would work for his father (either literally or an elder brother taking the title) in the anticipation that eventually the latter would provide the bride-wealth to allow him to marry and establish his own household. Because it was in the interest of the father to use his wealth to marry polygamously and maintain the son/ brother as a client providing the surplus labor on which the father's household depended, this could take some time, and it was not unusual for men to finally marry, if at all, only in their forties. If the Germans had not chosen to colonize this part of Cameroon in 1891, what might have happened to him? One can anticipate that such a man would either be stuck or have tried to use fictive kin links to become a client elsewhere, where he might have a better chance of establishing some autonomy through marriage. Given that large polygamous households are reported for this period, with twenty-plus wives, hundreds of children, and many unmarried male clients who might sexually serve the wives of the father but never be acknowledged as the father of such progeny, the degree of freedom appears to have been quite limited (cf. Warnier 1993). Into this situation came European colonial rule and the potential for access to independent wealth either by direct labor on European-owned plantations established on the coast about two hundred miles away, or by working as a servant or translator for a European officer or trader, or by joining the missions, going to school, and becoming a catechist or pastor. To a certain extent there was little choice in the matter, since chiefs were forced to provide annual quotas of labor for plantations and to serve the needs of German rule. But, if such men ever made it back to the Grassfields (the death rate was over 70 percent), they were physically and emotionally transformed. Unmarried client males no matter what their age would otherwise live an ephemeral existence living in the compounds of their "father," being fed still by their mother every evening, without proper clothing or head covering and ostensibly celibate and unmarried, unable to socially reproduce themselves. There is little doubt that there were revolts and that these "young males" were a source of unrest that was solved before colonial rule, by the expedient means of selling them out as slaves. After 1903, there are increasing reports of gangs of these young men returning, either from service with the German colonial army or from working on the coastal plantations, to challenge the hierarchy of the chiefs, bringing their own bride-wealth to marry and being blamed for their rapacious behavior. They wear cloth and beads and red berets; they own guns and provide blankets and enamel pots for their prospective wives. Yet these are the ones who survived the corvee labor on the plantations or sustained the colonial economy. In other words, a new materialization of the self occurs in a context of a massive expansion in the exploitation of surplus male labor by the colonial mode of production. Contrast this with the case of a young woman living in Yaounde, the capital of Cameroon, in 2003. She has met a sixty-five-year-old North American man on the Internet who has subsequently come to Cameroon and married her. Having applied to the relevant embassy for a visa, she is refused on the grounds that the official believes she has married the man in order to migrate to North America for economic reasons. She is genuinely shocked and confused by the idea that she does not love her husband, also by the officials' idea that as soon she gets there she would leave him. Not only is marriage her major social aim, but also as a jobless woman without skills, this remains an unlikely prospect for her in urban Cameroon. Do we decry the marriage as unfree in our macro analysis of global sexuality and migration or recognize it as fulfilling a dream of dignity that compensates for daily humiliation by the promise of autonomy, security, and material well-being? It seems not much has changed in a hundred years except the content of the "colonial regime," which defines the life chances of the young and marriage in Cameroon.

At this point we can draw further on Foucault's writings on technologies of the self (Martin et al. 1988; Warnier 2001). In any given materiality, Foucault argues that techniques of the body and instrumental techniques are also techniques of the self. Consciousness is therefore something formed through bodily acts of making and doing, in interaction with others. Acting toward others also means acting on oneself, which defines the space of power, that is, historically constituted governmentalities. This is the essential connection established by Foucault: that techniques of the self are also techniques of the other and that the internalization of such sensory materialities forms the subject in social and political analysis. You may not only be more or less material in your being; you may also be more or less aware of what that might be and its causation. While we have been influenced by Marx to see such variation in sequential, historical terms, usually as a contrast between premodern and modern, Foucault uses the contrast between subjectivity and subjectification to link techniques of the self to forms of practical activity in the same period—for example, how the emergence of public and private spheres in eighteenth-century Europe can be linked to reading, playing music, and new forms of sociality. In other words, Foucault shows that relating techniques of the body to something called society through "praxis" cannot be empirically identified except by specifying more precisely the articulation of knowledge and consciousness, how techniques of the self are objectified as material actions and how, combined, they relate to particular modes of governmentality and persons.

Warnier uses the example of the notables from the highlands of West Cameroon to describe the sort of discrepancy that can build up when people are subjectivized into different categories of person (Warnier 2001: 18). In his case, ancestral substances are quite literally body substances, and relationships between people are conceived metonymically through the bodily processes by which they are distributed, that is, digestion, regurgitaion, breathing, spitting, and ejaculation. Moreover, the principal ancestral substances are saliva, raphia wine, breath, semen, food, and palm oil; some of these are contained physically in the body, others in bags, bowls, and calabashes that are considered as extensions of that physicality. When people address the Fon, they place hands over the mouth so their breath and saliva will not be spat out and touch him. But he may pour raphia wine from his cup into their cupped hands so they can drink. Containing, storing, and circulating substances reach their apex in the dry season festival. As people assemble to dance, the Fon will take a mouthful of raphia wine and spray it out over the people in front of him. They rush forward so the droplets might fall on their backs and shoulders. In the next few moments, women in particular would do everything possible to ensure that he spits on them: conception of a child results, in locals' perception, as much through access to ancestral substance as through the mixing of male and female substances. The sexual act is described widely in central Africa as a form of cooking involving heat and the transformation of male and female substances into the fetus (de Heusch 1980). It is also widely believed that male semen feeds the fetus in gestation, that breast milk feeds it after birth. But this is not sufficient to make a human being. Ancestral substance in the form of breath/saliva from the Fon or lineage head or another source of wet substance (commonly visualized as coming from a stream at night and entering the woman's womb while she sleeps) completes the conception and makes the fetus alive and human. A woman will say this has happened when she feels the fetus kick inside her for the first time.

A Grassfields person is therefore at least dual and experienced as a combination of the substances making life, the product of a conjugal union and an ancestral substance. The occasion of the annual renewal and dispersal of substances also becomes a means to judge the moral and physical state of the Fon's body as the origins of these substances. Limits on their distribution can prevent the transformation of children into adults, of young men into household heads, of women into mothers. As the principal recipient of ancestral substances, the Fon absorbs them, stores them, and regurgitates them on demand. The fact that the body of the Fon is inalienable while its contents are alienable implies that his is the only body that acts as a practical means of circulating ancestral substances through the kingdom. All other bodies are to some degree or other literally imbued with his substance (in the past, because households were highly polygamous, a significant part of the population of a chiefdom could be derived biologically from the Fon's ancestry). They are pale shadows of the special body of the Fon, which renders theirs mundane. In the past slaves were the epitome of immaterial bodies; the unexpectedly dead and zombies were and still are the victims of witchcraft, which has literally "sucked out" their bodily substances and used them for the benefit of others. Bodies are also literally transformed in the process of acquiring a new status. Installation rituals are pragmatically concerned with making new bodies through ingestion. Initiates are literally physically reformed through the ingestion of special foods and medicines that will pass into the bloodstream, circulate through their bodies, and alter their composition. Materiality was therefore not only a relative matter of hierarchy, of gender, youth, age, and so on, but also a matter of deprivation and loss. We may think of materiality as existence in the world, but for others this is clearly not the case.

HIERARCHIES OF MATERIALITY

I am concerned therefore that we should not lose an understanding of the conditions of hierarchical materiality which defines how some may become more material than others and how exclusivity of access to material being may be a product of or an elimination from practical and intellectual activity. The irony is that if we can only become fully material through active participation, then it might seem that materiality is not an a priori condition upon which some causal inference can be drawn but is the result of our active participation (or lack of it, denial of it) in the circumstances of self-realization. But from a materialist stance, nature in this context is effectively materialized as mind-body, and hierarchies of materiality are formed through denial of full access to an embodied sense of self. Marx's view that success depends on the passage from embedded to disembedded to re-embedded social relations in reality becomes a number of alternative states of material being that constitute the person at different times or as different persons at the same time. The essential linkage between self-realization, materiality of being, and praxis occurs not in a mere sequence of actions, as in some technical activity, but in how they relate to a more general notion of existence. In the Lacanian sense that we apprehend our subjectivity as images—that the mirror teaches the child how he or she becomes visible, for himself or herself and others—self-consciousness is an acquisition achieved as a product of alienation, that is, the separation of self from other (Lacan 1978). Hence the well-known modernist theme that the ego must be seen as a function of misrecognition, an imaginary object dependent upon respectful recognition and esteem earned in the eyes of others. But if subjectivity is neither a passive reflection of an external "gaze" nor the immediate product of sensory activities but rather depends on how images of the person be-come recognized, then the formation of consciousness is a political act.

Colonialism was a project that actually relied on either failure or success in the struggle to exhibit the materiality of persons (cf. Cohn 1996). The notion that people were present only when named, indexed, censused, edu-cated, dressed, housed, or otherwise materially demarcated illustrates the potential for a greater or lesser sense of materiality to define a presence or to confer a form of consciousness that was otherwise deemed not to exist. The fact that colonial architecture, medicine, education, roads and transport, clothing, and food served to make the "native" visible in new and disturbing ways both to the ruler or ruled but more significantly to each other is a constant source of conflict between those, particularly the young, who ac-quired these material conditions with alacrity and those, particularly those in authority, who for various reasons resisted it. As is well known, the resisters were as often as not the wielders of colonial rule as those defined as traditional, since both, for different reasons, feared the aspirations of the young for a modernity that could not be satisfied. Bringing people into "the light of the day" is therefore not just a visual metaphor but had precise material implications of what links bodily form, modes of behavior, and states of consciousness for recognition (respectful or otherwise) to take place. The contrast between the abstractions of colonial authority and the temptations this provided for native conversion can be contrasted with the embodied practicality of ancestral physical renewal.

In the Cameroon Grassfields, contact with Europeans allowed indige-nous people, and particularly the young, access to different body substances from ancestral ones as a means of reproduction. From first contact with Europeans in the 1890s, young men and in particular young women wished to convert to Christianity by quite literally changing their bodies. If all could share in the body of Christ, then all could achieve spirituality through the salvation of their own personal body rather than by sharing that of the Fon. Quite literally this meant participating in the Christian ritual of baptism, of washing or anointing the body as a means of altering or individualizing its relationship to ancestral substance. If in some sense the Fon's breath/saliva "cooled" the violence of the sexual act, cleansed it, and gave life to the fetus, it seems that baptism and holy water shared the same potential to complete the conception of a person. Once conversion was achieved, it seems there was no great compulsion, at least among Catholic converts, to attend church or even take the sacrament when dying. Father Rogan, the head of the Catholic Mill Hill Mission in Cameroon, writing in his annual report in 1931, complained of the gross immorality of the West Cameroon Christians and said that recently only twenty-five out of four hundred Christians had come to mass at the church near Soppo. He continued in a shocked tone, "There are scores of adult Christians, men and women, living together. . . . the fact of young Christian girls giving birth to illegitimate children arouses no comment. If the girl chooses to name the father, Christian parents are satisfied with a fine" (Rogan 1931). If baptism had the effect of girls gaining control of their bodies, it seems to have had a major effect on their faith in the power of ancestrally ordered hierarchy. By working for German colonial officers or walking to the coast to work on the plantations, young men worked to consume European foods, wear their clothes, wash themselves with imported soap, and get drunk on German schnapps. Young girls would flee to the missions from polygamous households to be married to young catechists and be trained as good housewives. There they would be given blankets, cloth, enamel bowls, and other utensils to create a domestic household, to prepare food and clothe themselves according to their new Christian role. Numerous complaints are made by the older men deserted by their wives. "One expects one's wives to look after one's compound and to attend to one's food. The Roman Catholics come and take one's wives away and one is left neglected" (Jeffreys 1933). Such reports quite literally describe the transformation from dependence on lineage heads and fons to a more individualized and egalitarian resubstantiation of the body. Sally Chilver (personal communication) provides one story from 1916 about a party of catechumens seeking baptism, traveling in search of Catholic priests, and being welcomed and baptized at the seminary in Nkongsamba. One woman from the party returned home richly dressed in European cloth. She went to the market to show herself off and was mistaken for a "vision"—for someone who had been to another world and had returned with rich clothes. The fact that normally such access to occult powers was a privilege of male ancestral hierarchy doesn't seem to have interfered with her physical recategorization as a Christian. By 1929 such women had become well known in the Grassfields as prophetesses capable of healing and confronting suspected witches among those who came to see them. One such woman, called Munia, began to preach in the yard of the Basel Protestant Mission in Bali in 1929 and initiated her converts by bathing them fully clothed in the mission pond. Munia dreamed that God was going to send food and that there was no longer any need for women to prepare fields for planting. God would show them how to get salt for nothing (i.e., not to rely on men), how to heal the sick, and how to make sterile women fertile (O'Neil 1987).

It is perhaps not surprising that the missions were quickly seen as a threat by both the colonial authorities and the chiefs. But what was the nature of the threat posed by the missions to colonial support of traditional power? One of the earliest points of conflict is the appearance of European-style buildings in places where the young would congregate: by being so visible, the buildings could be used by the young as a base for asserting their power against the chiefs. Buildings made of sun-dried brick and with zinc roofs used materials that had to be transported often over one hundred miles by human porterage. Buildings were erected by the Catholic missions on chiefdom land, often without permission, in order to bring the "bush churches" closer to people and in contradiction to the chiefs who would only allow them and mission schools to be built near the palaces. Mission reports of the late 1920s and early 1930s provide evidence of a systematic strategy by the Catholic mission to secure land and build churches without permission from the chiefs, which in turn brought the missions into increasing conflict with colonial authority. On October 29, 1937, a meeting was held in Bafut, one of the major Grassfield chiefdoms, by the chief commissioner to resolve the dispute between the elders and the Catholic mission. The mission wanted to build more churches, and the elders refused to give them plots of land and wanted the illegally built churches torn down. The commissioner asked the elders to explain their antagonism to the churches. The first speaker, an aged counselor, said:

> The little experience we have had of the Roman Catholic converts in Bafut has antagonised us toward the mission. These Christians have caused a great deal of trouble. They declare that they are free from all restraint by us and refuse to follow any longer Bafut customs and traditions. As a result of the teaching he gets, a Christian refuses to recognize Bafut authority. Consequently we do not want the Roman Catholic mission here. They are disrupting the town. (Jeffreys 1933: 4)

Later on in the meeting, complaints are made of the young converts' attitude toward eating: "What annoys us is that they have joined us in our feasts, eaten our salt, but when it comes to their turn they refuse to reciprocate on the grounds that they are Christians. When their turn comes to provide the feast, they say as Christians they cannot remain as members and leave having eaten our feasts and paid nothing." Another complaint concerns the palm wine of chiefs: "If a messenger [*chinda*] is carrying it on the road people will get out of the way and leave the road clear. No one, not even a Quarter head will touch it but we have seen Roman Catholics snatch the calabash, smash it and spill the wine on the road."

The idea that young converts are strong and independent and take what they want shows up best in changing attitudes toward marriage. A girl given in marriage by her father will be approached and told, "Come to church and be free. You can stay where you like and then your father must refund the brideprice." To the chiefs, the Catholic missions were a sickness: wives refuse to provide food, girls refuse marriage and go to live in town, and young men go outside to work and refuse to follow tradition. Yet seventy years later the chiefships thrive, and you can hear similar complaints made by elders against the young, although now the complaints are focused on their attending nightclubs or the individualizing effects of their spending too long in the cities or abroad.

A MATERIALIST APPROACH?

What constitutes a materialist approach? The most obvious would be in this case the political economy of colonial and postcolonial transition. The "freedoms" experienced by participation in the colonial economy were founded on particular forms of coerced labor and the extraction of surplus value. For the majority of young male clients, the new freedoms ended in their deaths on the plantations or in labor gangs on the side of a road or a railway that they were forced to construct. For those that survived, the articulation of traditional marriage to the individualizing aims of the young either paradoxically and momentarily acted to enlarge the hierarchy of large polygamous households of senior elders or eventually broke them down into either more diverse patterns of competition for wives and land redistribution. A related and relevant issue would be how these emergent tendencies of the relative success of the colonial economy were made visible or realizable to all concerned, through clothes, food, zinc tin roofs, and missions built of sun-dried brick.

But this materialization of success brings us to the other side of the materialist argument stressed in this chapter. In the same way that Latour marginalized the substrate leading to the substantiation of microbes in Pasteur's discovery in 1864, the political economy is usually ignored because of its objective character. But rather as Marx's argument on the organic composition of capital is still the best way of understanding the exploitation of surplus labor value in modern capitalism, whatever one's individual experience of it may be, praxis provides the grounds on which people come to experience themselves in the eyes of others as more material, more massive and condensed, or as ephemeral and immaterial. Any particular form of such a praxis is a mediation in the sense that it boils down to the work of young male clients, which became an object for colonial competition, or the reproductive capacity of young women, access to which unexpectedly escapes the control of elders and missionaries alike. The attendant reality of massive exploitation, loss of life, and extraction of surplus labor has to be matched, therefore, by this other side of the materialist argument.

What can we glean from this ethnography about the conditions for new forms of self-realization? What we might think of some of these stories, such as the female prophetesses or the fate of the young woman in Yaounde, is simply not at issue, since it is new expectations of care, security, and dignity that we assume people are struggling for. But this can constitute a curious mixture of new forms of power as well as self-sacrifice. For example, impeding colonial subjects from understanding the conditions of their existence, blocking their self-realization, was achieved at first by preventing travel and movement except under conditions of extreme supervision and punishment. Not surprisingly, mobility is perhaps the key treasured personal right in postmodern Cameroon. So today is access to the Internet, phones, and digitized information. Cameroon, like much of the rest of West Africa, has one of the highest rates of use of mobile phones in the world, though it is also one of its poorer members. Self-realization is therefore a pragmatic issue rooted in what one can expect from the social relations and contacts available and the demands that can be exerted both upon them and by them.

CONCLUSION

Asking whether a materialist approach is possible raises a final issue. We began with Marx's belief that emancipatory knowledge is linked to the potential for self-realization. He wanted to delineate a threshold of acceptability, however utopian, below which a society cannot be regarded as minimally just or decent. We have more sophisticated renditions of such aspirations in liberal writers on justice who describe the conditions to achieve a freedom of capabilities. But Marx also started from the premise that "substantive freedom" depends on having access to a set of opportunities to choose from. The premise that basic civic and political rights are the best guarantees of such access to well-being also defines a liberal position. We are able to give weight to this argument from a materialist perspective in that the achievement of these aims involves a choice of different material opportunities. If a society is "developed" by the material conditions which ensure that certain capabilities are functioning, Marx's more determinist views would seem to have prevailed. As we have seen, there are several advantages to this sense of materiality, since it ensures presence by the acquisition of the basic means of a social life. However, historical experience convinces us that this is not sufficient and substantiates only the right of various authoritarian regimes to define a spurious legitimacy in the right to rule. Rather, it is the capacity to make choices, and the capabilities of self-realization implied therein that would constitute the materialization of an archaeology of freedom.

NOTE

I am particularly grateful for discussions with Stephan Feuchtwang and Jean-Pierre Warnier in writing this chapter.

REFERENCES

Appadurai, Arjun. 1986. *The Social Life of Things*. Cambridge: Cambridge University Press.

Cohn, Bernard. 1996. *Colonialism and Its Forms of Knowledge*. Princeton, N.J.: Princeton University Press.

de Heusch, Luc. 1980. "Heat, Physiology and Cosmogony: Rites of Passage among the Thonga." In Ivan Karp and Charles S. Bird, eds., *Explorations in African Thought Systems*. Bloomington: Indiana University Press.

Eagleton, Terry. 1997. *Marx and Freedom*. London: Phoenix Press.

Elster, John. 1985. *Making Sense of Marx*. Cambridge: Cambridge University Press.

Ingold, Tim. 2000. "On Weaving a Basket." In *The Perception of the Environment*. London: Routledge.

Jeffreys, M. D. W. 1933. "Roman Catholic Mission: Application for Site at Bafut." Bamenda Archive No. B. 516/33, provincial delegation, Bamenda, Cameroon.

Lacan, Jacques. 1978. *Ecrits*. Vol. 1. Paris: Editions du Seuil.

Latour, Bruno. 1998. *Pandora's Hope*. Cambridge: Harvard University Press.

Lemonnier, Pierre. 1993. *Technological Choices*. London: Routledge.

Leroi-Gourhan, André. 1993. *Gesture and Speech*. Trans. Anna Bostock Berger. Cambridge: MIT Press.

Martin, Luther H., Huck Gutman, and Patrick H. Hutton, eds. 1988. *Technologies of the Self: A Seminar with Michel Foucault*. Amherst: University of Massachusetts Press.

Marx, Karl. 1967. "Economic and Philosophy Manuscripts." In *Marx and Engels Collected Works*, vol. 3. London: Lawrence and Wishart.

——. 1973. *Grundrisse*. Harmondsworth: Penguin.

Marx, Karl, and Friedrich Engels. 1975. *Collected Works*. Vol. 5. London: Lawrence and Wishart.

Mauss, Marcel. 1950. "Les techniques du corps." In Claude Lévi-Strauss, ed., *Sociologie et Anthropologie*. Paris: PUF.

O'Neil, Robert. 1987. "A History of Mogamo, 1865–1940." PhD diss., Columbia University.

Rogan, M. 1931. Annual Report for the Diocese of Bamenda, Cameroon. Mill Hill Mission Archives, Mill Hill, London.

Warnier, Jean-Pierre. 1993. *L'esprit d'entreprise au Cameroun*. Paris: Karthala.

——. 2001. "A Praxeological Approach to Subjectivation in a Material. World." *Journal of Material Culture* 6.1:5–24.

Žižek, Slavoj. 2003. "Not a Desire to Have Him, But to Be Like Him." Review. *London Review of Books*, August 21.

Ownership gathers things momentarily to a point by locating
them in the owner, halting endless dissemination, effecting an identity.
—**MARILYN STRATHERN,** *Property, Substance, and Effect*

FRED MYERS

Some Properties of Art and Culture:
Ontologies of the Image and Economies
of Exchange

n the early 1970s, the Aboriginal artist and activist Wandjuk Marika asked
the Australian government to investigate the unauthorized use of Yolngu
clan designs on a variety of commodity forms, inaugurating a process of
recognizing indigenous "copyright" for such designs. Copyright, famously, is known to involve a particular formulation of materiality, distinguishing idea from concrete expression, with only the latter being subject to
ownership rights as a form of property.[1] However sympathetic to indigenous
concerns over controlling their culture, this treatment of design—and
culture—as a form of property involves understandings and practices of
materiality and subjectivity that are different from indigenous Aboriginal
relationships to cultural production and circulation. In exploring the significance, for material culture theory, of recent work on and events in the
development of notions of cultural property, one of my main concerns in
this chapter is the relevance of local understandings of objectification—or
objectness and human action—as embedded object-ideologies. I discuss the
limits of legal discourses of cultural property to capture and reflect indigenous Australian concerns about their relation to culture, to creativity, and
to expression.

The central thesis of this chapter is that materiality—as a theory of quality
of objectness—is not so much an issue of matter but is constituted, rather,
through ideological frameworks. Thus, the formulation of materiality (or

materialities) is varied and often conflicting around different understandings of subjects and objects. Nowhere is this more apparent—or palpable—
than in situations in which human beings attempt to secure, stabilize, or
even limit the flow of culture, to turn culture into property form. Rather
than proposing a theory of materiality, then, I am interested here in pursuing through ethnographic consideration the trajectory of local theories of
materiality as indigenous Australian paintings and designs move through
the Western art-culture system and the Western concept of property and as
different object-ideologies meet. My interest in this problem derives from
ethnography that indicates Aboriginal concerns over the control of socially
valued knowledge and its dispersal—through practices of secrecy, exchange,
invisibility, and immateriality. These practices clearly depended on the materialities of producing and circulating knowledge through voice, ritual, and
object-presentation and equally certainly did not anticipate the materiality
of mechanical and digital reproduction. Ultimately, I see this study as one
consideration of what happens when "culture" takes on new and varied
forms of materiality.

Ethnography abounds in the unexpected—ironies, complicities, and in-
completeness of action, the stuff of social life. Ethnography does not accept
the certainties of cultural constructs like "property" built on an assumption
of the radical difference—what Bruno Latour (1993) would call "purification"—between subjects and objects.[2] Over the last several years, I have
studied Aboriginal Australian cultural action and creativity in the arts by
following the life of objects and the worlds, institutions, and people they
bring together (or mediate).[3] This ethnography has been a response to the
Primitivism debates (Clifford 1988; Manning 1985; Price 1989; Rubin 1984)
that dominated the framing of this topic and ignored culturally meaningful
action on the other side of the West/rest divide. I have been concerned with
tracing the unintended developments of indigenous Australian art as a form
of intercultural production, caught up in complex networks and institutions
of collaboration.

Indigenous acrylic painting began in central Australia in 1971 as a form of
cultural production in the government settlement of Papunya. At a time
when government policies promoted a radical regime of cultural assimila-
tion, with its apparently implacable hostility to indigenous culture, Aboriginal painters found a sympathetic supporter in a schoolteacher with art

training, Geoff Bardon (see Bardon 1979, 1991). Bardon helped catalyze the Western Desert painting movement, which eventually placed its work in the most prestigious art galleries and venues in that country and elsewhere (Myers 2002). It was never imagined that Aboriginal image-making could be a contemporary fine art that would bring unprecedented recognition and visibility to Aboriginal people and their culture within the Australian nation, and we have much to learn from indigenous understandings of this outcome.

I am going to discuss three cases of scandal—"fraud" or "forgery"—in the Aboriginal art market, because these somewhat extreme and irregular cases help illuminate what happens when contact occurs between what I call a revelatory regime of value characteristic of indigenous Australians and the "Western art-culture system" (Clifford 1988). I emphasize that I am concerned with the specifics of the art-culture system, which cannot assimilate all the potential properties of indigenous painting to its own schemas. The cases of fraud provide cautionary tales, helping us to understand the limits of our theoretical constructs and the transformative consequences of reorganizations of value provoked as objects circulate across cultural borders and between regimes of value. These reorganizations flow from the provocative effect of putting ideas and expectations into material forms that are mediated through the specific historical structuring of the fine art market.

What emerges from these case studies are the problems of articulation between images as integral aspects of Aboriginal culture and two alternative systems of representation through which Aboriginal people have increasingly been forced to live and by which they might be both valued or devalued. The first is "art," which has offered a medium through which they have been able to make themselves visible on their own terms, more or less, intervening in the representations circulating "about" them. But their interventions cannot be understood apart from the *materiality* of painting and of "art" (that is, art's institutions and properties). The other point on this triangle is "cultural property," an important conceptual framework that has been put forward as a basis for claiming protection of indigenous and minority groups against cultural appropriation. The fundamental claim derives from the assertion that art (or culture) is " 'essential to' or 'constitutive of' or 'expressive of' the identity of the group" (Coleman 2003: 1). Frequently, claims for protection have been articulated by extending the regimes of copyright and intellectual property law, but these forms of protection raise many difficulties in the way they formulate intercultural activity (see Coleman 2003). Between them we are faced not only with three perspectives upon the nature of materiality, but also with the degree to which their consideration reveals both my own understandings and the more general Aboriginal conceptualizations of what might be implicated in the materiality of objects and images.

CASE 1: WANDJUK MARIKA

The first scandal occurred in the early 1970s, when Wandjuk Marika—the well-known Yolngu artist and activist from Arnhem Land in northern Australia—asked the Australian government to investigate the unauthorized use of his sacred clan designs on a variety of commodity forms, in particular on tea towels. Marika inaugurated a process of recognizing indigenous "copyright" for such designs, a process that has subsequently occurred in a number of well-known cases, involving the use of Aboriginal images on everything from T-shirts to carpets manufactured in Vietnam.[4]

In Wandjuk's words:

That was 1974.
Then I walked into one of the shops and I found the tea towel,
Published in Holland,
Which had my own sacred design on this tea towel, tablecloth.
When I walk into that shop, and when I saw it
I was shocked and break my heart.

I bought it, cost me maybe $10
And then I said to the shopkeeper,
"Look you don't charge me that much.
This is my own design, you have no right to sell it.
This is bad. This is my own design, my sacred design.
I will only buy that for $2, just for the cloth,
Because it is my own copyright design."

Then I was thinking very hard.
What shall I do, where shall I get the help,
Who's going to help to stop this copyright stealing?
Instead of painting their own painting, they always copy designs
From the traditional areas.

They don't know what the painting is.
They thought they are just pleasure paintings
But it's the symbol, the power, experience and knowledge.
After I found my own design on the tea towels I was shocked and I lose
my power to paint,
Lose my power for a number of years.

Yes, I was thinking and thinking;
I try and try and at last something was coming into my mind.
Ah, I said, I have to send this to the Prime Minister,
The former Prime Minister, which is Gough Whitlam.
Gough was Labor Prime Minister,
And I sent the two towels to Canberra to Prime Minister and I say, "OK,
I need help to setting up something to protect the copyright.
I need the lawyer or something,"
And they say to me "OK. Don't worry Wandjuk, we'll help you."
(Marika 1995: 118–119)[5]

Marika's claim evoked sympathy. By 1974, of course, few people who heard of his story would be disadvantaged by recognizing indigenous ownership on copyright grounds. More important, the translation of indigenous rights into the framework of copyright—or cultural property—seemed an intelligible "recontextualization" (Thomas 1991) of indigenous painting within the commodity regime. This recontextualization would transpose what might be seen as one set of signs and practices into another regime of value.[6]

Wandjuk objected not simply to commodification as a form of desacralization but more specifically to the display and use of designs by those without ritual authority to do so. The misuse affected him: he lost the power to paint. While he also perceived the effects of the commodity circulation of these forms, he *surely* must have imagined conditions or conventions under

1. Wandjuk Marika, Yolngu artist and cultural activist, as photographed by Juno Gemes in 1982. Copyright 1982 Juno Gemes.

which legitimate holders of these designs *could* circulate them, such as the famous Yirrkala bark petition for land rights to the Australian Parliament in 1963 (see Morphy 1992; Wells 1982; see fig. 2) and other ritual diplomatic exchanges such as the Arnhem Land *Rom* taken to Canberra in November 1982 (Wild 1986). Elsewhere, too, painters at Papunya Tula Artists in Central Australia imagined themselves able to exchange their designs for money or other objects. For now, I want to claim the case Wandjuk made as the one which best fits the understanding of intellectual copyright, in which the flow into commodification violates and harms his own relationship to inalienable property. It is also a case in which he narrates his own importance

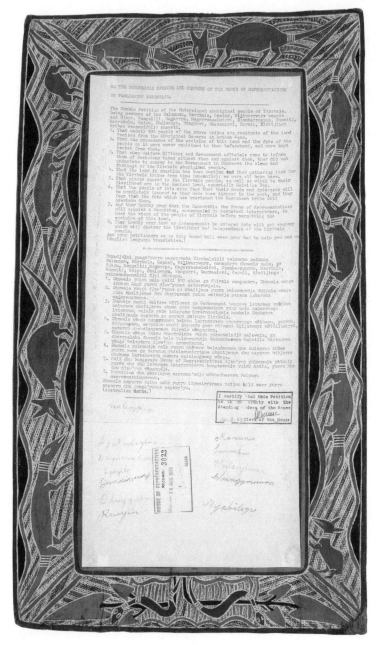

2. The Yirrkala bark petition, sent to the Australian Parliament in 1963, where it is still housed. Reproduced with permission of the Yirrkala community.

through his relationship to Gough Whitlam, then Australia's prime minister, as a guardian against the promiscuous dispersal of his clan's designs.

In order to understand this situation in terms closer to those of indigenous participants, it is critical to look at the relationship between local understandings of objects and human action—as embedded in practices of personhood, relatedness, and secrecy—and what happens with the regulation and classification of the new form of Aboriginal painting. The treatment of both design and culture as forms of intellectual property in the legal setting involves understanding ideas and practices of materiality and subjectivity—of object and subject—that are different from indigenous Aboriginal relationships to cultural production, creativity, and circulation. The "object ideology"[7] of this revelatory regime of value is organized around the practical consciousness of materiality as something brought forth into "sensory presence"—what Pintupi people mark with the concept *yurti*. Materiality is conceived as something objectified in revelation or transmission, rather than created de novo. That revelation of ancestral knowledge and events in material form, such as painting, ritual, or song, is colloquially known as "The Dreaming" (*tjukurrpa* in Pintupi).

As Wandjuk Marika suggests, it is possible to translate the social practices of indigenous image-making in terms of their resemblance to practices of intellectual property, of ownership and copyright, but only partly. Aboriginal people (Yarnangu) in Central Australia say that the story-song-design complexes of The Dreaming—and both the rituals and landscapes that are viewed as integral to them—are "held" (*kanyinu*) by various groups of people. Perhaps I can make this ontology clearer: The Dreaming is not the landscape itself or principally even an explanation of it, although that is one of its attributes. Rather, the landscape is the materialization of The Dreaming as a sensory form to be experienced (that is, *yurti*); it is a manifestation of The Dreaming, but not an account of what it *is* (see also Poirier 1996). The right to "show" (*yurtininpa*, "reveal" or "make sensorily present") a ceremony is in the hands of those we might call "owners" of that country and its associated Dreaming stories. It was on such grounds that the men I knew typically painted their own country—"making visible" or giving, in this way, components of their own identity (see fig. 3). But although they might "give," "reveal," or exchange them, the images remain (as Marika's statement points out) always a part, another extension or embodiment of those who

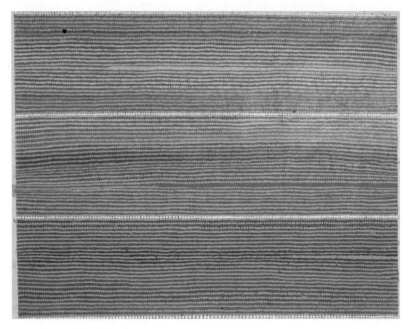

3. Turkey Tolson's painting *Straightening Spears*, 1991. Iconically representing spears through the image of dotted lines, this painting emphasizes the large number of men gathered in The Dreaming, straightening their spears at Ilingawurrngawurrnga and preparing to engage in battle. Copyright of Aboriginal Artists Agency. This version of the famous image has been made available by permission of the Robert Steele Gallery.

are custodians of these Dreamings and of The Dreaming itself, which is the identity ground of the painters. The right to conduct a symphony is not held to be a claim to composing it.

But the materiality of this knowledge—objectified in particular forms such as the landscape, ritual, or acrylic and bark painting—has distinctive consequences. Objectifications of Aboriginal myth and ritual knowledge have material qualities beyond the narrative structure; they have extension in space, insofar as the stories are linked to specific places, which may become an important material property in formulating a social identity among those who have rights to different stories located along the same ancestral path. Realized in sound and performance, stories and the ceremonies reenacting them—along with the associated paraphernalia and designs—can also be owned and exchanged (but not sold and purchased); rights to speak and transmit them can become the objects of social and political organization, and their material properties encourage distinctive strategies of concealment and transmission.

The concern of people in such a system is to limit dispersal, to control the potential or manifestations of The Dreaming (*tjukurrpa*). Understood as objectifications of ancestral subjectivity, manifestations of The Dreaming are further identified with certain persons and groups who have a kin-based obligation to control the rights to reproduce these images as well and to determine who can see them. Unlike with classical Western copyright, the images controlled here are not thought to be of people's own creation.[8] Again the nearest parallel might be the way the rights of a lineage to the profits made from a symphony are based on its ancestral composition, but the Aboriginal view does not emphasize the artistic activity of the painter.

This is a distinct system of value production that takes its integrity from its relationship to all other aspects of that society's values, constituting what Marcel Mauss called a "total social fact" (Mauss 1925). The Dreaming discursively and practically articulates personhood and ontology, mediating significantly the sociopolitical relations between people organized spatially (in territorially dispersed groups) and intergenerationally into a system of identity, of similarity and difference, of autonomy and relatedness (see Myers 1986). The production of images, within this framework and especially in ritual, is a fundamental medium in which a person's—or group's—autonomy can be expressed and drawn into relationship with others (see Myers 1986, 1988). I would call this a "revelatory regime of value."

Such a regime of value did not anticipate the ways in which technologies such as the market and mechanical reproduction could detach signs from those who make and circulate them. For Aboriginal people, it is not fundamentally objectifications of human creativity, then, which copyright proposes to regulate; copyright would be regulating rights to esoteric ancestral knowledge and creativity. And if it is not human or individual creativity that is at stake, we will also see that the mere potential for ownership (existence as a material object) does not achieve an easy placement in the fine art system.[9]

Waves of scandal and rumor have equally followed the entry of indigenous painting into the system of fine art, a recognition supposed to be accompanied by an emptying or subordination of political and ethnic value to those of a transcendental or formal aesthetics.[10] This subordination is not,

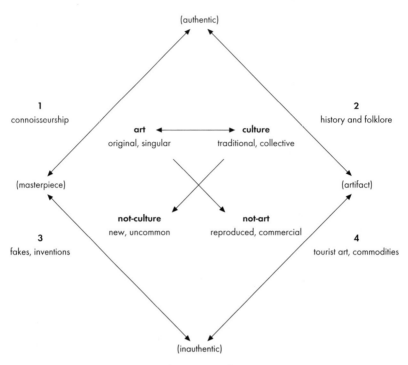

(authentic)

| 1 | | | 2 |
| connoisseurship | | | history and folklore |

art ⟷ culture
original, singular   traditional, collective

(masterpiece)   (artifact)

not-culture   not-art
new, uncommon   reproduced, commercial

| 3 | | | 4 |
| fakes, inventions | | | tourist art, commodities |

(inauthentic)

4. The Art-Culture System. Source: After James Clifford, *The Predicament of Culture* (Cambridge: Harvard University Press, 1988), 224.

however, complete, and what actually prevails is a contestation over the hierarchical organization of the values adhering to these objects. As indicated by Clifford's well-known diagram of the "art-culture system" (fig. 4), a classification as "art" involves an object being articulated as original, singular, and unique—values placing objects on the side of authenticity, in contrast to fakes or reproductions, on the one hand, and to the class of objects that are seen as traditional and collective, on the other hand. The classification of fine art, based on connoisseurship, markets, and art museums, recognizes a difference in human creativity and execution that has little value in the revelatory regime in which the production of Aboriginal art originates. Furthermore, the art-culture system supposedly does not recognize the racial or cultural identities of the artist. To be art, an object cannot be collective but should be expressive of a more sublime characteristic that subordinates other properties to individual creativity.

As Clifford noted, the art-culture system in this form has an ideological function. It constructs an anthropological image of the concept "humankind," perceived to be the source for "a universal human creative and aesthetic potential." This is "Art" within Roland Barthes's "Family of Man" (Barthes 1957)—in which all art is "human art." But this universalism becomes a contested terrain for those concerned with appropriation.

ART AND CULTURE. As Clifford's diagram (1988: 224) implies, the classifications "art" and "culture" are rooted in distinctive institutions such as art museums, art history, and art dealing, rather than (say) anthropology or natural history. This is an example of a regime of value, the hierarchical organization of values implicated in classification and institutionalization (for others, see Beidelman 1997; George 1999). Yet Aboriginal objects are not simply assimilated to this new context. The recontextualization of Aboriginal objects is also transforming the context of fine art itself, as the cases of scandal indicate.

IMAGININGS. In articulating their contemporary practices, Aboriginal painters in central Australia have drawn on a framework that is not particularly concerned with the usual sources of value that characterize "art" in the West. The movement of acrylic paintings into the purview of Western viewers and patrons challenges the ways in which cultural objects are familiarly formulated for us. They use an ontology and set of practices drawn from their own world of production, imagining their circulation in the terms of the local economy of exchange, the revelatory regime of value I described earlier. Their paintings, they often said, were being given "to Canberra," understood as either the site or country of the Australian federal government, on whom they were dependent, or their "bosses" or *mayutju*, who by virtue of this "giving" or "revelation" were thereby drawn into a relationship of both obligation and moral identity. For individual purchasers, the gift required appropriate compensation, which the painters recognized would necessarily mean money as the primary expression of value within that system. The painters expected that buyers would recognize that payment was for the revelation of Dreamings and not for the mere execution of the painting.[11] This is the significance of gestures such as one Pintupi man's claim that he should have been paid "four hundred thousand dollars."

For the Aboriginal people of remote Australia, forgery is "theft," not simply because the money-producing component of the image is diverted but because their designs are inalienable dimensions of their identity. But forgery can take other forms as well. What if the work is *not* an appropriation of specific indigenous designs?

Does it matter if a work is not produced by an Aboriginal person? In the first scandal story, the tea towel designs were clearly Yolngu. But there is also the case of the white Australian artist Elizabeth Durack, who painted pseudonymously using the invented identity of an Aboriginal man, Eddie Burrup (McDonald 1997: 7; McCulloch 1997a: 21, 22; S. McCulloch 1997c: 14–21). Although she did not appropriate specific indigenous designs, Durack entered her work in competitions of "Aboriginal art." The revelation of her circumstance provoked outrage in some Aboriginal quarters.[12] The journalist Lenore Nicklin reports:

> When Djon Mundine [a well-known indigenous curator] discovered that Eddie Burrup was really the 81-year old West Australian painter Elizabeth Durack, he was furious. Here was cultural appropriation at its worst. "It's a fucking obscenity," he said. "It's like Kerry Packer [a leading and aggressive Australian business man] pretending to be Mahatma Gandhi." (Nicklin 1997: 22)

Although many must have suspected that the large prices and attention being received by Aboriginal art would be an attraction for any white artist, Durack's invention does not appear to be a case of appropriating Aboriginal identity and images purely for profit. A member of a famous pioneering family and a longtime friend of Aboriginal people in western Australia, Durack described the invention of Eddie Burrup as more of an alter ego. McCulloch (1997c: 23) reports that "in creating Burrup, Durack felt, insofar as it was a conscious decision . . . that he became a conduit for her huge and somewhat eclectic reservoir of knowledge about the Aboriginal world." Durack saw painting as "Eddie" as working within the spirit of reconciliation and was shocked at the misunderstanding of the works and her reasons for doing them. One Aboriginal response was Mundine's: "She's from the squattocracy. Elizabeth Durack saying she mixed with Aboriginal people is like Prince Charles saying he mixed with nannies. I'm sure she played with Aboriginal children when she was a little girl, but she came home and slept between white sheets" (Mundine, quoted in Nicklin 1997: 22).

This judgment evaluates her Aboriginality (or lack thereof) and her right to participate as an Aboriginal person, policing the identity boundaries in a way that rejects a common Western fantasy of personal and artistic self-invention. Mundine's comments here reflect a position he has articulated frequently in relation to the growing number of "wannabes": one does not become "Aboriginal" simply by an act of invention.

But complex and hybrid identifications not confined to racial or ethnic identity[13] are coming to be more commonly acknowledged in contemporary Australia. Durack's close and enduring relationship with the Aboriginal people with whom she grew up elicited comment from Jeff Chunuma, a respected member of the Waringarri community. Less severe but still critical, disapproving but still her "son," Chunuma is reported to have passed on his community's response as follows: "You tell 'im 'e's got to come up here, sit down and talk to us. It's no good what 'e's doing. That old man behind her shoulder [referring to her adopted identity]. She got to stop doing that" (Jeff Chunuma, quoted in McCulloch 1997c: 19). The implication is that had she discussed her project with her supposed community, they might have supported her.

One gallery director, clearly operating in terms of the Western art-culture system, claimed the issue of identity was irrelevant. Echoing the common claims to art's universality, Edmund Capon (of the Art Gallery of New South Wales) declared, "I don't give a hoot who painted it. I care about the picture." "I don't see it as fraud," he said, "because the painting itself is going to be judged on the painting itself; it's not going to be judged on who painted it" (Capon, quoted in McCulloch 1997a: 2). To do otherwise would be to admit that indigenous painting was judged on different grounds than other "art" and to raise questions about whether it was really of a quality to be called "art."[14]

Mundine, speaking from a distance, correctly recognizes a larger picture in which Aboriginal people's right to control their culture and art is being transgressed. But actual relationship and geographical propinquity make a difference in the judgment. The reaction to Durack's impersonation was generally milder in the West—from both Aborigines and others who know the Duracks well from the family's longstanding pastoral connection with the Kimberley. Durack, they said, had been speaking for Aboriginal people through her art for years, and while her Aboriginal creation may have been misguided, it was based on altruistic motives and a genuine attempt at cultural bridge-building. (McCulloch 1997a: 2)

Durack's case is perhaps the most telling of them all, in that the scandal comes to question the cultural (racial or ethnic) identity of this art, its motivations, and its implications. Jeff Chunuma's comments make it clear that "ownership" is not necessarily racialized—that some sort of hybridity of local identity might be acceptable (in the form of adoption, initiation, or even intensive consultation), however much the art-market regime of value attempts at purification or denial of such relationships.

CASE 3: TURKEY TOLSON

Other examples of "forgery" or "fraud"—by which I mean paintings done by non-Aboriginals and passed off as "Aboriginal," or paintings signed by famous Aboriginal painters but not actually painted by them—have also weighed on the art market. For example, in the Kathleen Petyarre case (see McCulloch 1997d: 3), a painting that was said to have been done by her and that won a National Aboriginal Art Prize was later said to have been painted partly by her Welsh (white) husband. In another case, the famous Pintupi artist Turkey Tolson (see McCulloch-Uehlin 1997: 1, 4) signed paintings done by female relatives.

What is at stake when a work by a white person is passed off as executed by an Aboriginal person and becomes part of the prime minister's collection, or when one can't tell the difference between a painting done by an Aboriginal and one done by a white? Is a good painting a good painting, no matter who paints it? Most theorists of modern art would insist that this is the case.[15]

And what about Turkey Tolson's admission (fig. 5) that he signed works painted by others (his wife, for example)? Surely this admission affects the value of works he has signed, since his signature is no longer evidence of his execution and the paintings' part in *his* story. In Aboriginal terms, this is

Statutory Declaration

I, TURKEY TOLSON TJUPURRULA do solemnly and sincerely declare:-

- I have seen my daughter-in-law Leanne, my daughter Nellie and also Pamela and Elizabeth at Michael Hollow's Gallery painting canvasses.

- I have seen some of the canvasses as they have been painted inside the Gallery by the women.

- I have seen they do not sign these canvasses when they are finished. I have seen Michael Hollow pay the women $200.00 each for some of these paintings.

- I have gone down to Michael Hollow's Gallery and I have signed these paintings in the Gallery that the women have painted.

- Michael Hollow has told me to sign these canvasses that the women have painted. He has then payed (sic) me $200.00 for signing these canvasses.

- I am also currently painting some paintings for Henry at the camp.

- Henry gave me some canvasses and some paint on Easter Sunday.

- Henry has told me that my daughter and daughter-in-law can help me do the paintings.

- I have been with Henry when he has seen the women painting these canvasses at the camp.

- I have seen Henry at the camp every day since he gave me the canvasses on Easter Sunday.

- When at the camp Henry has asked me to change over with the women and to paint on these canvasses that the women have been painting on so that he can take a photograph of me painting on those canvasses.

- As those canvasses are finished by the women and me, Henry has asked me to sign them.

- I have seen that the women do not sign any of these canvasses.

- I have seen Henry pay the women $50.00 for these paintings.

- Henry pays me $150.00 sometimes, and sometimes $200 after I sign these canvasses.

- Henry has asked me to do 60 canvasses and sign them.

- Henry gave me the canvasses on Easter Sunday and asked me to complete them by Monday or Tuesday next week.

- I have seen the photograph attached to this statement and I know the person there to be the Henry I am speaking about.

- I know that Susan McCullough writes for The Australian newspaper and that she wants to tell this story in the newspaper to a lot of people.

- I agree to her telling the story in the newspaper.

Declared at: *ALICE SPRINGS IN THE NORTHERN TERRITORY OF AUSTRALIA*
Dated *15th day of APRIL 1999*

Before me:

TURKEY TOLSON

5. The statutory declaration made by Turkey Tolson in 1999, part of the furor over Aboriginal art's commercialization.

unproblematic because Turkey authorized this painting of his Dreaming and oversaw its correctness. What do people own, therefore, when they buy one of these paintings? Some art dealers, of course, might benefit in the short term, if they can have a few more "Tolsons" to sell, because this signature makes a painting worth more than others. But the revelation of the practice threatens the overall structure of investment.

The absolute Aboriginality of the painting is not compromised, because some authorized Aboriginal person did execute the painting. But the sincerity of the sign is threatened if a commercial motive appears to dominate. The Alice Springs art seller Michael Hollows replied to the allegations about Tolson's work by insisting that the artist substantially reworked any paintings to which he put his name, in that way making them properly—by market standards—bearers of his signature (McCulloch-Uehlin 1997: 4). What is evident is that "art" requires a deeper "authenticity" than (for example) "tourist souvenirs." In other cases, which I don't have time to discuss, the scandal erupts at the boundary of Aboriginality and money. Does an apparent motivation of the painters for monetary reward necessarily imply a loss of the genuine Aboriginality—and a corruption of their profound relationships to The Dreaming—that should underlie their projects, an alignment of Aboriginal painting's sincerity with art's proper, "from the heart" authenticity?[16] If so, then those who have celebrated acrylic painting as "fine art" on the modernist model[17] have been misguided to announce the "end of Aboriginality" (and a recognition of the painterly aesthetic strength of the work); for some, this "end" seems to threaten Aboriginal art (and culture) with the possibility of simple commodification, marked by named painters making simulacra of their earlier successful paintings at their dealers' behest. Surely what is taking place is not a simple commodification, not a reduction of objects to quantitative exchange value, but rather a reorganization of the hierarchy of values adhering to the objects.

Does Turkey's participation in these practices represent a compromise of some deep identity on his part? Or has he, rather, been caught up in an art-market game which has consequences for him, but whose ethics and standards are different from his? His paintings enter into an art market characterized by a race for "product," and a competition for "name" artists. The artists believe they have the right to sell to whomever they please, but by accepting this condition of alienability they find themselves uncomfortably placed in what they are discovering is the corruption of the system, in which dealers vie with each other for the affections, loyalties, and paintings of individual Aboriginal artists.[18]

SCANDAL

As the movement from the revelatory regime to the commodity world of culture and art proceeds, these difficult articulations give rise to the potential for the various scandals. Not only does the commodification of these images detach them from the controls under which their dispersal was traditionally regulated, but mechanical and digital reproduction present a further range of new materialities, far beyond those encountered by Marika in the use of clan designs on a tea towel in Brisbane. With the rise of connoisseurship and a fine art market (see Myers 2002) where claims to universal fine art dismiss Aboriginal content as irrelevant, the conditions are created for the multitude of hundreds of battles and scandals involving forgery, frauds, and the structuring of the art market for Aboriginal fine art. These threaten the security of the structure of economic value within a system that is now challenged by Aboriginal paintings that partially resist and partially accommodate both their commodification and their status as fine art. The articulation properly brings into question the reputations of some dealers, no doubt, but they also threaten the integrity of the Aboriginal painters. In these rumors and scandals, one may recognize struggles over fixing the place and limits of Aboriginal culture's very appropriation by the market.

NEGOTIATING IDENTITY

Marilyn Strathern eloquently summarized the promiscuous possibility of materiality and possession, drawing on the critical potential of insights from Papua New Guinea ethnography, which no doubt also reflect a local object ideology. "Ownership," she has written, "gathers things momentarily to a point by locating them in the owner, halting endless dissemination, effecting an identity" (1999: 177). Rather than simply detaching producers, objects, and owners, the movement of Aboriginal images is producing new identities. Litigants accuse legal representatives of Aboriginal organizations of appropriating producers' interests. Indigenous activists attempt to create new organizations to represent the copyright claims of indigenous artists. As such it is possible to see these scandals in a positive light, as a renegotiation of the boundaries of indigenous and other identities. Such renegotiations take place largely through the materiality of the types of mediations I have described here.

The scandals represent a significant moment in the conceptualization or institutionalization of cultural property, a social drama or struggle in which contested evaluations are made evident and hierarchies (or regimes of value) put to the test. This is the model of social fields (Turner 1974) where values, strategies, and resources are all up for grabs, where boundaries are made in the process of adjudication rather than assumed.

Intellectual copyright law may allow for compensation to occur for unauthorized use of designs, but—as most supporters of this remedy acknowledge—copyright does not fully represent what is at stake in the problematic circulation of acrylic paintings as cultural artifacts (see Coleman 2003). A range of values attaches to these objects, and at different times, different properties come into view as salient. Copyright payment cannot, for example, remedy the threat or harm to cultural identity, nor can it assuage memories of the history of genocide that erupts in the exploitation of sacred designs and objects. There is no question that for many viewers, owners, and producers of the paintings, the occasion within which they are going to be seen by whites makes this history a vital aspect of what they are. In any case, the question of what kind of objects these paintings might be is not resolved in the legal imagination, as the growing interest in the frauds, forgeries, and misrepresentations indicates. Aboriginal peoples' rights over their designs or even over the concrete objects themselves will be transformed, but not simply, absolutely severed by the act of sale.

The result is inevitably a complex and transient accommodation rather than a domination between the sense of ownership and meaning that paintings come to have as Aboriginal culture, as fine art and as cultural property. Each permeates and leaks into the other, subverting its internal integrity by becoming an "excess" that cannot be simply contained by the system of values that generated it.

So Aboriginal people objected to Elizabeth Durack's impersonation of an Aboriginal neither as a criminal act nor—despite some views—as a "theft" of identity as if identity were a form of property. The Aboriginal criticisms suggest that her painting as an Aboriginal was problematic because she hadn't negotiated it with a relevant Aboriginal community. This seems to reflect considerations similar to those that became visible when Euro-Australian artist Tim Johnson painted, *with* permission, using the dot style.[19] He did so not *as* an Aboriginal person, but through an identity Aboriginal people had accepted. While such a performance was acceptable to some—and it might not have been acceptable to all Aboriginal people with rights to those designs—this does not make it different from the situation of Aboriginal people performing their identities—a performance that is always dangerous and subject to counterclaim and retaliation.

If "Aboriginality" is not the principal content of the paintings, what is the threat from non-Aboriginal painters painting in an Aboriginal style, or disguising themselves as Aboriginal? The very possibility of fraud suggests that a painting's indexical connection to Aboriginal people and their cultural project can be faked in the sign's detachment from persons in the market. But this in turn contradicts the claim that this art is valued just because it is *good* art (not because it is good *Aboriginal* art), deserving of entry into the nonghettoized category of "contemporary art" and not merely "culture." Painting within the frame of "fine art," why can't white artists paint "Aboriginal art"?[20] Are we reaching a new stage in the detachability of these signs, as music reached earlier with schizophonia (see Feld 1995)?

What is at issue in this boundary activity are the possibilities of "corruption" (see Lomnitz 1993).[21] The Durack case, of impersonating an Aboriginal identity in painting, does not constitute a crime, but it may be the most upsetting of the cases for Aboriginal people.[22] Its salience is evident through the effect of these corrupting practices on indigenous self-production. Complaints from Aboriginal people framed in terms of copyright (see Johnson 1996b) and about the stealing of their culture conjoin with equally long-standing concerns for self-determination for indigenous people within Australia, which has typically meant securing the right to speak for themselves, to represent themselves. This is not just the backward-looking protection of "one's culture," conceived as a static object. What is sought is an uncorrupted sphere in which "Aboriginal people" can themselves communicate. For others to presume to speak in their voices corrupts Aboriginal people's opportunities for self-determination. To put it more analytically, forgery and fraud undermine the possibility of forming an identity. In the context of the Durack case, the question "Who are you?" is anything but rhetorical. However, while the local Kimberley community's assessment of Durack stands in some contrast to the more assertively essentializing identity politics of the national Aboriginal activists, the latter must defer to the former, at least officially, because the category of community member has priority in recognition of identity. The art market is necessarily less open.

Turkey Tolson's artwork is threatened by corruption, but not because he is painting for money per se. Most of the painters do that, and they have become a source of money for their relatives, whose demands are intense and never-ending. The issue lies less in the absolute qualities of money, abstractly considered, than in the properties of its delivery and temporal distribution. Aboriginal artists paint their identities in their paintings, and the paintings are exchanged for cash—but in the broadest terms, the painter is trying to manage this identity in the midst of an onslaught of desire. Turkey's work is threatened by corruption because the conditions of his presence in Alice Springs—his need for more *regular* money and the needs of his dealer for "product"—draw him away from the experiences that inform his painting. This is not an artifact of alienation or monetary exchange *tout court*, but of specific properties of its availability. Ultimately, the scandals revolve around the dispossession, appropriation, or corruption of the principal good that indigenous people may have in the contemporary cultural conjuncture—their identity.

The very existence of these objects and their circulation depend at least partly on the intentions of the Aboriginal participants. We know that many indigenous artists in central and northern Australia have agreed to—and even initiated—the circulation of some forms of their religious imagery in commodity spaces at the same time that they seem to insist on its retaining some of its indigenous meaning and value. This objectification has not been a simple matter. The sustaining of indigenous—or perhaps "traditional"?—notions of cultural authority and identity through copyright, urged by Wandjuk Marika as long ago as 1973 (see Isaacs 1995; Johnson 1996b; Marika 1986), *has* been an insertion of Aboriginal views into the broader Australian framework that governs cultural production and circulation. What seemed an unlikely and unrealistic wish on the part of older Aboriginal people—that the Euro-Australian society would recognize their culture if they revealed it to them; that the images would *have* power over those who see them—has proved more the case than anyone would have imagined. If anything, they underestimated the agency possessed by their paintings in Gell's (1998) sense. But this agency in part accrued from the fact that these paintings are now hybrid objects embedded in a complex and transformed network of actors and actants, many of whom are not Aboriginal.

The scandals, then, demarcate potentials to cause harm, a potential intrinsic to the materiality of this wider field in which they are now situated. Certainly such harm may occur from the mismanagement of cultural properties, but even with the best of intentions from all concerned, dangers can result from the very materiality of social action objectified into concrete form.[23] A relevatory regime of value constituted not only within a fine art market but simultaneously as an issue of cultural property must contain contradictions with problematic consequences.

CONCLUSION: ARTIFACTS OF MATERIALITY

Issues of property and proliferation are central to the debates about materiality initiated by Walter Benjamin (1968) in his famous essay "The Work of Art in the Age of Mechanical Reproduction." I do not see this process as unidirectional. The question here is whether the prestige of the fine art market can come to Aboriginal acrylic painting without its succumbing to the processes of alienation inherent in commodification—the complete detachment of these objects from their producers and those authorized to have them produced. Where commodification leads to such radical alienation, it is the people as much as the product that is lost.

The Aboriginal art scandals reveal more than the existence (and persistence) of object-ontologies; they also instantiate contestations. Which ideologies of materiality will prevail as the material forms that comprise Aboriginal art circulate through varying regimes of value that have their own hierarchies and legal regulations? Because object-ideologies are related —as in the case of the art-culture system—to specific institutions and practices, the properties of "art" and "culture" must be understood as determined and objectified in relationship to these social fields.

This is why the circulation of objects through different regimes can reveal what anthropologists have known, since Victor Turner's work on social dramas (1974), about the ways in which hierarchies of value are articulated (see also Miller 2003). The articulation of our systems of law and aesthetics with those of Aboriginal people produces some strange and unpredictable effects and dilemmas. My point is that the recognition of Aboriginal objects as art is a material practice—not simply an endorsement of Aboriginal culture, but a recognition of certain forms of its materialization within a specific institutional form and system of value (involving markets, museums, and collectors). There is, I am arguing, a practical conflation of discourses as well as new openings that might cut across the distinction between Aboriginal and white. Just as the expectations of specific understandings of creativity embedded in copyright may haunt Aboriginal producers, the entry of these new concerns may also transform the way in which copyright is conceived. These are equally potential effects of the materiality of Aboriginal art.[24]

The art-culture system and the category of fine art within it should be understood as a structure that "purifies" (in the sense of Latour 1993) the objects that enter it, detaching from them the properties irrelevant to their aesthetic order. The process is akin to what Max Weber observed on the autonomization of the domain of art (and religion, etc.), and Pierre Bourdieu's delineation of fields of cultural production. Yet these art scandals also bear witness to the continued eruption of Aboriginalities (externalities of the fine art field) as the materiality of indigenous practices and understandings resist the detachment of these objects from their authorizing ontology. The paintings cannot be separated from the persons identified with them—from the fundamental understandings of Aboriginal life, which are integral to their value as aesthetic. As others have also argued, the question of "authenticity" remains a critical component of the legitimation of indigenous art (Hoban 2002; Merlan 2001). In this way, Aboriginal art shares with Western fine art something like the "art for art's sake" idealism that positions the field of art production against the profit orientation or utilitarian aim of other fields (see Marcus and Myers 1995; Hoban 2002).

The issue of authenticity implicated in these scandals is not simply generated by the process of commodification, but is further motivated by the context of Australian multiculturalism and the governmental commitment to tolerance of cultural diversity that led to early support for Aboriginal painting in the first place (see Myers 2002; Merlan 2001). There is a suspicion that Aboriginal painters are not genuinely Aboriginal, but are really just like the rest of Australia—and therefore not deserving of any special consideration. That is, culture is no longer the basis for recognizing a special difference. This provides yet another leverage of cultural motion. Insofar as these scandals actually flow toward a suspicion of *cultural* difference altogether, they have flowed toward the other pole of differentiation: "race." The idea that "race" is the difference actually forecloses the promiscuous potential of indigenous art and becomes another way of delineating or containing the flow of Aboriginality that otherwise might threaten the preserve of "Whiteness" and "Blackness." The art scandals show the inability of the fine art world fully to commodify the works both because of indigenous understandings and also the growing politicization of identity itself. In this situation, where "whites" painted as "Aboriginals," Aboriginal critics and commentators had conflicting views as they sought to protect the integrity of this vital resource of hope. While there are no doubt those who would never agree, there were prominent indigenous people, usually closer to the Kimberley community, who were prepared to accept Durack's work if she observed the obligations of participation with indigenous communities.

The resolution of this tension is taking place through the production of a new category—"Aboriginal fine art." This new category or subfield of art production (Hoban 2002) is partly subordinated to fine art in general through its acceptance of the general standards of connoisseurship that make it still distinct from "ethnographic art." It is the product of a specific network of cultural actors and institutions, one that includes whites and Aboriginal people. As such it forms part of a larger network of recontextualization, of battles over power and cultural capital that aim to move what had been "ethnographic art" to the context of "art museums." What emerges are the limitations of any version of the category of fine art that fails to recognize the problems that "Aboriginal fine art" addresses. The placement of objects in the category "fine art" should better proceed through the clarification of local art histories, emphasizing the work of producers, rather than the simple judgment of collectors and dealers. What these stories have revealed is the foundations for Aboriginal painters' claim that they must retain an authority over objects that have been separated from them, commensurate with the continued attachment of their identity to those same objects.

NOTES

I would like to thank Jane Desmond, Faye Ginsburg, Judith Goldstein, Bruce Knauft, Rene Lederman, Daniel Miller, and T. O. Beidelman for their comments on earlier versions of this chapter. An earlier and shorter version was delivered at the 2002 American Anthropological Association Meetings panel on materiality, organized by Daniel Miller, and an expanded paper was delivered as the American Ethnological Society Presidential Lecture, April 23, 2003, in Providence, Rhode Island.

1. U.S. copyright law, for example, holds that one can copyright a specific expression (a book, a song composition, a poem) but not a general idea (see Vaidhyanathan 2001).

2. In this sense, I believe the modern world is "becoming susceptible to anthropological treatment"—in Latour's (1993) words—of the "seamless fabric of what I shall call 'nature-culture.'"

3. My understanding of Aboriginal life and painting is based on extensive fieldwork with Pintupi-speaking people in various communities of central Australia from 1973 to 1975, 1979, 1981, 1982, 1983, 1984, and 1988 and in a variety of shorter field trips and work with dealers, curators, collectors, and government representatives in Australia, France, and the United States during the 1990s. I have described these relationships and the ways in which they guided my understanding in Myers 2002.

4. In an early case, Aboriginal Artists Agency brought suit on behalf of an Arnhem Land artist, Yangarininy Munungmurra, against Peter Stripes Fabrics in New South Wales (1985) for adapting the artist's work to suit furnishing fabric. A second important case involved a group of Arnhem Land artists including Johnny Bulun Bulun against a T-shirt manufacturer in Queensland who had produced many shirts using their bark paintings, and more recently Bulun Bulun and his brother George Milpurrurru sued R&T Textiles Pty. Ltd. (1998) for importing and selling fabric printed featuring their work. The carpets case was heard as *Milpurrurru v. Indofurn Pty. Ltd.*, 1995. Other cases have involved the use of Aboriginal images on Australian currency.

5. See also Marika 1986.

6. The significance of Thomas's discussion of recontextualization is broad.

7. I am borrowing from the model of language ideology, as used by Schieffelin and Woodard (1998) and Silverstein (1979).

8. Indeed, Pintupi painters always insisted to me that their images "are not made up, not made by us. They are from The Dreaming."

9. As Joseph Sax (1999) has noted, the detachability of art objects from their creators is a problematic area for property law. Recent trends in the latter have limited the rights of owners to detach these commodities from the biographies of their producers.

10. Three articles have been published by others on the significance of these scandals and the problem of translating indigenous value into the field of Western art production: Coleman 2003, Hoban 2002, and Merlan 2001.

11. To be sure, Pintupi paintings can enter meaningfully into an aesthetic regime of value. I don't have time to discuss this here except to say that the virtuosity and success of acrylic painting is heavily indebted to the palpability of the sign vehicles (see Myers 1989). Discussions of these properties may be found in Morphy 1984 and 1992, while traditional central Australian image-making has been discussed by Meggitt (1962), Munn (1973), and Spencer and Gillen (1899).

12. Recent reports that the British Prince Harry had been using Aboriginal motifs in his paintings provoked another round of outrage and some interesting attempts to understand the place of Aboriginal claims and modern art. See Shadbolt and Collins (2003) and Jones (2003).

13. I am thinking of the ways in which many young people in Australia have adopted features of Aboriginality for their own, expressing themselves through indigenous music and values.

14. At a Radio National interview (August 18, 2000) occasioned by a major exhibition of Papunya Tula art, the questions from Michael Cathcart carried a probing nuance. Was this really fine art, or was it just a kind of sentimental recognition of Aboriginal culture? "Fred Myers," he asked me, "what's your take on this? Is it fair to see this kind of art as part of a world-wide phenomena in art, or do we need to see it within a purely Aboriginal context?"

15. For example, proponents of acrylic painting as fine art have insisted that Aboriginality doesn't matter, that who painted a work does not matter: this is just good art, or "I like the way they move the paint," as modern art dealer John Weber said (1989). This might imply that no special pleading is needed for *Aboriginal* art: that this is art that works in the modernist sense.

16. This is the view implied in the controversial Australian Broadcasting Commission (ABC) documentary for the Four Corners program *Art from the Heart?* Produced by Richard Moore and Jeremy Eccles, this documentary was broadcast by the ABC on May 25, 1999.

17. There is not enough space here to consider the complexity of Western stances toward so-called modern art—the varieties of modernism and doctrines they represent. "Formalist modernism" as set forth by Clement Greenberg and his followers is, after all, very different from the modernism that celebrates the primitive. I have explored some of these issues in other writing (see Myers 1994). What I think is "modernist" in total, and what links this problem to the considerations of Weber and Bourdieu, is the pursuit of an essential formulation of "art" in line with its autonomy as a field of cultural production.

18. These scandals have become part of Australia's national conversation with itself. The well-known Australian intellectual Germaine Greer decried such developments as "Selling off the Dreaming" (Greer 1997: 5; for a reply to Greer's controversial views, see McDonald 1997: 9). In her argument, Greer follows an earlier line of criticism set down by Anne-Marie Willis (1993), questioning "the progressive agency of Aboriginal art for Aboriginal people" (1993: 125). In fact, Greer's denunciation only delineates quite clearly the difficulties of managing two ongoing problems for the contemporary life of Aboriginal culture: its authenticity in contexts of co-presence with the market (commodification) and with white society itself (cultural identity).

19. For discussion of the Tim Johnson case, see Johnson (1997) and McLean (1998).

20. This argument was recently made in the context of Prince Harry's appropriation (see Jones 2003).

21. I should say that the use of the term *corruption* here is my own and that it is an external judgment of the way these processes affect the values of participants.

22. Turkey Tolson's willingness to sign paintings executed by his relatives is unproblematic for them.

23. The availability of acrylic paintings in the art market raises the question of how they are to be treated, by whose rules, and whether there are in existence meaningful regulations to manage these objects and the interests they represent in an adequate way. In summary, concern over cultural appropriation may involve (1) prevention of cultural degradation, (2) the preservation of cultural goods as valuable objects, (3) deprivation of material advantage, or (4) failure to recognize sovereign claims. How to convert these perceived injurious experiences into culturally meaningful bases for dispute and action is a significant problem. These more abstract considerations allow us to understand the cases of scandal because they clarify what the central values are that are under threat.

24. Copyright regulation itself is an unsettled domain. Recent work on copyright suggests not only that its formulations are historically varied and dependent on technological mediations (see Vaidhyanathan 2001), but also that regulations of the rights over culture and its expression are the specific results of human action mediated through institutional and social form. Certainly the relations between human subjects and their products cannot be understood as simply expressions of natural law. Rather, Aboriginal artists and activists like Marika insist that we apprehend the materiality that objectifies their culture in terms of the identity-producing ideology that informs it and is threatened by its conversion into a mere commodity stripped of these dimensions.

REFERENCES

Appadurai, Arjun. 1986. "Introduction: Commodities and the Politics of Value." In Arjun Appadurai, ed., *The Social Life of Things: Commodities in Cultural Perspective*, 3–63. Cambridge: Cambridge University Press.

Bardon, Geoffrey. 1979. *Aboriginal Art of the Western Desert*. Sydney: Rigby.

——. 1991. *Papunya Tula Art of the Western Desert*. Melbourne: McPhee Gribble.

Barthes, Roland. 1957. *Mythologies*. Paris: Éditions du Seuil.

Beidelman, Thomas O. 1997. "Promoting African Art: The Catalogue to the Exhibit of African Art at the Royal Academy of Arts, London." *Anthropos* 92:3–20.

Benjamin, Walter. 1968. "The Work of Art in the Age of Mechanical Reproduction." In Hannah Arendt, ed., Harry Zohn, trans., *Illuminations*, 217–251. New York: Schocken Books.

Clifford, James. 1988. *The Predicament of Culture*. Cambridge: Harvard University Press.

Coleman, Elizabeth. Forthcoming. "Aboriginal Art and Identity: Crossing the Borders of Law's Imagination." *Journal of Political Philosophy* 11.2.

Coombe, Rosemary. 1997. "The Properties of Culture and the Possession of Identity: Postcolonial Struggle and the Legal Imagination." In Bruce Ziff and Pratima Rao, eds., *Borrowed Power: Essays in Cultural Appropriation*, 74–96. New Brunswick, N.J.: Rutgers University Press.

Feld, Steven. 1995. "From Schizophonia to Schismogenesis: The Discourses and Practices of World Music and World Beat." In George Marcus and Fred Myers, eds., *The Traffic in Culture*, 96–126. Berkeley: University of California Press.

Gell, Alfred. 1998. *Art and Agency: An Anthropological Theory*. Oxford: Clarenden Press.

George, Kenneth. 1999. "Introduction: Objects on the Loose." *Ethnos* 64:149–150.

Greer, Germaine. 1997. "Selling off the Dreaming." *Sydney Morning Herald*, December 6.

Hoban, Caroline Holdstrom. 2002. "The Field of Art Production and Western Desert Acrylics." *Australian Journal of Anthropology* 12:178–190.

Isaacs, Jennifer. 1995. *Wandjuk Marika: Life Story, as Told to Jennifer Isaacs*. St. Lucia: University of Queensland Press.

Johnson, Vivien. 1996a. *Dreamings of the Desert: Aboriginal Dot Paintings of the Western Desert*. Adelaide: Art Gallery of South Australia.

———. 1996b. *Copyrites: Aboriginal Art in the Age of Reproductive Technologies*. Sydney: National Indigenous Arts Advocacy Association and Macquarie University.

———. 1997. *Michael Jagamara Nelson*. Sydney: Craftsman House.

———. n.d. "Cultural Brokerage: Commodification and Intellectual Property." Unpublished ms.

Jones, Jonathan. 2003. "Aborigines Are Wrong about Harry." *The Guardian*, August 20, 20.

Latour, Bruno. 1993. *We Have Never Been Modern*. Cambridge: Harvard University Press.

Lomnitz, Claudio. 1993. "Decadence in Times of Globalization." *Cultural Anthropology* 9.2: 257–267.

Manning, Patrick. 1985. "Primitive Art and Modern Times." *Radical History Review* 33:165–181.

Marcus, George, and Fred Myers. 1995. Introduction to *The Traffic in Culture: Refiguring Anthropology and Art*. Berkeley: University of California Press.

Marika, Wandjuk. 1986. "Painting Is Very Important (Story as Told to Jennifer Isaacs)." In Ulli Beier, ed., *Long Water: Aboriginal Art and Literature* (special issue of *Aspect* 34), 7–18. Sydney: Aboriginal Artists Agency.

Mauss, Marcel. 1925 [1990]. *The Gift: The Form and Reason for Exchange in Archaic Societies*. Trans. W. D. Halls. New York: Norton.

McCulloch, Susan. 1997a. "Artistic Licence or Fraud?" *Weekend Australian*, March 15–16.

———. 1997b. "Dreaming Art Awakens Overseas Demand." *The Australian*, April 10.

———. 1997c. "What's the Fuss?" *Australian Magazine*, July 5–6.

———. 1997d. "Galleries Stamp Beamish Name on Black Art." *The Australian*, December 24.

McCulloch-Uehlin, Susan. 1997. "Painter Tells of Secret Women's Artistic Business: I Signed Relatives' Paintings." *Weekend Australian*, April 17–18, 1999.

McDonald, John. 1997. "Putting Dr. Greer in the Picture." *Sydney Morning Herald*, December 13.

McLean, Ian. 1998. *White Aborigines: Identity Politics in Australian Art*. New York: Cambridge University Press.

Meggitt, Mervyn J. 1962. *Desert People*. Chicago: University of Chicago Press.

Merlan, Francesca. 2001. "Aboriginal Cultural Production into Art: The Complexity of Redress." In Chris Pinney and Nicholas Thomas, eds., *Beyond Aesthetics: Art and the Technologies of Enchantment*, 201–234. Oxford: Berg.

Munn, Nancy. 1973. *Walbiri Iconography*. Ithaca: Cornell University Press.

Miller, Daniel. 1987. *Material Culture and Mass Consumption*. Oxford: Blackwell.

———. 2003. "The Virtual Moment." *Journal of the Royal Anthropological Institute* 9:57–75.

Morphy, Howard. 1984. *Journey to the Crocodile's Nest*. Canberra: Australian Institute of Aboriginal Studies.

——. 1992. *Ancestral Connections*. Chicago: University of Chicago Press.

Myers, Fred. 1986. *Pintupi Country, Pintupi Self: Sentiment, Place, and Politics among Western Desert Aborigines*. Washington, D.C., and Canberra: Smithsonian Institution Press and the Australian Institute of Aboriginal Studies Press.

——. 1988. "Burning the Truck and Holding the Country: Forms of Property, Time, and the Negotiation of Identity among Pintupi Aborigines." In David Riches, Tim Ingold, and James Woodburn, eds., *Hunter-Gatherers, II: Property, Power and Ideology*, 52–74. London: Berg.

——. 1989. "Truth, Beauty and Pintupi Painting." *Visual Anthropology* 2:163–195.

——. 1994. "Beyond the Intentional Fallacy: Art Criticism and the Ethnography of Aboriginal Acrylic Painting." *Visual Anthropology Review* 10.1:10–43.

——. 2002. *Painting Culture: The Making of an Aboriginal High Art*. Durham, N.C.: Duke University Press.

Nicklin, Lenore. 1997. "Dream Meets Reality." *Bulletin* 8 July, 20–23.

Poirier, Sylvie. 1996. *Les Jardins du Nomade: Cosmologie, territorie et personne dans le désert occidental australien*. Munster: Lit Verlag.

Price, Sally. 1989. *Primitive Art in Civilized Places*. Chicago: University of Chicago Press.

Rubin, William. 1984. "Modernist Primitivism: An Introduction." In W. Rubin, ed., *"Primitivism" in 20th Century Art: Affinity of the Tribal and the Modern*, 1–84. New York: Museum of Modern Art.

Sax, Joseph. 1999. *Playing Darts with a Rembrandt: Public and Private Rights in Cultural Treasures*. Ann Arbor : University of Michigan Press.

Schieffelin, Bambi, Kathryn Woolard, and Paul Kroskrity, eds. 1998. *Language Ideologies: Practice and Theory*. New York: Oxford University Press.

Shadbolt, Peter, and Peter Collins. 2003. "Harry Paints His Way into Outback Row: Prince Accused of Stealing Aboriginal Motifs in Works." *The Guardian*, August 19, p. 3.

Silverstein, Michael. 1979. "Language Structures and Linguistic Ideology." In P. Clyne et al., eds., *The Elements: A Parasession on Linguistic Units and Levels*. Chicago: Chicago Linguistic Society.

Spencer, Baldwin, and Frank J. Gillen. 1899. *The Native Tribes of Central Australia*. London: Macmillan.

Spyer, Patricia, ed. 1998. *Border Fetishisms: Material Objects in Unstable Spaces*. New York: Routledge.

Steiner, Christopher. 2001. "Rights of Passage: On the Liminal Identity of Art in the Border Zone." In Fred Myers, ed., *The Empire of Things*. Albuquerque: School of American Research Press.

Sutton, Peter, ed. 1988. *Dreamings: The Art of Aboriginal Australia*. New York: George Braziller/ Asia Society Galleries.

Strathern, Marilyn. 1999. *Property, Substance, and Effect : Anthropological Essays on Persons and Things*. London and New Brunswick, N.J.: Athlone Press.

Thomas, Nicholas. 1991. *Entangled Objects: Exchange, Material Culture and Colonialism in the Pacific*. Cambridge: Harvard University Press.

Turner, Victor. 1974. *Dramas, Fields, and Metaphors*. Ithaca, N.Y.: Cornell University Press.

Vaidhyanathan, Siva. 2001. *Copyrights and Copywrongs: The Rise of Intellectual Property and How It Threatens Creativity*. New York: New York University Press.

Weiner, Annette. 1992. *Inalienable Possessions: The Paradox of Keeping-While-Giving*. Berkeley: University of California Press.

Wells, Edgar. 1982. *Reward and Punishment in Arnhem Land, 1962–1963*. Canberra: Australian Institute of Aboriginal Studies; Atlantic Highlands, N.J.: Humanities Press.

Wild, Stephen, ed. 1986. *Rom: An Aboriginal Ritual of Diplomacy*. Canberra: Australian Institute of Aboriginal Studies Press.

Williams, Raymond. 1989. *Resources of Hope: Culture, Democracy, Socialism*. London: Verso.

Willis, Anne-Marie. 1993. *Illusions of Identity: The Art of Nation*. Sydney: Hale and Iremonger.

MATTHEW ENGELKE

Sticky Subjects and Sticky Objects:

The Substance of African Christian Healing

T o what extent can religious practice be given over to a project of immateriality? According to Colleen McDannell (1995), it cannot. She
reads the history of Christianity as the tension between the material
and immaterial worlds: "In Christ there is a blurring of the material
and the spiritual; the sacred voice and the profane human body" (McDannell 1995: 5). She points to the story of the Golden Calf in Exodus 32, which
"tells Jews and Christians that when people lose their faith in God they
construct false images of the divine" (1995: 9). The Protestant Reformers in
England, in the reign of Henry VIII, were fervently against the ubiquity of
"human incrustations" (Phillips 1973: 70) in the Catholic Church. Objects
were dangerous because "nothing spiritual can be present when there is
anything material and physical" (Edwards cited in Aston 1988: 13).

A defaced fourteenth-century church panel was exhibited at the recent
Gothic: Art for England show at the Victoria and Albert Museum in London.
Sometime in the sixteenth century, the image had been scratched out. In its
place had been written a verse from the Bible. The Word had been used to
destroy the evidence of Catholic idolatry. But even though some English
iconoclast had indeed purged the panel of its idolatrous nature, it was still, to
the casual observer, an object. Whether or not its defacement was motivated
by the idea that "nothing spiritual can be present when there is anything
material and physical," it could still be hung on the wall. Stripped of its

theological and social dimensions (in a manner perhaps only museum exhibitions can accomplish), the materiality of the panel remained. In a "vulgar" sense (see Miller, this volume) the project of immateriality is difficult to accomplish.

The destruction of Christian art in Gothic England suggests something of greater importance in the study of religious materiality. Often, indeed inevitably, the repudiation of the material is a selective process. What sustains projects of immateriality in religious practice is always the definition of what counts as materially dangerous. Even Henry VIII tempered his position in the period between 1537 and 1543 (see Aston 1988: 234–244); by the time of his death the king had developed a sincere interest in the distinction between "abused" and "unabused" (Phillips 1973: 202) objects.[1] Indeed, no religion can do without material culture (Keane 1998; McDannell 1995; Tambiah 1984; see also Keane, Maurer, and Meskell's chapters in this volume). The question posed at the outset then becomes, as Webb Keane (1998: 29) might put it: *In what sense* can religious practice be given over to a sustained project of immateriality?

In the introduction to this volume, Daniel Miller suggests we can approach the commitment to immateriality best through "the messy terrain of ethnography." What matters in a museum exhibition documenting one strain of sixteenth-century iconoclasm is not the irreducible materiality of a church panel, but how its defacement expresses a logic of spiritual transcendence. When we investigate religious practice we see that not all material culture is alike. As other contributors to this volume show, the task then becomes the recognition of "relative" (see Rowlands) or "plural" (see Myers) materialities.

In this chapter I focus on the logic of materiality in the Masowe weChishanu Church, an apostolic Christian church with large followings throughout Zimbabwe. As I hope to make clear, the Masowe apostolics are committed to a project of immateriality. They want a religion in which things do not matter. Material culture in its various forms constitutes the single most important obstacle in developing a spiritual relationship with God. But as we might expect, the commitment to immateriality makes what things the Masowe do use in religious life all the more important. Here I focus primarily on the stuff of their healing—the objects and substances that Masowe prophets employ to cure people of their afflictions. Healing is of central importance in Zimbabwe to both African Christian and "traditional" religious practitioners. Because Masowe prophets and traditional healers use material things (and often the *same* things), how the authority of objects was defined as part of a Christian project of transcendence was a subject of some importance in the church. In this chapter I argue that the sincerity of the Masowe's commitment to immateriality depended on the ability to show that—as Miller puts it—some things are "more material than others."

A STICKY SUBJECT

As with many fieldworkers, my research was punctuated by a number of ailments, both real and imagined. As well-known healers, the Masowe prophets took a polite interest in my well-being. In an effort to maintain some critical distance from the church, however, I tried to be careful about what I shared regarding my health, and also what I took from the prophets when they did manage to extract a complaint or observe a symptom. This was not always easy, and on one occasion I found myself the recipient of one of their more significant preparations. It is called holy honey and, as far as the Masowe are concerned, it is the most effective spiritual medicine. While primarily used to fight the ill effects of witchcraft, it was thought the honey might also relieve my this-worldly ailments.

Holy honey is not simply honey. The exact ingredients are guarded by the church's prophets and elders, but as I worked my way through two jars of the stuff over the course of several weeks, I could detect in it hints of cooking oil and lemon juice. The honey is dark brown and viscous. It is sticky-sweet and has a tangy aftertaste (the lemons), with hints of smoke. Regardless of the ingredients or their preparation, however, I was told that what mattered was the blessing conferred upon it by the Holy Spirit. Indeed, holy honey, like all apostolic medicines, was understood to be powerful because of its spiritual properties. As a substance it did not matter.

The weChishanu's honey, perhaps like an Azande's *benge* (see Evans-Pritchard 1976: 122–148) or a Thai Buddhist amulet (see Tambiah 1984: 243–257), derives its importance from an immaterial quality. Apostolics would always insist to me that the Holy Spirit can cure someone's afflictions without the benefit of any "medicine" or blessed object. Nevertheless, holy honey occupies a privileged position in the religious imagination of the apostolics.

In contrast to the other medicines they might receive, honey was characterized as something like a smart drug: it just made you feel good. It gave you more energy throughout the day. It helped you think clearly. Some men told me it increased their sexual stamina. All things considered, and dutiful statements about the power of the Holy Spirit aside, if apostolics could have any healing treatment, it would be honey.

Yet there was something about holy honey that unsettled the apostolics. While its properties were understood as the result of a spiritual blessing, in practice they sometimes treated it as if these properties were inherent. Holy honey, qua honey, could do things. I got a clear sense of this the day I received a second jar in the course of my own "treatment." It was immediately after an early-morning church service one Wednesday in Chitungwiza, and I had promised to give a friend in the congregation a ride into Harare, where he worked, some 25 kilometers to the north. He knew I had the honey in the car, and he talked about it all the way into town, reminding me of its beneficial side effects and remarking on the fact that he was about to face a long and tiring day at work. As we pulled into the parking lot of his office he lingered for a moment. "Ah," he said. "Just one sip of that stuff might do me good." The prospects of a miserable day at work do not constitute an illness, as far as the Masowe are concerned. Nevertheless, by asking for a sip my friend made it clear in that moment how easy it is to slip from the principle of the immaterial to the lure of the physical. His request undercut the more general claim that apostolics made about healing substances. If God's blessing is what made honey a powerful spiritual medicine, and if its use was inspired for individual cases, then for my friend it ought to have been—to paraphrase E. E. Evans-Pritchard (see 1976: 147)—"just an ordinary thing, mere honey." Clearly, it was not. Its materiality mattered.

I want to use this vignette to frame a more general discussion of the apostolic disposition toward religious things, toward both material culture and immateriality. What makes my friend's request for honey interesting is the extent to which it highlights the weChishanu emphasis on the immateriality of religious practice. Apostolics are wary of spiritual materiel; religious things are dangerous things, and often betray shortcomings of faith. The manipulation of material culture is therefore a delicate matter in the church, and the reconciliation of the material and immaterial worlds is a process fraught with pitfalls. As I hope to make clear at the end of this chapter, honey both challenges and confirms this logic in a poignant way. That morning in the car, it was a sticky subject for my friend. It made him feel awkward, even embarrassed, given his religious commitments. In treating the honey as a thing, rather than an idea, he was undermining an important aspect of his faith. Before explaining this further, however, we need to consider more generally how the apostolics develop a systematic repudiation of the material dimensions of religion.

DOING WITHOUT:
THE EMERGENCE OF JOHANE MASOWE

During the winter of 1932, a young man called Shoniwa Masedza from Makoni District in Southern Rhodesia suffered a series of debilitating ailments, forcing him to give up his job working for a shoemaker near Salisbury. Shoniwa retreated to Marimba, a hill outside of Salisbury, where in a number of dreams he was visited by the Holy Spirit. God told Shoniwa he was now Johane Masowe—Africa's "John the Baptist." His mission was to bring the Word of God to African peoples, so that they might enter the Kingdom of Heaven. Baba Johane, as he came to be known, developed followings throughout a number of districts in Mashonaland over the next several years. In 1938 he began traveling south. Eventually he ended up in Port Elizabeth, South Africa, where he established the Apostolic Sabbath Church of God (ASCG).[2] When Johane left Mashonaland, however, he also left behind a group of his followers who developed a model of Christian faith based on some of his earliest preaching, distinct from what came to define the ASCG. That group that stayed behind is now called the Masowe weChishanu Church.

I want to highlight two aspects of the weChishanu's repudiation of material culture in religious practice. First, weChishanu Masowe do not recognize texts as sources of religious authority. In fact, they refer to themselves as "the Christians who don't use the Bible," and they do not allow it to be used in their church services. The weChishanu say that the Bible is unnecessary— that because their prophets speak with the power of the Holy Spirit, they have a "live and direct" connection with God. When Baba Johane started preaching, he emphasized this by telling his followers not to use the Book. In fact, there are some colonial documents in which he admits to telling his followers to burn the Bible, an admission that the elders I worked with were quick to confirm.[3] Within a few years Johane reversed his position on textual authority, claiming that he would need the Bible to convince South Africans (who were thought to be better educated than Africans in Southern Rhodesia) that he was truly Christian.[4] Some of his most influential elders did not agree with him. They saw his acceptance of the Bible as a pragmatic decision that undercut the principle of "live and direct." These elders broke with Johane and became the first group of weChishanu. "It's the Holy Spirit that actually formulated a Bible," as one weChishanu apostolic told me in 1999. "So . . . there is no point in using it. If it was the Holy Spirit that made all those speeches in the Bible, and yet the Holy Spirit is speaking now, it is better to listen to the Holy Spirit than to use the Bible." And so for the weChishanu the spoken word takes precedence over the written word. Elsewhere, I discuss this position in more detail (Engelke 2004b), but the point I want to make here is that rejection of the Bible is an indication of the apostolics' concern with material culture—about what it can and cannot do. Books, in this view, cannot provide for a personal relationship with God, and often serve to stand in the way. Faith must be "live and direct," constituted by its immateriality.

Following McDannell's analysis of Protestantism in the United States, we might say that the weChishanu consider themselves "strong" Christians because they claim to "grasp spiritual truths directly" (1995: 8). In fact, even more than some of their Protestant forebears, the Masowe mean to do without things. Inasmuch as European iconoclasts moved away from images, they replaced those images—as evidenced in the V&A *Gothic* exhibition—with the Book. "Protestants turned words into objects. During the nineteenth century, family Bibles [in the United States] became so lavish and encyclopedic that they functioned more like religious furniture than biblical texts" (McDannell 1995: 15; see also Coleman 1996). In Africa, the British and Foreign Bible Society also made the Book something of a fetish—and not only for African "heathens." The society's own operators often spoke about the Bible as a thing in itself, something that had agency (see Howsam 1991; Bradlow 1987). Today, as far as the Masowe are concerned, the Bible is no less a material impediment to faith than a Catholic icon. They see proof of this in fellow Christians in Zimbabwe and often noted to me how people in other churches seemed to treat the Bible as an end in itself, wrapped in expensive leather bindings, displayed prominently in one's living room, carried around like an oxygen tank. The weChishanu had no time for such "religious furniture."

The second aspect of the weChishanu's immateriality, and our primary concern in this chapter, is their emphasis on spiritual healing. I have already suggested in passing that weChishanu come to terms with the materiality of faith through practices of healing. At this point we can extend the discussion. WeChishanu talk about the troubles of Africa as the result of witchcraft and the continuing importance of ancestral spirits. Like many Pentecostal and charismatic churches on the continent, however, they want to "make a complete break with the past" (Meyer 1998; see also Engelke 2004a). Ancestral and other spirits may play an important role in everyday life, but this is something the weChishanu hope to get rid of. Serious illness, family strain, and unemployment can all be signs for the Masowe of the meddling and often nefarious interventions of *midzimu* (ancestral spirits), *ngozi* (avenging spirits), and *tokoloshi* (witchcraft familiars) in everyday life. Christian healing is the ultimate redress—the only way to make that "break."

As Jean Comaroff argues, healing in African etiologies is "fundamentally concerned with the reconstitution of physical, social, and spiritual order" (1980: 639; see also Janzen 1978; Turner 1968). For the Masowe these social orders must be reconstituted as Christian, so it is vital to recognize the threat of (as they call it) "African custom." It is not that the weChishanu deny the realities of witchcraft, then, or the sway of the ancestors. Indeed, healing churches throughout southern Africa "take belief in the power of witches, evil spirits and other mystical agents seriously and are for that reason, in the eyes of a large section of the public, able to provide help in cases where such agents are thought to be involved" (Schoffeleers 1991: 4). Healing is what draws most people to the weChishanu Church, and it is the key practice through which prophets maintain their authority. From the beginning of his mission, Johane saw ridding the world of witchcraft as one of his primary goals. He wanted to break with "African custom," to show that what he was doing was different from what spirit mediums or traditional healers could do. Joel Robbins (2003) has suggested that anthropologists studying Pentecostal and charismatic churches need to take this kind of emphasis on "breaks" seriously. The insistence on the immateriality of healing in the weChishanu Church supports Robbins's point. Indeed, we can trace how the apostolics understand their difference through the immaterial dimensions in the stuff of healing.

In a document in the state archives in Zimbabwe, Johane says: "Whilst staying on [Marimba] hill, I used to hear a voice saying, 'I have blessed you. Carry on with the good work. Tell the natives to throw away their witchcraft medicines.' "[5] Most such records in the colonial archives strip away the voices and imagery of religious figures. Cosmology was not the state's primary interest (Dillon-Malone 1978: 25). But other sources add dimensions to Masowe's concern with "witchcraft medicines" and further explain why getting rid of them is central to apostolic cosmology. Elders in the church told me numerous stories of Baba Johane's abilities, and in each the power of African Christian healing lies in its superiority to both Western biomedicine and "traditional" curative practices (spiritual and nonspiritual). For example, one elder from Highfields, in Harare, recalled a story his grandmother told him as a young boy:

> According to her, by [the early 1930s], when she joined Johane Masowe, one of her sons was very sick. And when she went to consult Johane, her son got better within three days. Yet she had moved around—she had gone to hospital and to other spiritual healers and to the n'anga [traditional healer] without any joy, until in three days' time Johane Masowe prayed for him and the boy was up and running.

This example of Johane's gift as a healer is mirrored in the narratives I collected during the course of my fieldwork. In one case, a young man I met suffered from severe stomach pains. He went to the doctor and got medicine for ulcers. This did not help. So he went to a traditional healer (Shona: n'anga) who gave him some medicines (Shona: muti). This did not help either. Unsure of what to do, his brother's wife's mother told him to try a Masowe prophet, so one Saturday, he went to a Masowe service in Chitungwiza. He was given something to drink out of a wooden bowl, but he did not know what it was. By the next morning, his stomach pains were gone. "The results were very chop-chop," he told me. Soon after, the prophet told him his pains had been caused by a relative jealous of his job in a music store. It was witchcraft. About a year later, after attending services and discussing the matter with elders, the young man joined the church.

The weChishanu mark their difference through narratives of healing. One aspect of their commitment to immateriality, then, is the rejection of traditional curative and occult practices—still represented in Johane's forceful image of the "witchcraft medicines."[6] Indeed, driven as it is by what they see as the desire for accumulation (cf. Geschiere 1997; H. West 2001), "witchcraft" is a catch-all phrase of scorn, shorthand for the dangerous things produced by unsaved Africans.

THE PLACES AND PRACTICE OF HEALING

Like those of many apostolic groups in southern Africa, the Masowe church services and healing sessions take place under open skies, the worshipers clothed in white robes. Both of these facts are folded into apostolic narratives about a "live and direct" faith. Where they pray and what they wear are part of the logic of immateriality. Apostolics refuse to erect church buildings because they say God's kingdom is "everywhere." It cannot be confined to a chapel. Moreover, buildings, like the Bible, are an impediment to spirituality. The weChishanu claim to have witnessed proof of this on countless occasions: fund-raising efforts and endless talk in other churches about their new chapels, or their need for a new chapel. "It's a wonder they find time to pray," one informant mused. Particularly during the colonial era this rejection of built spaces was tied also to more pragmatic concerns. WeChishanu and other Masowe groups were often persecuted by the state because they were perceived to be anti-colonial. Moving from place to place was a practical decision tied to larger cosmological concerns (cf. Mukonyora 2000; Werbner 1985). Today the Masowe still describe themselves sometimes as lost in the "wilderness."

In the absence of a built space, the white robes of the apostolics form a kind of phantom wall that define the perimeters of a service. These robes fall to one's feet, tied loosely at the waist, cut in as simple a fashion as possible. These robes are important to their wearers; they are material evidence of commitment to the faith. Yet the robes also embody something of the paradox of apostolic immateriality. What makes them special, according to my informants, is their simplicity. Robes must be made of cheap cloth, and they serve as a leveling device within the congregation. With such garments on, no one can tell who is rich and who is poor. Everyone is the same. In contrast to the smart suits one might see at other Christian churches, or the elaborate dress of an African spirit medium or n'anga, apostolic fashion is an anti-fashion. The robes are a clear statement that they should not matter.

Ritual and social life as a weChishanu apostolic is, without question, less materially oriented than that in most Christian churches in Zimbabwe. The weChishanu have no church buildings, no elaborate altars, and only simple robes. They do not even accept the Scripture of their scriptural religion. What is more, while prophets do not want to see their congregations live in poverty, they have never preached a gospel of prosperity (Green 1995; Maxwell 1998; Meyer 1998). Being a successful and faithful Christian does not, in their view, require the accumulation of commodities and material riches. As "strong" Christians, those "who use objects or images in their devotional lives or who feel that certain places are imbued with special power are seen as needing spiritual help or crutches" (McDannell 1995: 8).

Most weChishanu groups meet in small groves, perhaps by a river or, in cities and towns, by the side of a road. The average size of a congregation is only about one hundred people, but the better-known prophets in the urban areas can attract up to ten times that number. (I would estimate that in 1999, when I finished my fieldwork, there were approximately 100,000 Masowe apostolics in Zimbabwe.) In these larger congregations, about half of the people attending will not be members of the church—they come only for healing; so the sea of white robes one normally finds will be marked by pockets of everyday color.

Masowe healing sessions vary from one congregation to the next, but there is a general pattern as to what one can expect. Sessions are usually held after the main services on Fridays and Sundays. The more influential prophets will hold separate meetings on Saturday afternoons to accommodate the large numbers of people in attendance. When everyone has gathered in the grove or field, seated in a large circle with the men and women facing each other, a specially designated group of apostolics (called *vaimbi*, or "singers") will begin to sing. These songs, or "verses" as the Masowe call them, help soothe the congregation's afflictions. They are also a plea for the Holy Spirit to fill a prophet: "*Tauya Baba Kuzopona* [Father, we come here to be saved]." The singing might continue for an hour, interspersed with short monologues from a prophet about the power of God.

Eventually a prophet will ask those who have come for healing to stand up in accordance with their particular "illness." Can they not conceive a child? Are they estranged from their families? Have they lost their jobs? Do they have stomach pains? Are they mentally ill? When the sick have been accounted for, church elders call them off to one side of the main gathering. In many congregations, as the "patients" move off, they shuffle past a prophet, who lays on hands. The elders then arrange the people into long rows. The people bend down on their knees, and over the course of the next hour or so, they are given holy water and other blessings from God in the form of "medicines." They might also be given a sip of another "medicine"— as was the case in the example above of the young man who suffered the stomach pains of jealousy for working in a record store. It is in these sessions that one could expect to receive holy honey. More commonly, however, each person is given a sip of holy water and something else—some object or substance—that has been blessed and which they take away as part of a prescribed treatment.

When Masowe talk about the stuff they receive for healing, they often refer to it, as I have here, as "medicine." Indeed, the language of a healing session mirrors the language of a biomedical system. People come as "patients," they are "treated" in weekly "clinics," and, if necessary, they are watched over by church elders in makeshift "wards." Not all apostolic churches are comfortable with adapting medical terminology to describe what they do. For example, the John Maranke Church—another large movement in Zimbabwe and Zambia (see Jules-Rosette 1975)—does not allow its members to use biomedicine. Children in the Maranke Church are not vaccinated for measles and other diseases, and the Maranke would never go to hospital. During my fieldwork in 1999, a group of Maranke apostolics made the news when they overturned a government truck carrying medicine to treat victims of a cholera epidemic in an area where the church had a significant following.[7] The weChishanu apostolics do not understand this distrust of the medical system; they see it as a sign of "primitive" behavior, a lingering influence of "African custom." In fact, I often had Masowe apostolics—including prophets—ask me to provide them with aspirin, hydrocortisone ointments, and cough syrups. The weChishanu see no reason not to take advantage of medical science. Such medicines are, in fact, blessings from God of another kind—something that can supplement the more important work of spiritual healing. This is not to say the apostolics think of aspirin as a spiritual treatment. In fact, they see it as entirely natural. Medical doctors throw up no problems, theologically speaking, because they do not claim their authority from the spiritual world. This is the key difference between a medical doctor and a "traditional" doctor. The former present no cause for alarm because their material things carry no immaterial pretensions. So when someone is suffering from witchcraft, or because of an angered ancestral spirit, biomedicine may help relieve his or her symptoms. But it will never get to the root of the problem; it will never provide a cure. For that, spiritual intervention is required.

PEBBLES AND PRAYERS

To an apostolic, holy honey and aspirin are not substances of the same kind. The other ways in which Masowe refer to their spiritual medicines make this clear. Indeed, "the relation between material things and immaterial meanings . . . must be effected through speech" (Keane 1998: 28). For the weChishanu this is reflected quite literally in the religious terminology of their therapeutics. To wit, any medicine a prophet provides is known more precisely as a "prayer" (Shona: *muteuro*). Embodying the principle of a "live and direct" faith, apostolic medicines are spoken of as speech acts. They are prayers, not things. And so the difference between biomedicine and spiritual medicine is the latter's immaterial qualities.

The most common type of muteuro is the pebble, or small stone.[8] Any pebble or stone the size of a marble (or smaller) will suit the purposes of the church. I often saw elders collect them in the dirt around a congregational site in preparation for healing sessions. What patients are meant to do with the pebbles can vary. Each case is handled individually, so when one receives muteuro in this form, one also receives instructions for its use. For example, if a patient is suffering from stomach pains, she may be asked to place the pebble in a glass and to drink water from the glass three times per day (usually three full glasses in each sitting, for a total of nine glasses of water per day). The pebble conveys its spiritual blessing to the water, in effect creating holy water on the spot, without the burden of providing someone with a week's supply of it. Similarly, someone might be asked to place the pebble in the tub or bucket of water with which one bathes each morning. The muteuro helps the water cleanse the body of any spiritual impurities or afflictions. Not every spiritual remedy involves the manufacture of holy water. If someone has lost his job, or is looking for a job, he might be asked to place the muteuro in his wallet (although it should never touch money directly). Those taking a school exam or test at work can keep the muteuro in their pocket, to help them remember what they have studied. In one of the more unusual testimonies I collected, a man was made redundant from a factory job in Bulawayo. Subsequently, he came to Harare to consult a particular Masowe prophet. The prophet gave him a pebble and told him to mail it to a friend back in Bulawayo. On instruction, this friend then took the pebble and threw it over the perimeter wall of the factory. Within a few weeks, the man was reinstated in his job.

What makes pebbles and small stones special for Masowe weChishanu apostolics? To put it simply, the fact that they are not special. Pebbles are free, they are easy to gather, and they do not inspire envy or want—sentiments associated with witchcraft. Pebbles are also very practical. Water, I was told, is an effective medium for healing, but it is difficult to carry, especially in large quantities. (We will come back to water shortly.) It can also be hard to come by for congregations that do not have easy access to a river, borehole, or tap. For this reason, water is used sparingly, and only in the course of an actual healing session, where one 5-liter jug might last several weeks if doled out to the patients a sip at a time. Pebbles, on the other hand, are much easier to circulate. In most cases, elders will pass them out during a healing session immediately after the sharing of the water. They are durable, too. While no material thing is foolproof, pebbles come close. If you drop a pebble, you can pick it up. If you drop a cup of holy water, it might be gone forever—dissolving into the ground, or spilling into a crack in the floor. Pebbles do not break or split easily. They maintain their integrity in the face of regular use. Cloth and wood—long used in other Christian churches, and in other healing rituals—might tear or splinter or break. Pebbles are also easy for patients to keep track of. This is not always the case with other muteuro: We saw how even as I had the holy honey with me in the car the morning I drove that friend to work, it was difficult to keep it for myself. In another incident, a friend of mine in the church was given muteuro in the form of a mango paste. He made the mistake of leaving it in the kitchen, and his brother used it as chutney for an evening meal.

Pebbles also have the distinct advantage of not sparking any association with traditional African healing (either spiritual or medicinal).[9] The weChishanu might be comfortable using the language of biomedicine to describe their healing practices, but in their effort to break with "African custom" they would never use the language of a n'anga or spirit medium (Shona: *svikiro*). N'anga and spirit mediums use a variety of objects and substances in their healing practices, but pebbles are not among them. The weChishanu have therefore made something significant out of something that had no prior meaning in the social field of African therapeutics.

The paradox of the pebble is its being special-because-it-is-not. As a key symbol of Christianity it expresses the weChishanu's systematic repudiation of material culture. In many respects, the pebble is the most important thing in the church. Some might argue that an apostolic's white robes are the best representation of faith; robes are indeed valued by their wearers as a sign of commitment to the church. But a muteuro, and especially the pebble, is an index of the spiritual power of God; it is what makes donning the robes significant. Pebbles are the tools of evangelization. Whereas most Christian narratives place the Bible at the center of faith (Engelke 2003; G. West and Dube 2000), the Masowe would want to stress their muteuro as the evidence of Christian success. Having rejected the Bible, weChishanu objectify their faith in something that in and of itself has no social or cultural value. What better way to undercut the importance of material culture than to hold up as its archetype something you find in the dirt? Indeed, as I suggested at the beginning of this section, the very word apostolics use to signify their ritual medicines is meant to shift attention away from the question of materiality. A pebble is a prayer. It is part of the "live and direct" relationship with God that strong Christians ought to possess, a claim that "signification offers the subject an escape from materiality" (Keane 2001: 87).

IMMATERIAL DISTINCTIONS

The emphasis on "live and direct" faith and the rejection of the Bible leads the weChishanu to be dismissive of other Christian churches. When pressed, or in certain moods, Masowe apostolics might indeed claim that they are the only "true" Christians because they have seen past the false security of the Book. But in practice they are not much concerned with Christian objects other than the Bible, and they did not spend much time deriding any Christian brethren. They never spoke about the Catholic Church as too full of icons and ritual paraphernalia, for instance, and they rarely discussed the Pentecostal compulsion for "material success" (Maxwell 1998: 362) other than expressing their conviction that Pentecostal preachers con people out of their money. Rather, as I have already alluded to in the discussion of "witch-craft medicines," the Masowe directed their concern with objects against traditional healers and spirit mediums. This is something they brought up on a regular basis. Muti, or traditional medicines, were seen as bothersome and dangerous, and the Masowe took pleasure in talking about them as such. What healers and mediums used in their practices would always evoke dismissal, as much as the stuff of witchcraft. But muti also sparked anxiety because the weChishanu were concerned that people might think prophets are simply another kind of spirit medium.

Traditional healers and spirit mediums occupy distinct roles in the social field of Zimbabwean therapeutics, but they each differ as well from witches (who are considered categorically evil). Healers, or n'anga, may or may not have relationships with spirits that help them in their vocation (Chavanduka 1994: 46). Most, in any case, undergo training for the collection and prepara-tion of flora and fauna used as muti in treatments for patients (Reynolds 1996). Healers are neither good nor bad per se; some have reputations as being helpful, while others are said to be open to using their skills for malevolent purposes. Mediums, on the other hand, are normally under-stood as influential figures in the community. Indeed, the interventions of the ancestral spirits that speak through them are considered necessary for the maintenance of social order. "The most important quality of ancestral spirits is that they have the welfare of the people who live within their provinces at heart" (Lan 1985: 55). This is not to say that the authority of mediums goes uncontested: some have ended up being shot to death (see Ranger 1982). But mediums are, on the whole, prominent players in local and sometimes national politics.

The weChishanu do not deny that healers can use their skills to help alleviate people's ills, and they are well aware of the important role that mediums have played in the past. The problem is that these figures are not Christian: Whatever ends they achieve, the means are unacceptable. And because the "means" in most cases involve the significant use of ritual objects and substances, the weChishanu make an effort to distinguish their muteuro from the healer or medium's muti. If pebbles were the only muteuro, there might be little more to this case study. But set against this normative "spiritual medicine" are, as I have already noted, a number of more specialized substances that do not have the benefit of being empty signifiers. Many of the things prophets use are already meaningful. Of these, water and honey are two of the most important. Water and honey each highlight, in different ways, how apostolics differentiate the immateriality of muti and muteuro at the material level.

WATER, WATER EVERYWHERE

Studies of African healing in Zimbabwe have documented hundreds of plant and animal extracts used in the production of muti and the practice of divination (Gelfand et al. 1985; Reynolds 1996). In addition, water has been shown to occupy a special place in the therapeutic imagination, as many healers claim to learn their skills underwater, at the bottom of rivers; the most powerful healing spirits, called *njuzu*, are mermaids (see Reynolds 1996: 158–160). Rain as a key source of life and social order has also been studied in depth, in relation to both mediums (Lan 1985) and the Mwari cults (Ranger 1999). In my own research with mediums and n'anga, the importance of fluid substances in healing practices was particularly evident. Following Christopher Taylor's work on healing in Rwanda, I would argue that in Bantu cosmologies fluids mediate between "notions of causality" (1992: 36); to control the proper flow of fluids (water, humors) is to control the course of life and social well-being.

Water, then, is not a substance that Masowe apostolics can claim as their own, despite its historical importance to Christianity. Almost any religious figure in Zimbabwe might claim to benefit from water's properties. There is nothing necessarily Christian about it. This made one medium I knew in Harare particularly angry over apostolic claims to have privileged access to the spiritual world. This medium used *njuzu* (mermaids) to help cure the afflictions of the people who came to her, and she did not see why her reliance on water spirits was any different from an apostolic prophet's reliance on holy water. When I mentioned this to informants in the church, they always replied by saying that holy water was substantively different because it had God's blessing. Their answers suggested that water in and of itself did not have intrinsic qualities—that its meaning is imbued. This was the logic behind muteuro. At the same time, however, I would argue that it was precisely because water seemed to have "natural meaning" (see Keane 2001: 70–71, citing Grice 1957) that the apostolics did not belabor themselves over it. Water is meaningful in so many different religious contexts that the apostolics were able to resolve their anxieties over any parallel between their use of it with that of a traditional healer or medium's. In other words, the apostolics thought that water did have something of an intrinsic value, so it did not make sense to try to control the meanings people associated with it. Its ubiquity made it both a lost cause and nothing to worry about.

So from the apostolic point of view, the natural meaning of water is the opposite of the pebble. This difference is what makes them similarly un-problematic and begins to suggest how the Masowe see some things as "more material than others." Both are safe because both are mundane. As poles in a cosmology of material culture, they anchor the constellation of value in therapeutic things. But as is often the case, it is not the extremes that elicit the most interest and concern, because extremes are predictable. Their associations are easier to control. That which lies between the poles is more disconcerting, because it embodies the potential problems in the substance of healing. For the weChishanu, honey is the substance that best character-izes this tension, so I return to it here by way of conclusion.

A STICKY OBJECT

My friend who stressed the merits of honey on the way to work that Wednes-day morning might have been the most enthusiastic proponent of its use, but he was not alone. Honey has been an important substance since the first days of Johane's mission. During his illness, for example, through which he received the revelatory dreams on Marimba Hill, Johane claims to have survived on wild honey.[10] Much was made of this point when I collected oral histories from weChishanu elders. Today, when describing the groves and fields in which they pray, apostolics often refer to them as "lands of milk and honey." In those ritual spaces, the weChishanu can be heard to sing a verse, the simplicity and directedness of which is difficult to miss:

Uchi, uchi
uchi, uchi, uchi

Honey, honey
honey, honey, honey

This verse is used to soothe people when they are possessed by ancestral spirits, *ngozi*, or witchcraft familiars. Apostolics also use honey as a simile to describe any place that is particularly prosperous. After a good rainy season, for example, one apostolic from Chiweshe District said to me: "Our farms look like a land of milk and honey; the Holy Spirit has blessed us this year." Once, even, a friend of mine in the church referred to a Mercedes Benz as a "honey car" (Shona: *motokari weuchi*), a true sign of its prestige.

Within the wider socioreligious field, however, the holiness of honey breaks down. Honey produces comfort, to be sure, but it also produces anxiety. Its positive qualities are balanced by negative potentialities. Unlike pebbles—which the apostolics claim as their own—and water—which is so obviously salubrious—honey occupies a more ambiguous therapeutic role. Part of the problem is that mediums and n'anga also use honey, so the Masowe cannot claim it as their own. But neither does honey have the common currency of water. It is not so meaningful, in other words, that it becomes meaningless. If honey has intrinsic properties, they are less certain than those of water. So the Masowe do not want to cede the value of honey, unlike water, as something open to interpretation. While it is clear to them that the substance lends itself to Christian uses, there is nothing to stop a medium (such as the woman I mentioned in the previous section) from mounting a convincing case that it lends itself equally to "African customary" uses, as well. This is exacerbated by the nature of the substance: honey can be fermented; in fact, the process of fermentation is dependant upon its dilution, which is precisely what prophets and elders do to make it "holy."[11] But the apostolics forbid the taking of alcohol, particularly in its traditional forms, such as honey wine, millet beer, and the like. These alcoholic substances are in fact the most important offering one can give one's ancestors— the very kind of "African custom" Masowe hope to end. Now, the honey apostolics produce is not fermented. But in their appropriation of this substance as a powerful channel for spiritual healing, the weChishanu seem to be playing with fire.

The positive characterizations of honey described above help explain what drove my friend to ask for a sip of mine in the car that day. The negative characterizations should give us a sense of why talking about it was a sticky subject. He was talking himself into temptation. He was allowing for the possibility that the honey carried inherent properties. In the car, honey was not about a "live and direct" connection with God. It was about facing the workaday world. It was about the taste of honey, the hope for relief. In this instance my friend was treating it like aspirin or, worse yet, muti rather than muteuro. He was suggesting that its materiality mattered in a way that cut against the grain of his faith.

From honey as a sticky subject of conversation, then, we come to see honey as a sticky object. Within the realm of healing, it becomes the practical channel through which the Masowe articulate their exception to the rule that faith should be immaterial. It is their recognition that even strong Christians cannot divorce themselves from the material. Holy honey is both the testament and the test of faith. As I hope to have shown in this chapter, the extent to which religious communities objectify their authority through the use of things deserves attention as much for what it tells us about the immaterial world as it does about the persistence of the material one. The logic of Masowe cosmology is a logic of immateriality, but this will always involve a process of objectification. More than this, however, forms of objectification become the things through which immateriality can be both demonstrated and lost. As used by Masowe apostolics in Zimbabwe, honey, pebbles, and water suggest that materiality is a matter of degree and kind.

NOTES

Research for this chapter was supported by a Fulbright-Hays Doctoral Dissertation fellowship and the Graduate School of Arts and Sciences at the University of Virginia. Earlier versions of this chapter were presented at University College London, the 2003 AAA meetings in Chicago, and Goldsmith's College, London. I would like to thank the audiences at UCL and Goldsmith's (especially Phil Burnham and Catherine Alexander) for comments and Tracy Luedke for organizing the AAA panel. Maia Green, Rebecca Nash, and Harry West read the chapter with trademark acuity. I am afraid any shortcomings that remain are mine alone.
1. It should not be forgotten that Henry VIII's and Edward VI's iconoclasm also benefited the royal treasury: precious metals in the religious art and objects destroyed were melted down and recast, and bishop's lands were confiscated by the crown (see Phillips 1973: 97–100).
2. The ASCG later became the Gospel of God Church (see Dillon-Malone 1978); after Johane's

death in 1973 the Gospel of God Church split into two main factions, one of which is still known as the Gospel of God (with a base at Gandanzara, Zimbabwe—Shoniwa-Johane's boyhood home). The other is known simply (if somewhat confusingly) as the Johane Masowe Church (with a base in Lusaka, Zambia).

3. See "Statement by Shoniwa to Native Detective Zakia," November 1, 1932, National Archives of Zimbabwe file s138/22 (hereafter NAZ s138/22).

4. See the interview with Amon Nengomasha and Jack Dzvuke, NAZ file AOH/4.

5. See NAZ s138/22.

6. The term *witchcraft medicines* does not refer only to substances used by witches; Johane and his followers also used this term to refer to anything used by a spirit medium or traditional healer. This is evident in an interview with a certain Pauros Mugwagwa Musonza, in which he explains to the oral historian Dawson Munjeri how Johane's followers made him surrender his muti ("traditional" medicines). See NAZ file AOH/51.

7. "Cholera claims six Johane Marange sect members," *Zimbabwe Herald*, November 19, 1999, p. 1.

8. I am using the word *pebble* here because this is how the apostolics referred to them. Technically, however, not all the "pebbles" they used were in fact pebbles (rounded stones shaped by flowing water); some were chips of rock, some were crystalline. However, I could not discern a pattern to their use that reflected a conscious differentiation of material properties.

9. This would not be the case in West Africa, where stones do, in fact, play an important role in religious therapeutics and divination (see, for example, Jackson 1989)—or for that matter, so it seems, on the island of Sumba, Indonesia (see Keane 1998). As Terence Ranger (1999) has shown, rocks are an integral aspect of the southern African religious imagination, but more in terms of space and place than their materiality. Bengt Sundkler, too, has written of the Zionist prophet John Mtanti who in the mid-1920s found holy stones in a river to build "the new Jerusalem": "They looked like ordinary stones to ordinary people, but Mtanti discovered a message in them, or rather *on* them" (1976: 125). The message was a written one; each stone was marked by a letter of the Roman alphabet, to be deciphered as a source of biblical revelation. This case is again different from that of the Masowe. For Mtanti, only particular stones were of interest, and only because they charted a predetermined "supernatural drama" (Sundkler 1976: 135) which he was, in effect, reading—like the New Testament.

10. See NAZ s138/22.

11. I would like to thank Murray Last for discussing these points with me.

REFERENCES

Aston, Margaret. 1988. *England's Iconoclasts: Laws against Images*. Vol. 1. Oxford: Clarendon.

Bradlow, Frank. 1987. *Printing for Africa: The Story of Robert Moffat and the Kuruman Press*. Kuruman: Moffat Mission Trust.

Chavanduka, Gordon. 1994. *Traditional Medicine in Zimbabwe*. Harare: University of Zimbabwe Press.

Coleman, Simon. 1996. "Words as Things: Language, Aesthetics and the Objectification of Protestant Evangelicalism." *Journal of Material Culture* 1.1:107–128.

Comaroff, Jean. 1980. "Healing and the Cultural Order: The Case of the Barolong boo Rat-shidi." *American Ethnologist* 7.4:637–657.

Dillon-Malone, Clive. 1978. *The Korsten Basketmakers: A Study of the Masowe Apostles*. Manchester: Manchester University Press.

Engelke, Matthew. 2003. "The Book, the Church, and the 'Incomprehensible Paradox': Christianity in African History." *Journal of Southern African Studies* 29.1:297–306.

——. 2004a. "Discontinuity and the Discourse of Conversion." *Journal of Religion in Africa* 34.1/2:82–109.

——. 2004b. "Text and Performance in an African Church: The Book, 'Live and Direct.'" *American Ethnologist* 31.1:76–91.

Evans-Pritchard, E. E. 1976. *Witchcraft, Oracles, and Magic among the Azande*. Abridged ed. Oxford: Clarendon Press.

Gelfand, Michael, et al. 1985. *The Traditional Medical Practitioner in Zimbabwe: His Principles of Practice and Pharmacopoeia*. Gweru: Mambo Press.

Geschiere, Peter. 1997. *The Modernity of Witchcraft: Politics and the Occult in Postcolonial Africa*. Charlottesville: University Press of Virginia.

Green, Maia. 1995. "Why Christianity Is the 'Religion of Business': Perceptions of the Church among Pogoro Catholics in Southern Tanzania." *Journal of Religion in Africa* 25.1:25–47.

Howsam, Leslie. 1991. *Cheap Bibles: Seventeenth-Century Publishing and the British and Foreign Bible Society*. Cambridge: Cambridge University Press.

Jackson, Michael. 1989. *Paths toward a Clearing: Radical Empiricism and Ethnographic Inquiry*. Bloomington: Indiana University Press.

Janzen, John. 1978. *The Quest for Therapy in Lower Zaire*. Berkeley: University of California Press.

Jules-Rosette, Bennetta. 1975. *African Apostles: Ritual and Conversion in the Church of John Maranke*. Ithaca, N.Y.: Cornell University Press.

Keane, Webb. 1998. "Calvin in the Tropics: Objects and Subjects at the Religious Frontier." In Patricia Spyer, ed., *Border Fetishisms: Material Objects in Unstable Spaces*, 13–34. London: Routledge.

——. 2001. "Money Has No Object: Materiality, Desire, and Modernity in an Indonesian Society." In Fred Myers, ed., *The Empire of Things: Regimes of Value and Material Culture*, 65–90. Oxford: James Currey.

Lan, David. 1985. *Guns and Rain: Guerrillas and Spirit Mediums in Zimbabwe*. London: James Currey.

Maxwell, David. 1998. "'Delivered from the Spirit of Poverty?': Pentecostalism, Prosperity, and Modernity in Zimbabwe." *Journal of Religion in Africa* 28.3:350–373.

McDannell, Colleen. 1995. *Material Christianity: Religion and Popular Culture in America*. New Haven: Yale University Press.

Meyer, Birgit. 1998. "'Make a Complete Break with the Past': Memory and Post-colonial Modernity in Ghanaian Discourse." *Journal of Religion in Africa* 28.3:316–349.

Mukonyora, Isabel. 2000. "Marginality and Protest in the Wilderness: The Role of Women in Shaping Masowe Thought Pattern." *Southern African Feminist Review* 4.2:1–22.

Phillips, John. 1973. *The Reformation of Images: Destruction of Art in England, 1535–1660*. Berkeley: University of California Press.

Ranger, Terence. 1982. "The Death of Chaminuka: Spirit Mediums, Nationalism, and the Guerrilla War in Zimbabwe." *African Affairs* 81:349–369.

———. 1999. *Voices from the Rocks: Nature, Culture and History in the Matopos Hills of Zimbabwe*. Oxford: James Currey.

Reynolds, Pamela. 1996. *Traditional Healers and Childhood in Zimbabwe*. Athens: Ohio University Press.

Robbins, Joel. 2003. "On the Paradoxes of Global Pentecostalism and the Perils of Continuity Thinking." *Religion* 33:221–231.

Schoffeleers, Matthew. 1991. "Ritual Healing and Political Acquiescence: The Case of the Zionist Churches of Southern Africa." *Africa* 60.1:1–25.

Sundkler, Bengt. 1976. *Zulu Zion and Some Swazi Zionists*. Oxford: Oxford University Press.

Tambiah, Stanley Jeyarja. 1984. *The Buddhist Saints of the Forest and the Cult of the Amulets: A Study in Charisma, Hagiography, Sectarianism, and Millennial Buddhism*. Cambridge: Cambridge University Press.

Taylor, Christopher. 1992. *Milk, Honey, and Money: Changing Concepts in Rwandan Healing*. Washington: Smithsonian Institution Press.

Turner, Victor. 1968. *The Drums of Affliction: A Study of Religious Processes among the Ndembu of Zambia*. Oxford: Oxford University Press.

Werbner, Richard. 1985. "The Argument of Images: From Zion to the Wilderness in African Churches." In Wim van Binsbergen and Matthew Schoffeleers, eds., *Theoretical Explorations in African Religion*, 253–286. London: Kegan Paul International.

West, Gerald, and Musa Dube, eds. 2000. *The Bible in Africa: Translations, Trajectories, Trends*. Leiden: Brill.

West, Harry. 2001. "Sorcery of Construction and Socialist Modernization: Ways of Understanding Power in Postcolonial Mozambique." *American Ethnologist* 28.1:119–150.

BILL MAURER

Does Money Matter? Abstraction and
Substitution in Alternative Financial Forms

From reflection on the democratic possibilities of the revelation that money is "only" information (Hart 2001) to appreciation of the logics of circulation warranting the abstractions of contemporary finance (Lee and LiPuma 2002), analysts of contemporary monetary formations wonder what happens to the age-old question of how a material object can ever be adequate to abstract value when the object itself no longer seems to matter. In scholarly and popular venues, the story of money is repeatedly told as an evolutionary tale of greater and greater distance from actual things, of greater dematerialization, in a linear trajectory from barter, to metal coin, to paper backed by metal, to paper declared valuable by fiat, and, finally, to complex financial entities like derivatives, with future, not anterior, backing. The study of the social implications of these monetary transitions has a long and esteemed lineage from Aristotle through Georg Simmel to twentieth-century anthropology, sociology, and economics.

More broadly, however, because of its implications for the problem of the relationship between a material reality and abstract representation, money in the Western philosophical tradition has often served as the sine qua non of the problem of the possibility of truth itself. Specifically, as Marc Shell has shown, money has been the paradigmatic case of the model of truth as *adequatio intellectus et res*, whether understood as the adequation of a representation with an underlying and preexisting reality, or the bringing into relation of thought and matter, Word and Flesh, and so on (Shell 1978, 1982). Adequation cannot proceed without abstraction, since, in this model of truth, knowledge is attained by abstracting from the materiality of the world the intellectual generalities that make sense of it, or the spiritual or metaphysical forms that animate it. Money's role in mediating exchange, in this philosophical tradition, provides the model for other intellectual abstractions. Barter, in contrast, was direct, unmediated exchange of a quantity of one kind of thing for quantities of another. People bartering did not have to reason any more abstractly than the figuring of ratios (how many apples will get you a fish?). Once money appeared, and mediation by a third term entered the exchange operation, a new kind of abstraction had taken place. Or so the story goes. Traders (and analysts) got caught up in the curious dynamics of monetary equivalence, and the conundrum of money's very existence: how can everything be placed on one scale of value figured in terms of money, and how can this thing called money take on such mediating powers?

Anthropologists have long recognized, of course, that the "introduction" of money is never so simple an affair. Paul Bohannan's (1959) classic studies showed that other schemes of reckoning abstract value existed in Tiv society before "general purpose" money came on the scene. More recent writers document the complexity of the interactions between general and special purpose moneys (Akin and Robbins 1999). Others, in sociology, demonstrate that general purpose money, deemed to dissolve all things into the flat wash of monetary value, has never been as straightforward as it has seemed and that people in contemporary capitalist economies rarely actually regard all things as equally commensurate with money, and find ways of regarding money as itself plural and specific to certain expenditures (Zelizer 1997).

Even though it is so trite, however, the story of increasing abstraction always seems to cause flashes of revelation and previously unrealized connections when new kinds of actual exchange make explicit the disconnection between money and whatever substance or power is deemed to underwrite it. The debate over the introduction of the greenback in the nineteenth-century United States resonates with contemporary conversations about derivatives, as it does with Melanesian discussions about Western-style moneys' interface with other items. We—we all, in the field and in the texts that make up the corpus of knowledge on money—continually seem surprised by money's disconnect, or its failure "really" to capture worth. In his rich discussion of Melanesian currencies, Robert Foster concludes that Melanesians receive new national moneys in a manner that "exceeds the limits" of representation and abstraction, for "money can never represent or stand for anything else 'truly,' that is, fully and finally. . . . the issue is no longer one of representation's arbitrariness, but rather its ultimate failure. In other words, money is always representationally flawed" (Foster 1999: 230–231).

Attending to the representational failure of money occasions a reconsideration of the barter story. Marilyn Strathern has argued that assessments of barter as relatively unmediated hinge on a misrecognition of the mathematics and pragmatics of such exchanges. She finds that in Melanesia value hinges not on the commensuration of differences between things, but rather "a substitution of units" (1992: 185). These units are conceived "as body parts, from bodies (persons) which . . . must first be construed as partible," and also, therefore, as encompassing other things as well (ibid.). This process does not conjure objects separate from subjects, but partible persons/things and abstractable units that are substituted—not compared—with one another. This is not reification of the bourgeois kind, where comparison introduces numerical ratios between different goods to commensurate value and poses the problem of the adequacy of a representation (value) to its objects. Substitution instead creates homologies, and equivalence in the exchange of gifts "will always (can only) appear as a matching of units" made to become homologues of one another (171).

This chapter is a thought experiment. What if the abstraction of monetary mediation were really a form of substitution? What if the pragmatics of money—not what it does, but *how* it does—obscures that substitution because those pragmatics always seem to involve commensuration and calculation and, thus, comparison rather than substitution? The adequation of substance to value might then be seen as an indigenous analytical procedure that takes the attention away from homology and makes money appear to be, instead, a matter of abstraction and mediation. Let me be clear. Adequation relies on the higher-order generality of a calibrating metric to bring meaning to the matter of the world. Abstraction is an operation "above" matter, and is the animating force that gives that matter form. In this framework, money and truth serve interchangeably as models for one another and for that calibrating metric. They are analogous to one another, but superordinate to mere matter. Substitution, rather than organizing knowledge in terms of higher-order calibrations, operates through homologies that lie to one side of one another as well as alongside the materialities to which they maintain a relation. None is superordinate to another, nor to that which the model of adequation would maintain is the "underlying" reality.

Loosening the grip of adequation may also help to turn around the implicit assessments of abstraction in many discussions of money. Is there a sense in which it is grain futures, for example, that are irreducibly material, and grain itself which is highly abstract? Can we imagine a world where the problem of abstraction and adequation obscure the practical effectivity of money, despite, or because of, money's representational failures? Whither, then, social inquiry, a practice that defines itself in relation to the adequacy of its representations to a reality that supposedly precedes it? In other words, does acknowledging money's representional failure point up that of social inquiry, our intellectual currency, itself? To some, this may seem to be beating the dead horse of anthropology's engagement with reflexivity. Yet the fetishism of ethnographic information, rather than its enframings, still has a strong hold on the discipline, with Clifford Geertz's "another country heard from" still axiomatic even for forms of social inquiry based on interpretation and understanding rather than a positivistic quest for generalizable laws.

My central contention in this chapter is accepting that money essentially poses the problem of abstraction, and adequation presumes a starting-point analogous to and perhaps derived from the idea of a state of fallen grace, a world where matter and spirit are sundered, and only the divine can make the Word flesh. And yet, it is unclear whether we have ever left that state of grace, or whether, instead, continuing in the now of the assumption that we have done so permits other work to take place. Despite the continuous revelation that money is "just" abstraction or "mere" fiction, money continues to have efficacy. The distraction of adequation, I am suggesting, allows us to continue doing what we are doing despite our knowing full well what we do (Žižek 1989). To make the case, I will present two alternative money forms widely separated in time yet linked by a tradition in which the Word ought not be made flesh: the first standardized coin of the caliphate, and early-twenty-first-century tradable Islamic mortgage paper.

Consider a situation in which the adequation of word to flesh is not at issue, a situation in which the working out of monetary logics lies in the way of the questions one might pose to it, because that working out is expressing other questions that cut off questions of the flesh. The word and the coin figure somewhat differently in early Islam from the Greek and later Christian traditions examined by Shell. Between 693 and 697 C.E. (74–77 A.H.), the Umayyad caliph 'Abd al-Malik instituted a series of remarkable administrative reforms in an effort to Arabize the caliphate and infuse the empire with his moral authority. Besides reorganizing the taxation system, requiring the use of Arabic instead of Persian or Greek in the financial administration, building the Dome of the Rock in Jerusalem, and establishing a post office and new irrigation systems, 'Abd al-Malik instituted two important transformations of meaning and money. He commissioned a new edition of the Qur'an that included, for the first time, diacritical marks indicating the vowels; and he replaced the head of the sovereign on the coins of the caliphate with the Word of God. The latter was accomplished around 693 C.E. (74 AH). Indeed, the new coins inaugurated the new calendar by inscribing Hijra time and generalizing it throughout the caliphate and beyond.[1]

The new coins also used new metrics, thus contorting the distribution of bullion around the Mediterranean and contributing rather substantially to the caliphate's wealth (Grierson 1960). They also brought the gift of revelation and virtuous living to those who would use them in exchange, the Qur'anic inscriptions on them explicitly exhorting repentance and behavior within "the limits of Allah."[2]

The caliphate under 'Abd al-Malik faced a series of civil conflicts, rebellions, and wars, especially in Iraq and Persia, portions of which 'Abd al-Malik was able to bring under Umayyad rule after protracted struggle and intrigue. War broke out as well with Byzantium, when the emperor there refused to accept the circulation and use of the new money. Scholars of this period interpret 'Abd al-Malik's various reforms as the consolidation of a "new ideological policy" (Lapidus 1988: 61; see also Khalidi 1994: 84–85) and "successful symbolism" that gave the government a "symbolic form" designed to establish "a political and moral unity of all Arabs under Islam" (Hodgson 1974: 246), indeed, created "Muslim" as a generalized and extendable category of identification. Replacing the head of the sovereign with writing, and the writing of God besides, was "a daring innovation . . . and an iconographic stroke of genius," as the design was "at once highly abstract and immediately symbolic" (Hodgson 1974: 247).

But what if we consider the analytical tools of symbolism and ideology to be already exhausted, since both are bound to the logic of abstraction and adequation (a symbol is a symbol because it stands for something else "below" it, and ideology is the covering over of a set of "real" relations at the "base")? Perhaps then the conventional account of the coinage reforms is beside the point. When viewed together with the orthographic changes introduced into the Qur'anic text, the "symbolism" of the coins and the caliph's other accomplishments interrupts the form of symbol, meaning, and their relation that Shell found in monetary manifestations of Greek and Christian thinking.

The reign of 'Abd al-Malik took place during a "time of immense doctrinal flexibility" (Watt 1974: 61). One of the chief questions had to do with the standing of the caliph, revolving around the theological status of the very term, based on the Arabic root *kh-l-f*. The meaning of this root is "behind, in place," which transformed into "behind, in time," or "after" (Watt 1990: 57). The term *khalifa* occurs only twice in the Qur'an, referring once to Adam (2:30) and once to David (38:26). These references allowed the Umayyads to claim that they stood in the place of, after, Adam and David, and therefore had divine sanction for their rule.[3] In the civil wars of the time, the Umayyads' opponents objected that the first caliph, Abu-Bakr, refused the title *khalifa* of God in favor of *khalifa* of the Messenger of God (Watt 1974: 69). At issue was the degree of distance and emanation from the divine, but also the question of whether the caliph was an emanation from God at all, or, more momentously, an attribute, an unchanging essence at one with divinity. In his monetary reform, meanwhile, the caliph 'Abd al-Malik caused the phrase *khalifa Allah*, referring to himself, to be stamped on his new coins (Crone and Hinds 1986: 7).

Given that he understood himself as God's caliph, in a position analogous to that of Adam, David, or Muhammad, 'Abd al-Malik's orthographic reforms interlocked with his monetary reforms. Interpreted as an effort to Arabize the administration for the sake of symbolism and ideology, the orthographic reform, adding vowels to the Arabic script, also supposedly derived from the caliph's fear of ever speaking "incorrect Arabic," especially when reciting the sacred text (Abbott 1972: 4; Hitti 1937: 219–220), and from an apocryphal incident in which a Greek scribe urinated into an inkwell (Hitti 1937: 217). No simple rebellion, such an act constituted an affront on the very authority and legitimacy of the Qur'an itself. The first revelation given to Muhammad, the temporal beginning of the sacred text, appears near its end, and concerns the nature of "man," the movement of the pen in transcribing the Word of God, and the subsequent recitation of that transcendent Word: "Recite in the name of the Lord Who created. He created man from a clot. Read and your Lord is Most Honorable, Who taught to write with the pen, Taught man what he knew not" (96: 1–5).

The penning and recitation of God's Word was at the center of early Islamic philosophical debates in elliptical if not direct conversation with Christian claims of Jesus's divinity. The latter had only been made explicit recently, in the Anathemas of the Second Council of Constantinople in 553 C.E., less than a century before Muhammad's flight to Medina. According to the Second Council:

> If anyone does not confess that the Father and the Son and the Holy Spirit *are one nature or essence*, one power or authority, worshipped as a trinity of the same essence, one deity in three hypostases or persons, let him be anathema. For there is one God and Father, of whom are all things, and one Lord Jesus Christ, through whom are all things, and one Holy Spirit, in whom are all things. (Emphasis added)

The Qur'an counters, in a passage that echoes the first revelation about the pen and the clot and also invokes the name of the first identified caliph: "The similitude of Jesus before Allah is as that of Adam; He created him from dust, then said to him: 'Be.' And he was" (3: 59).

Jesus, then, was clearly a mere man, not God, a thing of dust. But what is the status of this divine call to "be"? If it is, like God, uncreated and eternal, but made manifest by God in Arabic speech and then penned in Arabic letters by his scribe Muhammad, and manifested in the materiality of spoken and written language, then might the call to "be" be homologous to the Christian understanding of the body of Christ, a manifestation of uncreated divinity made material in the flesh of the world? For the Mu'tazilites, a theological movement that arose in Basra in the middle 700s, just after the reign of 'Abd al-Malik, the status of the divine Word raised the question of the status of the Qur'an itself: was it, like God, uncreated and eternal, or was it created on the lips and in the penning gestures and inked letters of believing humans? The answer to the question would determine, among other things, the importance and relevance of exact pronunciation of the kind 'Abd al-Malik sought to inspire with standardized diacritical marks. To the Mu'tazilites, the doctrine of the uncreated and eternal Qur'an smacked of the doctrine of the Man-God made flesh in Jesus Christ: physical, yet eternal; material, yet uncreated (hence of a virgin birth).[4] For the doctrine of the uncreated and eternal Qur'an, the difference between the uncreated Qur'an and the Incarnation would be merely in the "modality of . . . manifestation" of the divine Word (Corbin 1993: 109).

The Mu'tazilites, in contrast, maintained a sharp distinction between the word-as-speech or the materiality of writing and speaking, on the one hand, and the Divine Idea, on the other. Prefiguring Saussure's distinction between *parole* and *langue* and indeed the metaphysical distinction between matter and form or *res* and *intellectus* that would preoccupy Christian thinkers wondering about the theological status of things like Jesus's foreskin or toenails (Shell 1995), the Mu'tazilites' doctrine that the Qur'an was created, not uncreated, stood together with the idea of divine immutability: God, strictly speaking, does not utter, for to utter is to effect a change in state, a difference from the originary moment, an iteration that creates alternatives (What to speak? To speak or to write? Which is primary, the Person or the Word?). The uttered word is not an attribute of the divine Word, but merely its expression. God is a oneness and not of the world or its words. Later, and in opposition to the views of the Mu'tazilites, Ibn Hanbal (780–855 c.e.) would argue that the word itself, in its very materiality on lips, and through pens and in ink, is transcendent; that God Himself speaks in the words of the Book which are thereby, as it were, Words. His disciple, Ibn Taymiyya, like others since, nonetheless equivocated on the status—created or uncreated—of human pronunciation of Qur'anic words.

Given the unsettled debates during and after the reign of 'Abd al-Malik over the status of words and the Word, the created and uncreated Qur'an, and the Christian doctrine of a God incarnate, can the monetary reforms be interpreted in terms other than symbolic or ideological? I suggest that in a time of doctrinal flexibility, 'Abd al-Malik's coins in themselves obviated in advance the apparent opposition between the philosophical positions that would later polarize the Mu'tazilites and the Hanbalis.[5] Both of those positions depend on a logic of anteriority and seriation that is simply beside the point for the *khalifa Allah* and his coins. For in 'Abd al-Malik's formulation, the caliph is not God's representative, but is instead an actual substantive attribute of the essence of God. Not an emanation from God like the soul of any human, the caliph is one with the divine, but on another scale. Therefore, the caliph's coin no longer requires the seal of any worldly sovereign, for the sovereign is no longer simply worldly at all. Instead, it carries the very word, or Word, of God. In so doing, it does not symbolize or stand for anything else. It is, with the other attributes of God, one with God. The word or Word is neither material nor ideational, but both and neither at the same time and in a worldly or transcendent oneness. Or, to be more precise, questions about material versus ideal were not part of the coins' pragmatic universe. The coins and the *khalifa Allah* are a pragmatic hedging of the question of the created or uncreated word. Sidestepping the problem of the inlibration of the Qur'an (was there an insubstantial and eternal Book *before* the Qur'an was penned, before revelation?), the *khalifa Allah* also obviated the problem of a ruler's worldly authority. Doing so permitted an appreciation of the double-sidedness of the apprehension of God as that which humans can never truly know and yet which they are obligated to experience and make material in the world through virtuous practices. The "hedging" here, then—the "sidestepping"—is just this sort of virtuous practice.

'Abd al-Malik similarly hedged the question of whether God or the caliph is foregrounded in the instantiation of the *khalifa Allah*. The root *kh-l-f* spatially locates an entity behind or in the background, and also places it temporally behind, or after. Seen from the perspective of a judge watching a two-person race from the finish line, the person spatially behind the other will also temporally follow that other and come in behind, or second, temporally after the first. Yet being spatially behind can either be the background from which the foreground springs out, or the shadow projected from the foreground, a hazy image of it. Being temporally behind can either be the second who follows, or the procession from the first. What is in the background therefore does not necessarily temporally foreground but might temporally proceed from what is in front. Which, here, is primary? Which is originary? Which is cause and which emanation? These sorts of questions were posed by 'Abd al-Malik's opponents, who were summarily executed for participating in the logic of the symbol (with meanings "behind" it) that had no truck with the coins of the *khalifa Allah*.[6]

I am suggesting that the coin of 'Abd al-Malik functions as a nonusurious supplement to the monetary semiotics presented by the Western metaphysical tradition. Playing on the Qur'anic prohibition of *riba*, glossed in the twentieth century as "usury" or "interest," but more properly translated "increase," I would like to suggest that the coin of 'Abd al-Malik does not add to or replicate so much as stand across that tradition, lying in the way of some of its suppositions and stopping its conceptual practices in their tracks. Like the Qur'an, it forbids the (exegetical) increase, expansion, or elaboration of the tradition of *adequatio intellectus et res*. It does so by confounding behind in time with behind in space, cause and effect, meaning and matter, while it stages the mutuality of temporal and spatial anteriority, and the substitutability rather than adequation of word and thing. In effect, it substitutes the problem of the imagination of coinage to that of the problem of the imagination of the deity.

SECURITIZING ISLAM

Islamic banking is a wholly twentieth-century phenomenon. While it emerged from nationalist and Islamist movements on the Indian subcontinent in the 1930s, and while those early movements resulted in the formation of Islamic banking institutions in the 1960s and 1970s, it came to fruition (and market share) only in the 1980s. Saudi royals have bankrolled many Islamic banking ventures and institutes, and Middle Eastern banks have experimented with interest-free models since the 1970s. But the contemporary Islamic banking movement has achieved its successes mainly through the efforts of South Asian and Arab immigrants to the United States and United Kingdom, as well as return migrants to Malaysia and the subsequent diffusion of Islamic economic knowledge and practices in the Malay/Indonesian speaking world.[7] Islamic finance is organized around debate over the Qur'anic prohibition of *riba*—or, more specifically, whether or not all forms of "increase" constitute the forbidden *riba*.[8] While that discussion remains unsettled, both theologically and in terms of Islamic banking's responses to conventional financial practices, the field has developed a number of contractual forms that provide funds for business and projects and home financing without the use of interest. Some are based on "administrative fees" in place of interest; others are based on profit- and loss-sharing arrangements. The former are generally seen as more "efficient" but perhaps "less Islamic," while the latter are seen as more "equitable" and "more pure" (see, e.g., El Gamal 2000; Saleh 1986).

The American Finance House–LARIBA drew up the first "Islamic mortgage" contract in 1987 for the purchase of a home in Madison, Wisconsin.[9] The contract was on a cost-plus model (*murabaha*)[10] according to which the finance company purchased the house and the client paid the cost of the house plus a pre-set and unchanging markup over a period of time. It was the pre-set and unchanging amount of the markup that distinguished this contract from a conventional interest-based mortgage.[11] Later mortgage products developed by the same company used lease-to-purchase agreements based on *ijara* contracts from classical jurisprudence. In an *ijara* contract, the homebuyer pays back a predetermined proportion of the principal each month, plus the bank's share of the "rent" the house would fetch on the local rental market. American Finance House–LARIBA continues to use *ijara* contracts, while its main competitor uses a cost-plus model.

In March 2001, the U.S. Federal Home Loan Mortgage Corporation, known colloquially as "Freddie Mac," signaled its support for American Finance House–LARIBA's Islamic mortgages by investing $1 million in existing American Finance House–LARIBA contracts. It has since invested a total of $45 million. Freddie Mac was created by an act of Congress in 1970 to create a secondary market for mortgages. As a "government-sponsored enterprise" (GSE), it is a wholly independent stockholder-owned corporation. The corporate Web site states, "Just as stock and bond markets have put investor capital to work for corporations, the secondary mortgage market puts private investor capital to work for homebuyers and apartment owners, providing a continuous flow of affordable funds for home financing. We like to call it 'linking Main Street with Wall Street.' "[12]

Freddie Mac's chief function is to purchase mortgages from lenders and securitize them. The process of securitization involves purchasing a number of individual mortgages, bundling them together, and then selling shares in the bundle to investors. The shares are abstract units of the bundle, not the individual mortgages within it, and can be valued according to factors such as the overall risk profile of the bundle, itself a function of the probability that individuals will default on their mortgages. The net effect is to spread the risk of default among a number of investors, rather than having it all fall on the lender, and to provide the lender with a market for mortgages. This generates liquidity for the mortgage market. For Freddie Mac, investing in Islamic mortgage alternatives fell under its mandate to expand opportunities for underserved populations to gain access to home ownership.[13]

Freddie Mac support has been hailed as an incredible milestone in the growing visibility and legitimacy of Islamic mortgage alternatives. Before September 11, 2001, Freddie Mac had begun to expand its purchase of Islamic mortgage alternatives. In August 2001, it invested $10 million to purchase lease contracts from Standard Federal Bank and United Mortgage of America in Detroit.[14] It is significant that the only new entrant into the field of Islamic finance in the United States since September 11, 2001, Guidance Residential, is a home financing company, which has already entered into an agreement with Freddie Mac for an initial commitment of $200 million.[15]

With Guidance, Freddie Mac has also begun to explore the securitization of Islamic mortgage alternatives for the purposes of creating securities for large investors who seek Islamically acceptable investment vehicles. One of my interlocutors once remarked that this creates an incentive for "organizations with the deep pockets" to step in. Securitization also makes Islamic mortgage alternatives scalable in a way they had not been before, when they were primarily local or regional affairs backed by small investors. Although American Finance House–LARIBA has a greater geographic spread, Guidance is quickly catching up. The profile of its client base is remarkably different, however: Guidance mortgage applicants tend to be poorer and male, while American Finance House–LARIBA applicants tend to be richer and to apply jointly (as husband and wife).

The problem here is that securitization seems to distance the object of the contractual agreement—the house—from the activity of buying and selling. Some Islamic financiers, namely, those who promote *ijara* contracts, decry this move. They argue that Islamic banking insists that exchange be explicitly rooted in the assets underlying it, and not abstracted from those assets. Here we see an incipient argument among Islamic bankers over abstraction versus substitution, an echo of the argument between the Mu'tazilites and the Hanbalis. One interlocutor has repeatedly stressed to me that what distinguishes Islamic banking from conventional banking is not simply the prohibition of interest, but the emphasis on "real, tangible" goods. *Ijara* leasing contracts are thus seen as more Islamically acceptable than *murabaha* cost-plus models because the amount paid on top of the principal each month is calculated from the fair market rent that the house would command, not an abstract or arbitrary markup "tied to nothing." At the same time, others argue that the securitization of mortgage paper will greatly increase the liquidity of this sector, as well as reduce the costs of an Islamic mortgage to the point where it will be a comparable expense to a conventional home loan. Hence, the future efficiency makes up for any sacrifice of equity, in the literal and figurative sense.

In his early and prescient study of the prohibition of *riba* (interest) and *gharar* (uncertainty, risk, speculation), Nabil A. Saleh (1986) argued that there would be two means of developing Islamic banking instruments. One would devise operational techniques that seem to "overturn the prohibitions of *riba* and *gharar*" through the niceties of legal reasoning and strategy. The other would stress adherence to the letter of the prohibitions in the name of ensuring the "legitimacy of its means and objectives" lest "the whole system . . . be perverted" (1986: 117–118). Saleh worried that the rift between these two approaches would eventually put the future of the field in peril. He also worried that the resort to legalistic stratagems, *hiyal*, allowed Islamic banks adopting the former approach to "achieve objectives which are not necessarily lawful [i.e., under Islamic law]" for the sake of "flexibility" (ibid.: 117).

There is a kind of casuistry in Islamic banking discussions about securitization that lies in the way of its analytical or religious assessment.[16] This casuistry may also explain the different client profiles of American Finance House–LARIBA and Guidance, as well as people's assessments (in interviews) that Guidance is actually "more shari'a compliant" than the former, despite the former's strict *ijara* model and the latter's more interestlike model. Writing within Islamic economics, Mahmoud El-Gamal notes, "As the field of 'Islamic economics' tries to find its place (within economics, social science, Islamic studies, or any other field) not only must we continue to differ in our opinion about the nature of the field, but we must also continue to misunderstand each other" (2000: 5). While these misunderstandings do little to hold back exchange, they constitute the very field of Islamic banking as an intellectual enterprise. On the one hand, the field is a straightforward debate over abstraction and its permissibility in Islamic law, like that over the status of the written word of the Qur'an. On the other hand, the field replicates the *form* of that debate. The field and the practices it supposedly warrants are detached from one another not by degrees of *abstraction*, but by what Roy Wager terms *obviation*: the intellectual field and the contractual practices "double back" on one another, even as they block or lie in the way of each other by continually laying upon each other new semantic or pragmatic relationships (Wagner 1978: 257). At any moment, Islamic banking is either the intellectual debates or the contractual practices. The one substitutes for the other depending on the venue and the work to be done, and, in the process of substitution and the layerings it facilitates, creates potential for new work. Thus, substitution and homology, not representation or symbol, govern "Islamic banking."

But at what point do legal stratagems become illegitimate? Can splitting legal hairs render an entire activity suspect? While the Maliki and Hanbali schools of jurisprudence have rejected *hiyal*, the Hanafi and Shafi have tended to accept it. If the "gate of *ijtihad*" (interpretation) is closed, then interpretation cannot proceed. Rather, *taqlid*, imitation, must be the chief means of attempting the creation of entities adequate to changing historical conditions. Yet *taqlid* for Islamic banking would mean imitating conventional economics, which contains forbidden elements like interest. Hence, substitution, not adequation, becomes the preferred analytical operation: one could either achieve Islamic banking through *taqlid*, with the imagined past of Islamic market relationships characterizing Muhammad's Mecca, or one could make a case for opening the gate of *ijtihad* and using its methods of reasoning by analogy (*qiyas*), comparing benefits and harms (*istislah*), and even, possibly, devising *hiyal*. While some Islamic bankers rely on imitation and substitution, others accept representation and abstraction. *Hiyal* and *qiyas* take center stage in the working out of practical problems and in speculative ruminations, and, indeed, the working out of whether this opposition is one of scale (lower-order problems versus higher-level ruminations) or kind (and, thus, more lateral than hierarchical). Meanwhile, however, when they are not debating the finer points of law but in the thick of the work of drafting a contract, people mix and match from among all four Sunni schools of jurisprudence and even occasionally from Shi'a jurisprudence. For example, many Islamic finance institutions offer the gamut of Islamic contracts, like *murabaha* and *ijara*, no matter their provenance and even if they are putatively mutually exclusive. Offering both under one roof mixes contracts considered to be "more" Islamic with ones considered to be "less" Islamic. Conventional banks with Islamic "windows" (like HSBC or Citibank) mix Islamic and conventional products and procedures. Is this acceptable in the name of efficiency and practicality? What is interesting from the point of view of the story of the Mu'tazilites is that no one today is being executed over such matters of dogma. It is not that practice trumps theory, however; it is that practice and theory mutually intertwine or densely lateralize to create the very field of "Islamic banking" itself. Occasionally, some throw up their hands in exasperation and demand a return to strict *taqlid* of classical Islamic practices. Others claim that only qualified *shari'a* scholars should issue *fatwas* on such matters, or, alternatively, that everyone should be skeptical of so-called *shari'a* scholars who may be in the pay of one or another agency. These claims are rejected, incidentally, by those whom a quantitatively oriented sociologist, looking merely at the demographic data, might peg as "more conservative," such as Guidance's applicant pool. In the meantime, however, when the sources of authority are not being called into question, work is getting done. Contracts are being drawn up. Innovations are being made. And Islamic banking and finance trundle along. I am interested in this meantime, and I want to develop an analytic in the meantime, as well.

I am arguing that Islamic banking is casuistic in the classical sense of the term. It is a form of moral practical reason that takes place "whenever extraordinary new issues arise" (Keenan 1996: 123), and, like casuistry, it takes the form of analogies to actual cases rather than the quest for algorithms adequate to all cases. It involves a working, practical knowledge and a "thick" understanding of particular problems and situations.[17] It depends on a conception of *shari'a* as dynamic, not static, and *fiqh* as "not a compendium of religious duties but a system of subjective rights" (Asad 2003: 242). Furthermore, the performative force of the sorts of debates and questionings discussed above operates not simply as the product of ethical judgment or deontics, for those debates are a form of practical activity that works to "cultivate virtuous thought and behavior" (ibid.: 246). The *practice* of virtue—of trying out arguments and methods of securitization for Islamic mortgage contracts—lies in the way of the (very Christian) question of whether Islamic banking is mere ideology or true belief.

ADEQUATION AND ABSTRACTION

In a series of remarkable works, Marc Shell, to whom I referred earlier, has put forward arguments about the semiotics of money (*seme* from the Greek for both word and coin). Greek coinage posed the problem of the relationship between face value (intellectual currency) and substantial value (material currency), inscription and thing. In the tradition Shell examines, the problem of money is thus homologous to problems of knowledge, of the adequation of *intellectus* to *res*, thought to world. Kant defined truth as "the agreement of knowledge with its object"[18] and took the object to be not a real, sensuous thing in the world but an object of knowledge.[19] Money materializes this problem of knowledge, specifically around the relationships between its value and its medium, and the inscriptions on it and its substance. Can a coin, as material substance, ever be adequate to its value in exchange? And where does such value reside—in the metallic substance itself, or in the ideas inscribed on the die and impressed in the metal? Nietzsche's assault on metaphysics remained stamped with their *charakter* (the die used to produce the obverse impression on a coin):[20] "Truths are . . . metaphors worn out and without sensuous power; coins which have lost their impressions and now matter only as metal, no longer as coins" (quoted in Shell 1978: 154). Shell demonstrates, too, that Heidegger, even in his arguments against the notion of truth as the adequation of *intellectus* and *res* and in favor of a notion of truth as "unconcealment" (*aletheia*), still depended on the monetary metaphor and "propositions about coins" that neglect the coin's own status as a proposition (ibid.; see Shell 1982: 162–177).[21]

Shell traces this same problem through beliefs and practices in Christendom concerning the adequation of the divine Word to the world, and, particularly, the theological and epistemological problem of the Word-made-flesh in the body of Jesus, nearly universally understood in Christendom since the sixth century to be God. Shell proposes that we cannot outthink the idea that matter is ontologically prior to thought and language, or its flip side, that thought is prior, and that coinage is given value only by the sovereign mind (just as bread becomes the Eucharist only through the spiritual animation of transubstantiation).[22]

Now if, as Shell (1978, 1982) has argued, Western metaphysics, from Plato to Heidegger, took commodity money as the paradigmatic case of knowledge defined as the appropriateness of a representation to reality, Marxism saw in commodity money the motor of the abstraction of exchange, labor and time, such that social abstraction could itself function as a total form of domination under capitalism. But why should adequation and not some other operation be the foundation of epistemology? Moishe Postone argues that Marx's theory is neither strictly determined by the world in which it was situated, nor outside of it in such a manner as to presume that it could build the world anew (Postone 1993: 140–142). Marx located the historical dialectic "within the framework of a historically specific social theory"; thus, his analysis of capitalism, "his own social context," simultaneously implied a "turn to a notion of the historical specificity of his own theory" (Postone 1993: 140). So, people would base their theories of truth on adequation right at the moment when universal commodification made all things/people fungible with one another via the medium of money. The reflexivity of Marx's argument, according to Postone, is immanent to its object, the capitalist society of Marx's time, yet nonidentical to it. "*Capital*, in other words, is an attempt to construct an argument that does not have a logical form independent of the object being investigated, when that object is the context of the argument itself" (ibid.: 141). Presumably adequation, the appropriateness of a representation (here, critical) to its reality (here, capitalism), would be a mode of knowledge historically specific to the abstractions of capitalism as Marx sought to unfold them in his corpus.

Yet Postone is unable to account for the apparent transhistoricity of the model of truth as the agreement of thought with matter. Alfred Sohn-Rethel (1978: 58–67) proposed that the invention of coinage in ancient Greece gave rise to philosophy, because the coin's reality as at once material and abstraction immediately suggested the problem of knowledge as the adequation of the idea to matter and subordinated the latter to the former. In a footnote, Postone attempts to get around the awkward problem of the apparent historical continuity of Western metaphysics' preoccupation with adequation and money by claiming that, as the commodity form was not generalized in ancient Greece, it was not totalizing in such a manner as to render abstract labor a total mode of social domination (Postone 1993: 156n). To Postone, Sohn-Rethel's thesis is insufficiently historically grounded. Postone here follows Lukács, according to whom ancient Attica, despite its coinage, did not experience "certain aspects of reification . . . as universal forms of existence; it had one foot in the world of reification while the other remained in 'natural' society" (Lukács 1971: 111).[23] What had been an argument about kinds of social formations thus transmogrifies into an argument about the extent of reification and degrees of distance from "natural" society.

Contemporary "alternative" financial forms like Islamic banking are utterly preoccupied with the promise (or premise) of such natural societies, whether they be imagined as spaces of primitive barter, the bazaars and guilds of Arabia during the time of Muhammad, or even the pure market imagined to have been envisioned by Adam Smith and supposedly now made possible by information technologies and the wiring of the planet.[24] In speculating about the presence or possibility of such natural alternatives, they visualize themselves as doing so from a state of fallen grace: with both feet, as it were, mired in reification. The apparent impossibility of a return to "nature" demands that the attempt be made and continually throws up the question of whether we really have left the state of grace or whether we've simply repressed it, only to have it return in unlikely places. Islamic banking, in fact, hinges on those moments of revelation and the repressed's return. It seeks a unity, a moment where the Word has no business being adequate to any thing because it is perfect in itself, and a moment where the world need not approach the Word because it is already one with—not part of, but homologous to—its oneness. In Islam, this state of unity at every level of scale is called *tawhid*.

From the disciplinary location of anthropology, or from the position of Postone's exegesis of Marx, Shell's tracking of the history of metaphysics through the problem of adequation and money is remarkable in its temporal and cultural scope. Like Kant, Shell leaves unasked an anthropological question of specificity that would make two demands. First, what is the specificity of the cultural and historical location of these conceptual creditors who have lent Kant a definition? Second, what is the specificity of Kant's world that would have made this borrowing possible and intelligible to Kant's contemporaries and intellectual heirs? Reading Shell, however, one gets the sense that the identity of money and metaphysical speculation is everywhere and anywhere we care to look in the Western tradition; and yet, again, there is a fascination, indeed a revelatory moment, in assuming this claim. But how does the function of adequation allow Shell to place Plato's and Heidegger's coins on either side of a copula, rendering them equivalent? The answer proposed in this chapter concerns a mathematics of equivalence and a metaphysics of presence organized under the sign of the Word-made-flesh. Alternative operations of equivalence, in other monetary practices organized through homological unity rather then reduction to zero, eclipse those mathematics and metaphysics.

ANTHROPOLOGICAL *TAWHID*

Roy Wagner concludes *The Invention of Culture* with the following exhortation:

> The presentation of the anthropological "literature" as "fact," "data," or "knowledge" must be tempered with the kind of interpretation . . . that will bring the fascinating and mutual invention of anthropologist and "native" alike into awareness. . . . Voltaire observed that if God did not exist it would have been necessary to invent Him. And, like the theologians of the Islamic Muta'zilla [*sic*], I would add that if God *does* exist, this makes it all the more necessary that we invent him, for invention is the form of our experience and understanding. (Wagner 1975: 159)

This chapter has attempted to take up Wagner's call. "The anatomy of invention, the implications surrounding it, and the responsibility it entails must be articulated openly and publicly" (Wagner 1975: 157). This is a *duty*, Wagner writes, an ethical obligation that is "our only alternative to being victimized by the inventors and manipulators of secular reality" (157–158). I take Wagner to mean that the making explicit of invention as the quintessential human "thing to do" (159) means that anthropology, and social inquiry generally, must abandon its claims to find new facts, reveal hidden truths, pull back veils, or make adequate representations. These moves presuppose a regime of facticity wedded to logics of anteriority that may not be as consistent as they at first appear. The alternatives examined here could well be written about more conventionally, as having always been within the metaphysics of anteriority, adequation, and abstraction. They often do restage the dynamics of the Greeks and Christians who worried so much about the relation between the Word and the world.

Yet taking the thought experiment of this chapter to its provisional end, for some Islamic bankers and their clients the problems suggested by the coins and the mortgage securities do not matter. What matters more is the unity of creation, the oneness of the universe and God, and the practical activity that cultivates a virtue homologous to that oneness. Each of these elements is understood and made efficacious not in terms of a relation of adequation, but in terms of their mutual substitutability. What these alternative currencies do is immanent to conventional finance and analytical practice as well. This demands an anthropology that comes to grips with its own evidentiary claims as moral claims, and as referential yet without being wedded to any anterior or grounding real, as functioning within a logic of homology and substitution rather than representation as such. This may seem like familiar territory to a discipline still recovering from debates in the 1980s over representation. Abandoning an anterior ground, some fear, means we can no longer talk about real events, histories, politics, or ethics. But reference need not be grounded on or modeled after the apparent self-evidence of perception. Histories, for that matter—past events—are never completed in the past. The unfair privilege of new angles that reveal the wholeness of some object is that they still retain a grounding authority in some ultimate real, and, thus, their privilege. An internal critique, not content to remain within the defined boundaries of the object, lies more at the threshold, feeling the pull of the limited but mutual creativity of critique and its objects. Spirit versus matter, representation versus reality, becomes a nonoperative question. The cases presented here are what they are entirely through their material displacements, yet those displacements only matter in their mutual formation: coins, contracts, conventional finance, and this chapter alike.

NOTES

1. The Hijra calendar enumerates the lunar years beginning with Muhammad's flight from Mecca to Medina in 622 C.E.

2. The verses used included 9:33 and 9:122: "He it is Who sent His Apostle with guidance and the religion of truth, that He might cause it to prevail over all religions, though the polytheists may be averse," and "They who turn (to Allah), who serve (Him), who praise (Him), who fast, who bow down, who prostrate themselves, who enjoin what is good and forbid what is evil, and who keep the limits of Allah; and give good news to the believers." See Blair and Bloom 1999: 223–224.

3. See, generally, Donner 1999, Watt 1974, and Crone and Hinds 1986.

4. Presumably women do not create but rather merely carry or bear.

5. Daniel Miller points out that the "two sides" here are reminiscent of the token and commodity theories of money explored by Keith Hart (1986). What is interesting here, as in Hart's work, is not so much one to the exclusion of the other, but their being welded together despite their apparent opposition.

6. See Watt 1990, especially 57ff.

7. My account differs somewhat from Kuran 1997, Vogel and Hayes 1998, and Saeed 1999, but this is not the place to delve into the different genealogies of Islamic banking available in the academic literature. This matter will be addressed in my forthcoming book on the subject.

8. For instance, is interest on productive as opposed to consumptive loans forbidden? Is equity from the appreciation of the value of a property a form of forbidden increase? Is bartering lower-quality items for a lesser quantity of a higher-quality type of the same item forbidden? The examples are endless.

9. See Abdul-Rahman and Abdelaaty 2000; Abdul-Rahman and Tug 1999; Ebrahim and Hasan 1993.

10. Islamic banking and finance employs Arabic terms from classical jurisprudence for its contractual forms.

11. Two Middle Eastern financial companies attempted to offer Islamic financial services in the United States as well, but with limited success, as did a small financial services company based in Houston. The Saudi firm Dallah al-Baraka opened a subsidiary in California in 1988, only to move shortly thereafter to Chicago and shift its emphasis from consumer finance to real estate and industrial investment. The United Bank of Kuwait (UBK) opened a mortgage company, al-Manzil, in 1998, but closed shop in 2000. MSI, an outgrowth of the Islamic Circle of North America, offered various loan products to consumers based on lease-to-purchase and co-ownership models in the Houston area, but never achieved the visibility or scale of the American Finance House. Unlike MSI and the American Finance House, however, UBK and al-Baraka lacked a constituency in the communities in which they attempted to operate, and, as a result, could not mobilize the networks that the other two companies had tapped into through community connections, mosques, and political and social organizations. Significantly, UBK's entry into Islamic home finance in the United States did spark an interpretive ruling from the Office of the Comptroller of the Currency (OCC) that has had enduring significance for the field. It will be discussed later in this chapter.

12. "Twelve Frequently Asked Questions about Freddie Mac," available at http://www.freddiemac.com/corporate/about/twlvquest.html, last accessed August 21, 2003.

13. Indeed, Freddie Mac's involvement with Islamic home finance came under the rubric of its "Summer of Homeownership" initiative which sought to bring greater access to underserved populations, particularly lower-income individuals and immigrants. According to some estimates less than 60 percent of Muslims in the United States are homeowners, compared to the U.S. average of 69 percent (Thomas n.d., n. 9).

14. Freddie Mac press release, August 10, 2001, "Freddie Mac, Standard Federal Bank Announce New Islamic Home Financing Initiative for Michigan Families," available at www.fred diemac.com/news/archives2001/sohinitiative0810.htm. See also "Freddie Mac Provides Lease-Purchase Mortgages for Muslims," *International Real Estate Digest*, September 4, 2001.

15. See "Islamic Home Financing Starting the Nation's Capital," *The Minaret*, July–August 2002, 19–20.

16. Experts on Islam at this point may well question my invocation to casuistry, and feel exasperated by my recitation of sources and traditions in a manner somewhat inconsistent with their understanding of "Islam." They will claim that I am not accurately recounting or specifying, that I have played fast and loose with the "facts," etc. The issue is not, however, who can lay claim to authoritative versions of the truth (based on closer readings, more complete knowledge, "original" sources, more "context"). Rather, in making the charge in these terms, such experts would be replicating the debate that goes on all the time among Islamic bankers. It is this formal replication that is my object and method—that is, it is this formal repetition of the debate within Islamic banking that this chapter attempts to incite, while obviating the quest for descriptive accuracy.

17. Such forms of analogical moral reasoning are also characteristic of those monotheisms that do not presume the materialization of the deity, but have nevertheless had an important albeit contentious place in Catholic doctrine.

18. Kant adopted St. Thomas Aquinas's conception from the *Summa Theologica* (I, q.16, a.2) and *Quaestiones Disputatae de Veritate* (q.1, a.1). Given Thomas's attribution of this definition, Shell is to be forgiven for repeating that Thomas obtained his concept of truth from the ninth-century Jewish philosopher Isaac Israeli (c. 832–c. 932 C.E.; Shell 1982: 135). Arguably, instead, this definition comes not from this Jewish Neoplatonist but rather the tenth-century Muslim Ibn Sina (Avicenna) via the latter's reflections on Aristotle. See Altmann and Stern 1958: 58–59 and their translation of Isaac's text.

19. See Kant 2003: 97. In fact, Kant is actually probably closer to the (tautological) Thomist conception than not, since the section of the *Summa* on adequation seeks to demonstrate that truth resides in the intellect, not the senses. Incidentally, Kant's "touchstone" metaphor is monetary in origin; a touchstone is what you use in a money-changer's balance to determine whether a coin is true or false.

20. See Shell 1978: 64. In Plato's *Philebus* (25a), Socrates analogizes "classification and minting: 'We ought to do our best to collect all such kinds as are torn and split apart, and stamp a single *charakter* on them' " (Shell 1978: 62n).

21. The essential Heidegger here is "On the Essence of Truth," which begins with and carries its argument forward through a series of propositions about "true coin" and "counterfeit coin," the latter of which "is something real . . . [and therefore] the truth of the genuine coin cannot be verified by its reality" (1949: 321). Heidegger continues, "What do 'genuine' and 'true' mean here? Genuine coin is that real thing whose reality agrees with . . . what we always and in advance 'really' mean by 'coin.' Conversely, where we suspect false coin we say: 'There is something not quite right here' " (ibid.).

22. Shell (1995) notes the connection between communion tokens and coinage, both materially and iconographically.

23. Postone does not criticize Lukács's invocation of natural society here; rather, he criticizes Lukács's assumption that labor lies outside the social ground of capitalism (Postone 1993: 156n) rather than existing within capitalism as "its own social ground" (ibid.: 151). This is an essential move for Postone's larger argument to unseat Lukács's proletarian version of standpoint epistemology.

24. Some Islamic economics scholars note with approval Smith's moral philosophy.

REFERENCES

Abbott, Nabia. 1972. *Studies in Arabic Literary Papyri*. Vol. 3, *Language and Literature*. Chicago: University of Chicago Press.

Abdul-Rahman, Yahia, and Mike Abdelaaty. 2000. "The Capitalization of Islamic (Lariba) Finance Institutions in America." Paper presented at the Fourth International Harvard Islamic Finance Information Program Conference, September 30.

Abdul-Rahman, Yahia, and Abdullah Tug. 1999. "Towards Lariba (Islamic) Mortgage Financing in the United States: Providing an Alternative to Traditional Mortgages." *International Journal of Islamic Financial Services* 1.2 (July–September). Available online at http://www.islamic-finance.net/journal.

Akin, David, and Joel Robbins. 1999. *Money and Modernity: State and Local Currencies in Melanesia*. Pittsburgh: University of Pittsburgh Press.

Altmann, A., and S. M. Stern. 1958. *Isaac Israeli: A Neoplatonic Philosopher of the Early Tenth Century*. Oxford: Oxford University Press.

Asad, Talal. 2003. *Formations of the Secular: Christianity, Islam, Modernity*. Stanford: Stanford University Press.

Blair, Sheila, and Jonathan Bloom. 1999. "Art and Architecture: Themes and Variations." In John Esposito, ed., *The Oxford History of Islam*, 215–267. Oxford: Oxford University Press.

Bohannan, Paul. 1959. "The Impact of Money on an African Subsistence Economy." *Journal of Economic History* 19.4:491–503.

Corbin, Henry. 1993. *History of Islamic Philosophy*. Trans. Liadain Sherrard. London: Kegan Paul International.

Crone, Patricia, and Martin Hinds. 1986. *God's Caliph: Religious Authority in the First Centuries of Islam*. Cambridge: Cambridge University Press.

Donner, Fred. 1999. "Muhammad and the Caliphate: Political History of the Islamic Empire up to the Mongol Conquest." In John Esposito, ed., *The Oxford History of Islam*, 1–61. Oxford: Oxford University Press.

Ebrahim, Muhammed Shahid, and Zafar Hasan. 1993. "Mortgage Financing for Muslim-Americans." *American Journal of Islamic Social Sciences* 10.1: 72–87.

El-Gamal, Mahmoud. 2000. "The Economics of 21st Century Islamic Jurisprudence." In *Pro-*

ceedings of the Fourth Harvard University Forum on Islamic Finance, 7–12. Cambridge: Harvard Islamic Finance Information Program.

Foster, Robert J. 1999. "The Legitimacy of Melanesian Currencies." In David Akin and Joel Robbins, eds., *Money and Modernity: State and Local Currencies in Melanesia*, 214–231. Pittsburgh: University of Pittsburgh Press.

Grierson, Philip. 1960. "The Monetary Reforms of 'Abd al-Malik." *Journal of the Economic and Social History of the Orient* 3:241–264.

Hart, Keith. 1986. "Heads or Tails? Two Sides of the Coin." *Man* (n.s.) 21:637–656.

——. 2001. *Money in an Unequal World*. New York: Texere.

Heidegger, Martin. 1949. "On the Essence of Truth." In Werner Brock, ed., *Existence and Being*, 292–324. Chicago: Henry Regnery Co.

Hitti, Philip K. 1970/1937. *A History of the Arabs from the Earliest Times to the Present*. London: Macmillan.

Hodgson, Marshall. 1974. *The Venture of Islam: Conscience and History in a World Civilization*, vol. 1: *The Classical Age of Islam*. Chicago: University of Chicago Press.

Kant, Immanuel. 2003. *Critique of Pure Reason*. Ed. and trans. Norman Kemp Smith. London: Palgrave Macmillan.

Keenan, James. 1996. "The Return of Casuistry." *Theological Studies* 57:123–139.

Khalidi, Tarif. 1994. *Arabic Historical Thought in the Classical Period*. Cambridge: Cambridge University Press.

Kuran, Timur. 1997. "The Genesis of Islamic Economics: A Chapter in the Politics of Muslim Identity." *Social Research* 64.2:301–337.

Lapidus, Ira. 1988. *A History of Islamic Societies*. Cambridge: Cambridge University Press.

Lee, Benjamin, and Edward LiPuma. 2002. "Cultures of Circulation: The Imaginations of Modernity." *Public Culture* 14.1: 191–213.

Lukács, Georg. 1971. *History and Class Consciousness: Studies in Marxist Dialectics*. Trans. Rodney Livingstone. London: Merlin Press.

Postone, Moishe. 1993. *Time, Labor, and Social Domination: A Reinterpretation of Marx's Critical Theory*. Cambridge: Cambridge University Press.

Saeed, Abdullah. 1999. *Islamic Banking and Interest: A Study of the Prohibition of Riba and Its Contemporary Interpretation*. Leiden: Brill.

Saleh, Nabil A. 1986. *Unlawful Gain and Legitimate Profit in Islamic Law*. Cambridge: Cambridge University Press.

Shell, Marc. 1978. *The Economy of Literature*. Baltimore: Johns Hopkins University Press.

——. 1982. *Money, Language and Thought*. Berkeley: University of California Press.

——. 1995. *Art and Money*. Chicago: University of Chicago Press.

Sohn-Rethel, Alfred. 1978. *Intellectual and Manual Labor: A Critique of Epistemology*. Atlantic Highlands, N.J.: Humanities Press.

Strathern, Marilyn. 1992. "Qualified Value: The Perspective of Gift Exchange." In Caroline Humphrey and Stephen Hugh-Jones, eds., *Barter, Exchange and Value: An Anthropological Approach*, 169–191. Cambridge: Cambridge University Press.

Thomas, Abdulkader. n.d. "Methods of Islamic Home Finance in the United States: Beneficial Breakthroughs." Unpublished ms.

Vogel, Frank, and Samuel L. Hayes III. 1998. *Islamic Law and Finance: Religion, Risk, and Return*. The Hague: Kluwer Law International.

Wagner, Roy. 1975. *The Invention of Culture*. Englewood Cliffs, N.J.: Prentice Hall.

——. 1978. *Lethal Speech: Daribi Myth as Symbolic Obviation*. Ithaca, N.Y.: Cornell University Press.

Watt, W. Montgomery. 1974. *The Majesty That Was Islam: The Islamic World, 661–1100*. New York: Praeger.

——. 1990. "God's Caliph: Qur'anic Interpretations and Umayyad Claims." In *Early Islam: Collected Articles*, 57–63. Edinburgh: Edinburgh University Press.

Zelizer, Viviana. 1997. *The Social Meaning of Money*. Princeton, N.J.: Princeton University Press.

Žižek, Slavoj. 1989. *The Sublime Object of Ideology*. London: Verso.

HIROKAZU MIYAZAKI

The Materiality of Finance Theory

In this chapter, I seek to redefine what counts as materiality in the social studies of economics and finance. My point of departure is two recent projects: James Carrier and Daniel Miller's call for attention to the "growing influence of the discipline of economics" (Carrier 1998: 7), which they term "virtualism" (Carrier and Miller 1998), and Michel Callon's discussion of the role of economics in the market, that is, "the essential contribution of economics in the performing of the economy" (Callon 1998b: 23).

Both projects have effectively brought economic theory into view as an ethnographic subject, albeit from two very different standpoints. The goal of this chapter, however, is to demonstrate ethnographically that both are predicated on a narrow view of materiality that focuses on the problem of fit between economic theory and economic realities. Both therefore miss other materializing potentials of economic theory. I suggest that ethnographic investigations of economic theory should not be limited to such concern with the relationship between economic theory and economic realities, narrowly defined. Rather, I suggest that ethnographers pay attention to how different kinds of objectification of economic theory open and close theory's own materializing potential.

Drawing on my ethnographic fieldwork in a trading room of a major Japanese securities firm, I investigate both obvious and less obvious ways that finance theory was objectified and materialized. These included translations of state-of-the art academic articles on financial economics, various research projects surrounding the importation and refinement of financial economics, and even the trader's own self-image as social reformer. Ultimately, I suggest that an ethnographic study of finance theory must expand its analytical scope to incorporate its own research as one further instance of the materialization of finance theory.

CONCRETE PROCESSES OF ABSTRACTION

In their discussion of virtualism, Carrier and Miller draw attention to the abstractions of both economy and economic knowledge. The target of their critique is the greater role economists and economic theory play in the world (see also Fourcade-Gourinchas and Babb 2002). According to Carrier and Miller, this is a consequence of a longer-term process of the "disembedding" of economy (see Carrier 1998b: 2, following Polanyi 1957) and also a cause of the intensification of that process (see Carrier 1998: 6–8). The virtualism of economic abstraction is for them "a practical effort to make the world conform to the structures of the conceptual," that is, a "tendency to see the world in terms of idealised categories, a virtual reality, and then act in ways that make the real conform to the virtual" (Carrier 1998: 5; see also Miller 1998: 196). The danger of such abstractions, they assert, lies in the fact that "virtual reality . . . displays a uniformity and logicality that necessarily departs from the uncertainty of the real world, with its unanticipated influences and unknowable future, not to mention the factors that can be known and anticipated but are ignored in the governing program" (Carrier 1998: 7). As Miller has noted more recently, the impetus behind this argument was an awareness that "it was time we stopped thinking of economics as the study of economies. Instead, what needed to be emphasized was the degree to which economics and other abstract models were managing to accrue such power that they were able to transform actual economic practices, making them accord more with these same models" (Miller 2002: 229).

Michel Callon also challenges the notion of economics as an objective description of the real economy. But unlike Carrier and Miller, who focus on the distance between economic theory and economic realities, Callon draws attention to the substantial role economics plays in the market. Drawing on Marie-France Garcia's study of a strawberry market in rural France, Callon shows how a specific "configuration" (22) of spatial arrangements, standardization and calculating devices transformed a space saturated with preexisting social relations into "a space of calculability" (20). Callon points out that this configuration was based on "the pure model of perfect competition proposed in economics handbooks" (22). From this perspective, Callon pronounces, "Yes, *homo economicus* does exist" (22), albeit within the network of economic theory, calculative instruments, and other "framing" devices (16–19; see also Callon 1998a).

Donald MacKenzie has recently extended Callon's thesis to analyze what he terms the "performativity of finance theory" (MacKenzie 2001: 130). MacKenzie asserts, "Finance theory itself has played an important role in its assumptions becoming more realistic" (MacKenzie 2001: 133). The convergence between finance theory and the market, according to MacKenzie, takes place in particular through an operation known as arbitrage (see MacKenzie 2001, 2003a, 2003b; Mackenzie and Millo 2003).

In arbitrage, a trader simultaneously trades two assets whose prices are dependent on each other, such as a contract for a given commodity in the cash market and a contract for future delivery of the same commodity, in order to take advantage of any price discrepancies between the two. Arbitrage is a fundamental operation in financial economics: almost every pricing tool for derivatives trading is predicated on the computation of "fair" or "arbitrage-free" values (see, e.g., Hull 1997: 12–13; Neftci 2000: 13–14).

In theory, at least, because arbitrage opportunities are found by simulating conditions in which there are no arbitrage opportunties, and then acting on those simulations, arbitrage drives the market to reach that arbitrage-free state. As MacKenzie asserts:

> Finance theory is itself drawn on by modern arbitrageurs, so arbitrage is a key issue for the 'performativity' of economics: the thesis that economics creates the phenomena it describes, rather than describing an already existing "economy." . . . To the extent that arbitrageurs can eliminate the price discrepancies that finance theory helps them to identify, they thereby render the theory performative: price patterns in the markets become as described by the theory. (MacKenzie 2003b: 350–351)

Callon's and MacKenzie's treatment of economic theory draws on Callon's own earlier work as well as the work of Bruno Latour, John Law, and other scholars of science studies who have long sought to dislocate theory and abstraction, more generally, from the divide between the ideal and the material (see, e.g., Callon 1986; Latour 1987; Law and Mol 1995; Pickering 1995). As Latour puts it, "We will never cut off the abstractions or the theories from what they are abstractions or theories *of*, which means that we will always travel through the networks along their greatest length" (Latour 1987: 243). These writers have been devoted to describing theory as an "entanglement" of acts of abstraction with instruments, interests, and other forms of materiality (cf. Thomas 1991). In this view, theory ceases to be an entity independent of the contexts of its use as well as of the process of its making.

In this respect, Callon's and MacKenzie's treatment of economic theory and of its articulation with the calculative practices surrounding it represents a radical departure from the conventional separation of economic theory from economic realities in mainstream anthropological and sociological critiques of economic theory. Economic anthropologists and sociologists have long focused their energy on refuting neoclassical economics (see, e.g., Dalton 1963; Dore 1983; Granovetter 1985; Polanyi 1957; Sahlins 1972). They have taken "the market as an ideological model rather than an empirical core to economic activity" (Miller 2002: 219; see also Carrier 1997; Dilley 1992). From the latter perspective, as Miller argues, Callon's treatment of economic theory not only departs from the reality of economic practices but also reifies economic theory: "Callon writes from the basis of an economists' vision, which has at its heart the assumption that most transactions within the capitalist world are indeed market transactions and that his task is to understand the mechanisms that allow them to work as markets. As a result, Callon follows the economists in mistaking a representation of economic life for its practice" (Miller 2002: 219). From Miller's perspective, in other words, although ethnographers should study the process by which economics has achieved its preeminence, they must also be careful not to replicate in their analysis economists' impulse to drive the world to emulate their models (see also Miller 1998).

In contrast to both lines of argument, in this chapter I do not privilege the relationship between economic theory and economic realities as the locus of materialization. Rather, I draw attention to other forms of objectification of economic theory such as learning, justification, and extension, and to other ways that theory materializes. From this perspective, the work of Callon, MacKenzie, Carrier, and Miller can be seen as yet another kind of objectification of economic theory with its own materializing effects. This broadened scope of inquiry into the materiality of economic theory may also allow us to understand in more ethnographic terms how economic theory sustains its force despite its distance from economic realities.

OBJECTIFYING FINANCE THEORY

My investigation draws on ethnographic research I completed between 1998 and 2001 on a team of traders in a major Japanese securities firm I will call Sekai Securities. Sekai Securities's derivatives team was established in 1987.[1] The initial purpose was to promote futures and options among the firm's institutional clients as new investment tools. The team hired a number of applied mathematicians and engineers and subsequently engaged in extensive research on financial economics. Some of these mathematicians and engineers also traded derivatives as proprietary traders, that is, traders who invest the firm's own assets. An examination of the team's diverse activities reveals that these traders made a wide range of uses of finance theory, and in the process, finance theory materialized in both obvious and not-so-obvious ways.

LEARNING

The team's initial modality of engagement with finance theory was that of learning (cf. Rohlen 1992). The team approached finance theory as an explicit object of learning. This was partly because many of the mathematicians and engineers recruited to join the team did not know much about finance, and partly because Japanese securities firms like Sekai perceived themselves as latecomers to global financial markets already dominated by U.S. firms (see Miyazaki 2003; Miyazaki and Riles 2005). In this modality, finance theory was objectified as new knowledge from the United States.

As part of its effort to promote derivatives trading in the Japanese markets, the team devoted itself to preparing numerous educational documents for institutional investors. In order to prepare these documents, members of Sekai's derivatives team read English-language books on derivatives, from standard academic texts such as John Cox's and Mark Rubinstein's *Options Markets* (1985) to more practical texts such as John Murphy's *Technical Analysis of the Futures Markets* (1986) and Jack Schwager's *Market Wizards* (1993). Some of these books had been translated by other market participants by that time. In other cases, members of the team translated and later published them. Researchers at Sekai's research wing, whose main task was to develop financial products and trading models for Sekai's institutional clients, also translated and published state-of-the-art articles by U.S. scholars and published them in the industry's journals (e.g., Rubinstein and Leland 1981). From my point of view, all of these translations and promotional documents can be understood as instances of finance theory's materialization.

Likewise, the team's research projects also materialized finance theory in their own way. During the early 1990s, many members of the team participated in collaborative projects with U.S. business school professors. Although these projects did not yield much direct profit to the firm, the team nevertheless invested heavily in them. From the mid-1980s to the mid-1990s, Sekai's research wing established partnerships with U.S. business school professors and their consulting firms (cf. Bernstein 1992: 292–293). Sekai regularly funded these professors' research projects, hired them to conduct in-house seminars for their traders in Tokyo, and also sent researchers and computer scientists to California to develop various trading models.

For example, in 1992, the team collaborated with a professor at the University of California, Berkeley, business school. The official object of this collaboration was to develop a pricing model and a pricing program for certain kinds of options known as "exotic options." In the early 1990s, foreign investment banks in Tokyo introduced these options to Japanese institutional investors, and Sekai Securities followed by introducing them as well. Exotic options are those tailored to a particular investor's needs and contain elements that make their pricing complicated. The central problem in pricing exotic options concerned how to solve more complicated differential equations than those contained in standard options pricing formulas. Sekai sent a young trader from its derivatives team and a researcher from its research wing to work with a business school professor for approximately five months on solving these equations. Sekai paid the professor $3,000 a day for this work. The young trader recalled in April 2000 that upon his return, the team was able to price exotic options competitively vis-à-vis foreign investment banks by using a solution he had developed when he was in California.

A senior trader, an applied mathematician trained at the University of Tokyo who had overseen this project, told me in 2000 that from his point of view, the main purpose of the project had not been to invent new solutions but rather to convince the young trader, a recent graduate from a computer engineering program at a lesser university, to accept the senior trader's general solution to the differential equations required for the pricing of these exotic options. The senior trader insisted that he had already known the solution because he had solved similar differential equations as a graduate student in applied mathematics. What is interesting from my perspective is that this personal rivalry between the two traders over theoretical problems prompted an international collaborative project, which in turn translated into handsome financial support for a U.S. academic while also reconfirming the privileged status of financial economics as knowledge imported from the United States into the Japanese markets.

JUSTIFICATION

In the volatile market environment of the late 1980s and early 1990s, derivatives trading often became a target of public criticism, and Sekai traders deployed their knowledge of financial economics to defend their trading practices. The controversy surrounding index arbitrage was a case in point. When a market for futures on the Nikkei 225 Index, a Japanese premier stock index, opened at the Osaka Stock Exchange in 1988, traders at U.S. investment banks in Tokyo discovered that these index futures were significantly overpriced relative to the price of the index. Thus, there were numerous arbitrage opportunities in this market. After U.S. investment banks launched arbitrage trading in the Japanese markets, Sekai's derivatives team followed suit and began engaging in index arbitrage (see Miyazaki 2003).

When the stock market crashed in February 1990, however, index arbitrage emerged as a target of public criticism. Market commentators explained the crash as a consequence of securities firms' irresponsible practices of index arbitrage trading. In response, the founder of Sekai's derivatives team (whom I will call Aoki in this chapter) and his traders wrote numerous papers defending their trading practices. Some of these were written at the request of the Osaka Stock Exchange. Others were written out of the traders' frustration with the tendency of the firm's management to entertain the dominant view of index arbitrage as the cause of the crash.

What is interesting for present purposes is the way Aoki and his traders resorted, in these papers, to textbook definitions of the role of arbitragers in the market. The traders repeatedly argued that arbitrage served to make the cash market and the futures market correlate better so that the futures market could better serve risk management purposes. They also asserted that even if they themselves did not engage in index arbitrage, other market participants would quickly take advantage of arbitrage opportunities. Underlying this view was an assumption that arbitragers are an intrinsic part of the market's internal price adjustment mechanism. Although this price adjustment function was not necessarily at the forefront of any trader's daily concerns (see also Buenza and Stark 2002), Sekai traders became material embodiments of that function in their defenses of arbitrage trading.

In the view of many traders, arbitrage opportunities virtually disappeared from the Nikkei 225 index futures market by 1992 (see Avril 2000: 156). One can interpret this fact as evidence of what MacKenzie has termed finance theory's performativity: index arbitrage, as an instantiation of the theory that there is a "fair" and "arbitrage-free" relationship between the cash market and the futures market, may have effectively made the market arbitrage-free (cf. Miyazaki 2003: 258). My point, however, is that it is important to understand how finance theory also became materialized in a much more obvious fashion, in the traders' efforts to justify index arbitrage in economic terms.

EXTENSION

Another material effect of finance theory was its own extension. In the aftermath of the financial scandals and the failure of major Japanese financial institutions in the late 1990s, market commentators celebrated financial economics as an essential tool for economic reform of all kinds. This situation presented a new opportunity to Sekai derivatives specialists. Following Sekai's merger with a U.S. financial conglomerate in 1999, Tada, who had succeeded Aoki as the head of Sekai's derivatives team, joined a small investment fund. Tada's new work concerned an emerging field of finance known as "private equity," that is, investment in companies whose securities are not listed on stock exchanges. Tada's fund invested in a variety of business ventures ranging from a *takoyaki* (fried-octopus) restaurant chain to an importer of U.S. cosmetic products. The fund also developed a number of securitization schemes—schemes to consolidate and turn assets such as real estate, bad loans, and future cash flows into tradable securities. In the spring of 2000, Tada mentioned a variety of other potential targets of securitization with much excitement. For example, Tada told me that he planned to develop a scheme to securitize medical fees for hospitals. He also mentioned other "mispriced" investments ranging from golf course memberships to tax-exempt religious organizations as possible targets of securitization (see Miyazaki 2003: 260–261).

What interests me for present purposes is the way arbitrage served as a guiding metaphor for Tada's new investment schemes (see Miyazaki 2003: 260). At first glance, none of these investment schemes resembled the sort of index arbitrage trading Tada and his traders had been engaged in during the late 1980s and early 1990s. In index arbitrage, traders would construct their trading positions by computing a "fair" and "arbitrage-free" price relationship between interrelated assets. In these new investment schemes, in contrast, Tada extended the arbitragers' impulse to find an arbitrage opportunity, that is, a "mispriced" asset, to those markets in which he could only intuitively know the asset's divergence from its "fair" price. In our conversations in 2000 and 2001, Tada described these schemes as part of his own personal commitment to make Japanese society more efficient and rational. The implicit linkage between arbitrage and the ideal of an "efficient" and "rational" market that had been backgrounded in his work in index arbitrage was now foregrounded for him, as it had been in Sekai traders' polemical writings defending arbitrage.

MacKenzie has drawn attention to the role of traders' faithlike commitment to the ideal of the efficient market (and lack thereof) in financial markets (see MacKenzie 2001: 129–130). But his discussion of the role of such faithlike commitment is constrained by his privileging of the relationship between economic theory and economic realities. In the case of Tada's investment schemes, Tada's faithlike commitment to finance theory may not have resulted in the kind of convergence between theory and its object, that is, the market, that MacKenzie anticipated; indeed, some of Tada's investment schemes failed miserably. However, this commitment nevertheless generated a particular kind of self-image and subjectivity for Tada.[2] It allowed him to imagine himself as a social reformer and to engage in a set of associated utopian dreams (see Miyazaki 2003: 261; Miyazaki n.d.). My point is that ethnographic studies of finance theory must pay attention to these various forms of objectification of finance theory as instances of the materialization of finance theory, regardless of the actual fit between the theory and the market. It is through these mundane forms of deployment of finance theory, and not always through the spectacular convergence between the theory and the market, that the theory solidifies.

TOWARD AN ANTHROPOLOGY OF FINANCE THEORY

Callon and MacKenzie critique anthropologists for insisting that economic theory is an inadequate descriptive and analytical tool for understanding real markets. What Callon and MacKenzie share with both anthropologists and economists, however, is that their inquiry into economic theory centers around the relationship between economic theory and economic realities.

One way to move away from this attachment to the relationship between economic theory and its object, the market, is to observe the ways in which economic theory becomes materialized in its diverse uses in market practices, broadly defined. In this chapter, I have discussed various instances of materialization of finance theory in the career trajectories of Sekai derivatives specialists. These instances of materialization range from the team's translation work and other publications, to Tada's utopian dreams, to his metaphorical extension of arbitrage, to interventions in various facets of Japanese society. These materializations may at first glance seem both obvious and insignificant to both economists and anthropologists, whose concern focuses on the validity of economic theory as a descriptive and analytical tool for studies of economic realities. However, once economic theory is apprehended ethnographically as an object of learning, an instrument for justification, or a tool for social reform in addition to a descriptive and analytical tool, it becomes evident that the materiality of economic theory goes beyond questions regarding the realization of theoretical assumptions in the economy.

These forms of objectification of finance theory (e.g., learning, justification, and metaphorical extension) are different from the objectification of economic theory as an instrument for "formatting" the market described by Callon and critiqued by Miller, on the one hand, and the objectification of economic theory as the antithesis of economic realities proposed by Miller and implicitly critiqued by Callon, on the other. Both of the latter kinds of objectification are predicated on a narrow conception of materiality associated with the problem of the possibility of convergence between economic theory and economic realities. The ethnographic material discussed above demonstrates that this is only one of many materializing potentials of economic theory.

These other objectifications of finance theory in turn demand attention to the publication and popular consumption of massive volumes of academic and non-academic writings on financial economics in Japan and elsewhere as yet another materialization of finance theory. In the context of my ethnographic research, for example, numerous popular books written by Japanese academics and traders not only have facilitated the wider circulation of financial economic knowledge but also have represented the authors' personal efforts to capitalize financially on broader popular fascination with financial economics (see, e.g., Ishii 2000; Kariya 2000; Konno 2000; Mikami and Yotsuzuka 2000; Yoshimoto 2000).

Likewise, in the academic context of which this chapter is part, it can be said that social theorists' writings on financial economics constitute yet another kind of objectification of finance theory and its materialization. In response to the recent waves of financial crises, from the currency crises in Southeast Asia, Latin America, and Turkey to the failure of long-term capital management and the collapse of Enron, many social theorists have turned to finance economics as a subject of inquiry. Their inquiry has been focused on what they see as a radical shift in the character of global capitalism, and in this context derivatives have become the ultimate example of economic abstraction and hence the subject of intensive philosophical contemplation (see, e.g., Comaroff and Comaroff 2000; Coronil 2000; Lee and LiPuma 2002; LiPuma and Lee 2004). From my perspective, these too can be understood as material effects of finance theory, alongside popular books about finance and Tada's utopian dreams. Therefore Callon's and others' objectification of economic theory, along with the recent work on financial economics in social theory, surfaces as yet another materialization of economic theory.

What are the implications of these observations for ethnographic studies of theory more broadly (cf. Boyer 2001; Riles 2004a)? In writing on Taylorism, the literary scholar Martha Banta reflects on the difficulty of writing about theory without reproducing the theory's own "totalizing" propensity (cf. Miyazaki 2004). Speaking of her own " 'history' of the culture of theorizing" she notes, "It is a history that continues to replicate itself in our own desire to gain totalizing control over literary structures, by whose means we might gain control . . . over the systematized worlds in which we speak, make money, wield power, love, live, and die" (Banta 1993: xi). Banta strives to resist this tendency by focusing on narratives surrounding theory. In other words, Banta seeks to counter theory's propensity for abstraction and totalization with narrative's inherent propensity for complexity and excess (cf. Stewart 1996).

From the perspective of my discussion above, what is difficult about economic theory as a subject of ethnographic investigation is not its propensity for abstraction and totalization. Rather, the difficulty concerns a feature of anthropological abstraction: the persistent emphasis on the relation between economic theory and economic realities (see Strathern 1995). I have suggested that the work of Callon, MacKenzie, Carrier, and Miller perpetuates this particular abstraction and associated view of materiality. By drawing attention to other forms of objectification of economic theory, I have sought to develop a broader scope of ethnographic inquiry into the materialization of economic theory.

I want to emphasize at this juncture, however, that I am not merely suggesting that ethnographers study how economic theory takes on different meanings and serves different instrumental purposes in different contexts of appropriation (see Appadurai 1986; especially Kopytoff 1986; see also Thomas 1991). The purpose of this chapter is not to propose a "mapping" project of this kind but to show how different kinds of objectification of economic theory open and close different materializing potentials of that theory. For example, I have sought to demonstrate how the objectification of economic theory by Callon, MacKenzie, Carrier, and Miller entails a narrow view of its materiality. In contrast, my ethnographic account of market practices points to other forms of objectification of economic theory and their associated materializing effects. My point is that these "narrow" and "broad" approaches can be seen as two contrasting modalities that open and close different aspects of economic theory and hence generate different effects.

My insistence on seeing academic writings side-by-side with other forms of materialization of economic theory in market practices resonates with the efforts of Douglas Holmes and George Marcus, Bill Maurer, and Annelise Riles to bring into view parallels between economic knowledge and anthropological knowledge (see Holmes and Marcus 2005; Maurer 2002a, 2002b, 2003; Miyazaki and Riles 2005; Riles 2004b; see also Thrift 1996). These writers have drawn attention not only to anthropologists' "complicity" with their subjects (see Marcus 1998) but also to "analytical forms" that anthropologists share with their subjects (see, in particular, Maurer 2002a; Riles 2004b). I suggest that an ethnographic investigation of economic theory must begin with recognition that anthropology's own form of objectification, like many other objectifications in market practices, entails a particular notion of materiality and is itself an instance of the materialization of economic theory.

NOTES

My fieldwork in Tokyo was supported by the American Bar Foundation and the Abe Fellowship Program of the Social Science Research Council and the American Council of Learned Societies with funds provided by the Japan Foundation Center for Global Partnership. I thank Stephen Hilgartner, Michael Lynch, Bill Maurer, Daniel Miller, Janet Roitman, and especially Annelise Riles for their helpful comments on earlier drafts of this chapter.
1. Derivatives are a class of securities whose value is linked to the underlying value of assets traded in cash markets. Futures and options are primary examples of this class of securities. A futures contract is a contract to buy or sell an asset on a pre-specified future date at a pre-specified price. An option is a right to buy or sell an asset at a pre-specified price, and the buyer of an option may exercise the right before its "expiration date."
2. My concern with subjectivity echoes Ellen Hertz, Karin Knorr Cetina and Urs Bruegger, and Caitlin Zaloom's attention to the production of various forms of subjectivity and sociality in financial markets (see Hertz 1998; Knorr Cetina and Bruegger 2000, 2002; Zaloom 2004).

REFERENCES

Appadurai, Arjun, ed. 1986. *The Social Life of Things: Commodities in Cultural Perspective.* Cambridge: Cambridge University Press.
Avril, Philippe, 2000. *Nihon no ekuiti deribatibu* [Equity derivatives in Japan]. Tokyo: Shigumabesu Kyapitaru.

Banta, Martha. 1993. *Taylored Lives: Narrative Productions in the Age of Taylor, Veblen, and Ford*. Chicago: University of Chicago Press.

Bernstein, Peter L. 1992. *Capital Ideas: The Improbable Origins of Modern Wall Street*. New York: Free Press.

Boyer, Dominic C. 2001. "Foucault in the Bush: The Social Life of Post-Structuralist Theory in East Berlin's Prenzlauer Berg." *Ethnos* 66.2:207–236.

Buenza, Daniel, and David Stark. 2002. "Tools of the Trade: The Socio-Technology of Arbitrage in a Wall Street Trading Room." Columbia University Center on Organizational Innovation Working Paper.

Callon, Michel. 1986. "Some Elements of a Sociology of Translation: Domestication of the Scallops and the Fishermen of St. Brieuc Bay." In John Law, ed., *Power, Action, and Belief: A New Sociology of Knowledge?* 196–229. London: Routledge and Kegan Paul.

——. 1998a. "An Essay on Framing and Overflowing: Economic Externalities Revisited by Sociology." In Michel Callon, ed. *The Laws of the Markets*, 244–269. Oxford: Blackwell.

——. 1998b. "Introduction: The Embeddedness of Economic Markets in Economics." In Michel Callon, ed., *The Laws of the Markets*, 1–57. Oxford: Blackwell

Carrier, James G. 1997. Introduction. In James G. Carrier, ed., *Meanings of the Market: The Free Market in Western Culture*, 1–67. Oxford: Berg.

——.1998. Introduction. In James G. Carrier and Daniel Miller, eds., *Virtualism: A New Political Economy*, 1–24. Oxford: Berg.

Carrier, James G., and Daniel Miller, eds. 1998. *Virtualism: A New Political Economy*. Oxford: Berg.

Comaroff, Jean, and John Comaroff. 2000. "Millennial Capitalism: First Thoughts on a Second Coming." *Public Culture* 12.2:291–343.

Coronil, Fernando. 2000. "Towards a Critique of Globalcentrism: Speculations on Capitalism's Nature." *Public Culture* 12.2:351–374.

Cox, John, and Mark Rubinstein. 1985. *Options Markets*. Englewood Cliffs, N.J.: Prentice-Hall.

Dalton, George. 1961."Economic Theory and Primitive Society." *American Anthropologist* 63.1:1–25.

Dilley, Roy. 1992. "Contesting Markets: A General Introduction to Market Ideology, Imagery and Discourse." In Roy Dilley, ed., *Contesting Market: Analyses of Ideology, Discourse and Practices*, 1–34. Edinburgh: Edinburgh University Press.

Dore, Ronald. 1983. "Goodwill and the Spirit of Market Capitalism." *British Journal of Sociology* 34.4:459–482.

Fourcade-Gourinchas, Marion, and Sarah L. Babb. 2002. "The Rebirth of the Liberal Creed: Paths to Neoliberalism in Four Countries." *American Journal of Sociology* 108.3:533–579.

Granovetter, Mark. 1985. "Economic Action and Social Structures: The Problem of Embeddedness." *American Journal of Sociology* 91.3:481–510.

Hardie, Iain. 2004. " 'The Sociology of Arbitrage': A Comment on MacKenzie." *Economy and Society* 33.2:239–254.

Hertz, Ellen. 1998. *The Trading Crowd: An Ethnography of the Shanghai Stock Market*. Cambridge: Cambridge University Press.

Holmes, Douglas, and George Marcus. 2005. "Cultures of Expertise and the Management of Globalization: Toward the Refunctioning of Ethnography." In Aihwa Ong and Stephen Collier, eds., *Global Assemblages: Technology, Politics, and Ethics as Anthropological Problems*, 235–252. Malden, Mass.: Blackwell.

Hull, John. 1997. *Options, Futures, and Other Derivatives*. 3rd ed. Upper Saddle River, N.J.: Prentice-Hall.

Ishii, Itaru. 2000. *Fainansharu enjinia: Kinyu kogaku no ninaitetachi* [Financial engineers: Practitioners of financial engineering]. Tokyo: Kodansha.

Kariya, Takeaki. 2000. *Kinyu kogaku towa nanika? Risuku kara kangaeru* [What is financial engineering? With special reference to the problem of risk]. Tokyo: Iwanami-shoten.

Knorr Cetina, Karin, and Urs Bruegger. 2000. "The Market as an Object of Attachment: Exploring Postsocial Relations in Financial Markets." *Canadian Journal of Sociology/Cahiers canadiens de sociologie* 25.2:141–168.

——. 2002. "Global Microstructures: The Virtual Societies of Financial Markets." *American Journal of Sociology* 107.4:905–950.

Konno, Hiroshi. 2000. *Kinyukogaku no chosen: Tekunokomasuka suru bijinesu* [The challenge of financial engineering: The techno-commercialization of business]. Tokyo: Chuokoron-shinsha.

Kopytoff, Igor. 1986. "The Cultural Biography of Things: Commoditization as Process." In Arjun Appadurai, ed., *The Social Life of Things: Commodities in Cultural Perspective*, 64–91. Cambridge: Cambridge University Press.

Latour, Bruno. 1987. *Science in Action: How to Follow Scientists and Engineers through Society*. Cambridge: Harvard University Press.

Law, John, and Annemarie Mol. 1995. "Notes on Materiality and Sociality." *Sociological Review* 43.2:274–294.

Lee, Benjamin, and Edward LiPuma. 2002. "Cultures of Circulation: The Imaginations of Modernity." *Public Culture* 14.1:191–213.

LiPuma, Edward, and Benjamin Lee. 2004. *Financial Derivatives and the Globalization of Risk*. Durham, N.C.: Duke University Press.

MacKenzie, Donald. 2001. "Physics and Finance: S-Terms and Modern Finance as a Topic for Science Studies." *Science, Technology, and Human Values* 26.2:115–144.

——. 2003a. "An Equation and Its Worlds: Bricolage, Exemplars, Disunity and Performativity in Financial Economics." *Social Studies of Science* 33.6:831–868.

——. 2003b. "Long-Term Capital Management and the Sociology of Arbitrage." *Economy and Society* 32.3:349–380.

MacKenzie, Donald, and Yuval Millo. 2003. "Constructing a Market, Performing Theory: The Historical Sociology of a Financial Derivatives Exchange." *American Journal of Sociology* 109.1:107–145.

Marcus, George. 1998. *Ethnography through Thick and Thin*. Princeton: Princeton University Press.

Maurer, Bill. 2002a. "Anthropological and Accounting Knowledge in Islamic Banking and Finance: Rethinking Critical Accounts." *Journal of the Royal Anthropological Institute* 8.4:645–667.

——. 2002b. "Repressed Futures: Financial Derivatives' Theological Unconscious." *Economy and Society* 31.1:15–36.

——. 2003. "Uncanny Exchanges: The Possibilities and Failures of 'Making Change' with Alternative Monetary Forms." *Environment and Planning D: Society and Space* 21.3:317–340.

Mikami, Yoshihiro, and Toshiki Yotsuzuka. 2000. *Hejji-fando tekunoroji: Kinyugijutsu to toshisenryaku no furontia* [Hedge fund technology: The frontiers of financial technology and investment strategies]. Tokyo: Toyokeizai-shinposha.

Miller, Daniel. 1998. "Conclusion: A Theory of Virtualism." In James Carrier and Daniel Miller, eds., *Virtualism: A New Political Economy*, 187–215. Oxford: Berg.

——. 2002. "Turning Callon in the Right Way Up." *Economy and Society* 31.2:218–233.

Miyazaki, Hirokazu. 2003. "The Temporalities of the Market." *American Anthropologist* 105.2: 255–265.

——. 2004. *The Method of Hope: Anthropology, Philosophy, and Fijian Knowledge*. Stanford: Stanford University Press.

——. n.d. "Economy of Dreams: The Production of Hope in Anthropology and Finance." Unpublished ms.

Miyazaki, Hirokazu, and Annelise Riles. 2005. "Failure as an Endpoint." In Aihwa Ong and Stephen Collier, eds. *Global Assemblages: Technology, Politics and Ethics as Anthropological Problems*, 320–331. Malden, Mass.: Blackwell.

Murphy, John. 1986. *Technical Analysis of the Futures Markets: A Comprehensive Guide to Trading Methods and Applications*. New York: New York Institute of Finance.

Neftci, Salih N. 2000. *An Introduction to the Mathematics of Financial Derivatives*. 2nd ed. San Diego: Academic Press.

Pickering, Andrew. 1995. *The Mangle of Practice: Time, Agency, and Science*. Chicago: University of Chicago Press.

Polanyi, Karl. 1957. "The Economy as Instituted Process." In Karl Polanyi, Conrad M. Arensberg, and Harry W. Pearson, eds., *Trade and Market in the Early Empires: Economies in History and Theory*, 243–270. New York: Free Press.

Riles, Annelise. 2004a. "Property as Legal Knowledge: Means and Ends." *Journal of the Royal Anthropological Institute*.

——. 2004b. "Real Time: Unwinding Technocratic and Anthropological Knowledge." *American Ethnologist* 31.3:392–405.

Rohlen, Thomas. 1992. "Learning: The Mobilization of Knowledge in the Japanese Political Economy." In Shumpei Kumon and Henry Rosovsky, eds., *The Political Economy of Japan*, vol. 3: *Cultural and Social Dynamics*, 321–363. Stanford: Stanford University Press.

Rubinstein, Mark, and Hayne E. Leland. 1981. "Replicating Options with Positions in Stock and Cash." *Financial Analysts Journal* 37.4:63–72.

Sahlins, Marshall. 1972. *Stone Age Economics*. New York: Aldine.

Schwager, Jack D. 1993/1989. *Market Wizards: Interviews with Top Traders*. New York: Harper-Business.

Stewart, Kathleen. 1996. *A Space on the Side of the Road: Cultural Poetics in an "Other" America*. Princeton: Princeton University Press.

Strathern, Marilyn. 1995. *The Relation: Issues in Complexity and Scale*. Cambridge: Prickly Pear Press.

Thomas, Nicholas. 1991. *Entangled Objects: Colonialism, Exchange and Material Culture in the Pacific*. Cambridge: Harvard University Press.

Thrift, Nigel. 1996. "Shut Up and Dance, Or, Is the World Economy Knowable?" In P. W. Daniels and W. F. Lever, eds., *The Global Economy in Transition*, 11–23. Harlow: Longman.

Yoshimoto, Yoshio. 2000. *Kinyukogaku mane-gemu no majutsu* [The magic of the money game in financial engineering]. Tokyo: Kodansha.

Zaloom, Caitlin. 2004. "The Productive Life of Risk." *Cultural Anthropology* 19.3: 365–391.

WEBB KEANE

Signs Are Not the Garb of Meaning:
On the Social Analysis of Material Things

H ow can we both understand things and do full justice to their materiality? The effort seems still to be haunted and confounded by such ancient dichotomies as form and substance, essence and accident, matter and spirit. Old habits die hard, and a host of promised poststructuralist and postmodern redemptions have not entirely shaken themselves free of their conceptual genealogies. Perhaps, as some have argued, we can't shake these dichotomies because they are so deeply part of our metaphysics of presence (Heidegger 1962), or then again, perhaps it's because we are so entrenched in reified consciousness (Lukács 1971)—because we have always been heirs of the Greeks or, conversely, because we are now capitalist moderns. In either case, we would be facing a tall order indeed.

MATERIALITY AS A SEMIOTIC PROBLEM

But consider a more specific arena: the lingering effects of certain models of the sign. Here efforts to rethink materiality are still commonly hampered by certain assumptions built into the lineage that runs from Ferdinand de Saussure to poststructuralism. Guided by these assumptions, we tend to divide our attention between things and ideas. Those whose attention centers on things may be tempted to relegate ideas to an epiphenomenal domain, subordinated to real, tangible, stuff. Conversely, attention to ideas often seems to render material forms into little more than transparent expressions of meaning. And the more social analysis stresses the intentions, agency, and self-understandings of humans (following, for instance, Weber 1978), the more it tends to reproduce the very dichotomy between subject and object it might better be putting under critical scrutiny (Keane 2003).

This chapter aims to develop an approach to signs for which the practical and contingent character of things is neither subordinated to, nor isolated from, communication and thought. It aims to shake off what has been described as "one of [Saussure's] most durable legacies" (Irvine 1996: 258), the radical separation of the sign from the material world. The result should be a better understanding of the historicity *inherent* to signs *in their very materiality*.

OBJECTS AS A PROBLEM FOR SUBJECTS

Throughout this chapter I will return to the example of clothing, which has an indisputably intimate relationship to persons—not just their appearance and social identities, but even their gestures and smell (Stallybrass 1996). Given this intimacy, we should perhaps wonder why anyone would think of clothes as superficial. Or worse: in 1854 the American Transcendentalist Henry David Thoreau famously wrote, "I say, beware of all enterprises that require new clothes, and not rather a new wearer of clothes" (1971: 23). What's to fear? Beneath Thoreau's moralizing of things lie implicit and, today, widespread assumptions about signs. Thoreau's moralism dwells on the ways in which clothing marks social distinctions, subjects us to the vagaries of fashion, and displaces our proper concern with the immaterial. He observes that "there is greater anxiety, commonly, to have . . . clean and unpatched clothes, than to have a sound conscience" (1971: 22). Clothes form a material outside that distracts us from the spiritual inside, with the result that, in Thoreau's words, "We know but a few men, a great many coats and breeches" (1971: 22). In this ironic rhetoric, we may hear something in common with the words of Thoreau's junior by one year, Karl Marx. Recall how Marx (1967) famously appropriated "fetishism," a concept that had until then been restricted to comparative religion, in order similarly to accuse his contemporaries of inverting the proper relations between animate and inanimate things.

But there is more. Caring about clothing gives us over too much to the opinion of others. Thoreau's discussion of clothing ends with an attack on fashion (1971: 25), which forces us to acknowledge the authority of others, whether that be the distant arbiters of style or the opinion of our neighbors. For Thoreau, the distinction between inner and outer provides ontological support for his individualism, which sees in social relations a threat to personal authenticity. For both Thoreau and Marx, despite their obvious political differences, the misapprehension of material things is not merely a mistake—it has grave consequences. It leads us to invert our values, imputing life to the lifeless and thereby losing ourselves. The proper understanding of material signs has moral implications. These hinge both on a particular understanding of the subject's fundamental interiority and on the subject's relations to other people, to the extent that they are mediated by signs. Signs are viewed, like other people, as thoroughly external to, or even at odds with, that interiority.

Thoreau's remarks about clothing suggest an important theme running from nineteenth-century Protestantism to the high modernist aesthetic of, say, the Austrian architect Adolf Loos a half century later. Thoreau would surely have welcomed Loos's assertion that "the evolution of civilization is tantamount to the removal of ornament from objects of use" (quoted in Gell 1993: 15), with its celebration of function over appearance, its rejection of surfaces not just as superfluous but as immoral.

Why should materiality be a moral question? Part of the answer involves the historical fate of a particular ontology that defines subjects in opposition to objects (Keane 1996, 2002). But there is a more specific manifestation of this ontology, in background assumptions about the sign common to much Western social theory. If social and cultural analysts still find it difficult to treat objects as no more than illustrations of something else, as, say, communicating meanings or identities, it is because we remain heirs of a tradition that treats signs as if they were merely the garb of meaning—meaning that, it would seem, must be stripped bare. As this tradition dematerializes signs, it privileges meaning over actions, consequences, and possibilities. Yet we must be wary of merely reversing this privilege and thereby inadvertently reproducing the same dichotomy. Drawing on semiotic concepts such as iconicity and indexicality, and the ideologies that organize them in representational economies, I'd like to suggest some alternatives.

SIGNS IN THEIR CAUSAL RELATIONS

I want to argue that certain semiotic concepts can help clarify the relationships between causal and logical dimensions of material things in society, between contingency and meaning. Because this word is used in so many different ways, a brief word on what semiotics, as I use it, is *not*. One of the most original uses of Charles Sanders Peirce's key concept of the "indexical sign" is Alfred Gell's *Art and Agency* (1998). Despite this, Gell claims to eschew semiotics per se. This because he identifies semiotics with "language." This won't do for understanding things, he says, because he wants to attend to the qualities of the object itself. He writes, "We talk about objects, using signs, but art objects are not, except in special cases, signs themselves, with 'meanings'; and if they do have meanings, then they are part of language" (1998: 6). Fair enough; the problem here is that Gell too quickly assimilates "sign" to "meaning," "meaning" in turn to "language," and "language" to something like "coded messages." In this, Gell seems to accept Saussure's (1959) structuralist model of language, as consisting of signifieds which are encoded in the form of arbitrary signifiers, in order to be transmitted to someone else, who decodes them and thereby recovers the signified meanings.

Indeed, this model is of little help in understanding objects. But we can go further: it's not even a good account of language. Saussurean "semiology" (not "semiotics") also makes it hard to perceive the role that language does play vis-à-vis material things. First, it treats language as something that exists in a plane of reality quite distinct from that in which any nonlinguistic things (material or conceptual) are found. It connects to those things only as objects of reference and denotation. Second, by seeing language only as coded meaning, Saussurean semiology fails to see the role linguistic practices play in the objectification of things, a point to which I will return at the end of this chapter. The problem is, semiotics has too often been treated, especially in cultural studies, as merely about the communication of meanings. Perhaps for this reason, Gell's use of the concept of index doesn't develop its articulation with other aspects of the sign. As a result, I would argue, he doesn't fully explore the social and historical implications of the index. Instead he seeks a direct road to the transhistorical domain of cognition. I would like to show how semiotics can help us restore these social and historical dimensions to the analysis.

In contrast to those who treat signs as coded messages, Peirce located signs within a material world of consequences.[1] He insisted that concrete circumstances were essential to the very possibility of signification. Thus he criticized Hegel's idealism with these words: "The capital error of Hegel which permeates his whole system . . . is that he almost altogether ignores the Outward Clash. . . . [This] direct consciousness of hitting and getting hit enters into all cognition and serves to make it mean something real" (Peirce 1958: 43–44).[2] Peirce offers a way of thinking about the logic of signification that displays its inherent vulnerability to causation and contingency, as well as its openness to further causal consequences, without settling for the usual so-called materialist reductionisms. To see this we need to recognize how the materiality of signification is not just a factor for the sign *interpreter* but gives rise to and transforms modalities of action and subjectivity *regardless* of whether they are interpreted. I want to argue that this openness should be central to any theoretically principled effort to understand the historical dynamics of material things.

The Peircean model of the sign has two features I want to bring out here. First, it is processual: signs give rise to new signs, in an unending process of signification. This point is important because it entails sociability, struggle, historicity, and contingency. This interpretation of the model offers a challenge to the facile but commonplace claim that to take things as signs is to reduce the world to discourse and its interpretation, to give in to the totalizing imperative to render all things meaningful. Second, the Peircean model devotes considerable attention to the complex range of possible relationships among signs, interpretations, and objects. For purposes of material analysis, I will be concerned with relations between signs and their possible objects of signification, which can be one of resemblance (*iconicity*), actual connection (*indexicality*), or rule (*symbolism*).[3]

The best-known social analyses of materiality focus on production. Since production is, in a brute sense, a cause of the product, these analyses often work with some version of indexicality. Take, for instance, Marx's distinction between the product of nonalienated and alienated labor. We could call the former indexical, insofar as the weaver can see herself in the cloth she weaves because it bears the evident stamp of her work. By contrast, alienated labor fails to index labor, since the industrial worker doesn't recognize himself in the factory output. In Bertrell Ollman's characterization, nonalienated human powers "exist in their product as the amount and type of change which their exercise has brought about. The degree of change is always proportionate to the expenditure of powers, just as its quality is always indicative [that is, iconic] of their state. . . . Man's productive activity leaves its mark . . . on [and thus is indexed by] all he touches" (1971: 143). In what is otherwise a vastly different approach, Heidegger also emphasizes the contrast between practical activity and the contemplative or theoretical attitude, and he favors the former for what seems to be its indexical character. He writes, "The shoemaker . . . understands *himself* from his things [the shoes]" (quoted in Munn 1986: 275, n. 12).[4] But indexicality is only one dimension of modes of signification. What I want to turn to now is the role of resemblance in the inherently social and historical character of material things.

BUNDLING AND THE OPENNESS OF OBJECTS

"She likes red," said the little girl.

"Red," said Mr. Rabbit. "You can't give her red."

"Something red, maybe," said the little girl.

"Oh, something red," said Mr. Rabbit.

—CHARLOTTE ZOLOTOW, *Mr. Rabbit and the Lovely Present*

One of the most sophisticated and far-reaching uses of iconicity in ethnographic analysis is Nancy Munn's (1986) account of a Melanesian system of production, consumption, and exchange. Her analysis gives a special role to those sensuous qualities of objects which have a privileged role within a larger system of value.[5] Their significance is borne by certain qualities beyond any particular manifestations in any specific objects. As Mr. Rabbit observes, redness must be embodied in something red. But the little girl's intuition is right too: for someone who likes red, in theory any number of quite different objectifications will do. Similarly for Gawans, according to Munn, "lightness," for instance, can pertain to canoes, garden plots, decorations, bodies, and so forth.

Mr. Rabbit reminds us that qualities must be embodied in something in particular. But as soon as they do, they are actually, and often contingently (rather than by logical necessity), bound up with other qualities—redness in an apple comes along with spherical shape, light weight, sweet flavor, a tendency to rot, and so forth. In practice, there is no way entirely to eliminate that factor of copresence, or what we might call *bundling*. This points to one of the obvious, but important, effects of materiality: redness cannot be manifest without some embodiment that inescapably binds it to some other qualities as well, which can become contingent but real factors in its social life. Bundling is one of the conditions of possibility for what Kopytoff (1986) and Appadurai (1986) called the biography of things, as the qualities bundled together in any object will shift in their relative salience, value, utility, and relevance across contexts.

One of the reasons Munn focuses on qualities, I think, is that it permits her to find identities among quite distinct things (canoes, garden plots, and so forth). Any analysis of signs in society needs to provide an account of how entities that are materially different in their qualities or, minimally, in their spatiotemporal coordinates, count as *the same thing*, without simply reproducing the conventionalism exemplified by the type-token relationship in structuralist linguistics—without assuming, that is, that people go around with a code book or set of rules in their heads. Abstracting qualities from objects offers a way of bringing discrete moments of experience into an overarching value system on the basis of habits and intuitions rather than rules and cognitions. But it is the cultural totality that makes it possible for Munn to speak of these instances as being "the same." That is, there is still some governing principle that makes of possible instances realizations of the same thing, and thus the possibilities—and recognizability—of future actions.

Icons in and of themselves remain only unrealized potential. In Munn's analysis, for instance, lightness partakes in a network of possible causal relations. To give food away rather than eating it fosters exchange relations with expansive potential across social space and into future time. What is given value by the specific aesthetic in which lightness plays this pivotal role are *causal* relations (eating food makes it unavailable for exchange). These relations are, for instance, registered by effects on the body: one who eats instead of giving comes to have a heavy and sluggish body. The very objectualization and thus legibility of iconicity (sluggishness), in this case, entails indexicality (the causal effects of eating). But these causal relations would still hold even if no one took them to be socially significant, being, say, in America rather than Melanesia.

If the properties of a material thing exist even if never taken as iconic elements of a sign, the reverse is also the case. An icon can resemble an object that doesn't exist—a map, say, of a fantastic land, or a cloud that looks like a unicorn. Since all objects have qualities, *any* given object potentially resembles *something*. This means any object can suggest possible future uses or interpretations. The artist's preliminary sketch for a sculpture makes use of this characteristic openness of iconicity as a means of discovery, "suggesting . . . new aspects of supposed states of things" (Peirce 1955: 106–107). The object in this case plays a role in the creation of something new that is not reducible to the acting subject's intentions. Rather, the interaction between the possibilities suggested by form and the taking up of that suggestion by the sculptor are a version of what Bruno Latour (1993) calls hybrids. Moreover, since resemblance is underdetermined, icons require some further guidance to determine how exactly they are similar to their objects. After all, even an ordinary portrait photograph is normally flat, immobile, and much smaller than its subject (see Pinney 1997). This guidance is thoroughly enmeshed with the dynamics of social value and authority—they are not merely external and supplementary to the force of iconicity.

CLOTHING AND POSSIBILITY

Take the example of clothing. The openness of iconicity was at work when colonial subjects turned Western shirts upside down and wore them as pants; it is at work when European tourists buy "ethnic cloth" and hang it on the wall as art. Resemblance, however, can only be with respect to certain features, and therefore depends on selection. To hang a flat, rectangular ikatted waist cloth from the Indonesian island of Sumba as wall art encourages one to overlook its bilateral inversion, since the images at each end are upside down relative to one another—the viewer tends to look only at those that are "right-side up." Determining what features count toward resemblance commonly involves larger questions of social value and authority. This is especially easy to see in colonial clashes. For instance, the Western sense of propriety, in colonial southern Africa, was offended by multifunctional apparel (Comaroff and Comaroff 1997: 270). Accustomed to one set of clothes for dining and another for gardening, one kind of textile to cover tables and another beds, Europeans were scandalized when Tswana used the same blankets as garments, ground cover, market bundles, and baby carriers. In time, a successful hegemony would restrict such potential uses, constraining which iconic possibilities would be recognized in practice.

Iconicity is only a matter of potential. The realization or suppression of that potential cannot be ascribed simply to the qualities of the object in themselves. There must always be other social processes involved. These processes may involve varying degrees of self-consciousness and control. Semiotic analyses have tended to favor the more strictly regimented domains as royal or liturgical ritual, high fashion (Barthes 1983), or connoisseurship (Bourdieu 1984). But there are far less well organized dimensions to social life. Even in the more controlled domains, however, since those material qualities that are suppressed do persist, objects bring the potential for new realizations into new historical contexts (see, e.g., Thomas 1991).

SEMIOTIC IDEOLOGY

One of the fundamental distinctions between icon and index concerns the nature of the inferences they will support. An icon tells us something about the qualities of its object but not whether that object actually exists. An index affirms the actual existence of its object, but not what, exactly, that object is. In different ways, each in itself "assert[s] nothing" (Peirce 1955: 111). Therefore, as Alfred Gell (1998: 14–15) and others have observed, making sense of indexicality, for instance, commonly involves ad hoc hypotheses. The observation is useful because it doesn't require us to assume everyone goes around with a preexisting code or cultural rule book in their heads. Yet the social power of indexicals demands some further account of their social regimentation or at least their recognizability—their coherence across discrete moments of intuition. Indexicality must be furnished with instructions (Hanks 1996: 46–47). It is semiotic ideology that helps do that.

By *semiotic ideology* I mean people's background assumptions about what signs are and how they function in the world.[6] Such assumptions help determine, for instance, what people will consider the likely role that intentions play in signification to be, what kinds of possible agent (humans only? animals? spirits?) exist to which acts of signification might be imputed, whether signs are arbitrary or necessarily linked to their objects, and so forth. Thorstein Veblen's (1912) notion of conspicious consumption, for instance, seems on the face of it to be a clear-cut example of indexicality. One appreciates the value of a classical education or high-heeled shoes by recognizing their lack of utility, and from that draws the inference that someone who can afford to dispense with utility must hold a certain status. But this recognition is mediated by what you assume about the world. Knowing Latin or wearing high heels are not useful, for example, only if you believe Latin doesn't have magical power or that height is immaterial to selfhood. Semiotic ideologies are thus concerned not just with signs per se but with what kinds of agentive subjects and acted-upon objects might be found in the world. There is no reason to conclude, however, that semiotic ideologies are total systems capable of rendering all things meaningful. Indeed, I would suggest below that the openness of things to further consequences perpetually threatens to destabilize existing semiotic ideologies.

THE OPENNESS OF THINGS
IS INHERENTLY HISTORICAL

What do material things make possible? What is their futurity? How might they change the person? As the references to Thoreau and Loos above suggest, there are times when these questions become urgent. For example, missionary history across the colonial world shows a persistent and troubling tension between the hope that clothing will change people, and the danger that people once clad will invest their clothing with too great a significance (Comaroff and Comaroff 1997: 223; Hansen 2000: 26, 30–32; Spyer 1998). On the one hand, proper dress is essential to the inculcation of modesty, propriety, and civility. Yet how much should one hope clothing will transform people? Not so much that they forget it is but a surface that can be removed. There are many dangers. They may, for instance, become frivolous and vain. Colonial writing is replete with depictions of dandified or otherwise ridiculous natives. Morality thus depends on the correct understanding of the materiality of things and the immateriality of persons, a balancing act that invites perpetual anxiety.

It is not only missionaries who are unsettled by the question of how much change we ought to expect from a change of clothes. Transvestitism, after all, is serious business. In Indonesia, the capacity of Buginese *bissu* to mediate between the world of the living and the dead, for instance, requires mixed gendered dressing. And certainly new historical ambitions seem to demand new clothes. Across the Malay world, to convert to Islam required that one take on new kinds of clothing and food regulations, which is one reason people figured the same must be true of Christianity (Aragon 2000; Taylor 1997). By the end of the nineteenth century, young nationalists in the more urban parts of the Dutch East Indies were asserting their modernity and new capacities through sartorial transformations, and in the twentieth they resisted calls for a Ghandi-like return to indigenous cloth (see Schulte Nordholt 1997, especially the chapters by van Dijk, Danandjaja, Mrázek, Taylor).

We must be clear: at issue here is not just the expression of "identities." For instance, clothing cannot be understood without the experience of comfort and discomfort, both physical (see, for instance, Banerjee and Miller 2003) and social (Elias 1994). And these have little to do with meaning, expression, identity, nor even, as Marcel Mauss (1979) would remind us, with some universal phenomenology of bodily experience. We drape ourselves in habit, competence, and constraint—with what clothing makes possible. Sumbanese cloth allows the comforting gesture of draping it protectively around oneself, as they say, like a hen huddled against the rain. The man's waistcloth leaves legs free to straddle a horse; his headcloth is good for everything from wiping sweat off the neck to transmitting magical power to asserting his individuality (Keller 1992). Men and women's clothing has no pockets. But special objects can be hidden in their folds. And the very insecurity of this draping can be played to advantage. One man told me how he got rid of a powerful talisman that, while useful, was becoming dangerous. Knowing it would be even more dangerous if he intentionally disposed of it, he folded it into his waistcloth and started on a long cross-country trip. Somewhere, perhaps in crossing a river, the talisman was lost, as it were, accidentally on purpose. We could say he thereby elicits the very agency of the thing. At the other end of the spectrum, Indonesia's early nationalists struggled against the discomfort of tight shoes and neckties in their effort to open up new possibilities. For them, "wearing a Western suit with tie did facilitate a handshake instead of a humble *sembah* [a respectful Javanese gesture of greeting], and wearing trousers did lend itself to sitting on a chair instead of being seated on the floor" (Schulte Nordholt 1997: 15).

New clothing makes possible or inhibits new practices, habits, and intentions; it invites new projects. Nicholas Thomas (1999) observed that the adoption of the so-called poncho by western Polynesian Christians didn't merely *express* their new modesty; in practical terms, by offering new ways of covering themselves, it made it *possible*. If we are to treat things "in their own right," and not just as the tangible garments draped on otherwise invisible and immaterial ideas, we must consider their forms, qualities, practical capacities, and, thus, their place within causal relations. For if, in Marilyn Strathern's (1988) terms, objects are revelatory, it is not simply because people say so, nor even because the anthropologist can impute to people certain beliefs. If things mediate our historicity, we cannot be content to ask only what meanings people attribute to them now. And even of those meanings, we must be attentive to the ways in which they are (for the time being) regimented and brought into relation to other things—much of this being the task of social power.

CLOTHING TAKEN TO BE MEANINGFUL

Material signs in themselves, unaided by semiotic ideologies and the various modalities of social regimentation, assert nothing. And social analysis that depends on assertions—that tries to "read" signs—is commonly confined to the retrospective glance. It works best for highly regimented systems of socially conventional signs. Indeed, in their most totalizing form, concepts such as culture, discipline, episteme, and hegemony are responding to the constant struggle within societies to regiment signs by taking the outcome as a given. But as I have been stressing here, the semiotic character of material things means that outcome is not, in principle, settled. It is not simply that their meanings are underdetermined, but also that their semiotic orientation is, in part, toward unrealized futures. Take the most ordinary of things. George Herbert Mead remarked, "The chair is what it is in terms of its invitation to sit down" (1934: 279). What interests us as embodied actors rather than, say, spectators, is the chair's instigation (by virtue of its form, that is, iconic suggestion) to certain sorts of action—and, thus, its futurity. This instigation may be most powerful when actors are least aware of it, something typical of what Daniel Miller (1987) calls "the humility of objects." And as instigation, the chair can only invite actions, not determine them: people in the colonial Indies may not have responded even if the Dutch had permitted them to rise from their floor mats. To realize some of the potentials of things, and not others, is the stuff of historical struggles and contingencies. The reason this seemingly obvious point is worth stressing is that it points us beyond the retrospective character of common ways of understanding signs, seeking to read them in terms only of what they presuppose and express.

What did Western dress worn by people of the Indies in the early twentieth century index? What possibilities did people hope to effect by a change of clothes? Acceptance of European culture, a desire to be part of a sophisticated world, acquiescence to Dutch rule, assertions of equality to Europeans, hostility to Islam, rejection of village society, being modern, access to fungible wealth, or short-sighted extravagance? And why did some of these attempts at cross-dressing fail and others succeed? When the Dutch, for instance, refused to acknowledge Indonesians' sartorial assertions of equality, they were helped by a semiotic ideology that told them clothing is merely skin-deep—a message of little consequence.

Semiotic ideologies are vulnerable, not least by their exposure to the openness of things. Consider the effects of what I have called bundling. Necessarily embodied in some particular objectual form, a given quality is contingently (rather than by logical necessity or social convention) bound up with other qualities—redness on a cloth comes along with light weight, flat surface, flexibility, warmth, combustability, and so forth. There is no way to eliminate (nor, entirely, to regiment) that factor of co-presence or bundling. This points to one of the obvious, but important, effects of materiality: redness cannot be manifest without some embodiment that inescapably binds it to some other qualities as well, which remain available, ready to emerge as real factors, as it crosses contexts. Western slacks treat the legs independently of one another. This permits a longer gait than does a Javanese sarong, inviting (but not determining) athleticism and giving them the potential for becoming socially realized conventions, that is, symbols understood as icons, of, say, "freedom." In Indonesia they have tended to be more expensive than the sarong as well, and thus indexical of relative wealth and, by extension, urban life. But now that the sarong has come to be purposefully deployed as a conventional symbol of Islam (indexical, but only by decree), slacks also threaten to be indexical of the not-wearing of sarong.[7]

These associations provide raw material for ideological consolidation. Middle-class men in Indonesian cities today have a rule-governed sartorial repertoire: a neotraditional outfit for weddings, safari suit for official meetings, long-sleeved batik shirt for receptions, shirt and tie for the office, sarong and *pici* for Friday prayers (Danandjaja 1997; van Dijk 1997). These are coordinated with bodily habituses: the Javanese *sembah*, sitting on mats and eating with hands while in neotraditional clothes; firm handshake, direct eye contact, chairs, and utensils in office attire; Islamic *salam* while in sarong. This cluster of habits, expectations, and constrained possibilities is the outcome of several generations of semiotic regimentation and stabilization. In addition to the direct effects of government regulations over its vast civil service, other responses reinforced them. For instance, a popular "uniform fever" swept Indonesia in the 1970s, as people at the margins of citizenship sought to distinguish themselves from the anonymous masses by identifying themselves sartorially with the bureaucracy (Sekimoto 1997). Some people took to wielding uniforms as apotropaic talismans against corrupt police and vigilantes (Danandjaja 1997). It is against the background of such self-consciously communicative and highly systematized treatments of clothes that other modes of emblematization emerge, such as the taking on of more Middle Eastern styles of head covering by women (Brenner 1996). Now, in these tightly regimented circumstances, a communication model of the sign actually does a great deal to explain style. But not all social life in all domains is so tightly controlled and totalized. If we take signs to be expressive of meanings, we must be prepared to ask under what historical circumstances, and guided by what semiotic ideology, that is possible.

This consolidation, I think, is what Georg Simmel meant by saying that "style is always something general" (1950: 341). Without denying the complexity of the idea of style, we might take from this comment an insight into how a relatively stable style produces a certain orientation toward the future.

Style allows one to recognize, across indefinitely many further occasions, instances of "the same thing." But the work of selecting and stabilizing the relevant bundles of iconicity and indexicality, the semiotic ideology this involves, is a project that can in principle never be completed, or fully consolidated (on the limits of totalization, see Laclau and Mouffe 1985). As such, semiotic ideology is necessarily historical.

CLOTH MADE TEXT

I began by arguing against language- or text-based approaches toward material things. Yet we also know that things can, *under some circumstances*, be treated as meaningful in textlike ways. This should lead us to take textuality *not* as a model for signification, but rather as that which needs to be explained (see Silverstein and Urban 1996). What are the conditions, for instance, under which cloth does or does not come into view as a bearer of iconography, with meanings that can be "read"? Sumbanese ikats are only produced in a small number of villages, although they circulate through exchange and are highly valued across the island. Some aspects of meaning don't travel well: the fact that the smell of indigo dye vats is iconic of rotting flesh (Hoskins 1989) is quite significant in weaving villages but not elsewhere. Even in weaving villages, explanation of motifs was restricted to male specialists, not the women who actually wove. In central Sumba, where weaving was carried out but the technique of ikatting forbidden, ikatted textiles were ritually, economically, and socially potent, but their imagery drew little attention. The functions of Sumbanese cloth shift by turns from wrapped garment to folded exchange valuable, open curtain, shroud draped on a corpse, shield against ritual heat, suspended banner, object of verbal exegesis, hidden relic, and, nowadays, art on a wall. In the past, once a cloth was off the loom, there were few normal uses in which the imagery was laid out and made clearly visible as a whole. Most uses reveal only fragments of the pattern, in constant motion. In practice, the qualities that come to the fore are brightness and busyness, fragility or durability (depending on context), capacity to block light and retain heat, softness, absorbency, ease of manipulation, and bilateral symmetry (see Keane 1997b: 80–81).

Under what conditions, then, do iconology and exegesis become significant? In old Sumba, the most common ikat motifs included *patola* designs drawn from Indian trade cloth, dragons from Chinese porcelain, and rampant heraldic animals from Dutch coins (Adams 1969). These require little exegetical knowledge beyond an awareness that they index the power of distance, conveyed through the capacity of objects to move across space and time. In recent decades, however, enormous attention has been drawn to motifs (but not, for instance, their repetition across the cloth, which gets overlooked). What has changed? Cloth is increasingly encountered as a plane parallel to the stance of the viewer. That is how they are displayed by sellers, illustrated in books, and hung on collectors' walls. They are visible as rectangular frames, taken in at a single glance, with a top and bottom. As frames for imagery, cloths become instances of the category "traditional" art. They enter a series that also includes Balinese painting and Javanese shadow puppets, which encourages cross-reference among them. Commercial competition is also driving a focus on motifs, one of the main ways of differentiating producers and allowing them to display esoteric knowledge to the buyers (see Myers, this volume). Motifs (and some of their formal features, such as the jagged edges produced by the ikat dyeing technique) readily circulate independently of waist-clothes or their technologies, to T-shirts and murals. Discrete motifs become objects of discourse. This discourse plays a crucial role in objectifying cloth as bearer of motifs. Exegetical talk itself is becoming an indexical icon of male authority and of the "tradition" embodied in the commodified cloth (Forshee 2000).

WORDS AND THE OBJECTUALIZATION OF THINGS

I have been arguing against approaches to material things that privilege language, or even received notions of meaningfulness, as their model. By emphasizing the mediating role of semiotic ideology in the consolidation of objects as components of social life, I have also tried to bring out the historicity implicit in semiotics. I want briefly to sketch out one illustration of historical transformation and objectualization in which language *does* play a critical role.

It has been observed that the formal organization of Sumbanese cloth seems to echo that of other material forms in Sumba (Adams 1980). And, as Émile Durkheim and Mauss (1963) recognized long ago, such forms offer privileged sites for the expression or concretization of social structures and cultural meanings. Yet, as Michel Foucault (1972: 44) observed, "one cannot speak of anything at any time." What makes textile, village, or house readily available for talk about cultural meanings in objectual form, with what material consequences? Here I want to turn from clothing to architecture.

I have suggested (Keane 1995) that the concreteness of the house as a cultural object, that is, as a repeatable, relatively stable, and intertextually rich representation (see, for instance, Bourdieu 1979), derives in part from certain features of the ways of speaking that purportedly refer to it. In Sumba, these features include an emphasis on canonical poetic forms such as parallelistic couplets and schematic list-making, and a pragmatic structure that tends to create a powerful center within the ritual performance that can be linked to nonvisible, and normally absent, agents such as ancestor spirits (Keane 1997b). The various discursive possibilities afforded by the house take as their authorizing foundation, interpretative content, and structural guide verbal performances that seem to trace a pathway through the house, naming its parts one by one. This verbal structure is shaped, in turn, by certain presupposed conditions for ritual speech. Chief among these is the invisibility and possible nonpresence of the spirit addressees, for whom the space of ritual encounter must be mapped out in order to guide them into the presence of the speakers—hence the diagrammatic character of the verbalized house. That is, the materiality of the house comes to the fore as a response to a certain material condition—the invisibility of interlocutors.

How does this help us understand the consolidation of material things as social objects? I argue that the significance of the material qualities of the house—and thus the "bundling" of distinct material qualities provided by the objectualization of the house as a unified entity—changes when the conditions for ritual speech change. For self-consciously modern Christians, the spirits cease to be real addressees. Their invisibility ceases to be a materially objective reality. Yet ritual speech persists, increasingly as a text understood as carrying traditional wisdom and Sumbanese ethnic identity. The materiality of its poetic form reproduces the structure of the house, but now as the object of reference, rather than as the sequence for a potential realtime unfolding of an encounter with invisible agents. This unfolding, I should note, did not in the past require that there be an actual house to match the verbal structure—any virtual house, even a mat on the ground, meeting proper ritual baptismal conditions, could serve. But as the use of ritual texts shifts—from addressing spirits in order to bring about consequential encounters, to entextualizing cultural meanings in order to render them visible and interpretable—so do the relations to materiality they presuppose.

This is part of a general shift in semiotic ideology distinguishing and linking words and things. If, for example, ritual speech (ideologically) functions to refer to the world, the felicity of reference depends on the physical existence of actual houses that match those which are being denoted. Any apparent mismatch between words and the world reinforces the sense that they exist in separate and self-contained domains. No amount of *ritual* felicity can bring about changes in the *material* qualities of the house being referred to. At the same time, as contemporary Sumbanese increasingly come to see their immediate surroundings in terms of the material absence of exemplars of what is now thought of as the traditional house, something else is going on. On the one hand, they may perceive the lack of the appropriate physical structures as indicating the loss of tradition; they may even work to preserve token houses of the proper type. On the other hand, as Protestants, they are learning that verbal prayers are merely the outward expression of sincere inner thoughts that are, in essence, wholly immaterial, like the soul who intends them (Keane 1997a, 2002). They deny any significance to the material form that their words take. Language, like sacrificial goods, has become "merely symbolic" and thus ideologically dematerialized. In short, an explicit ontological claim, reinforced by new liturgical speech practices, along with a host of other mundane practices of modernity,[8] underwrites the transformation of the dominant semiotic ideologies within which the objectivity of material things comes to play its emergent social roles. Whereas language should not be the privileged theoretical model for a semiotics of material things, discursive practices *do* play a crucial role in ideological *consolidation* or semiotic regimentation (Silverstein 1996) in rendering objects legible, full of stabilized "meaning."

The idea of semiotic ideology should not be taken to imply totalization. Different orders of semiosis are differently subject to determination or autonomous logics. Thus the more indexical aspects of any configuration of signs will be more subject to direct transformation in response to material circumstances, whereas a system of conventions is subject to quite distinct modes of determination and transformation. Technological change may quietly alter the genetic content of the food on our table and labor economics the sources but not the look of our clothes. Meanwhile, legal rights are being reshaped in highly public verbal debates, whose outcome depends on the dynamics of argument, precedence, and party politics. Each of these processes involves very different temporalities, social logics, and consequentialities. But since even the most conventional signs are instantiated in material forms, they are, at least to that extent, subject to material causality. Conversation requires a shared language and a medium of communication; yam prestation requires a garden; the phone call requires electricity and a telephone—something so obvious as to be commonly overlooked.

OBJECTS AND THE POSSIBILITIES OF SUBJECTS

I have argued elsewhere that matter and materialism pose special difficulties for mainstream Protestants (Keane 1996, 2001). The effort to regulate certain verbal and material practices, and the anxieties that attend them, center on the problem of consolidating a human subject that is at its core independent of, and superordinate to, the world of mere dead matter (this greatly simplifies a complex story). What for anthropologists is a problem of social and cultural analysis—how to understand material things within human society—is faced by these missionaries as a practical problem—how to free humans from false relations to things, as in fetishism, animism, or naturalistic materialism. This view of signs has roots in an ontology that goes back before either Protestantism or modernity, to be sure, but it reaches a particularly strong and influential expression in their alliance, as expressed by the quotations above from Thoreau and Loos. It underwrites much of our contemporary social theory as well.

To take clothes in particular, and objects more generally, as expressions of meanings that really lie elsewhere is to depend on certain assumptions not just about objects, but about signs. Clothing seems most superficial to those who take signs to be the clothing of immaterial meanings. Like clothing, in this view, the sign both reveals and conceals, and it serves to mediate relations between the self and others. These are the very grounds on which Thoreau and many other Protestants and modernists are suspicious of clothing and, often, of semiotic mediation altogether. In unmediated transparency they hope to discover unvarnished souls and naked truth.

Iconism and indexicality function by virtue of meta-level semiosis. First, the very existence of a sign as such, for an interpreter, depends on a mode of proto-objectification. That is, before an object of signification can be specified, something must first be specified as a sign. And in the process, its objects must be determined to be objects. It is a historically specific semiotic ideology that determines what will count for the interpreter and actor as objects and in contrast to what subjects. A yam prestation that falls short of expectations, or a telephone call not returned, may index malevolent human intentions, an individual's forgetfulness, the disfavor of spirits, abstract social forces, one's own fate, mere happenstance, or something else altogether, only with reference to a specific ideological context that makes these plausible and relevant inferences. Thus the Protestant anxiety about the relative autonomy of the human subject from the material world constrains what will count as signs, as intentions, and as actions—excluding, like Weber, such things as the contingent materiality of things from the proper domain of the human. A semiotic analysis of the social power of things would thus demand an account of the semiotic ideologies and their discursive regimentation that enter into or are excluded from the processes by which things become objects, for these are the same processes that configure the borders and the possibilities of subjects.

NOTES

This chapter has benefited from the comments of Judith Irvine, Adela Pinch, and Christopher Pinney, and was completed during a fellowship year at the Center for Advanced Study in the Behavioral Sciences (Stanford, Calif.).

1. A useful selection from Peirce's vast, complex, and mostly unfinished and unpublished writings is Peirce 1955. For (necessarily selective) appropriations of Peirce in the context of contemporary cultural and social analysis, see Daniel 1996, Lee 1997, Parmentier 1997, and Silverstein 1976.

2. Note that he seems to be saying not that this "consciousness" provides the meaning of the cognition, but rather that it gives that meaning its reality effect.

3. The "symbol" here includes those arbitrary social conventions, such as Saussure's "language," which have dominated cultural analysis. For Peirce, symbols can encompass icons and indexes. For instance, the arrow on a "one way" traffic sign is legible only because we have conventions for understanding arrows. But we take it be indexical, as pointing in the actual direction we should go, in the here and now.

4. Compare Lukács: "[T]he diversity of subjective attitudes orientates praxis toward what is qualitatively unique, toward the content and the material substratum of the object concerned. . . . theoretical contemplation leads to the neglect of this very factor" (1971: 126).

5. She calls these *qualisigns*, a Peircean category of iconicity.

6. This idea expands on the concepts of "linguistic ideology" (Schieffelin, Woolard, and Kroskrity 1998) and "ethnosemiotic assumptions" (Parmentier 1997).

7. As pointed out in note 3 above, symbols can be taken as iconic or indexical.

8. These practices include the handling of money (Keane 2001), the effort to speak sincerely (Keane 1997a, 2002), and the treatment of exchange valuables as symbolic of abstract social values (Keane 1996, 2001).

REFERENCES

Adams, Marie Jeanne. 1969. *System and Meaning in East Sumba Textile Design: A Study in Traditional Indonesian Art*. New Haven, Conn.: Yale University Southeast Asian Studies.
——. 1980. "Structural Aspects of East Sumbanese Art." In James J. Fox, ed., *The Flow of Life: Essays on Eastern Indonesia*. Cambridge: Harvard University Press.
Appadurai, A. 1986. "Introduction: Commodities and the Politics of Value." In *The Social Life of Things: Commodities in Cultural Perspective*. Cambridge: Cambridge University Press.
Aragon, Lorraine V. 2000. *Fields of the Lord: Animism, Christian Minorities, and State Development in Indonesia*. Honolulu: University of Hawaii Press.
Banerjee, Mukulika, and Daniel Miller. 2003. *The Sari*. Oxford: Berg.
Barthes, Roland. 1983/1967. *The Fashion System*. Trans. A. Lavers and C. Smith. London: Jonathan Cape.
Bourdieu, P. 1979/1970. "The Kabyle House, or the World Reversed." In *Algeria 1960*. Trans. R. Nice. Cambridge: Cambridge University Press.
——. 1984/1979. *Distinction: A Social Critique of the Judgement of Taste*. Trans. Richard Nice. Cambridge: Harvard University Press.
Brenner, Suzanne. 1996. "Reconstruction of Self and Society: Javanese Muslim Women and 'the Veil.' " *American Ethnologist* 23:673–697.
Comaroff, John L., and Jean Comaroff. 1997. *Of Revelation and Revolution*, vol. 2: *The Dialectics of Modernity on a South African Frontier*. Chicago: University of Chicago Press.
Danandjaja, James. 1997. "From Hansop to Safari: Notes from an Eyewitness." In Henk Schulte Nordholt, ed., *Outward Appearances: Dressing State and Society in Indonesia*, 249–258. Leiden: KITLV Press.
Daniel, E. Valentine. 1996. *Charred Lullabies: Chapters in an Anthropography of Violence*. Princeton, N.J.: Princeton University Press.
Durkheim, E., and M. Mauss. 1963/1903. *Primitive Classification*. Trans. R. Needham. Chicago: University of Chicago Press.

Elias, Norbert. 1994/1939. *The Civilizing Process*. Trans. Edmund Jephcott. Cambridge: Blackwell.

Forshee, Jill. 2000. *Between the Folds: Stories of Cloth, Lives, and Travels from Sumba*. Honolulu: University of Hawaii Press.

Foucault, M. 1972/1969. *The Archaeology of Knowledge and the Discourse on Language*. Trans. A. M. Sheridan Smith. New York: Pantheon.

Gell, Alfred. 1993. *Wrapping in Images: Tattooing in Polynesia*. Oxford: Clarendon Press.

——. 1998. *Art and Agency: An Anthropological Theory*. Oxford: Clarendon Press.

Hanks, W. F. 1996. *Language and Communicative Practices*. Boulder, Colo.: Westview.

Hansen, Karen Tranberg. 2000. *Salaula: The World of Secondhand Clothing and Zambia*. Chicago: University of Chicago Press.

Heidegger, Martin. 1962/1927. *Being and Time*. Trans. J. Macquarrie and E. Robinson. New York: Harper and Row.

Hoskins, Janet. 1989. "Why Do Ladies Sing the Blues? Indigo, Cloth Production, and Gender Symbolism in Kodi." In Annette B. Weiner and Jane Schneider, ed., *Cloth and Human Experience*. Washington: Smithsonian Institution Press.

Irvine, J. T. 1996/1989. "When Talk Isn't Cheap: Language and Political Economy." In D. Brenneis and R. K. S. Macaulay, eds., *The Matrix of Language: Contemporary Linguistic Anthropology*. Boulder, Colo.: Westview.

Keane, Webb. 1995. "The Spoken House: Text, Act, and Object in Eastern Indonesia." *American Ethnologist* 22:102–124.

——. 1996. "Materialism, Missionaries, and Modern Subjects in Colonial Indonesia." In Peter van der Veer, ed., *Conversion to Modernities: The Globalization of Christianity*, 137–170. New York and London: Routledge.

——. 1997a. "From Fetishism to Sincerity: Agency, the Speaking Subject, and Their Historicity in the Context of Religious Conversion." *Comparative Studies in Society and History* 39:674–693.

——. 1997b. *Signs of Recognition: Powers and Hazards of Representation in an Indonesian Society*. Berkeley: University of California Press.

——. 2001. "Money Is No Object: Materiality, Desire, and Modernity in an Indonesian Society." In Fred C. Myers, ed., *The Empire of Things: Regimes of Value and Material Culture*. Santa Fe: School of American Research Press.

——. 2002. "Sincerity, 'Modernity,' and the Protestants." *Cultural Anthropology* 17:65–92.

——. 2003. "Self-Interpretation, Agency, and the Objects of Anthropology: Reflections on a Genealogy." *Comparative Studies in Society and History* 45:222–248.

Keller, Edgar. 1992. "Head-dresses as a Medium of Self-Expression in Laboya: Sumbanese Attire in Historical Perspective." In Marie-Louise Nabholz-Kartaschoff, Ruth Barnes, and David J. Stuart-Fox, eds., *Weaving Patterns of Life: Indonesian Textile Symposium 1991*. Basel: Museum of Ethnography.

Kopytoff, Igor. 1986. "The Cultural Biography of Things: Commoditization as Process." In A. Appadurai, ed., *The Social Life of Things: Commodities in Cultural Perspective*. Cambridge: Cambridge University Press.

Laclau, Ernesto, and Chantal Mouffe. 1985. *Hegemony and Socialist Strategy: Towards a Radical Democratic Politics*. London: Verso.

Latour, Bruno. 1993. *We Have Never Been Modern*. Trans. C. Porter. Cambridge: Harvard University Press.

Lee, Benjamin. 1997. *Talking Heads: Language, Metalanguage, and the Semiotics of Subjectivity*. Durham, N.C.: Duke University Press.

Lukács, Georg. 1971/1922. "Reification and the Consciousness of the Proletariat." In *History and Class Consciousness: Studies in Marxist Dialectics*. Trans. R. Livingstone. Cambridge: MIT Press.

Marx, Karl. 1967/1887. *Capital: A Critique of Political Economy*. Trans. Samuel Moore and Edward Aveling. New York: International.

Mauss, Marcel. 1979/1950. "Bodily Techniques." In *Sociology and Psychology: Essays*. Trans. B. Brewster. London: Routledge and Kegan Paul.

Mead, George Herbert. 1934. *Mind, Self, and Society from the Standpoint of a Social Behaviorist*. Chicago: University of Chicago Press.

Miller, Daniel. 1987. *Material Culture and Mass Consumption*. Oxford: Basil Blackwell.

Mrázek, Rudolph. 1997. "'Indonesian Dandy': The Politics of Clothes in the Late Colonial Period, 1893–1942." In Henk Schulte Nordholt, ed., *Outward Appearances: Dressing State and Society in Indonesia*. Leiden: KITLV Press.

Munn, Nancy. 1986. *The Fame of Gawa: A Symbolic Study of Value Transformation in a Massim (Papua New Guinea) Society*. Cambridge: Cambridge University Press.

Ollman, Bertell. 1971. *Alienation: Marx's Conception of Man in Capitalist Society*. Cambridge: Cambridge University Press.

Parmentier, Richard J. 1997. "The Pragmatic Semiotics of Cultures." *Semiotica* 116 (special issue).

Peirce, Charles Sanders. 1955. *Philosophical Writings of Peirce*. Ed. Justus Buchler. New York: Dover.

——. 1958. *Collected Papers of Charles Sanders Peirce*, vol. 8: *Reviews, Correspondence, and Bibliography*. Cambridge: Harvard University Press.

Pinney, Christopher. 1997. *Camera Indica: The Social Life of Indian Photographs*. Chicago: University of Chicago Press.

Saussure, Ferdinand de. 1959. *Course in General Linguistics*. New York: Philosophical Library.

Schieffelin, Bambi B., Kathryn A. Woolard, and Paul V. Kroskrity, eds. 1998. *Language Ideologies: Practice and Theory*. New York: Oxford University Press.

Schulte Nordholt, Henk. 1997. Preface to *Outward Appearances: Dressing State and Society in Indonesia*. Leiden: KITLV Press.

——, ed. 1997. *Outward Appearances: Dressing State and Society in Indonesia*. Leiden: KITLV Press.

Sekimoto, Teuo. 1997. "Uniforms and Concrete Walls: Dressing the Village under the New Order in the 1970s and 1980s." In Henk Schulte Nordholt, ed., *Outward Appearances: Dressing State and Society in Indonesia*, 307–337. Leiden: KITLV Press.

Silverstein, Michael. 1976. "Shifters, Linguistic Categories, and Cultural Description." In

Keith H. Basso and Henry A. Selby, eds., *Meaning in Anthropology*. Albuquerque: University of New Mexico Press.

——. 1996. *Indexical Order and the Dialectics of Sociolinguistic Life*. Austin: Texas Linguistic Forum (SALSA III).

Silverstein, Michael, and Greg Urban, eds. 1996. *Natural Histories of Discourse*. Chicago: University of Chicago Press.

Simmel, Georg. 1950/1923. "Adornment." In Kurt H. Wolff, ed., *The Sociology of Georg Simmel*, 338–344. New York: Free Press.

Spyer, Patricia. 1998. "The Tooth of Time, or Taking a Look at the 'Look' of Clothing in Late Nineteenth-Century Aru." In Patricia Spyer, ed., *Border Fetishisms: Material Objects in Unstable Places*, 150–182. New York: Routledge.

Stallybrass, Peter. 1996. "Worn Worlds: Cloth and Identity on the Renaissance Stage." In Margreta de Grazia, Maureen Quilligan, and Peter Stallybrass, eds., *Subject and Object in Renaissance Culture*. Cambridge: Cambridge University Press.

Strathern, Marilyn. 1988. *The Gender of the Gift: Problems with Women and Problems with Society in Melanesia*. Berkeley: University of California Press.

Taylor, Jean Gelman. 1997. "Costume and Gender in Colonial Java, 1800–1940." In Henk Schulte Nordholt, ed., *Outward Appearances: Dressing State and Society in Indonesia*. Leiden: KITLV Press.

Thomas, Nicholas. 1991. *Entangled Objects: Exchange, Material Culture, and Colonialism in the Pacific*. Cambridge: Harvard University Press.

——. 1999. "The Case of the Misplaced Poncho: Speculations Concerning the History of Cloth in Polynesia." *Journal of Material Culture* 4:5–20.

Thoreau, Henry D. 1971/1854. *Walden*. Ed. Lyndon Shanley. Princeton, N.J.: Princeton University Press.

van Dijk, Kees. 1997. "Sarong, Jubbah, and Trousers: Appearance as a Means of Distinction and Discrimination." In Henk Schulte Nordholt, ed., *Outward Appearances: Dressing State and Society in Indonesia*, 39–83. Leiden: KITLV Press.

Veblen, Thorstein. 1912. *The Theory of the Leisure Class: An Economic Study of Institutions*. New York: Macmillan.

Weber, Max. 1978. *Economy and Society: An Outline of Interpretive Sociology*. Trans. E. Fischer et al. Berkeley: University of California Press.

SUSANNE KÜCHLER

Materiality and Cognition:
The Changing Face of Things

T orn between notions of an embodied and a hardwired mind, the study of cognition has long been the silent victim of a distinction between the phenomenal and the noumenal that emerged from the Enlightenment to drive a theory of culture in which not things, but humankind, is at the helm.[1] The world as experienced and the world as ontologically framed have remained in tension, despite a long line of scholarship devoted to situating thought at the heart of the individual and of culture. Confidence in the notion of an embodied mind, thought to have finally replaced an ousted Cartesian dualism, was shattered when the electronic simulation of the mind showed that it may radically differ from what we have thus far imagined or successfully built a model for. The reason for placing this question mark over existing models of mind is consciousness, whose explanation is still one of the most hotly contested issues of our time.[2] Thus, despite an avalanche of detailed and coordinated studies of human cognition, we are faced today with an apparently insurmountable clash between those who assume a body-driven mind and those who assume a mind driven by its neurologically verifiable existence.[3]

The problem over where to position mindfulness certainly has a long and complex history, yet arguably it stems from the perceived need to situate an explanation of mind squarely within a theory of culture designed in the image of man.[4] Textbooks on culture reiterate Marvin Harris's (1975: 661) definition of culture as the "pattern of behaviour and thought learned and shared . . . of a societal group." This notion of culture as "sets of learned behaviour and ideas" reduces to a product the things that result from learned behavior.[5] Not generally mentioned is Edward Tylor's (1913) classical definition of art as "capabilities," an understanding made evident in one of the most widely used textbooks on culture, which goes as far as stating that "culture" does not refer to behavior or to such products of behavior as tools, art, and other artifacts. Instead, culture is thought to be made up of shared, prescriptive understandings that reside in people's minds, "never in the artifacts themselves" (Swartz and Jordan 1976: 53).[6]

These views may appear dated in the light of more recent studies that have returned things to a framing of culture where they work as images that make shared learning possible (cf. Bourdieu 1977; Keane 1997). Yet despite the readmission of the material into anthropological analysis over the last two decades, we have progressed embarrassingly little in understanding how things and thought, whether embodied or not, relate to each other in conditioning a conscious mind.[7] The trouble is that, as Daniel Sperber laments in his *Explaining Culture*, although anthropology has reconsidered its position and admitted things into the remit of culture, it continues to assume that there are irreducibly cultural things that do not correspond to the types of things that are talked about in nonsocial sciences—types of things such as clans, lineages, myths, rituals, but also art, which are denied any correspondence with biological or psychological types (1997: 376). Cognitive anthropology, following in the wake of structuralist analysis and the theory of the "habitus," has certainly tried to seek out the correspondence of mental and cultural representations, yet the things that act as carriers of thought have fared little better in cognitive anthropology than in conventional analyses, at least partly because they are regarded as "representations" that package what already exists in the mind.[8]

Things are allowed back into the analysis of culture, but only as long as they serve as targets for a mind eager to project itself onto mirrorlike surfaces. This position has left us bereft of analyses that concern themselves with how thought accompanies things and try to determine the nature of this thought that dwells with things. This lack in studies of the materiality of cognition betrays a residual distaste for the material as the generally *Ungeistige*, or inanimate, which can be rescued only through a perceptual approach capable of foregrounding the intelligent eye.

Why does a cognitive approach to culture need things at all, or conversely, why should a study of things concern itself with issues of cognition? The more conventional answer regards this need on a priori grounds: for it is things that create cognition, both as a Kantian subcategory that organizes the way we experience the world, and as embodied aspects of past peoples from which we learn to think in particular cultural ways. Yet there is another reason, too, for why cognitive approaches need things. The reason lies in the technological advent of the electronic image, which is displacing the word as the primary vehicle of knowledge transmission. We no longer believe it credible that we know how to operate efficiently in a given social environment via information granted to us through the spoken or written word, for images are now known to be far more economical and thus faster tools of transmission, allowing Barbara Maria Stafford (1996: 39) to argue that "perception is a significant form of knowledge, perhaps even the constitutive form."[9]

Advances in the technical capacity of neuroscience to model the processing of image-based thought has turned the study of the mind into a highly specialized affair. The emerging complexity of the mind/brain/body/thing nexus has undoubtedly impacted the social sciences, forcing its retreat to safer territory. Never has the cognitive approach been as shunned as it is today. Yet persistent rumors abound that leaving the division of labor on mind and matter intact would be a grave mistake (Stafford 1996; Gell 1998; Latour 1999), because on the back of technological innovations that model intelligence in things, new ways of thinking about the nature of consciousness are being made possible. To the surprise and dismay of disciplines devoted to the study of man, the modeling of cognition now thrives on the material analogue of perception in computer simulation. Indeed, as Stafford (1996) pointed out, as intelligence is designed into everyday products we are reminded of the premodern notion that there is no inanimate matter. Yet what are the things where thought can dwell, and what is the nature of this thought from which knowledge rises like clouds of smoke?

The animation of things is nothing new but is synonymous with the age of the machine.[10] Today, however, new sensing, networking, and automating technologies are created with the sole purpose of vivifying "dead" objects by making them responsive to human need and emotion. No longer is technology just "out there" at our disposal for enchanting the world.[11] Instead, it is designed to be "inhabited," to be lived in and thought with. In its most recent articulation, wireless computing, a bright new world of unlimited connectivity and transparent communication, promises the end of the nineteenth-century legacy of inscrutable persons and gated communities. We are presented with the dream of a world in which attachment is facilitated by images that are vehicles of associative thought.

Yet although the advent of this technology promises to fulfill our dream of ultimate control over matter, it also carries a radical challenge to our most trusted assumptions about things. In a world of silicon life-forms it no longer makes sense to ask how a thing can only be an object of discursive thought. Displaced at a stroke are interpretative skills that have been the hallmark of the humanities since the birth of the Enlightenment. We have to ask how a thing can be "thoughtlike," or "how thought can conduct itself in things," and construct master methodologies that do justice to manifold and relational complexes no longer contained within a framework of discrete objects and subjects. The radical shift implied in this move is the subject of this chapter.

First and foremost, this shift exposes culture as an obsolete explanatory factor for the material. Since Émile Durkheim, generations of scholars have crafted "the social life of things" out of preoccupation with the social life of man. For too long we have lived with the notion that the material is receptive to concepts that are projected onto it. This projectionist fallacy, the oppositional framework of culture and objecthood in which objects merely serve as substitutes for persons, falls apart as animated things, although responsive to human need and emotion, become effective in managing connective and analogical relations.

The acknowledgment that our assumptions about materiality have to be revised to accommodate a new economy of knowledge technology is not new. Indeed, as a common strand of argument it unites the writings of Bruno Latour (1999) on science, of Alfred Gell (1998) on art, and Barbara Stafford (1999) on eighteenth-century art history. They all argue that a concern with materiality must proceed independently of the question of culture. Latour alerts us to methodologies that seek out the complexity of innovation from within the relational qualities of the material, pointing out new ways of overcoming the oppositional thinking that for too long has separated the world of social things from the world of science. Gell, in his much misunderstood chapter on style in *Art and Agency* (1998), evoked methodologies that handle relations in what he termed the "interartifactual domain" in ways that expose the analogical quality of these relations. Stafford (1999) further elaborates the theme of connectivity and resemblance by taking the analogical force of the visual and the material as a platform from which to rethink how we create attachments in a world in which subjects and objects do not stand in opposition to each other.

The shift implied in the advent of the intelligent object, however, exposes assumptions not just about objects, but also about cognition. Anthropology, like many of its neighboring disciplines, has tended to pick and choose when it comes to addressing what things may reveal about thought. A coherent theory of cognition relevant to the humanities and social sciences has never existed, yet one single dominant issue has come to prevail in studies of culture. This, of course, is memory, or rather a model of memory deeply entrenched in the Enlightenment's rediscovery of an ancient technique of recollection that supplanted discursive thought with images (Kwint and Breward 1999; Forty and Küchler 1998; Young 1993). An almost fanatical pre-occupation with the memorial capacity of objects ensued, precisely when, ironically, the real significance of this model of memory, which had long served to legitimize the management of archives and museums, lost its significance within an impending intellectual economy in which proprietary rights were no longer extended to things, only to resources.[12] More recently, studies of techniques of recollection have given way to a concern with spontaneous recollection, with consciousness and attention.[13] It is no accident that such studies have revived the long-neglected work on the mnemic image by the early-twentieth-century art historian Aby Warburg, whose *Mnemosyne Atlas* was a testimony to images' capacity to fashion connections that emerge as thought. It is perhaps in relation to the nature of thought that moves through things that the lack of sensitive ethnographies of materiality is felt most strongly.[14]

Nothing from within the disciplines devoted to the study of thinking and learning would prepare one for the importance of an ethnography of materiality. For psychology—and, since the 1970s, cognitive psychology—has mapped out an approach to materiality based on the premise that the form it takes in culture is governed by unconscious, embodied, and habituated actions.

The failure of cognitive psychology to take on the exploration of conscious and spontaneous thought had devastating consequences for those working on issues of materiality. For if conscious, intentional thought is not just something attributed to people but is somehow part of the sensuous, performative, and formal properties of things, anthropology and its neighboring disciplines are faced with the most radical challenge yet to existing methodologies.

We are, arguably, at the threshold of a new age—not just of intellectual economy and of new ways of managing knowledge but also of materiality, in which not objects but images reign. The implications of this change for the material world are registered in a realm that is most immediate to our experience—the world of fabric, of textiles and clothing.

An overwhelming body of interdisciplinary scholarship has grown around the diverse subjects of cloth and clothing over the last decade.[15] One is tempted to allude to the observations by Walter Benjamin (1969) and Claude Lévi-Strauss (1969) that when phenomena grip the public imagination in such a manner, the public fascination resonates in an ending process that Benjamin likened to the sun setting beyond the horizon. While Benjamin was alluding to the disappearance of the public face of the storyteller in the face of print and photography, and Lévi-Strauss to the notion of primitivism in the face of the end of colonialism, we may witness in the overwhelming attention given to both textiles and clothing a sign that they are changing in some fundamental manner before our very eyes. What we may be faced with is clearly the end not of textiles and clothing, but of our trusted assumptions about them as "shifting ephemera on the surface of life" (Hollander 1993: xv), as trivial and fleeting expressions of a seriousness that resides elsewhere. We think quite readily of textiles and clothes as entirely social and psychological phenomena, as tangible and three-dimensional material for the interpretation and translation of emotions, manners, or habits. In subordinating clothes to the study of man—as illustrations and metaphors of the body within—we seem to have lost sight of the seriousness of textiles as images in their own right. We now are impelled to face up to this seriousness (see also Keane in this volume).

INHABITING TECHNOLOGY

When I first approached the topic of clothing and textiles as a new sensing, networking, and automating technology, I assumed the new textiles would belong to the genre of the robotic devices with which we have become familiar since the first automata emerged in the late 1800s. Yet the reality could not be more different, for the development of miniaturized forms of electromagnetic devices has largely involved cloth surfaces, commonly known as I-wear or intelligent clothing. Fashion, as Bradley Quinn (2002: 98) has pointed out, has been chosen as a vehicle for technology because "it is versatile, mobile, universal and adaptable and can act as a conduit for a body area network, which provides the backbone for intelligent clothing."

Who would have thought that cloth—of all things, the hallmark of craft and domesticity—would become the vehicle of cutting-edge design and technology? Since Victorian days, quilting and embroidery and certainly weaving—in a sense the whole gamut of textile culture, and this despite the fact that the cloth industry was central to the Industrial Revolution and the foundations of modernity—have been relegated to the backwaters of modernity, seen as suitable only for the young and the feeble-minded as quasi-educational pastimes that instill a sense of discipline, selflessness, and service (Parker 1984). For those who grew up in the 1960s, quilting and embroidery gained a new face—symbolizing love, peace, color, personal life, and a rejection of materialism—and became rebellious gestures against a hierarchical, puritanical, masculine establishment. Thinking in, through, and with cloth surfaces, however, remained an essentially feminine, if characteristically shallow, occupation of intelligence and creativity that thrived in the shadow of an ontology of cognition emulating depth and cumulative and text-based learning.

Yet all this may be about to change: we are finding ourselves in the midst of a technological revolution that brings to the fore the interface of cloth surfaces and the conduction of thought. While robotic gadgets using hidden electronics or microchips for animation have had a rather long history, reaching back, in their simplest form, to the animated toys of the late eighteenth century, the idea of animating material surfaces in ways that become progressively independent of interior devices is by contrast rather new. It took center stage only in the early 1980s with the so-called data glove, which was fitted with specially treated optical fibers that ran along the backs of the fingers, sending signals to a central processor. The animated surface had its first public outing in the Museum of Modern Art in New York in 2001, when computer keyboards and mobile phones imprinted on cloth were highlighted at an exhibition where cloth was not just the *cover* for electronic equipment but where cloth *was* the electronic equipment.

The cloth itself is made from fibers, such as nylon or polyester, that have been coated in carbon, or in one of a variety of metals, in order to make them more conductive. It is connected to a tiny circuit board containing a 5-volt battery and a chip no bigger than the nail on a person's little finger. When the material is touched, it completes an electrical circuit, allowing current to pass through it. This is picked up by the chip, which processes the signals using specially designed software and transmits them to an electronic device, such as a telephone, a computer, or a television set. The secret lies in the knitted pattern of the fibers: when touched, they determine how the electrical signals pass through, thus revealing where the contact was made.

The MOMA exhibition was the first appearance of this new type of fabric, which could be used to make the wearable computers that science fiction writers have dreamed of. Called ElekTex, the fabric has been created by Electro Textiles, a tiny company based at Pinewood Studios, near London, which researches, develops, and licenses interactive soft switching solutions for innovative product opportunities. The possibilities for "technologized" clothing have emerged as smaller, cheaper, and more powerful electronic components, wireless communication, and portable computers have become available (Quinn 2002: 98).

Gadgets made from ElekTex are, in one sense, reassuringly normal. The buttons on cloth-based television remote controls change channels, just as the ones on conventional remotes do. "It surely feels like a fabric, but it's more than that": so ElekTex presents itself on the Web. It is introduced as an intelligent technology capable of electronic sensing, heralding a new generation of product opportunities. "You can fold it, scrunch it or wrap it, according to your need." Lightweight, durable, flexible, and cost competitive, ElekTex promises (its creators claim) to change the way we live. "Welcome to the future," heralds ElekTex. "Welcome to a new soft world."

Yet normality still appears a long way off, as most electro-textiles have not advanced much beyond prototyping and military application (Quinn 2002: 98). A *New York Times* headline, however, foresees "electric threads that cosset you" as a future essential for the "smart dresser" (Eisenberg 2003). Used in car upholstery, electro-textiles could sense a passenger's weight and tell an air bag to adjust its force accordingly. Fleece versions of the electronic cloth could keep anyone snuggled under them toasty at a football game. Blood pressure sensors incorporated into the fabric could register changes by altering the color and pattern of the fabric. Tomorrow, your clothing will detect whether your body temperature is giving signs that you are getting sick and, if so, will contact the doctor for you. Your suitcase will let you know what clothes it contains. Clothes will tell you that you have forgotten your keys, or warn you when your wallet is stolen; a jogging suit will put you through your paces or accumulate the impressions of a place like an external memory store.

In the field of intelligent clothing, everything is possible. Various innovative products are already available on the market today, such as stockings that hydrate and energize the leg, stain-proof tiles, antibacterial socks, and uv-resistant swimwear. Timberland has brought out the "men's Venetian loafer," a shoe designed as a "smart comfort system" which distributes pressure evenly and has an expandable sole with flexible grooves that allow for natural movement.

Most of the uses we imagine for intelligent clothing are already in existence as prototypes. Munich-based Infineon Technologies last year presented its first solutions for wearable electronics and smart textiles. It developed microelectronic components that are directly connected to electrically conducting fiber and sewn into clothing, thus directly integrating the electronics in the textiles to ensure comfortable, highly wearable "smart" clothing. One application that will be marketable in the near future is a voice-controlled mp3 player whose electronics are directly integrated into the fabric of clothing and packaged to withstand even being laundered. A growing field is techno-medicine worn directly on the body. De Montfort University in Leicester is developing a fabric which contains electrodes that are sensitive to body changes and gases and can detect possible cancerous growth. Other fabrics can, through "micro-encapsulation," give off perpetual aromas that can either be simply pleasant or have healing properties. Also being developed is a Lycra suit containing tiny inflatable capsules that act as artificial muscles which can give elderly people support and mobile stability.

Although there is still a gap between fashion and sophisticated technology, several research laboratories have set out to fill this gap by exploring intelligent clothing's immediate and future possibilities. The World Wide Web is a good guide to laboratories such as MIT's Media Lab, the recently closed Starlab, Charmed Technology, Luminex clothing, International Robotics Jackets, and International Fashion Machines, all of which have set out to "fashion" technology. The alliance between the industries of fashion and information technology is best illustrated with the development of International Robotics Jackets by IRI, which recently patented the "fiber-optic animated motion technology." Its solid-state fiber-optic insertion and animation process is compact and lightweight and can, when inserted into the lining of fabric, provide high-brightness displays of corporate logos, graphics, and messages on any surface, from garments, shoes, or toys to furniture, curtains, and professional clothing, to name just a few of the seemingly unlimited possibilities.

For Stafford (1996), the appearance of an animate surface that is capable of "conducting" thought recalls pre-eighteenth-century visual and, essentially, analogical modes of learning, but refigured now in an actual object. Yet besides allowing us to rethink issues surrounding the role of the visual, the reappearance of analogy has other far-reaching consequences, as it directs us to revisualize how we create attachments in terms of connections and resemblances linking what may appear distinct. The value assigned to objects no longer relies on interpretative frames that uncovered interior, hidden states; now, rather, it hinges on what Alfred Gell (1998) called the abductive quality, or the cognitive "stickiness," of images that have become the focal point of attachment. As we enter exhibitions or watch ads that cater for this new immediate consumption of things as the sole focus of a rather spontaneous attention, we could begin to feel liberated from the trappings of disciplinary knowledge that prevent us from ever fully "owning" a thing we do not really know or understand.

The new responsive fiber surface calls into question existing theoretically framed perspectives on artlike surfaces, such as those of Renaissance art, which offered a view onto another world; or those of a surrealist art, which prided itself on providing surfaces that had no "beyond"; or those of conceptual art, designed as a surface onto which we can project our own thoughts. The responsive textile surface, on the contrary, serves as the carrier of thought, and thus makes us think in terms of associations that are no longer unique and discrete, but that are couched in the materiality of the thing within which the image dwells. We have not yet even begun to realize the full implication of the dawning of a material approach to thinking and knowing, yet we sense that it will certainly revolutionize the way we have regarded what appeared as merely decorative and ornamental.

"Smart" textiles are, intriguingly, simultaneously "art" textiles, reversing the long-standing put-down of textiles as "craft-art." As intelligent textiles begin to be integrated into contemporary artworks, and used by fashion designers rather than commercial labs, artists and designers will be put into a new position. The development of responsive textile art will lead to questions about the role of the artist as researcher and about the importance of collaborations and networks between artists, scientists, programmers, and engineers. Yet while artworks claim to actually make relationships between forms that we have to acknowledge, the new textiles point out that we can no longer ignore their ability to do these things.

The importance of the technologically designed "intelligent object," however, reaches well beyond a vision of a new bright future ruled by connectivity, not division. The insight that thought can conduct itself in things allows us to question whether the capacity of objects to be thoughtlike is merely a product of a new technological development, and thus unprecedented in history. The patterned weave that effects conductivity in techno-textiles suggests, to the contrary, that the model on which conductivity is based is derived from things that fill the storerooms of our museums yet have largely failed to be analyzed other than as objects of discursive thought. The advent of the intelligent object may not just herald a new future, but also offer us unprecedented opportunities both to open up a new perspective on things previously regarded as mute, and to question the nature of the thought that conducts itself in things.

THINGS IN MIND

It is by now a truism that images are good to think with (Bloch 1991; Stafford 1996; Lévi-Strauss 1969); yet we are still far from certain about the nature of the thought that wraps itself in iconic form. The most heavily trodden field is linguistic iconicity, where language acts as a sort of veil with the effect of allowing any number of choices in interpretation (Sperber and Wilson 1986: 9ff). Such are the productiveness of metaphorical statements that much work has been devoted to unraveling the indexical or logical nature of linguistic iconicity, so as to explain how metaphors can be effectively deployed in social contexts (Sperber 1977; Tilley 1999). Visual and material iconicity, on the other hand, leaves comparatively little to the imagination and, given its often brute factuality, remains largely mute in analysis so long as we are prepared to acknowledge connectivity as intrinsic only to words, not to things.

Our museum storerooms are filled with objects whose woven or linear surfaces appear to be merely "decorative" and of little or no consequence for those concerned with the more "serious" matters of life. It is their abstract surface pattern that sets these objects apart from more naturalistic representations in a way that recalls nineteenth-century distinctions between craft and art and appears to prohibit an analysis that moves much beyond the cognitive appraisal of symmetry.[16] Pattern drawn in a continuous motion on a plane surface has faired particularly badly compared with the analysis of geometric information couched in more naturalistic form (Layard 1936; Munn 1973).[17] We readily cherish the knowledge that paintings in fifteenth-century Italy were openly searched for geometric riddles and valued for the complexity of problem solving they showed, and that artists in Italian Renaissance culture were also respected mathematicians (Baxandall 1975), yet we lack analyses that extend this exploration to things that have fallen out of the category of art because of their apparent utilitarian value.[18]

The question of whether we can maintain such divisive approaches has been rekindled with the analysis of one such "utilitarian" object which existed in the shadow of the burgeoning field of pre-Columbian art history which recognized Maya glyphs as art, but turned a blind eye to the *khipu*, which seemed merely an extension of folk craft (Ascher and Ascher 1981). The khipu is an assemblage of colored knotted cords used by the Inca for census and bookkeeping around the time of the Spanish conquest. Each consists of a main two-ply cord made of wool or cotton, with others suspended from it, which in turn may have yet further pendants—without any prescribed limit to the branching. The meaning of a khipu is determined by the length and color of the cords, the way the cords are connected together, and the types of knots in each knot cluster, as well as by the relative placement of the knots—each aspect being part of a logical-numerical data recording system. The knots served as "counters" that, together with color and string, packaged magnitude or quantitative information in number form, translated into a visual label; the khipu thus allowed for the easy and portable transmission of complex knowledge. Recent work on the khipu underscores the importance of dispelling the long-standing assumption that they constituted a simple utilitarian and mnemonic device (Quilter and Urton 2002). Taking the tactility of the knotted cords at face value, Quilter and Urton (2002) propose that the material characteristics of the label entails a synthesis of word and number; it is the material label assigned to quantitative information that allows one to extend the analysis of the khipu as a system of counting to one of narrative "accounting."

It is largely on the back of khipu that a disciplinary field known as "ethno-mathematics" has emerged from the interdisciplinary work of American folklore studies (Ascher 1991; Urton 1997; Eglash 1999). It is to this hinterland of mathematics, and its prospects for those whose work involves the decorative, the material, and the kinesthetic that I want to turn now.

At stake is the analytical purchase of tracking mathematical ideas that may have informed the making of things, even if applied intuitively. Often derided as lacking systematic application, which only an established theory can assure, intuitive mathematics is found to underlie knowledge technologies such as navigation, tracking, and mapping, as well as the types of estimation and calculation found in mundane tasks such as grocery shopping (Lancy 1983; Lave, Murtaugh, and de la Roche 1985; Ascher 1991). Ethno-mathematics attracted those engaged in establishing the universality of human cognition against the backdrop of an evolutionary and developmental theory of cognition that found many followers in the wake of the demise of behavioral psychology (Piaget 1952; Zaslavsky 1973; Hallpike 1979; Mimica 1988; Crump 1990; Wassmann and Dasern 1994).

Embattled in proving or disproving the merit of an externalized and abstracted theory of mathematics over practical, applied cognition, those who work in this field have remarkably never lost sight of the data on which their theories came to be founded. These data are taken from diverse areas such as music, poetry, and dance; from art and architecture; from cosmology and ethno-science; and from games and chance (Crump 1990: vii; see also Gombrich 1984). They display the nature of what in anthropology we have come to call "formulaic thought," which is typically found in ritual contexts and yet classically represented in things that derive their predicating potency from their analogical relation to the most ordinary aspects of everyday life. Yet although such things are clearly closely guarding the secrets of the close relationship between thinking and being in culture, neither anthropology nor its neighboring disciplines have allowed ethno-mathematics into the inner circle of theory making. The reasons are complex but may stem from hesitating to adopt a philistine attitude toward a subject matter that, on the face of it, is accessible only to specialists.

It may once have sufficed to show, when evidence points to a reliance on fingers and material tokens for counting, that mathematical thinking abounds even in the absence of abstract mathematical reasoning. To pin the degree of abstraction of mathematical principles and the abandonment of embodied or material counters on an evolutionary and developmental scale has certainly been tempting (see Piaget 1952; Butterworth 1999). I believe, though, that the questions bound up with objects that play such an obvious role in thinking are too important to be assigned to the dustbin in this manner. One such question concerns the orthodoxy of mathematical thinking and its reliance on the tangibility inherent in the making of things that have definite material qualities.

THE PROBLEM WITH MATHEMATICS

As we generally associate mathematics with arithmetic, it is useful to recall its much wider scope. Mathematics utilizes sets of intuitions, such as number, angle, distance, volume, direction, length, symmetry, space, probability, dimension, smoothness, infinity, and many others. It gives these intuitions a precise language and a method for making exact deductions, calculations, and analogies. It also presents the complications and richness of these ideas, and the structures required to represent them.

The trouble with mathematics, in fact, is not to be found in its subject matter but is couched in the recent history of the discipline, which has turned its back on its own reliance on material representation in favor of a mentalist perspective (Banchoff 1990; Barrow 1992). No other theoretical development in mathematics had as much impact on the science and technology of today as the invention of topology, but conversely, no other part of mathematics has witnessed as systematic a forgetting of its roots in modeling and representation. Topology is the study of how objects retain their shape under deformation; it involves the rethinking of geometry from an observable reality to a logical system in which multiple perspectives reflect a "decentered" spatial cognition. As the new science of geometry, topology found its breakthrough in the nineteenth century with the modeling of the Klein bottle and the Rieman surface, both representing two-dimensional non-Euclidean geometry in shapes that have become archetypal for twentieth-century modernism (Mankiewicz 2000: 126–132).

The study of topology was long in the making. Ever since Euclid's *Elements* appeared in the third century B.C., Euclidean geometry had been heralded as the most perfect of mathematical systems. However, one assumption continued to provoke mathematicians to question the basic premise of Euclidean geometry. This was Euclid's fifth postulate, which states (Mankiewicz 2000: 126): "If a straight line falling on two straight lines makes the interior angles on the same side less than two right angles, the two straight lines, if produced indefinitely, meet on that side on which the angles are less than the two right angles." In the eleventh and the thirteenth century, but particularly from the seventeenth century onward, numerous attempts were made to disprove this postulate.

What was all the fuss about? Quite simply, it was the nature of space itself that was at stake. Euclid's geometry had rested on a one-point perspective embedded in a mechanical worldview where all internal matters could be observed and causally explained by external factors. Establishing a self-consistent geometry other than Euclid's meant that mathematics could branch out into logical paper worlds defined in terms of internal, relational factors. A nonmechanical conception of space was born which has made it possible to regard geometric representations as transformations that were now explained in terms of connectivity between regions of space, and with the rise of computing such transformations could be tracked. New genetics, new biology, and new physics have all been made possible by the question of self-organization invoked by the new study of topology (Barrow 1992).

The fact that geometric objects retain their properties under deformation was known and applied to an understanding of organic forms by D'Arcy Wentworth Thompson (1961) in his work *On Growth and Form*. Thompson turned the recognition of the reality of nonmechanical systems of transformation into a tool, known as the Venn Diagram, whose usefulness in tracking the generative capacity inherent in the formal properties of objects inspired Claude Lévi-Strauss to develop his theory of structuralism (1963) and spawned a generation of scholars who, even after the demise of structuralism, held firmly to the notion of transformation of manifold form.

Science preferred to forget the roots of its pathbreaking discovery in the making of simple models (Stafford 1991). This did not mean, however, that representation itself ceased to play a role in mathematical thinking. On the contrary: the twentieth century witnessed boundary-crossing collaborations between artists, designers, architects, and mathematicians as never before. The close relation between mathematics and art is recalled by Max Bill (1995: 7), who famously stated, "Just as mathematics provides us with a primary mode of cognition, and can therefore enable us to apprehend our physical surrounding, so too, some of its basic elements will furnish us with laws to appraise the interactions of separate objects, or groups of objects, one to another. Again since it is mathematics that lends significance to these relationships, it is only a natural step from having perceived them to desiring to portray them. This in brief is the genesis of a work of art." The possibility of a visual mind that feeds on images, once merely an esoteric brief for artists, had become a common expectation (Emmer 1995).

The common interests of modernist art and mathematics merge in the visualizing of the fourth dimension. Belief in a fourth dimension encouraged artists to depart from visual reality and to reject the system of one-point perspective that for centuries had portrayed the world as three-dimensional. The full impact of the visualization of the fourth dimension was realized in mathematics only with the advent of computer modeling. Its rediscovery by mathematics was inspired by works such as those produced by the American artist David Brisson, who developed the concept of hypersolids in the 1950s and produced perspective and orthogonal projection drawings as well as three-dimensional models of four-dimensional polytopes (Brisson 1978). His *Hyperanaglyph*, a four-dimensional form projected onto three dimensions, established him as a leader in the visualization of higher solids. In 1975 he coined the term *hypergraphics*, which came to denote both a concept and a technical process which transcended traditional methods of making images with new methods of visualization that could blend contemporary thinking in art and science. Much of the hypergraphic artwork is mathematically precise and enhanced by materials, colors, surfaces, textures, methods of construction, and so on (Banchoff 1990).

There is, as Max Bill (1995: 8) suggested, a danger in mistaking this suggestion modernism provokes—that art is based on principles of mathematics—for an assumption that art is a plastic or pictorial interpretation of the latter. In fact, mathematics and art are analogous processes of concrete thinking, "the building up of significant patterns from the ever changing relations, rhythms and proportions of abstract forms, each one of which, having its own causality, is tantamount to a law onto itself" (ibid.). In her most recent work, Marcia Ascher (2002: 3) speaks of "mathematical ideas" that are "integrated into the contexts in which they arise, as part of the complex of ideas that surround them" (Asher 2002: 3). Navigation, calendrics, divination, religion, social relations, or decoration all rest on mathematical ideas without those ideas emerging as a category or as distinct groupings of algebra, geometry, model building, or logic.[19]

Arguably, the investigation of art and mathematics has been hindered, rather than helped, by the seeming ubiquity of mathematics in cultural activity: in the construction of houses and other buildings, in the making of textiles and baskets, in the turning of flat pieces of cloth or animal skins into clothing or shoes that fit, in the making of calendars to mark seasons, in the planning of storage facilities or the layout of gardens and fields, in the depiction of kinship relations, or in ornamentation, as well as in spiritual or religious practices that are often aligned with patterns occurring in nature or in ordered systems of abstract ideas. Frequently intuitive, but not explicitly stated as such, mathematical ideas appear to be as much an undercurrent of social life as religious ideas are. Despite the interesting proposition that it could be mathematical ideas that provide the connection between ritual and everyday thought, math is as much the product as the precedent of these forms of praxis.

THE ART OF DESCRIBING

There are many potential mathematical ideas that can be shown to be essential to a host of situations. What such situations have in common is that they demand forethought that goes beyond mere practical logic to the description of what is known to connect a present moment with a future state. Navigation is one such situation where descriptive knowledge based on individual experience must be made accessible to others in a way that is transferable from a situation in the past to another one in the future; maps or models, such as the stick charts of the Marshall Islanders described by Marcia Ascher, are ways of representing relations in space from a perspective that is not egocentric (Ascher 2002: 89–125; Alpers 1984).

Such modeling of spatial relations brings to the fore an art of describing that captures knowledge not in classificatory form, but in a relational and analogical mode. Marshall Islanders' sea charts thus depict through a geometric arrangement of sticks and shells the interplay of oceanographic phenomena and landmasses. The islanders deploy an idealized version, called *mattang*, of shapes and motions in the sea and at the land-sea interface as an explanatory model that teaches how to connect analogical space to the spatial relations known through experience (Ascher 2002: 97). The *mattang*'s idealized geometry of swell interactions are then translated into other stick charts, called *meddo*, where the lines and curves visualize the actual result of the wind and sea interaction in and around a group of real atolls, which vary in size, shape, and underwater topography (ibid.: 116).

The art of describing thus brings into focus the salient connection between things. Carlo Ginzburg (1983) famously described this kind of knowledge as involving lower-level intuitive thinking, commonly found among hunters who use material clues to project a likely future outcome. While arguably inherently linked to intentional, strategic thinking, descriptive knowledge, if not captured in physical models or maps, must be spontaneously recallable for it to be useful and deployable as a technical skill. Where secrecy overrides the need for public access, it usually befalls specialists to securely handle such knowledge in ways that allows outcomes of situations to be predictable.

We could assume that a deeply personal and emotional involvement in descriptive knowledge would cancel out the role of analogical models. Yet there is only a small step between knowing how to describe what is or is likely to happen and securing that it does happen. Analogical models involving mathematical ideas are thus as likely to be utilized in divination as they are in other situations that appear to have a purely utilitarian value (Ascher 2002: 5–7). It is interesting that formulaic thinking invested with personal and emotive qualities tends to utilize binding, possibly due to its textured, tangible, but also transformative and thus simultaneously concrete as well as abstract quality (see Küchler 1999; Strohecker n.d.).

Like the Andean khipu, the Caroline Islander's knotted coconut frond has both numerical as well as topological features that count and thus give an account of knowledge which is not overt, but whose very description serves to shed light on a possible future (Ascher 2002: 6–8). The Caroline Islands are an archipelago of small atolls situated in Micronesia. Although its numerous islands are separated by vast stretches of ocean, all inhabitants share a concern with divination to gain information and understanding about ongoing or future happenings. Divination creates, through a series of knots, an analogous space inhabited by destiny spirits whose journey shows up directions to be taken as much as a Marshall Islander's stick chart paves the way through the ocean. The following description of procedure is taken from Marcia Ascher's recent *Mathematics Elsewhere*:

> To begin a divination session, the diviner splits the young leaves of coconut trees into strips, and then they or the client makes a random number of knots in each strip. The knotted strips are placed in a pile from which four strips are randomly selected. The first of the strips is held between the thumb and the forefinger, the second between the forefinger and the middle finger, and the third between the next fingers, respectively. Finally the knots on each strip are counted, returning, however, to a count of 1 each time a count of 4 is exceeded. (2002: 8)

From the first two strips a pair of counts is obtained that is precise in its numerical value; this value, in turn, is analogous to the particular relational value of destiny spirits. Together, numerical value and place value offer information from an analogical perspective on points of connection in the world of the unseen from which favorable or unfavorable consequences of distant events can be deduced.

Curious as it may appear, the example reveals the interrelation of hand or finger movement, the gestured conception of geometric space (in this case of knots), and the apprehension of number skills (Butterworth 1999: 244–246). Neurologically situated in the motor cortex, the gestured representation of numerosity underscores the importance of the tactility and textured quality of counters. We thus have come back full circle to topology, a science that appears to all outsiders impossibly abstract yet rests on the tangible qualities of the knot.

The material quality of bound surfaces, of drawn or placed lines, or of woven planes thus may resonate with thought of a particular kind. Though quite unspecific in nature, while making tangible and visible connections that lie at the heart of the art of describing, the textured surfaces of things carry what may be called formulaic thought. Through the embedding of formulaic connections that are made materially manifest in things, things can become the starting point for realizing such connections in other domains of life. Formulaic, materialized thought makes possible associative strings, fashionably described by the term *abduction*, that connect up the word of the material with the world of humankind. Our understanding of what facilitates such mindfulness thus cannot proceed without the study of materiality.

CONCLUSION

Far from being unprecedented, the advent of the intelligent object reaches back to premodern notions of animate matter whose artificial evocation drove Enlightenment's art and industry. The creation of conductive materials, however, fuses the material and the mindful in a new way that will provoke a radical rethinking of the models upon which we have based our understanding of cognition.

No longer can we regard things as passive receptacles of discursive thought; rather, as we have indeed long suspected, thought can conduct itself in things, and things can be thoughtlike. Arguably, we have, in the past, made the mistake of taking this claim too literally, by assuming that this thought that resides in the surface of things would equal words, concepts, or even categories. Intelligent objects have shown to us already that the kind of thought that dwells in the surfaces of things is often abstract, conductive, and connective in nature. It is this connectivity, essential to the art of describing, which has become of vital importance in capturing how things partake not just in thinking, but also in the shaping of knowledge. Fields that long were regarded out of bounds for those engaged in the study of humanity, such as mathematics, may become a new gateway for opening up the study of the material to the study of cognition and vice versa. Those who defined *Homo sapiens* as a toolmaker may have been right for more reasons than they knew.

NOTES

1. This point was made by Barbara Maria Stafford (1991) in the introduction to her *Body Criticism*, which discusses the rise of anatomical collecting in the early nineteenth century. In the Enlightenment, of course, humankind *was* at the helm of culture.

2. See Rosenfield (1992: 4) in relation to memory. See Edelman 1992 for a theory of an embodied mind.

3. The opposing positions have become synonymous with Dan Sperber's "The Epidemiology of Representation" (reprinted in his *Explaining Culture*, 1997) for the "brain" camp and Gerald Edelman's *Bright Air, Brilliant Fire* (1992) for the embodiment camp.

4. For a general overview of the history of the theory of mind, see S. Rose 1995.

5. See Schultz and Lavenda 1987: 5.

6. See also Johansen's 1992 article "Materielle oder matererialisierte Kultur?"

7. For a pathbreaking account of images as driving the economy of mind, see Bloch's 1991 article, "Language, Anthropology and Cognitive Science"; a converse, body-centered approach is found in Warnier's 2001 article, "A Praxeological Approach to Subjectification in a Material World."

8. There is now a vast cognitive anthropology literature available, of which the most central are Hirschfeld and Gelman 1994; Boyer 1994; and Whitehouse 2001. On issues of representation, see Hall 1997.

9. See also Bloch 1991.

10. Bredekamp (1995) on the Kunstkammer and the evolution of nature, art, and technology.

11. In Alfred Gell's (1992) sense.

12. We now are accustomed to subscribing to electronic resources such as search engines or to purchase programs that offer access to resources.

13. See S. Kingston 2003.

14. I have made this point in relation to the *malanggan* material in my own work; see Küchler 2002.

15. The main journal in this field is called *Fashion Theory*, and Berg publishes a book series titled "Dress, Body, Culture." An additional field has developed around the study of cloth, and two journals are currently dedicated to it: *Textile: The Journal of Cloth and Culture* and *Textile History*. There are also several professional associations related to this interest with their own journals: the Costume Society of Great Britain, the Costume Society of America, the International Textile and Apparel Association, and the Textile Society of America.

16. For a critical approach to pattern, see Gell 1998. On symmetry, see Washburn and Crowe 1992.

17. For a new perspective on this, see Eglash 1997.

18. See Kemp 2000; Henderson 1983; Field 1997; Emmer 1995.

19. See Ascher 2002: 4. There is no space for developing this point, but there is an interesting argument to be had about Kant—i.e., that mathematics cannot a priori be a category; it must be itself a product of objectification.

REFERENCES

Alpers, S. 1984. *The Art of Describing*. New Haven: Yale University Press.

Ascher, M. 1991. *Ethno-mathematics: A Multicultural View of Mathematical Ideas*. Pacific Grove, Calif.: Brooks/Cole.

——. 2002. *Mathematics Elsewhere*. Princeton, N.J.: Princeton University Press.

Ascher, M., and R. Ascher. 1981. *The Code of the Quipu*. Ann Arbor: University of Michigan Press.

Banchoff, T. 1990. *Beyond the Third Dimension*. New York: Freeman.

Barrow, J. 1992. *Pi in the Sky: Counting, Thinking and Being*. Oxford: Oxford University Press.

Baxandall, M. 1975. *Painting and Experience in Fifteenth-Century Italy*. Harmondsworth: Penguin.

Benjamin, W. 1969. *Illuminations*. Ed. H. Arendt, trans. H. Zohn. New York: Schocken Books.

Bill, M. 1995/1949. "The Mathematical Way of Thinking in the Visual Arts of Our Time." In M. Emmer, ed., *The Visual Mind*. Cambridge: MIT Press.

Bloch, M. 1991. "Language, Anthropology and Cognitive Science." *Man* (n.s.) 26.2:183–198.

Bourdieu, P. 1977. *Outline of a Theory of Practice*. Cambridge: Cambridge University Press.

Boyer, P. 1994. *Cognitive Perspectives of Religious Symbolism*. Cambridge: Cambridge University Press.

Bredekamp, H. 1995. *The Lure of Antiquity and the Cult of the Machine: The Kunstkammer and the Evolution of Nature, Art, and Technology*. Trans. Allison Brown. Princeton, N.J.: Princeton University Press.

Brisson, D., ed. 1978. *Hypergraphics: Visualizing Complex Relationships in Art, Science and Technology*. Boulder, Colo.: Westview.

Butterworth, B. 1999. *The Mathematical Brain*. London: Macmillan.

Crump, T. 1990. *The Anthropology of Number*. Cambridge: Cambridge University Press.

Edelman, G. 1992. *Bright Air, Brilliant Fire: On the Matter of the Mind*. New York: Basic Books.

Eglash, R. 1997. "Bamana Sand Divination: Recursions into Ethnomathematics." *American Anthropologist* 99.1:112–122.

Eglash, R. 1999. *African Fractals: Modern Computing and Indigenous Design*. New Brunswick, N.J.: Rutgers University Press.

Eisenberg, A. 2003. "For the Smart Dresser, Electric Threads That Cosset You." *New York Times*, February 6.

Emmer, M., ed. 1995. *The Visual Mind: Art and Mathematics*. Cambridge: MIT Press.

Field, J. V. 1997. *The Invention of Infinity: Mathematics and Art in the Renaissance*. Oxford: Oxford University Press.

Forty, A., and S. Küchler. 1998. Introduction to A. Forty and S. Küchler, eds., *The Art of Forgetting*. Oxford: Berg.

Gell, A. 1992. "The Technology of Enchantment and the Enchantment of Technology." In J. Coote and A. Shelton, eds., *Anthropology, Art and Aesthetics*. New York: Oxford University Press.

——. 1998. *Art and Agency*. Oxford: Oxford University Press.

Ginzburg, C. 1983. "Clues: Morelli, Freud, and Sherlock Holmes." In Umberto Eco and Thomas Sebeok, eds., *The Sign of Three: Dupin, Holmes, Peirce*. Bloomington: Indiana University Press.

Gombrich, E. 1984. *The Sense of Order*. London: Phaidon.

Hall, S. 1997. *Representations: Cultural Representation and Signifying Practice*. London: Sage.

Hallpike, C. R. 1979. *The Foundations of Primitive Thought*. Oxford: Clarendon Press.

Harris, M. 1975. *Culture, People, Nature: An Introduction to General Anthropology*. New York: Harper and Row.

Henderson, L. 1983. *The Fourth Dimension and Non-Euclidean Geometry in Modern Art*. Princeton, N.J.: Princeton University Press.

Hirschfeld, L., and S. Gelman, eds. 1994. *Mapping the Mind: Domain Specificity in Cognition and Culture*. Cambridge: Cambridge University Press.

Hollander, Anne. 1993. *Seeing Through Clothes*. Berkeley: University of California Press.

Ingold, T. 2001. "Making Culture and Weaving the World." In P. M. Graves-Brown, ed., *Matter, Materiality and Modern Culture*. London: Routledge.

Johansen, U. 1992. "Materielle oder materialisierte Kultur?" *Zeitschrift für Ethnology* 117:1–15.

Keane, W. 1997. *Signs of Recognition*. Berkeley: University of California Press.

Kemp, M. 2000. *Visualisations: The Nature Book of Art and Science*. Oxford: Oxford University Press.

Kingston, S. 2003. "Form, Attention and a Southern New Zealand Lifecycle." *Journal of the Royal Anthropological Institute* 9.4:681–709.

Kline, M. 1953. *Mathematics in Western Culture*. Harmondsworth: Penguin.

Küchler, S. 1999. "Binding in the Pacific: The Case of Malanggan." *Oceania* 69.3:145–157.

——. 2002. *Malanggan: Art, Memory and Sacrifice*. Oxford: Berg.

Kwint, M., and C. Breward, eds. 1999. *Material Memories: Design and Evocation*. Oxford: Berg.

Lancy, D. F. 1983. *Cross-Cultural Studies in Cognition and Mathematics*. New York: Academic Press.

Latour, B. 1999. *Pandora's Hope*. Cambridge: MIT Press.

Lave, J., M. Murtaugh, and O. de la Roche. 1985. "The Dialectics of Grocery Shopping." In B. Rogoff and J. Lave, eds., *Everyday Cognition*. Cambridge: Harvard University Press.

Layard, J. 1936. "Maze Dances and the Ritual of the Labyrinth in Malekula." *Folklore* 47:123–170.

Lévi-Strauss, C. 1963. *Structural Anthropology*. Trans. C. Jacobson and B. G. Schoepf. New York: Basic Books.

——. 1969. *Totemism*. London: Pelican.

Mankiewicz, R. 2000. *The Story of Mathematics*. London: Cassel and Co.

Mimica, J. 1988. *Intimations of Infinity: The Mythopoeia of the Iqwaya Counting System and Number*. Cambridge: Cambridge University Press.

Munn, N. 1973. *Walbiri Iconography: Graphic Representation and Cultural Symbolism in a Central Australian Society*. Ithaca, N.Y.: Cornell University Press.

Parker, R. 1984. "Femininity as Feeling." In *The Subversive Stitch: Embroidery and the Making of the Feminine*. London: Womens Press.

Piaget, J. 1952. *The Child's Conception of Number*. London: Routledge and Kegan Paul.

Quilter, J., and G. Urton, eds. 2002. *Narrative Threads: Accounting and Recounting in Andean Khipu*. Austin: University of Texas Press.

Quinn, B. 2002. *Techno Fashion*. Oxford: Berg.

Reyna, S. 2002. *Connections: Brain, Mind and Culture*. London: Routledge.

Rose, S. 1993. *The Making of Memory: From Molecules to Mind*. New York: Anchor Books.

Rosenfield, I. 1992. *The Strange, Familiar, and Forgotten: An Anatomy of Consciousness*. 1st ed. New York : Knopf.

Schultz, E., and R. Lavenda. 1987. *Cultural Anthropology*. New York: St. Paul.

Shore, B. 1996. *Culture in Mind: Cognition, Culture, and the Problem of Meaning*. Oxford: Oxford University Press.

Sperber, D. 1977. *Rethinking Symbolism*. Cambridge: Cambridge University Press.

——. 1997. *Explaining Culture*. London: Routledge.

Sperber, D., and D. Wilson. 1986. *Relevance*. Oxford: Blackwell.

Stafford, B. 1991. *Body Criticism: Imaging the Unseen in Enlightenment Art and Medicine*. Cambridge: MIT Press.

——. 1996. *Good Looking: Essays on the Virtue of Imagery*. Cambridge: MIT Press.

——. 1999. *Visual Analogy: Consciousness as the Art of Connecting*. Cambridge: MIT Press.

Strohecker, C. n.d. "Why Knot?" PhD diss., Epistemology and Learning Group, Media Arts and Sciences, Massachusetts Institute of Technology.

Swartz, M., and D. Jordan. 1976. *Anthropology: Perspectives on Humanity*. New York: Random House.

Thompson, D. W. 1961. *On Growth and Form*. Abridged ed. Cambridge: Cambridge University Press.

Tilley, C. 1999. *Metaphor and Material Culture*. Oxford: Berg.

Tylor, E. B. 1913. *Primitive Culture: Researches into the Development of Mythology, Philosophy, Religion, Language, Art and Custom*. 5th ed. London: Murray.

Urton, G. 1997. *The Social Life of Numbers: A Quechua Ontology of Numbers and Philosophy of Arithmetic*. Austin: University of Texas Press.

Warnier, P. 2001. "A Praxeological Approach to Subjectification in a Material World." *Journal of Material Culture* 6.1.

Washburn, D., and B. Crowe. 1992. *Symmetries of Culture*. 2nd ed. Seattle: University of Washington Press.

Wassmann, J., and P. R. Dasern. 1994. "Yupno Number System and Counting." *Journal of Cross-Cultural Psychology* 25.1:78–94.

Whitehouse, H., ed. 2001. *The Debated Mind: Evolutionary Psychology versus Theoretical Ethnography*. Oxford: Berg.

Young, J. E. 1993. "The Counter-Monument: Memory against Itself in Germany." In *The Texture of Memory: Holocaust Memorials and Meaning*. New Haven: Yale University Press.

Zaslavsky, C. 1973. *Africa Counts: Number and Pattern in African Culture*. Boston: Prindle.

NIGEL THRIFT

Beyond Mediation: Three New Material
Registers and Their Consequences

WHAT IS INSIDE IS ALSO OUTSIDE

This chapter is concerned with the changing nature of materiality insofar as that is the result of new infrastructures which question our usual concept of mediation because they are neither "inside" nor "outside" but are the work of mediation itself.[1] In particular, I will concentrate my gaze on the production and reproduction of new kinds of materiality through new paratextual machineries that both embody particular notions of scientific cognition and simultaneously distribute them by creating generalized surfaces. I will argue that this kind of materiality is moving on apace, and that it is producing new levels of universal experience, a new set of infrasensible realities that are both incarnate instrumentalities (Sobchack 1992) *and* new means of imagining the world.[2] I will develop this thesis of invention within convention through the examples of three different registers: screen, software, and (in less detail) body. In other words, what surrounds us and is embedded in us is increasingly something approximating the machine reality so beloved in the nineteenth century. But this is a reality that depends on the new senses of "human" and "material" that have now begun to exist—new "natural" attitudes that are effacing the old body politic and constructing a different kind of physic (Protevi 2001).

Of course, it would be very easy to depict developments like these as just further chapters in the disenchantment of the world, in which all human life becomes absorbed by scientific knowledge, an account which has a long pedigree (most famously, Sellars 1963). As Jürgen Habermas (2003: 106) puts it, "The vanishing point of this naturalization of the mind is a scientific image of man drawn up in the extensional concepts of physics, neuro-physiology or evolutionary theory, and resulting in a complete desocialization of our self-understanding as well." But I think that such depictions of the atrophy of the senses and mind are wrong, not only because, as Habermas himself points out, they confuse the stated and usually hyperbolic goals of research programs with reality—and are often absurdly reductionist to boot—but also because they are predicated on stable conceptions of what it is to be human and material and even calculative which are, I think, descried by the developments themselves, as well as by the voluminous anthropological record (e.g., Ascher 2002; Verran 2001). New materials produce new surfaces. New frames produce new forms of calculation. New avenues for, and com-binations of, the senses are called into being. Perhaps if these things could be measured, we would find more senses, more possibilities for thinking.

In general, I want to argue that these three different registers all are different forms of reanimation of the world which involve the active media-tion of machines[3] of various kinds in sending new kinds of life to us, chang-ing the nature of "us" as a result (Thrift 2004). But, more than that, the whole world of "dead" matter is transformed into an animistic cosmos, rendered as pure expression, thereby producing uncanny echoes with the naturalistic epicurean worldview summarized and extended by Lucretius,[4] but a worldview brought into existence by mechanical invention. As Moore (2000: 68–69) puts it in relation to the cinema in a passage which can easily be generalized out:

> Things and people are made of the same atomic material, just as in the cinema they are made of the same celluloid material. . . . celluloid takes on the animistic character of the atom, the single element that fashions the universe. Film images, including those of people, are things, and all things on celluloid are thereby reanimated and thus directly expressive.

This chapter is in three main parts, each of which considers a different register. The first two parts concentrate on the evolution of two different generalized surfaces and the way that these surfaces have been composed by a continuous interplay between practical use and theoretical appreciation, each feeding off the other to produce new sensoria. One way of looking at these developments is to think of them as a new set of surfaces gradually covering the world, a kind of second skin of new forms of attention, of new body parts calling forth new counterparts—of something, to quote Wordsworth, "far more deeply interfused."[5] So the first part of the chapter looks at *screens* and at the way in which this surface has been laid down over time. A full history is not possible in the confines of a short article, so instead I therefore concentrate on one of the earliest and most influential attempts to produce a "screenic" sensorium, namely German psychophysics. I will attempt to trace out just a few of the many ways that psychophysics intervened in a developing screenic consciousness, especially via the medium of film. The subsequent part of the chapter considers the advent of another generalized surface which has taken place since the 1940s: *software*. Particular consideration is given to the way that this development is producing a new layer of mechanical writing which is increasingly directing the world, a writing which is itself informed by a broad-ranging set of theories, most notably theories that appeal to biology. Then, in the third and concluding part of the chapter, I will argue that it is possible to see another generalized surface now starting to be laid down as a result of a whole series of linked developments, one that depends on a wholesale reworking of the human body. This reworking has consequences that are only now being thought through but promise even greater changes in the sense of material.

What seems certain is that developments like these are privileging different conceptions of materiality which emphasize a much greater sense of (to take in a much overused word) performativity. A more flexible sense of what the world is is being extemporized by "nonhuman" actors which are increasingly acting within the corral that used to be called human, making new materials that are not one thing or the other but weave together elements of both.

SCREEN: SHOWING THOUGHT

Screens showing various forms of photoplay have become a constant of Western societies, especially since the last decades of the nineteenth century. But in recent years, a complete ecology of screens has become apparent which can be thought of as a vast geographical web of perception, a vast epistemic apparatus, and a new form of inhabitation. Screens are one of the constants of everyday life, communicating, informing, entertaining, affecting life, simply being there providing ground. Their grip is constant and unremitting. In her book *Ambient Television*, Anna McCarthy (2000) lists just some of the locations where screens now routinely crop up, including in bars, hotel lobbies, airport lounges, and doctor's waiting rooms. To these one might add all the other screens that inhabit our lives now; computer screens in all their diversity, the screens on the back of aircraft seats, and even, presaging things to come, large roadside advertising screens and screens that cover the whole of buildings, making it difficult to decide what a wall consists of.

In many cases, it is difficult to know what these screens are doing as they vie for our attention. Are they simply visual chaff? Are they a means of redefining what counts as touch and grip, remembering Walter Benjamin and Maurice Merleau-Ponty's strictures on the tactility of vision and their understanding of motility as intentionality, as itself a kind of body? Are they practical renditions of the kinds of redefinition of the sign put forward by Gilles Deleuze and Félix Guattari and others which attempts to resuscitate semiology as a set of machinic assemblages that can include biological codings or organizational forms, assemblages in which the sign is transmuted into a moving form of expression, a vector of subjectivation?

One way of thinking about screenness is to regard it as one of the chief exemplars of the first coherent wave of postsocial relations. Thus, a number of authors argue that we have come to live in a "postsocial" world in which social principles and relations are "emptying out" and being replaced by other cultural elements and relationships, and most notably objects, which are not only increasing in volume and so becoming present in just about every encounter but also changing their character, becoming something like an interactive and constantly unfolding second skin.

> Postsocial theory analyses the phenomenon of a disintegrating "traditional" social universe, the reasons for this disintegration and the direction of changes. It attempts to conceptualise postsocial relations as forms of sociality which challenge core concepts of human interaction and solidarity, but which nonetheless constitute forms of binding self and other. The changes also affect human sociality in ways which warrant a detailed analysis in their own right. (Knorr Cetina 2001: 520)

This is an interesting view, but it has its problems. Most obviously, it conjures up the idea of a "traditional" world in which the social did not work through and with objects, as if this were possible. An alternative way of thinking usually takes as its starting point the work of Gabriel Tarde at the turn of the nineteenth and twentieth century (see Latour 2002; Toews 2003) and works forward to modern manifestations like actor-network theory. In this conception, the social, understood as a series of consolidated and persisting social facts, does not exist. Rather, endlessly changing and contingent compositions emerge out of a complex of difference and repetition which necessarily involves all manner of combinations of humans and nonhumans. Such a view continually calls into question what those categories might mean and continually insists upon a symmetry of avidity and possession between them.

Whatever the case may be—and I incline to the latter point of view—Knorr Cetina takes as one of her chief examples of postsociality the screen. For her, the screen constantly calls forth a need to be attended to: it is a "wired, programmed, and content-filled, textually elaborated surface that fascinates through its ability to frame and present a world" (Knorr Cetina and Bruegger 2002: 397), or at least worldlike features which conform to many of the strictures of writers like Schutz (a certain tensioning of consciousness, a specific form of self-experience, a specific form of sociality, and a specific time horizon). This the screen does through its ability to produce particular forms of "awakeness" which may be more or less intense but which grip attention at some level even though they may involve the loss of conventional representational function.[6] The screen, in other words, is not a terminus of perception. Some experiences may be reduced by its flicker, but others are amplified (Kracauer 1960).

But what I think is missing from this account (and from many others, I should add) is any sense of the theoretical foreplay that has brought screenness about. It is as if the object is somehow inviolate when, in fact, it has a long intellectual history which is itself determinate of the sensorium that now exists. Many full and only half-formed theories have intertwined with the practical history of screenness, producing what it is that we know now of and sense as a particular form of attention. I will take but one example out of the many prehistories of the screen that are now becoming available (e.g., Crary 1999): the set of theories that became known as psychophysics.

Though now largely forgotten, the German psychophysical tradition was for a long time a major element of Euro-American thought. It formed a bedrock of ideas about how the physical and mental world were co-constituted. It arose from the increasing tendency of psychological research to orient itself toward the empirically grounded natural sciences rather than self-observation—psychology had been regarded as a branch of philosophy—and is usually counted to have begun with the work of Gustav Theodor Fechner, who argued in *Elemente der Psychophysik* (1860) that everything which can be perceived by introspection had an objective organic correlate. Therefore, stimulated physical changes were bound to produce alterations in the activity of psychic perception. In turn, this view made it possible to carry out all manner of experiments by systematically varying the intensity of particular stimuli and then following the perception of differences. Probably the best-known psychophysicist was Wilhelm Wundt (1832–1920), who argued for a physiological psychology that was concerned exclusively with "an investigation of empirically groundable relations between physiological processes" (cited in Schluchter 2000: 67). Wundt had been a research assistant to Hermann von Helmholtz and had a varied career, including appointments at Heidelberg, Zurich, and Leipzig. At Leipzig, he established the first experimental psychological laboratory in the world. Wundt was particularly known for making the distinction between what he called perception and apperception. *Perception* was the term reserved for early-forming pre-aware responses to the world, the responses that allow us to hit a tennis ball or drive a car. Then, after perception, comes the fuller, more reflective consciousness of *apperception*. The investigation of perception blossomed, with the result that the time structure of the body began to be explored in much greater detail, often using the new technologies of movement. For example, it was shown that the brain anticipates and interpolates properties like motion and color in advance of the actual event (the famous "phi effect").[7]

Other important psychophysicists included Emil Kraepelin, who laid the foundation for the study of experimental psychopathology by establishing schools at Heidelberg and Munich, and Hugo Münsterberg, an émigré to the philosophy department at Harvard University.[8] It is difficult now to understand how influential psychophysics was at the time. The reasons for this eminence were threefold. First, it stated a new and robust kind of material-ism[9] through a sustained "campaign against consciousness, volition, intro-spection and other distinctive aspects of mind" (Daston 1982: 88). Indeed, in the most extreme case, any notion of an active will was jettisoned. Second, its tenets were simple enough that they traveled easily and widely. Thus psycho-physical ideas made their way across the Euro-American world—and indeed most noticeably to North America[10]—but also traveled across many different and diverse intellectual fields, into general social and cultural theory, into economics, into dance, and so on. Third, these ideas were associated with major changes in the experience of the world. It is to this latter point that I now want to move, for one area where psychophysics was influential was in the interpretation of the practice of photography and then moving pictures. And, as part of that more general movement, I think it is possible to argue that shards of psychophysical thinking sank into the ambient background of everyday life and have stayed there ever since, revealing themselves only on the off chance, as the photograph and moving pictures have transmuted into a more general "screenness" which is now so pervasive that it surely counts as a background to everyday life, a "qualculative" screenness that lies some-where between interpretation and calculation.

Elements of this translation happened early on. Take the case of Münster-burg (Andrew 1976, 1984). He can be seen as a part of the history of the formation of a vast epistemic apparatus of screenness which rises in con-junction with the invention of cinema (Crary 1999). Münsterburg strove to find a method for analyzing and measuring the emotions, which is par-ticularly relevant to this chapter's first theme of screenness because he linked it to the evolving medium of film (or what he called photoplay) in which "the perception of movement is an independent experience which cannot be reduced to a simple seeing of a series of different positions" (cited in Sob-chack 1992: 207). For him, measuring emotion was a psychophysical quest: "Motion is to a high degree the product of our own reaction. Depth and movement come to us in the moving picture world. . . . We invest the impression with them" (cited in Bruno 2002: 259). Thus, for Münsterburg, film is a visceral event which by mobilizing bodily sensation mobilizes the passions. Film therefore makes an impression which first comes into the visual field as bodily sensation. As he puts it (cited in Crary 1999: 313):

Impressions which come to our eye at first awaken only sensations. But it is well known that in the view of modern physiological psychology our consciousness of the emotion itself is shaped and marked by the sensations which arise from our bodily organs. As soon as such abnormal visual impressions stream into our consciousness, our whole background of fusing bodily sensations becomes altered and new emotions seem to take hold of us.

According to Münsterburg, what is seen at the movies, including motion, is produced in a mental process of binding. Speaking of this "spectatorial imperative," Münsterburg therefore claims that "the objective world of outer events . . . [is] adjusted to the subjective movements of the mind. The mind develops memory ideas and imaginative ideas; in the moving pictures they become reality" (cited in Bruno 2002: 259). And that process may take very little time at all as time grabs space; "not more than a sixteenth of a second is needed to carry us from one corner of the globe to the other, from a jubilant setting to a mourning scene. The whole keyboard of the imagination may be used to serve the emotionalizing of nature" (cited in ibid.: 260–261).

Psychophysics could not have existed without the invention of a set of machines that both constituted and revealed a certain kind of attention, acting as theoretical statements, means of representation, and proofs of efficacy within a general ideo-motor network of forces (Crary 1999). The machines were more than simple intermediaries: they were part and parcel of how attention was thought, for they constituted part of a

> shifting and intervening space of socially articulated physiological functions, institutional imperatives, and a wide range of techniques, practices, and discourses relating to the perceptual experience of a subject in time. Attention here is not reducible to something. The attention in modernity is constituted by these forms of exteriority, not the intentionality of an autonomous subject. Rather than a faculty of some already formed subject, it is a sign, not so much of the subject's disappearance as of its precariousness, contingency and insubstantiality. (Crary 1999: 45)

Since Münsterburg's day, psychophysical considerations of movement and image have, if anything, become more apposite. Even as they have sunk into the taken-for-granted background of the screen, their interpretation and operation has become a part of that constantly moving preconscious frontier between action and cognition in which so much of what is attended to first shows up.

I will end this section with a speculation. Psychophysical ideas have continued to reverberate, not least in providing, in their experimental fervor, the ground for much modern cognitive science. But early on in the twentieth century they were already meeting significant opposition from those opposed to such extreme physiological reductionism, most notably from Henri Bergson. Bergson's doctoral thesis (1913), *Time and Free Will*, is in large part a critique of psychophysical ideas and a reformulation. For Bergson (1913: 70),

> all psychophysics is condemned by its origin to revolve in a vicious circle, for the theoretical postulate on which it rests [that quantity can be equated to quality] condemns it to experimental verification, and it cannot be experimentally verified unless its postulate is first granted. The fact is that there is no point of contact between the unextended and the extended, between quality and quantity. . . . In truth, psychophysics merely formulates with precision and pushes to its extreme consequences a conception familiar to common sense. As speech dominates over thought, as external objects, which are common to us all, are more important to us than the subjective states through which each of us passes, we have everything to gain by introducing into them, to the largest possible extent, the representation of their external cause. And the more our knowledge increases, the more we perceive the extensive behind the intensive, quantity behind quality, the more also we tend to thrust the former into the latter, and to treat our sensations as magnitudes.

Bergson's thought was equally influential, and his ideas, too, have come down to the present in everyday life. Indeed, I think one could argue that the large part of recent thinking that has simply been a rerun of a number of Bergson's ideas on time and evolution has been able to bubble up because so many of its tenets have also become present in the screenic sensorium—objections to, and reformulations of, psychophysics converted into material presuppositions. It might even be that the psychophysical conception represents one take on the screen, stressing its ability to produce a measurable and functional intensity, while Bergson's take (or at least Deleuze's later reinterpretation) represents a more qualitative format based on the idea of what is surely an impossible level of absorption (Crary 1999). Each conception hails a different kind of screenic subjectivity.

ANOTHER VIEWPOINT: WRITING THOUGHT

I have considered the genesis of screenness. I now want to turn to a different kind of background, one invented more recently, namely software (Thrift and French 2002). There is considerable argument about what software does consist of, but what is sure is that it is part of a vast epistemic apparatus rather like screens, though one that is, both literally and metaphorically, far less easy to see. The technical substrate of Euro-American societies has altered decisively as software has come to intervene in nearly all aspects of everyday life and has become a part of the taken-for-granted. Yet, as a term in general use, "software" dates only from the 1950s. Its genesis was, of course, bound up with the invention of the first electronic computers and, more particularly, the first use of these computers for business applications in the late 1950s, a development which in turn led to the growth of companies specializing in the supply of software (Hayles 2003). At the time, it referred to just a few lines of code[11] that acted as a bridge between input and output. But particularly over the last twenty years, software has grown from a small thicket of mechanical writing to a forest of code covering much of the globe in a profusion of over two hundred different languages. Code runs all manner of everyday devices, from electric toothbrushes to microwave ovens, from traffic lights to cars, from mobile phones to the most sophisticated computers.

This gradual evolution of the original few kernels of software into what Clark (2001) aptly calls "wideware" is surely extraordinarily important for understanding the current direction of Euro-American cultures, and especially the nature of Western cities. Increasingly, spaces like cities—where most software is gathered and has its effects—are being run by mechanical writing, are being beckoned into existence by code. Yet, remarkably, this development has gone almost unrecorded. Why might that be? Four immediate reasons come to mind.

First, software takes up little in the way of visible physical space. It generally occupies micro-spaces. Second, software is deferred. It expresses the copresence of different times, the time of its production and its subsequent dictation of future moments. So the practical politics of the decisions about production are built into the software and rarely recur at a later date. Third, software is therefore a space that is constantly in between, a mass-produced series of instructions that lie in the interstices of everyday life, pocket dictators that are constantly expressing themselves. Fourth, we are schooled in ignoring software, just as we are schooled in ignoring standards and classifications (Bowker and Star 1999). Software very rapidly takes on the status of background and therefore is rarely considered anew.

It would be easy at this point to fall back on some familiar notions to describe software's grip on spaces like cities. One would be hegemony. But that notion suggests a purposeful project, while software consists of numerous projects cycling through and continually being rewritten in code. Another notion would be haunting. But again the notion is not quite the right one. Ghosts are ethereal presences, phantoms that are only half there and that usually obtain their effects by stirring up emotions—of fear, angst, regret, and the like. Software is more like a kind of traffic between beings, wherein one sees, so to speak, the *effects* of the relationship. What transpires becomes reified in actions, body stances, general anticipations (Strathern 1999). Software is best thought of, then, as a kind of absorption, an expectation of what will turn up in the everyday world. It is, in other words, a part of a "technological unconscious" (Clough 2000), a means of sustaining presence which we cannot access but which clearly has effects, a technical substrate of unconscious meaning and activity. "It is, after all, against the natural unity of self-heard voice that Derrida places technicity, the machine, the text, writing—all as bearers of unconscious thought" (Clough 2000: 17). Increasingly, therefore, as software gains this unconscious presence, spaces like cities will bear its mark, bugged by new kinds of pleasures, obsessions, anxieties, and phobias which exist in an insistent elsewhere (Vidler 2000; Thrift 2001). Software quite literally conditions existence, but very often "outside of the phenomenal field of subjectivity" (Hansen 2000: 17).

There is a more general reason, as well, that software remains so little considered. We still cleave to the idea of spaces like the city as populated by humans and objects that represent each other via words and images, which makes it very difficult to mark this new territory. Software does not fit this representational model, for its text concerns words doing things, determi-

does Hegemony ever suggest this?

nate presentations in particular contexts "below the 'threshold' of representation itself" (Hansen 2000: 4). Because software "affects our experience first and foremost through its infrastructural role, its import occurs prior to and independently of our production of representations" (ibid.: 4). Seen in this paratextual way, software is perhaps better thought of as a series of "writing acts" (rather than speech acts) of a Bakhtinian or Derridean kind, which have a "heuretic" rather than an analytic dimension (Ulmer 1989), based upon the inventive rather than the analytic, in which language is both message and medium. Thus:

> Within the previous instauration, founded on the alphabet, the only way to access theory *per se* was through metaphor, every concrete manifestation of the idea being equivalent to its deformation. Metaphors were necessary because the intellect was otherwise incapable of grasping the idea of true illumination. With the new instauration, the artefacts of theory are no longer metaphors. Instead, the object is no longer the deformation of the idea, but is its real embodiment. Now the idea, or thought, rests within, or out of, the object itself. (Lechte 1999: 141)

It is something of a moot point whether this means that software—as a nonrepresentational form of action—"does not rely on the activity of thinking for its ontogenesis" (Hansen 2000: 19) or whether it is simply another kind of distributed thinking in which yet more human functions are delegated into "the automatic, autonomous and auto-mobile processes of the machine" (Johnson 1999: 122), as part of a process of externalization and extension of the vital based, for example, on the apprehension of the human body as simply "too slow" (Stiegler 1998). Whichever the case, what we can see is that what counts as "life" itself comes into question as new material syntheses emerge and embed themselves (Doyle 1997).

The term *software* is not an easy one to work with for one more reason. In the literature, all kinds of different meanings of *software* are routinely conflated, with the result that different kinds of efficacy are muddled up. Thus, at the most general level, software is often considered to be part of a more general structure of writing, a vast Derridean intertext which has gradually become a system without edges and which includes all manner of "coded" writings rooted in a base cybernetic metaphor (Johnson 1992; Hayles 2003; Kay 2000). In such a conception, software is both a measure of how writing is now done and a new kind of cultural memory based upon discourses of information as pure digital technique. In a second guise, software can be considered as another step in the history of writing as a supplement to spoken language: here we have Derrida's critique of phonocentrism and logocentrism made flesh (Derrida 1998; Aarseth 1997).

> An ever-increasing number of people are spending more hours per day using written—that is, keyboard—language rather than spoken language. Within a few years, computers will be enriching nearly every household of the developed world. Human life in these countries is centering on, and contracting to, electronic text and international networking, and moving away from speech. Soon written language might be more prominent world-wide than spoken language. A different sort of language is emerging from this artificial interfacing: an "oral-written language" occupying a special position between spoken and written language. Computers now regularly communicate with one another, too, through writing—that is, through written programming languages—without human mediation. Writing has, in this way transcended humanity itself. We have redefined the very meaning of writing itself. (Fischer 2001: 316)

Within this general shift, software can be thought of as a set of new textualities: programming languages, e-mail and other forms of "netspeak" (Crystal 2000), and software packages, each with their own textual protocols and paratexts, which have produced their own linguistic turn. Then, in a third guise, software can be thought of as the product of the actual writing of code, as the outcome of the "practised hands" (McCulloch 1996) of a comparative handful of people who are able to mobilize skills that even now are difficult to describe to produce effective forms of code (Lohr 2001). Such skillful interaction between humans and machines has been the object of numerous studies in the human-computer interaction (HCI) and computer-supported cooperative work (CSCW) literatures which all show that there is no straightforwardly observable exchange between discrete purified entities called "human" and "machine" but rather a series of conversations which demonstrate that software is not a simple intermediary, but rather a Latourian "mediary" with its own powers. Then software has one more guise. It can be couched as the guts of a set of commodities: Web sites, software packages, games, animated movies, and so on, which are dispensed via the medium of screenness and have become part of a more general cultural ambience. In contemporary societies, the ubiquity of the screen reciprocally guarantees software's cultural hold, letting it assume an important role in most interactions.

To summarize, whatever its exact guise, software clearly stands for a new set of effectivities—agents of "material complexification," to use Hansen's (2000) phrase—which have added a whole set of new whorls and ridges to the business of life.

As with the screen, software comes loaded up with a theoretical background which has very often sunk into the interstices of the lines of code. The background I want to concentrate on here is that provided by biological theories of various kinds. Almost since its inception, the biological and the informational have been intertwined in software. Right at the birth of the modern computer, the new machines were framed in biological terms. For example, from the 1940s John von Neumann had been interested in the connections between computational logic and biology. The classic *First Report on the EDVAC* (1945) likened electronic circuits to neurons and the input and output part of the design to organs. Since those early days, biological metaphors have, if anything, become more prevalent in the world of software and computation. In some senses, this prevalence should not be thought of as surprising. After all, many early cybernetic and systems theory metaphors were in part drawn from reductive notions of the workings of the biological domain, and one might argue, as Sedgwick (2003: 105) has, that the problem was that the "actual computational muscle" was not as yet available to operationalize them. And biology itself has seen a long, drawn-out war between those who believe that the biological domain can be reduced to a set of computations and those for whom the organism cannot be reduced to the sum of its parts. For the former group of biologists, at least, cybernetic models were simply a natural extension of machinic thinking which had clear and obvious antecedents in the nineteenth century (but might even be traced farther back, to the Cartesian separation of man from machinelike animals). This kind of thinking finds its latest incarnation in a "predictive biology" which hopes to model the behavior of individual cells in computers (and then tissues, organs, and even organisms).

Thus, software writers' initial flirtations with the biological may be seen as nothing more than business as usual, but with a slightly more exotic tinge.

But, at the same time, these flirtations were also expressing a need for something more. As software became more complex, reductive models became increasingly inappropriate. Software more and more resembled a kind of ecology in which thickets of new code surrounded the strands of legacy code which often stayed unchanged through many versions of a package. And as the sheer length of code became a problem in its own right, all kinds of unexpected interactions and hidden errors came into play. The constant tinkering of numerous programmers started to produce programs large enough and complex enough to make it possible to regard programs as forming their own ecologies, complete with various niches and evolutionary tendencies and even forms of symbiogenesis. The result was that programs have increasingly come to be framed as environments in their own right, motivated by quasi-biological principles. Interestingly, such descriptions are used both by those only interested in programs as manifestations of narrow technique and by those who argue that programs occupy the realm of something more. For example, Nardi and O'Day (1999) want to argue for the creation of healthy "information ecologies" which will exhibit several biological principles: systemic interrelation, diversity, coevolution, keystone species, and the importance of local habitation.

Added to this, new algorithms were introduced which were clearly modeled on biological lines. The longest-running tradition of this kind of work is to be found in the so-called genetic algorithm and the more general phenomenon of evolutionary computing (Mitchell 1996). Though there were antecedents, it is generally agreed that genetic algorithms were invented by John Holland in the 1960s as a way of mixing natural and artificial systems (Holland 1975). Holland introduced a population-based algorithm that ran on evolutionary lines and could therefore produce programs that were able to do massively parallel searches (in which many different possibilities are explored simultaneously), that were adaptive, and that sought out complex solutions. In evolutionary computation, the rules are typically based on an idea of natural selection with variations induced by crossover and/or mutation. However, evolution has not been the only biological metaphor used to motivate computer programs. Another has come from neuroscience. Connectionism, which includes such models as neural networks, denotes the writing of computer programs inspired by neural systems. In connectionism, "the rules are typically simple 'neural' thresholding, activation spreading, and strengthening or weakening of connections. The hoped-for emergent behaviour is sophisticated pattern recognition and learning" (Mitchell 1996: 4). It would be possible to go on, but hopefully the point is made: among the rustle of many computer programs, biological analogy now holds sway.

To summarize, on a whole series of levels, one of the most prevalent theoretical descriptions of programming environments is now a biological one. And this description operates at a number of levels: as a means of framing programs, as a means of framing wider technological systems, and as a means of making assumptions about how the world turns up. Perhaps it is no surprise, then, that the next logical step is now being made: to try to produce "artificial" "life," either in the form of programs that exhibit lifelike agency in silico, so to speak, or in the form of robots which, through physical extension, are able to take on certain characteristics of bodily intelligence which are otherwise impossible to reproduce (Thrift forthcoming).

A FINAL VIEWPOINT: THE BODY THOUGHT ANEW

The message of this chapter has been that the object surfaces which interpose with our bodies are forming a new kind of carapace, a set of informational surfaces which, by dint of the combination of machine and theory, creates a new "inside" which is also simultaneously an "outside": "Everywhere, prophylactic skins slip into the space between people and things, forming seductive planes of contact as well as protective barriers" (Lupton 2002: 41). In turn the proliferation of these generalized surfaces and the reworkings of inside/outside that they bring with them is producing a new apprehension of materiality, a materiality that involves a kind of reanimation of the world through all manner of intentional objects (Attfield 2000; Marks 2000).

But we cannot stop there. Though this conclusion is necessarily speculative, it is grounded in recent developments which suggest another twist to the tale. For the biological body is itself under renovation, producing a further generalized surface and a further meshing of the inside and the outside in new and viscous combinations of "natural" attitude.

Additions to and modifications of the human body used to be restricted to relatively simple tools like spectacles, walking sticks, artificial limbs and block shoes, simple means of intervention such as various forms of contraception, the use of opiates, and primitive vaccinations, and simple means of decoration like cosmetics. But new additions and modifications to the human body range far and wide, taking in a whole series of interventions which lie somewhere between the prosthetic, the medical, and the cosmetic, including routine laser eye treatment, transplantations that now include not only heart and lungs but may also soon include the face, cochlear implants, all manner of interventions in the manipulation of embryos, the growth of new organs, various kinds of haptic engineering, mass chemical mood alteration through so-called pharmacological scalpels (e.g., Prozac, Ritalin), the cure of sexual dysfunction (e.g., Viagra), new methods of plastic surgery, genetic and pharmacogenomic diagnosis and manipulation, the mass use of body imaging technologies, and so on. Over the longer term, technologies like nanotechnology may also have an impact.

In turn, these changes are the basis of huge and growing "health care" industries whose economic impacts are highly significant. The pharmacology and biotechnology industries form one strand of this industrial complex. Another strand is formed by various forms of biomechanics, bioengineering, and medical instruments more generally. Finally, a large part of the information technology industry is increasingly taken up with biological applications and analogies (e.g., biomimetics). Other nascent industries may well become relevant in the future.

In other words, there is every reason to believe that we are only at the very start of developments in "technology inhabiting us" (Virilio 1998: 24), which will produce considerable change in accepted notions of what it is to be embodied as the body becomes a dynamic map of sociotechnical change—a tendency only heightened by wide-ranging anxieties about body image (e.g., around both obesity and eating disorders), which are both symptom and cause.

Such developments have already raised a whole series of pressing questions: What new technologies or combinations of technologies (e.g., nanotechnology, robotics, wearables, wireless, chemicals, genetics, pharmacogenomics) are most likely to have an impact on the human body in the next ten years? How can technologies be designed to interface better with the human body (e.g., through the growth of interactive personalized technologies which are increasingly able to react to bodily states like emotions)?

What aspects of human performance (e.g., hearing, eyesight, touch, endurance, memory, confidence and other forms of emotional literacy, appearance and attractiveness, sexuality) are most likely to be extended in the next ten years, and with what social consequences? What are the ethics of the new body-changing technologies (e.g., of mass mood manipulation through chemicals like Prozac and Ritalin [Breggin 1993; Healy 1997, 2002; Fraser 2003; Mertzl 2003])? What are the social consequences when technology allows those with money to ever more explicitly buy enhanced bodily performance—longer life spans, for example, and general alleviation of the effects of aging—and leaves those without money with no such prospects? How will people think about their bodies and minds when they will be increasingly able to track the condition of, intervene in, and even design aspects of them?—in other words, how robust are our notions of, for example, human nature, gender, and ethnicity? What will happen to systems of health care as "health" is increasingly aligned not just with freedom from illness but with choices about what kind of "better than well" (Elliott 2003) body to inhabit? What decisions will government have to take to avoid new forms of biological inequity, and what counts as democracy under these conditions? The list of questions and corresponding dilemmas could be extended almost indefinitely.

What seems clear is that the next change in the nature of materiality will be concentrated here. For what is being shown up is the inbuilt human tendency to change the environment being extended into the body, with the result that human embodied experience—that experience which is still so often considered to be a constant even as surfaces like screens and software have questioned its reach and meaning—is being decisively changed. Key human affordances are now being altered. This is phenomenology with the addition of chemical, surgical, computational, and genetic prostheses. This is Merleau-Ponty and Edmund Husserl and Martin Heidegger on drugs.

It is possible to produce a whole series of important warnings about the politics of this kind of surface. There are warnings about corporate and government power. Large corporations' and governments' power to define what counts as human—the politics of life itself (Rose 2001)—has entered a new phase. There are warnings about overstatement. For example, the increase in diagnostic power that is currently being brought about has not produced a corresponding increase in prognostic power (Webster 2002).

There are warnings about risk, as "science has acquired the power to define situations beyond what it knows about them" (Santos 1995: 47). And there are warnings about coherence: these developments may not add up and, at least in the first instance, are more likely to produce piecemeal changes in experience. At the same time, these developments have produced a heartening counter-politics which I want to end on. For though it is true that the surfaces of materiality are being changed in line with the interests of the powerful, I hope to have shown in the previous section that what is actually emerging is something much less direct and much more nuanced, a materiality which still retains spaces for contingency, complexity, and a sense of wonder.[12] Previous generalized surfaces like screen and software have in part been defined by an active counter-politics (from all manner of alternative and subversive uses of film to the open source software movement), and the same is happening with the inhabitation of the body. For example, patients are attempting to produce their own embodied experience by demanding a much greater say in not only the treatment of the disease they are suffering from but also how it is researched (e.g., Callon, Méadel, and Rabehoraisoa 2002). Though these may be small events, they have the ability to produce large consequences. Further, they remind us not only that "thoughts are no less physical than objects, thinking is no less physical than acting" (Brown 2003: 162) but also that thinking is now bound up with objects to such an extent that "everyday life presents us not with phenomenology's reduction of the world to consciousness, but with consciousness reconceived as something dispersed throughout the material world" (ibid.: 188).

NOTES

This chapter is a summary and extension of arguments that have unfolded over a number of papers now. It is very much a product of joint action. I would particularly like to thank Bruno Latour, Danny Miller, John Urry, and Sarah Whatmore for inspiration and encouragement. Parts of the section "Another Viewpoint: Writing Thought" draws on Thrift and French 2002 and is reprinted with permission.
1. The section heading is taken from Goethe, cited in Merleau-Ponty 1964: 58.
2. Through a project that they called the "naturalisation of phenomenology," the late Francisco Varela and others attempted to add the findings of cognitive science to phenomenology in ways which bear some remarkable similarities to the general tendencies that I want to describe, but my claim is that their work should be seen as part of a more general cultural process.
3. Of course, one of the important questions now becomes exactly what a "machine" is.

4. Famously put in the passage in *De Rerum Natura*: "If the spirit is not ruled by necessity in all its acts, if it escapes domination and is not reduced to total passivity, it is because of this slight deviation of atoms, in a place and time determined by nothing" (cited in Hadot 2002: 120). It is becoming something of a commonplace to identify the point at which materialism both breaks free and simultaneously stultifies with Marx's doctoral thesis on Epicurus and Democritus (e.g., Bennett 2000; Tiffany 2000). In that thesis, Marx only half-animates the world. He uses Epicurean philosophy (itself derived from the naturalistic theories of the Prescoratics, and especially Democritus) to show that the "sensuous appearance" of the world is built into its very character and is not just a subjective impression. But then, falling back on Democritus's earlier work, he only allows that sensuousness limited play, so he ends up with a standard philosophical anthropology in which exaltation, enchantment, and derangement are marked as the preserve of the human. "By the time Marx gets done with it, the fighting spirit of matter has settled down into the bodies of men" (Bennett 2000: 120). Marx therefore loses touch with the appreciation of agency within nature that Epicurus's fundamental atomic property of swerve affirms.

5. After all, it is worth remembering that skin is itself a multilayered, multipurpose organ that "shifts from thick to thin, tight to loose, lubricated to dry, across the landscape of the body. Skin, a knowledge-gathering device, responds to heat and cold, pleasure and pain. It lacks definitive boundaries, flowing continuously from the exposed surface of the body to its internal cavities. It is both living and dead, a self-repairing, self-replacing material whose exterior is senseless and inert while its inner layers are flush with nerves, glands and capillaries" (Lupton 2002: 29).

6. Knorr Cetina and Bruegger (2002) use appresentation rather than representation to refer to much of the content of screens, in that what is being displayed does not derive from any confirmed correspondence with the world but rather consists of instantaneous and relentless information continually flashing up. In making this distinction, they uncannily echo Wundt's distinction between apperception and perception (see below).

7. Consciousness, in other words, takes time to construct; we are "late for consciousness" (Damasio 1999: 127). In the 1960s, this insight was formalized by Libet using the new body recording technologies. He showed decisively that an action is set in motion before we decide to perform it: our "average readiness potential" is about 0.8 seconds, although cases as long as 1.5 seconds have been recorded. In other words, "consciousness takes a relatively long time to build, and any experience of it being instantaneous must be a backdated illusion" (McCrone 1999: 131). Thus, "much of our mental lives are lived in a twilight world of not properly conscious impulses, inklings, automatisms, and reflexive actions. . . . Our brains seem designed to handle as much as possible at a subconscious level of awareness, leaving focal consciousness to deal with tasks which are either particularly difficult or novel" (McCrone 1999: 135). Of course, none of this is meant to suggest that conscious awareness is just a cipher. Rather, we can say that the preconscious comes to be more highly valued and, at the same time, conscious awareness is repositioned as a means of focusing and sanctioning practice.

8. Where he maintained a laboratory!

9. Which, it might be added, a number of its adherents then spent much time and effort trying to deny.

10. See, for example, James 1890, which takes in many German psychophysical experiments but also expresses considerable skepticism about the mechanistic outlook they transmit.

11. One of the pressing empirical questions becomes exactly what is left of this theory once it has been put through the mangle of practice, and especially all the subsequent testings and additions which distort any vision. To my knowledge, no ethnographic work has directly confronted this question.

12. Currently there are many attempts to reinstate exaltation, enchantment, and derangement into materialism in a way already prefigured by writers like Bela Balasz and Walter Benjamin (cf. Andrew 1976, 1984), not least by exploring the poetic dimension as a kind of stuttering diagnostic (but see Abu-Lughod 1999). We cannot escape the fact that our means of depicting the world is bound up with what we take the world to be. But it is not the case that this is just a simple depiction of the real by the imagination. For material substance is "a medium that is inescapably informed by the pictures that we compose of it. We are confronted with the idea that a material body, insofar as its substance can be defined, is composed of pictures, and that the conventional equation of materialism and realism depends on the viability of the pictures we use to represent an invisible material world" (Tiffany 2000: 9). But what is slowly being realized is that there are other "songlines" too, songlines which are not drawn just through media like the body and the movement of air but also through the screen, software, and other mundane para-ethnographic apparatuses (Holmes and Marcus 2004; Miyazaki and Riles 2004) which all add their own determinations. What comparatively recent developments like the screen and software have also demonstrated is the degree to which, even in what may initially seem like tightly structured environments, encounters can produce their own unpredictable, indefinite but still crucial baggage, "a quality of 'thisness,' an unreproducible being-only-itself, that stands over and above its objective definition" (Massumi 2002: 222) and cannot be reduced to one or the other. What we see unfolding, then, is a sense of materiality which is prompting some striking equivalents to the spiritual exercises of Hellenistic philosophy. For what is being aimed at—in among manifolds that may appear cold and impersonal—are arts of living that emphasize transformation but can also acknowledge the simple pleasures of existing, all set within the context of a definition of human existence which has become ever more expansive (Hadot 1995, 2002; Thrift 2001).

REFERENCES

Aarseth, E. J. 1997. *Cybertext: Perspectives on Ergodic Literature*. Baltimore: Johns Hopkins University Press.

Abu-Lughod, L. 1999. *Veiled Sentiments: Honor and Poetry in a Bedouin Society*. Updated ed. Berkeley: University of California Press.

Andrew, J. D. 1976. *The Major Film Theories: An Introduction*. Oxford: Oxford University Press.

——. 1984. *Concepts in Film Theory*. Oxford: Oxford University Press.

Armstrong, T. 1998. *Modernism, Technology and the Body: A Cultural Study*. Cambridge: Cambridge University Press.

Ascher, M. 2002. *Mathematics Elsewhere: An Exploration of Ideas across Cultures*. Princeton, N.J.: Princeton University Press.

Attfield, J. 2000. *Wild Things*. Oxford: Berg.

Balazs, B. 1970. *Theory of the Film: Character and Growth of a New Art*. New York: Dover.

Bennett, J. 2000. *The Enchantment of Modern Life: Attachments, Crossings and Ethics*. Princeton, N.J.: Princeton University Press.

Bergson, H. 1913/2001. *Time and Free Will: An Essay on the Immediate Data of Consciousness*. New York: Dover.

Blumenberg, H. 1983. *The Legitimacy of the Modern Age*. Cambridge: MIT Press.

Bowker, G. C., and S. L. Star. 1999. *Sorting Things Out: Classification and Its Consequences*. Cambridge: MIT Press.

Breggin, P. 1993. *Toxic Psychiatry*. London: Fontana.

Brown, B. 2003. *The Sense of Things: The Object Matter of American Literature*. Chicago: University of Chicago Press.

Bruno, G. 2002. *Atlas of Emotion: Journeys in Art, Architecture and Film*. New York: Verso.

Callon, M., C. Méadel, and V. Rabehoraisoa. 2002. "The Economy of Qualities." *Economy and Society* 31:194–217.

Clark, A. 2001. *Mindware: An Introduction to the Philosophy of Cognitive Science*. Oxford: Oxford University Press.

Clough, P. T. 2000. *Autoaffection: Unconscious Thought in the Age of Technology*. Minneapolis: University of Minnesota Press.

Crary, J. 1999. *Suspensions of Perception: Attention, Spectacle and Modern Culture*. Cambridge: MIT Press.

Crystal, D. 2000. *Language and the Internet*. Cambridge: Cambridge University Press.

Damasio, A. 1999. *The Feeling of What Happens: Body and Emotion in the Making of Consciousness*. New York: Vintage.

Daston, L. 1982. "The Theory of Will versus the Science of Mind." In W. Woodward and T. G. Ash, eds., *The Problematic Science: Psychology in Nineteenth Century Thought*, 88–115. New York: Praeger.

Deleuze, G. 1993. *Difference and Repetition*. New York: Columbia University Press.

Derrida, J. 1998. *Archive Fever*. Chicago: University of Chicago Press.

Doyle, R. M. 1997. *On Beyond Living: Rhetorical Transformations of the Life Sciences*. Stanford: Stanford University Press.

Elliott, C. 2003. *Better Than Well: American Medicine Meets the American Dream*. New York: Norton.

Fischer, S. R. 2001. *A History of Writing*. London: Reaktion.

Fraser, M. 2003. "Material Theory: Duration and the Serotonin Hypothesis of Depression." *Theory Culture and Society* 20:1–26.

Habermas, J. 2003. *The Future of Human Nature*. Cambridge: Polity Press.

Hadot, P. 1995. *Philosophy as a Way of Life*. Oxford: Blackwell.

———. 2002. *What Is Ancient Philosophy?* Cambridge: Harvard University Press.

Hansen, N. 2000. *Embodying Technesis: Technology Beyond Writing*. Ann Arbor: University of Michigan Press.

Harrington, A. 1996. *Re-enchanted Science: Holism in German Culture from Wilhelm II to Hitler*. Princeton, N.J.: Princeton University Press.

Hayles, K. 2000. *How We Became Posthuman*. Cambridge: MIT Press.

———. 2003. *Writing Machines*. Cambridge: MIT Press.

Healy, D. 1997. *The Antidepressant Era*. Cambridge: Harvard University Press.

———. 2002. *The Creation of Psychopharmacology*. Cambridge: Harvard University Press.

Holland, J. 1975. *Adaptation in Natural and Artificial Systems*. Ann Arbor: University of Michigan Press.

Holmes, D., and G. Marcus. 2004. "Cultures of Expertise and the Management of Globalization: Toward the Re-functioning of Ethnography." In A. Ong and S. Collins, eds., *Global Assemblages*. Malden, Mass.: Blackwell.

Ihde, D. 1979. *Experimental Phenomenology*. New York: Paragon.

James, W. 1890/1950. *The Principles of Psychology*. 2 vols. New York: Dover.

Johnson, C. 1992. *System and Writing in the Philosophy of Jacques Derrida*. Cambridge: Cambridge University Press.

Johnson, J. 1999. "Ambient Technologies, Meaning Signs." *Oxford Literary Review* 21:117–134.

Kay, C. 2000. *Who Wrote the Book of Life? A History of the Genetic Code*. Stanford: Stanford University Press.

Kittler, F. 1999. *Gramophone, Film, Typewriter*. Stanford: Stanford University Press.

Knorr Cetina, K. 2001. "Postsocial Relations: Theorizing Sociality in a Postsocial Environment." In G. Ritzer and B. Smart, eds., *Handbook of Social Theory*, 520–537. London: Sage.

Knorr Cetina, K., and U. Bruegger. 2002. "Inhabiting Technology: The Global Lifeform of Financial Markets." *Current Sociology* 50:389–405.

Kracauer, S. 1960. *Theory of Film: The Redemption of Physical Reality*. Princeton, N.J.: Princeton University Press.

Kwa, Chunglin. 2002. "Baroque and Romantic Conceptions of Complex Wholes in the Sciences." In J. Law and A. Mol, eds., *Complexities: Social Studies of Knowledge Practices*, 23–52. Durham, N.C.: Duke University Press.

Latour, B. 2002. "Gabriel Tarde and the End of the Social." In P. Joyce, ed., *The Social in Question: New Bearings in History and the Social Sciences*, 117–132. London: Routledge.

Lechte, J. 1999. "The Who and What of Writing in the Electronic Age." *Oxford Literary Review* 21:135–160.

Lohr, J. 2001. *Go To: Software Superheros from Fortran to the Internet Age*. New York: Basic Books.

Lupton, E., ed. 2002. *Skin: Surface, Substance and Design*. New York: Princeton Architectural Press.

Marks, L. 2000. *The Skin of the Film: Intercultural Cinema, Embodiment, and the Senses*. Durham, N.C.: Duke University Press.

Massumi, B. 2002. *Parables for the Virtual: Movement, Affect, Sensation*. Durham, N.C.: Duke University Press.

May, J., and N. J. Thrift, eds. 2001. *TimeSpace*. London: Routledge.

McCarthy, A. 2000. *Ambient Television*. Durham, N.C.: Duke University Press.

McCrone, B. 1999. *Going Inside: A Tour Around a Single Moment of Consciousness*. London: Faber.

McCulloch, M. 1998. *A Digital Craft: The Practised Digital Hand*. Cambridge: MIT Press.

Merleau-Ponty, M. 1964. "The Film and the New Psychology." In *Sense and Non-Sense*. Evanston, Ill.: Northwestern University Press.

Mertzl, J. M. 2003. *Prozac on the Couch: Prescribing Gender in the Era of Wonder Drugs*. Durham, N.C.: Duke University Press.

Mitchell, M. 1996. *An Introduction to Genetic Algorithms*. Cambridge: MIT Press.

Miyazaki, H., and A. Riles. 2004. "Failure as an Endpoint." In A. Ong and S. Collins, eds., *Global Assemblages*. Malden, Mass.: Blackwell.

Mol, A. 2002. *The Body Multiple: Ontology in Medical Practice*. Durham, N.C.: Duke University Press.

Moore, R. D. 2000. *Savage Theory. Cinema's Modern Magic*. Durham, N.C.: Duke University Press.

Munsterburg, H. 1916/1970. *The Film: A Psychological Study*. New York: Dover.

Nardi, B. A., and V. L. O'Day. 1999. *Information Ecologies: Using Technology with Heart*. Cambridge: MIT Press.

Protevi, J. 2001. *Political Physics: Deleuze, Derrida and the Body Politic*. London: Continuum.

Rose, N. 2001. "The Politics of Life Itself." *Theory Culture and Society* 18:1–30.

Santos, B. 1995. *Towards a New Common Sense: Law, Science and Politics in the Paradigmatic Transition*. London: Routledge.

Schluchter, W. 2000. "Psychophysics and Culture." In S. Turner, ed., *The Cambridge Companion to Weber*, 59–80. Cambridge: Cambridge University Press.

Sedgwick, E. K. 2003. *Touching Feeling: Affect, Pedagogy, Performativity*. Durham, N.C.: Duke University Press.

Sellars, W. 1963. *Science, Perception and Reality*. Altascadero, Calif.: Ridgeview Press.

Sobchack, V. 1992. *The Embodied Eye: A Phenomenology of Film Experience*. Princeton, N.J.: Princeton University Press.

Stiegler, B. 1998. *Technics and Time 1: The Fault of Epimetheus*. Stanford: Stanford University Press.

Strathern, M. 1999. *Property, Substance and Effect*. London: Athlone Press.

Thrift, N. J. 2004. "Summoning Life." In P. Cloke, P. Crang, and P. B. Goodwin, eds., *Envisioning Geography*, 81–103. London: Arnold.

——. 2004. "A Geography of Unknown Places." In J. S. Duncan and N. Johnson, eds., *A Companion to Cultural Geography*, 121–136. Oxford: Blackwell.

——. Forthcoming. "Electric Animals: New Models of Everyday Life." *Cultural Studies* 18:461–482.

Thrift, N. J., and S. French. 2002. "The Automatic Production of Space." *Transactions of the Institute of British Geographers*, n.s., 27:309–335.

Tiffany, D. 2000. *Toy Medium: Materialism and Modern Lyric*. Berkeley: University of California Press.

Toews, D. 2003. "The New Tarde: Sociology after the End of the Social." *Theory Culture and Society* 20:81–98.

Turner, S. P. 2002. *Brains/Practices/Relativism: Social Theory after Cognitive Science*. Chicago: University of Chicago Press.

Ulmer, G. 1989. *Teletheory*. London: Routledge.

Verran, H. 2001. *Science and an African Logic*. Chicago: University of Chicago Press.

Vidler, A. 2000. *Warped Space: Art, Architecture and Anxiety in Modern Culture*. Cambridge: MIT Press.

Virilio, P. 1998. *Open Sky*. London: Verso.

Webster, A. 2002. "Innovative Health Technologies and the Social: Redefining Health, Medicine and the Body." *Current Sociology* 50:443–457.

Zimmerman, A. 2002. *Anthropology and Antihumanism in Imperial Germany*. Chicago: University of Chicago Press.

The overstuffed interiors of the second half of the nineteenth
century belonged to the same epoch as the thoughts born in them
and yet were not their contemporaries.
—SIEGFRIED KRACAUER, *History: The Last Things before the Last*

CHRISTOPHER PINNEY

Things Happen: Or, From Which
Moment Does That Object Come?

C learly things make people, and people who are made by those
things go on to make other things. The central question, however, is not whether this does or doesn't happen, but in what kind
of way it happens. What is the modality of this relationship?
Should we think of the process of objectification as akin to the smooth
curves of an oscilloscope, binding people and objects ever closer, or can the
alien and haunting presence of the things that we have made also produce
disjunction and incoherence?

While I agree with much of the critique developed in this book, I find the
solution that appears to hover over it troubling, for in its vision of a more
modest humanity, and one which exists in harmony with those things it
creates, it reinvents an old wheel (which turns too smoothly), rather than
creating a new one. It reinvents an old wheel through its continuing attachment to suture and contemporaneity, what the editor terms in his introduction "a dialectical republic in which persons and things exist in mutual self-
construction and respect for their mutual dependency." Here I will attempt
to delineate how one might advance the critique a stage further by suggesting that in addition to critiquing dominant models of "culture" and "society," we need also to question their epistemological bedfellows: "history"
and "contemporaneity."

The grounds for the critique are clear enough, and most of the contributors to this volume agree on most of what immediately follows. We must start by accepting what I take to be Bruno Latour's central point: that any engagement with materiality must *supercede* the question of culture, rather than oppose it in the name of objecthood. To argue for the "object" powers of objects (as do various forms of technological determinism), or conversely for the personlike power of objects (as does Gell in *Art and Agency*), is simply to intensify the work of "purification"—that is, the impossible separation of subjects and objects, humans and nonhumans. What appear to be opposites (humans and nonhumans) are complementary pairs in a space from which we need to escape.

Consequently, any discussion of materiality that starts and ends with the object is doomed to fail. In configuring materiality as objectness, it accidentally champions one half (objects) of a binary whose other half (subjects) it wishes to attack. Hence it intensifies the work of purification and does not advance the argument. On this, I think, all contributors are agreed.

The purification of the world into objects and subjects cannot be easily undone. It is especially difficult for anthropology, since, as the editor remarks in his introduction, any anthropology that seeks an empirical and ethical grounding will always have to respect the deeply entrenched purificatory dichotomies of its informants.

But this undoing is made doubly difficult by the obvious fact that the human sciences are themselves—historically and epistemologically—a reflection of the self-same process of purification. Bruno Latour has correctly observed that since Émile Durkheim the belief that objects "offer only a surface for the projection of our social needs and interests" has "been the price of entry into the sociology profession" (1993: 52). The artifact becomes an empty space, of interest only because of the "meanings" that invest it with significance. In the battle between the object world and the world of human relations, it is the latter which (through a circular procedure) inevitably triumphs: "To become a social scientist is to realize that the inner properties of objects do not count, that they are mere receptacles for human categories" (1993: 52).

A short-term history might invoke such observations as the starting point for a self-redemptive project in which anthropology seeks to correct the Durkheimian error. We might invoke Marilyn Strathern's wonderful account (1990) of the demise of the object with the rise of a social anthropology and go back to that presocial, pre-Durkheimian practice in search of clues for an alternative possible future. This I understand to be the solution that hovers over this volume: the possibility of a renewed anthropology that has benefited from a process of self-correction.

A historically deeper investigation would suggest that a far more radical assault is required, one that might abolish anthropology and other human sciences altogether. Martin Heidegger makes the following observation in his essay "Age of the World Picture":

> The more extensively and the more effectually the world stands at man's disposal as conquered, and the more objectively the object appears, all the more subjectively, i.e., the more importunately, does the *subiectum* rise up, and all the more impetuously, too, do observation of and teaching about the world change into a doctrine of man, into anthropology. (1977: 133)

The more objectively the object appears, the more subjectively the subject arises, and the more our teaching about the world turns into a doctrine of man, into anthropology. The birth of the object as the domain of the non-human, and the birth of man, are thus coincident. They are symmetrical movements in opposite directions in the process of purification that Latour describes so well. Anthropology as "a doctrine of man" will not get us anywhere in resolving our dilemma: like Durkheimian sociology, it is the problem.

LATE PURIFICATION

From this perspective the recent preoccupation with objects' and images' "social lives" might be seen as a version of what we might term Late Purification. Ostensibly concerned with objects and materiality (and indeed celebrated as being apparently concerned with this), it also entails the further colonization by the social and the subject. Tiring of the totality of the "social," objects are initially invoked as an oppositional domain but quickly succumb (for the reasons that Heidegger and Latour outline) to the hegemonic strategies that dominate social enquiry. Caught within the dichotomous world of purification, they can only ricochet between the essentialized autonomous object and the dematerialized space of things whose only graspable qualities are their "biographies" and "social lives."

For all their brilliant insight, Arjun Appadurai's stress on the "social life" of objects and Nicholas Thomas's investigation of objects' promiscuity might be seen—with the benefit of Latourian hindsight—as the outcome of a particular obsession with the figure of a purified person, with a human-besotted vision of reality. In Appadurai's case, endowing objects with quasi-human characteristics by conceding them a "life" and multiple careers ultimately reinscribes culture's potency through its ability to infinitely recode objects. Likewise, Nicholas Thomas writes that "as socially and culturally salient entities, objects change in defiance of their material stability. The category to which a thing belongs, the emotion and judgement it prompts, and the narrative it recalls, are all historically refigured" (1991: 125). The artifact is eviscerated in the all-powerful context of history or culture. I should note, however, that in a recent article Thomas (1999) revises his earlier position in favor of a view of artifacts as "technologies that created context anew." It also needs to be conceded that my own earlier work has stressed what Elizabeth Edwards described as photography's "polysemous nature, lack of fixity and context-dependent modes of making meaning" (Edwards 2001: 14).[1]

The fate of objects in the Appadurai and Thomas accounts is always to live out the social life of men, or to become entangled in the webs of culture whose ability to refigure the object simultaneously inscribes culture's ability to translate things into signs and the object's powerlessness as an artifactual trace. Narratives of the social lives of things, they reaffirm the agency of those humans they pass between.

While the demolition of the essentialized object was an urgent necessity, the declaration of objects' and images' emptiness has become a proof for an anthropology committed to the victory of the cultural over the material, and of the discursive over the figural. Such strategies might be seen as an enduring manifestation of the "linguistic turn," the humanities-wide preoccupation with the arbitrary and conventionalized nature of social meaning. Part of the radicality of the linguistic turn consisted in its critique of neo-Romantic fictions of the autonomous object and of self-present meaning. However, it might be argued that in its material-cultural incarnation the stress on the cultural inscription of objects and images has erased any engagement with materiality or visuality except on linguistic terms.

A similar powerlessness of the image is apparent in much writing about art, and a consideration of this notion will permit me to introduce my chief concern in this piece: the need to abolish "contemporaneity" as a contextual alibi within historiography.

THE GINZBURG PROBLEM

The historian Carlo Ginzburg, in his attempt to understand the tradition of visual analysis associated with the Warburg Institute, identified one aspect of this problem in his observation that "the historian reads into [images] *what he has already learned by other means*" (1989: 35; emphasis added). For Ginzburg (following Gombrich [1963]) this was a reflection of a "physiognomic" circularity: just as physiognomists' readings of faces tell us only about the classificatory system that informs the readings (rather than about the relationship between the face and character), so we unwittingly claim to find evidence in the visual that in fact we have discovered elsewhere.

Ginzburg's point mirrors Strathern's: much as we might wish to foreground materiality, we will have recourse to explanations recuperated through other (linguistic) means; or, as Strathern puts it, "Making social (or cultural) context the frame of reference had one important result. It led to the position that one should really be studying the framework itself. . . . the artifacts were merely illustration" (1990: 38).

In an Indian context the phenomenon which is usually referred to as the "muscular Ram" provides a good illustration of this. The cultural commentator Anuradha Kapur (1993) has advanced a celebrated argument that the rise of a violent and masculinist Hindu chauvinism in the 1980s has been paralleled in popular picture production by the muscularization of the deity Ram. Earlier textual and visual representations of him as effete and androgynous have given way to images of him as a hypermasculinized apocalyptic figure who is frequently depicted towering over the projected Ramjan-mabhumi temple which its supporters hope will be built on the site of the Babri mosque in Ayodhya in north India, demolished by Hindu activists in December 1992.

Kapur localized the images as the organic reflection of chauvinist sentiment in Ayodhya. In her account she captions these images "poster from Ayodhya" as though they were symptoms whose malignancy and relevance lay exclusively in their geographic occurrence at the site of the destruction of the Babri mosque.

But there are many ways in which Kapur's argument might be qualified. For instance, the transformation is much less sharp than she suggests, for androgynous images of Ram are still popular and still produced in huge numbers. A more complex account might stress the pan-Indian linkages and commercial determinants that are also relevant to these images.

Though it is enormously stimulating and raises issues of great political importance, the critical focus on these images is nevertheless a victim of a textual historiography that establishes its evidence "by other means." Because it has decided in advance that these images are a visual manifestation of an ideological force, it is unable to catch hold of the ways in which the materiality of representation creates its own force field. Consequently, a very straightforward Durkheimianism emerges in which the image somehow draws together and exemplifies, as a social representation, everything which can be identified as potentially determining it, and which the historian wishes to have deposited in the image as the validation of his or her supposition.

The example of Kapur's reading of the Ram images reveals the inextricable linkage between culture and history, locality and time: to make an argument about images circulating in Ayodhya is intrinsically to invoke a specific time of circulation from which a putative historical trajectory is then extrapolated.

Imposing interpretations reached "by other means" has become second nature for a variety of cultural commentators because of the compelling consensus that specific times and specific objects can be conjoined (just as specific "cultures" and specific objects can be), and the one explained in terms of the other.

This mode of contextualizing objects first seems to have appeared in late-eighteenth-century Germany. We can glimpse something of its historical genealogy in Homi Bhabha's exploration and critique of Bakhtin's analysis of Goethe's *Italian Journey* (1786–1788), and in the emergence of what Bhabha terms "national time-space."

For Bakhtin, Goethe succeeded in creating a "national historical time" grounded in the specificity of an Italian place and time. Italianness is made to speak in the tolling of bells that mark the passage of time: "The bells ring, the rosary is said, the maid enters the room with a lighted lamp and says *Felicissima notte. . . . If one were to force a German clockhand on them, they would be at a loss*" (cited in Bhabha 1994: 143). In Bakhtin's account, historical time is spatialized: the microscopic examination of everyday Italy reveals its Italianness in its fullness and singularity, in a paradigm of "strong-culture" which has also had its adherents within anthropology and whose genealogy, via Johann Gottfried von Herder, places it close to Goethe.[2] However, Bhabha, by contrast, wishes to draw attention to the disjunctions and doubleness that this vision attempts to paper over. For Bhabha "the space of the modern nation-people is never simply horizontal" (1994: 141). Instead (in a remarkable echoing of Kracauer; see below) we must attend to its "ambivalent temporalities," its "disjunctive time," and a "ghostly repetition."

The fictive national time-space Bhabha critiques will already sound familiar to anthropologists as an echo of Herderian cultural particularity. Anthropology was born as, and in many respects remains, a Herderian critique of a universal (Kantian) philosophy (Zammito 2002). "What one nation holds indispensable to the circle of its thoughts has never entered into the mind of a second, and by a third has been deemed injurious," Herder wrote in *Reflections on the Philosophy of History of Mankind* (1784–91).[3] Endowing objects with social lives, or valorizing the peculiar intimacy between a historical moment and object, are simply extensions of that particularity to the material world.

But what happens if we abandon this assumption and start looking for what is rendered "deceptive" and "inexplicable" by the current dominant paradigm? What if, instead of assuming that objects and culture are sutured together in national time-space, we start looking for all those objects and images whose evidence appears to be "deceptive" and whose time does not appear to be "our" time?

DECEPTIVE EVIDENCE

The scholarship of the art historian Francis Haskell enables us to see that almost simultaneously alongside the rise of the Herderian and Hegelian suturing of objects with culture and history there arose a critique of this possibility.

Edgar Quinet, who was one of the first to link image and epoch (and who in 1824 had translated Herder into French), also drew attention to important disjunctions. He was struck by the incommensurability of the "sombre severity" of the political regime of Venice and the liberating imperatives of its art: "If you look only at the government you get the impression that the whole of Venetian society must have been administered by a ceaseless reign of terror.... If ... you examine its art, you assume that these [men's] ardent imaginations can only have flourished in a regime of excessive freedom" (cited in Haskell 1993: 364).

Quinet's assumption that objects may be "unrevealing" of their cultural context (Haskell 1993: 366), found a later echo in the journalist-turned-folklorist and art historian Champfleury's ridiculing of "second-hand Hegelian notions" that every time the artist took up his palette or his chisel he would exclaim that "the state of mind of my contemporaries will emerge from each stroke of my brush" (Haskell 1993: 377, citing Champfleury).

CATARACTS OF TIME

A similar skepticism was subject to a much more rigorous examination by Siegfried Kracauer in his final, posthumously published work, *History: The Last Things before the Last* (1969). In this book he mounts a fierce critique both of Hegelian historicism and of other varieties of more workaday historicity.

"We tacitly assume," Kracauer noted, "that our knowledge of the moment at which an event emerges from the flow of time will help us account for its occurrence." This, as I suggested above, is the ground of the Ginzburg problem. Substitute "image" for "event": we assume the image will somehow embody the moment; we form a judgment of the moment and then read into the image what we have already determined "by other means."

According to Kracauer, it is no coincidence that it is anthropologists and art historians who have been most acutely aware of the problems underlying such assumptions, and then he goes on to discuss the art historian Henri Focillon, Focillon's student George Kubler, and the anthropologist Claude Lévi-Strauss.

Kubler (1962) urged the engagement not with the March of (a single) Time, but with the shapes of many times, and concluded that "the date of a specific art object is less important for its interpretation than its 'age,'" meaning its position in the sequence to which it belongs, and that these sequences have time schedules all their own.

In a parallel manner, Lévi-Strauss explored in *The Savage Mind* the possibility of histories "of different magnitudes [each of which] organizes specific data into a sequence which sets a time of its own" and concludes that "the dates belonging to any one of these classes are irrational [to each other]" (1962: 345, cited by Kracauer 1969: 145).

Kracauer then relates an experiment conducted by Sigmund Diamond at Harvard. He required students to "investigate different areas of American history and periodize the courses of events." The students came from different backgrounds—political history, literature and so on—and when they compared their periodizations they discovered (of course) that they did not coincide.

All this is background to Kracauer's analysis of the "nonhomogeneity" and "uncontemporaneous" nature of time. Contemporaneity is the most powerful trope of the homogenous empty time (which the social sciences assume) and which can be sliced crossways in order to reveal the myriad and intimate relations between everything occurring at any one given moment. This is the fallacious idea that, as Kracauer puts it, events which take place at a particular moment "are supposed to occur then and there for reasons bound up somehow, with that moment" (1969: 141).

To make time "uncontemporaneous" is to insist on its multiplicity and difference, and on what Kracauer termed the "cataracts" of time. Time, he concluded, was not a single river or a mighty cascade. It is a series of cataracts, each pursuing their own uncontemporaneousness in incoherent trajectories.[4] As with the "over-stuffed interiors of the second half of the nineteenth century" and the "thoughts born in them" invoked at the start of this article, cultural phenomena may inhabit "the same epoch" and yet may not be each others' "contemporaries."

THE RECURSIVE ARCHIVE

What may seen puzzlingly abstracted questions assumed a highly empirical specificity during the course of a project that I recently completed (Pinney 2004). That study of printed Hindu images from the late nineteenth century to the present inquires what a "visual history" of India might be. It refuses to use images as illustrations of something already established elsewhere and asks whether it is possible to envisage history as in part determined by struggles occurring at the level of the visual. For my purposes here, the visual is metonymic of a much larger domain of materiality.

Rather than visual culture as a mirror of conclusions established by other means, I try to present the outpouring of numerous Indian-run chromo-lithographic presses as an experimental zone where new possibilities and new identities are forged. The visual is also shown to be a zone in which new narratives are established that may be quite disjunct from the familiar stories of a nonvisual history.

Alongside the attempt to confront Ginzburg's problem of a physiognomic circularity (in which the image simply becomes the validation of what has been determined by other means), my study also investigates the disjunctures between images and their historical location.

I was forced to confront this disjunction in the first place because of the recursive nature of image production. Within the commercial industry of popular picture production, artists maintain large personal archives of many thousands of images, stretching back to the late nineteenth century (indeed, these archives were one of the major resources in my historical study). When presented with a request for a certain type of image from a publisher, most artists will turn to the repertoire of image solutions that they have filed in their own archives. The image they then produce in response to the commission is likely to be a "pastiche" of previously existing images.

One consequence of this generalized and profound recursivity is an extreme difficulty in finely matching images with historical and cultural contexts. My study consequently entailed a criticism of those analysts who seek to read images in an overly "epidemiological" manner as specific symptoms of time-sensitive conditions.

As an alternative (and very much under the guidance of Strathern's writing), I attempted to delineate an approach that treats images as unpredictable "compressed performances" caught up in recursive trajectories of repetition and pastiche whose dense complexity makes them resistant to any particular moment. My intention is not to suggest that images are completely unrelated to everyday history: the study is replete with such historical connectivity. What I argue is that images are not simply, always, a reflection of something happening elsewhere. They are part of an aesthetic, figural domain that can constitute history, and they exist in a temporality that is not necessarily coterminous with more conventional political temporalities.

In this respect, Jean-François Lyotard's writing on "figure" is of great potential value to those working toward a theory of "material culture." For Lyotard, "figure" invokes a field of affective intensity. Escaping some of the demands of meaning as signification, "figure" stands in a relation of "radical exteriority to discourse" (Carroll 1987: 30). Contrasting "figure" with "discourse," which strives for "linguistic-philosophical closure" and is "limited to what can be *read*, identified, and given meaning within a closed linguistic system" (ibid.), Lyotard evokes through "figure" not a realm of decodable meanings, but a zone where "intensities are felt."

Indeed, "materiality" might be defined as that (figural) excess, or supplementarity, which can never be encompassed by linguistic-philosophical closure. Thomas Docherty perceptively describes our "consistent inability to accept the alterity of the world as alterity" and the desire "to see it (instead) as a comprehensible sign, a sign whose evidential value and truthful meaning is located less in the (self-evidential) object itself and more in the linguistic subject of consciousness" (1996: 157). Where there is what he terms the "premature translation of things into signs" and the triumph of semiology over corporeality, there is no space for materiality, no space for the disjunction between object and epoch that figural excess reveals.

Culture and contemporaneity entail the assumption that objects are empty. Empty objects will only acquire (linguistic) "meanings" (this paradigm assumes) as a consequence of movement through (or more precisely by habitation within, in a moment of stasis) culture or history—history, that is, as something perceived as being structured by the possibility of contem-

poraneity. This, I have suggested, is the current dominant mode of addressing objects from within anthropology and historiography; and it this which
I have attempted to criticize.

The object of the critique will, I hope, by now be clear enough. But what
of an alternative? Must we forever remain imprisoned in the dichotomous
tautologies of purification, or can we imagine alternative ways of encounter-
ing materiality?

In the context of the Hindu chromolithographs that I have described
above, Roland Barthes's concept of "wavy meaning" suggested an alternative
way of proceeding that engaged with the manner in which the materiality of
the archive and its images impresses itself upon the surrounding world.
While these images are in certain contexts amenable to recoding, they can
never be plucked from that pathway and sutured in any simplistic way with
the "sociological" or "political" reality of any particular historical moment.

In his brilliant and strangely ignored reading of Bataille's *The Story of the
Eye*, Barthes (1982) made the point that most histories of objects are not
histories of *the object* at all. He recalls narratives, supposedly of objects, with
titles like *Memoirs of an Armchair*, or *The History of My Pipe*, and argues that
these are in fact stories of objects passed from hand to hand. Likewise one
might say that a conventional historiography that determines the nature of
images "by other means" simply passes objects from historical moment to
historical moment, discovering that the object exemplifies its own particular
historical moment.

By contrast, *The Story of the Eye* is, Barthes argues, a true object tale. This
pornographic narrative was first published in 1928 and elaborates a fluid
transubstantiation between a common network of objects constellated by a
saucer of milk, a human eye, a skinned bull's testicle, and the moon. Barthes
terms this a "spherical metaphoricity": "The Eye's substitutes are declined in
every sense of the term: recited like flexional forms of one word; revealed like
states of the one identity; offered like propositions none of which can hold
more meaning that another; filled out like successive moments in the one
story" (1982: 120). This declensional, "wavy" form of story comprising a
series of avatars follows a pathway where "its essential form subsists through
the movement of a nomenclature" (ibid.: 121), a narrative which emerges as
a series of settings for the further unfolding of the complex identity of the
central object. In the case of *The Story of the Eye*, the story takes us to a park

at night merely in order that the moon can shine on a stain on Marcelle's sheet, Madrid is visited only so that a bullfight might occur and the eye might transmute into a bull's testicle, and so on.

The narrative itself is a mere mise-en-scène for the appearance of various avatars (or declensions) of the central eye/testicle/moon object. The "vibrations" of this object (though perhaps, following Michel Serres and Latour, we should say "quasi-object") create a new "wavy meaning," a new indeterminate object agency, as it passes "down the path of a particular imagination that distorts but never drops it": Its *sound* remains the same (1982: 119).

In my study of Hindu chromolithographs I conclude that the precondition for the complex task of escaping the tautology of making images pass "from hand to hand" ("by other means") is the recognition that the "complex identity" of the visual and material will always "exceed" the present in the ways that Kracauer, Lyotard, and Barthes start to delineate.

ONLY DISCONNECT

To address materiality, I have argued, is to confront a tradition of subordinating objects and images to culture *and* history. The intransigence of the object has been submerged in the analytic surety of the power of humankind—that is, those who make culture and history, or those other frames within which we chose to dissolve the problem of the object and annul its enfleshed alterity.

The necessity of deterritorializing culture is now widely understood (thanks largely to Gilles Deleuze and Appadurai), the benefits of (as Kracauer argued) making history "uncontemporaneous" is just at the point of beginning to be understood, but the task of making objects once again material still seems almost impossible. The problem we face is how to think outside of that "context" whose historical emergence has been briefly sketched above: how to think more like Mount Hageners, for whom an image "contains its own prior context" (Strathern 1988: 33).

If the understanding of images' "social life" stresses their malleability, their suppleness in the face of changing time and place, I would like to reintroduce the presence, "tension" (as a limit to tensility), or "torque" of the image and explore the ways in which its time is never necessarily that of the audience. "Do not knock," Adorno labels his discussion of what he calls the "implacable . . . demands of objects" in *Minima Moralia*. "What does it mean for the subject," he asks,

> that there are no more casement windows to open, but only sliding frames to shove, no gentle latches but turnable handles, no forecourt, no doorstep before the street, no wall around the garden? . . . The new human type cannot be properly understood without an awareness of what he is continuously exposed to from the world of things about him, even in his most secret innervations. (1978: 40)

Technology, Adorno argues, subjects men "to the implacable, as it were ahistorical demands of objects" (1978: 19).

The point here is not to engage in further "purification" and argue "for" the object. Clearly there is a dialectical process of (what heuristically we might term) subjects making objects making subjects. But to stress the smoothness of this dialectical process is to take us back to the "national (or cultural) time-space" of eighteenth-century Germany. I would rather stress instead the disjunctures and fractures in this process and the likelihood of uncontemporaneous practices in which (just as Kracauer argued there are "cataracts" of time) there are cataracts of objects never fully assimilable to any "context." Instead of a context that can be sliced sideways (either traversely under the rubric of "culture" or horizontally under the rubric of a contemporaneous "history"), it may be more appropriate to envisage images and objects as densely compressed performances unfolding in unpredictable ways and characterized by what (from the perspective of an aspirant context) look like disjunctions.

For this reason I find Adorno more useful than Bourdieu. Adorno can sound like Bourdieu at times, but his suggestion that technology subjects men to "the implacable, as it were (subjunctive) ahistorical demands of objects" is especially provocative. Adorno's space of the "ahistorical" should be understood not in a purificatory or Nietzschean sense as a space beyond time and contingency, for it is clear that he is not arguing for transcendental objecthood.[5] Rather, I interpret him as arguing for the demands—of what we might term materiality, or figural excess—demands which can never be subsumed to the conventional culture-object space of post-eighteenth-century historiography. Here I understand Adorno's argument as paralleling Kracauer's and as a claim for an engagement with the "discontinuous world of ruptures and rejections" (Koch 2000: 115) constituted by objects. One might also reach this point via phenomenology, with its stress on the alterity of an enfleshed world, or Lyotardian notions of "figure." All share the assumption that there is an alterity (or "torque") of materiality that can never be assimilated to a disembodied "linguistic-philosophical closure," "culture," or "history."

If we are, indeed, in search of a new wheel, we should understand that we also have much to lose through the seductive charms of circularity, and smoothness of rotation. A very different sort of device, capable of more complex analytic configurations, and characterized by jolts and disjunctions, may be what is required.

NOTES

1. For a critique of the way in which my own *Camera Indica* (Pinney 1997) repeats this problem, see Pinney in Buchli 2002.
2. And note Goethe's readiness to create a space of cultural expertise: "So far I have seen only two Italian cities and only spoken to a few persons, but already I know my Italians well" (Goethe 1970: 68).
3. See Bunzl 1996: 20: "Embodying a unique genius or *Geist*, each *Volk* formed an organic whole, the values, beliefs, traditions and language of which could only be understood from within by entering into the viewpoint of the member." However, for a critique of the notion of Herder as the founder of modern cultural anthropology, see Hann 2002.
4. See Koch 2000: 114–120 for a suggestive discussion.
5. See Beatrice Hanssen's discussion of Adorno's critique of the manner in which "historical contingence and transience" escaped Heidegger's grasp and the way in which the "insidious 'natural growth'" intrinsic to Hegel's conception of world history negated transience (1998: 14, 16).

REFERENCES

Adorno, Theodor W. 1978 /1951. *Minima Moralia: Reflections from Damaged Life*. Trans. E. F. N. Jephcott. London: Verso.
Appadurai, Arjun. 1986. *The Social Life of Things*. Cambridge: Cambridge University Press.
Barthes, Roland. 1982/1963. "The Metaphor of the Eye." Reprinted as an appendix to Georges Bataille, *Story of the Eye*. Harmondsworth, U.K.: Penguin.
Bhabha, Homi K. 1994. *The Location of Culture*. London: Routledge.
Buchli, Victor. 2002. *The Material Culture Reader*. Oxford: Berg.
Bunzl, Matti. 1996. "Franz Boas and the Humboltian Tradition." In George W. Stocking Jr., ed.,

Volksgeist as Method and Ethic: Essays on Boasian Ethnography and the German Anthropological Tradition (History of Anthropology 8). Madison: University of Wisconsin Press.

Carroll, David. 1987. *Paraesthetics: Foucault, Lyotard, Derrida*. London: Methuen.

Docherty, Thomas. 1996. *Alterities: Criticism, History, Representation*. Oxford: Clarendon.

Edwards, Elizabeth. 1998. "Review of *Camera Indica*." *Visual Anthropology Review* 14.2.

———. 2001. *Raw Histories: Photographs, Anthropology, and Museums*. Oxford: Berg.

Ginzburg, Carlo. 1989. "From Aby Warburg to E. H. Gombrich: A Problem of Method." In *Clues, Myths and the Historical Method*. Baltimore: Johns Hopkins University Press.

Goethe, J. W. 1970/1786–1788. *Italian Journey*. Trans. W. H. Auden and Elizabeth Mayer. Harmondsworth, U.K.: Penguin.

Gombrich, E. H. 1963. "The Social History of Art." In *Meditations on a Hobby Horse*. London: Phaidon.

Hann, Christopher M. 2002. "All *Kulturvolker* Now? Social Anthropological Reflections on the German-American Tradition." In Richard G. Fox and Barbara J. King, eds., *Anthropology beyond Culture*, 259–276. Oxford: Berg.

Hanssen, Beatrice. 1998. *Walter Benjamin's Other History: Of Stones, Animals, Human Beings, and Angels*. Berkeley: University of California Press.

Haskell, Francis. 1993. *History and Its Images: Art and the Interpretation of the Past*. New Haven, Conn.: Yale University Press.

Heidegger, Martin. 1977. "The Age of the World Picture." In *The Question Concerning Technology and Other Essays*. Trans. William Lovitt. New York: Harper and Row.

Kapur, Anuradha. 1993. "Deity to Crusader." In Gyandendra Pandey, ed., *Hindus and Others: The Question of Identity in India Today*. New Delhi: Viking.

Koch, Gertrud. 2000. *Siegfried Kracauer: An Introduction*. Trans. Jeremy Gaines. Princeton, N.J.: Princeton University Press.

Kracauer, Siegfried. 1969. *History: The Last Things before the Last*. New York: Oxford University Press.

Kubler, George. 1962. *The Shape of Time: Remarks on the History of Things*. New Haven, Conn.: Yale University Press.

Lamb, Jonathan. 2001. "Modern Metamorphoses and Disgraceful Tales." *Critical Inquiry* 28.1:133–167.

Latour, Bruno. 1993. *We Have Never Been Modern*. Trans. Catherine Porter. London: Prentice Hall.

———. 1999. *Pandora's Hope: Essays on the Reality of Science Studies*. Cambridge: Harvard University Press.

Lévi-Strauss, Claude. 1962. *La Pensée sauvage*. Paris: Plon.

Lyotard, Jean-François. 1971. *Discours, figure*. Paris: Klincksiek.

Pinney, Christopher. 1997. *Camera Indica: The Social Life of Indian Photographs*. Chicago: University of Chicago Press.

———. 2004. *"Photos of the Gods": The Printed Image and Political Struggle in India*. London: Reaktion.

Strathern, Marilyn. 1990. "Artefacts of History: Events and the Interpretation of Images." In Jukka Siikla, ed., *Culture and History in the Pacific*. Helsinki: Finnish Anthropological Society.

Thomas, Nicholas. 1991. *Entangled Objects: Exchange, Material Culture, and Colonialism in the Pacific*. Cambridge: Harvard University Press.

——. 1999. "The Case of the Misplaced Ponchos: Speculations Concerning the History of Cloth in Polynesia." *Journal of Material Culture* 4.1.

Zammito, John H. 2002. *Kant, Herder, and the Birth of Anthropology*. Chicago: University of Chicago Press.

CONTRIBUTORS

Matthew Engelke is a lecturer in the Department of Anthropology at the London School of Economics. His research interests include Christianity in Africa, the history of anthropology, and human rights. He is also the editor, with Marshall Sahlins, of the Prickly Paradigm Press.

Webb Keane is an associate professor in the Department of Anthropology, University of Michigan. His research has ranged from the island of Sumba (eastern Indonesia), to Dutch colonial missions, to urban nationalists and literary figures in early twentieth century and contemporary Indonesia. He is the author of *Signs of Recognition: Powers and Hazards of Representation in an Indonesian Society* (University of California Press, 1997) and articles on material culture, social and cultural theory, exchange and commodities, national language politics, and religion.

Susanne Küchler is a reader in material culture and anthropology at University College London. She has worked extensively on memory and art, with special reference to Oceania. She has recently directed an ESRC-funded research project titled "Clothing the Pacific" (R000 23 91 98) and is currently completing manuscripts on pattern in the Pacific as well as on mathematical quilts in Polynesia.

Bill Maurer is an associate professor of anthropology at the University of California, Irvine. He is the author of *Recharting the Caribbean: Land, Law and Citizenship in the British Virgin Islands* (University of Michigan Press, 1997) and *Mutual Life, Limited: Islamic Banking, Alternative Currencies, Lateral Reason* (Princeton University Press, 2005), as well as the editor of *Gender Matters: Re-Reading Michelle Z. Rosaldo* and *Globalization Under Construction: Governmentality, Law, and Identity*. His research concerns the anthropology of finance, law, and money.

Lynn Meskell is an associate professor in the Department of Cultural and Social Anthropology at Stanford University. She is founding editor of the *Journal of Social Archaeology*. Some of her recent books include *Private Life in New Kingdom Egypt* (Princeton University Press, 2002), *Embodied Lives: Figuring Ancient Mayan and Egyptian Experience* (with Rosemary Joyce; Routledge, 2003), *Object Worlds in Ancient Egypt: Material Biographies Past and Present* (Berg, 2004), and *The Companion to Social Archaeology* (edited with Bob Preucel; Blackwell, 2004).

Daniel Miller is a professor of material culture at the Department of Anthropology, University College London. Recent books include *The Sari* (with Mukulika Banerjee; Berg, 2003), *The Dialectics of Shopping* (University of Chicago Press, 2001), and an edited volume, *Home Possessions* (Berg, 2001). His current research includes projects on value and political economy, loss and separation in London, and poverty and communications in Jamaica.

Hirokazu Miyazaki is an assistant professor of anthropology at Cornell University. He has conducted fieldwork in Fiji and Japan and has written on the place of hope in knowledge formation. He is the author of *The Method of Hope: Anthropology, Philosophy, and Fijian Knowledge* (Stanford University Press, 2004) and is currently completing a book entitled *Economy of Hope: Anthropology, Finance, and Japan*.

Fred Myers is a professor and chair of anthropology at New York University. His interests in material culture, circulation, and value have grown from his engagement with Western Desert Aboriginal people in Australia and are developed in two recent books: an edited volume, *The Empire of Things:*

Regimes of Value and Material Culture (SAR Press, 2001), and a study of the development and circulation of Aboriginal acrylic painting, *Painting Culture: The Making of an Aboriginal High Art* (Duke University Press, 2002).

Christopher Pinney is a professor of anthropology and visual culture at University College London. His research has focused on industrial workers in India, South Asian visuality, and the representation of early cultural encounters. He has held visiting positions at the Australian National University, the University of Chicago, and the University of Cape Town. His publications include *Photos of the Gods: The Printed Image and Political Struggle in India* (Reaktion, 2004) and (coedited with Nicolas Peterson) *Photography's Other Histories* (Duke University Press, 2003).

Michael Rowlands is a professor in material culture at University College London. His current research includes a comparison of UNESCO and Islamic-inspired approaches to cultural restoration in Mali and a Getty-funded project on innovation and change in material culture in Cameroon since 1700 A.D. Recent publications include articles on cultural rights and cultural property (Verdery and Humphrey 2004), the unity of Africa (O'Connor and Reid 2003), and heritage and modernity in Djenne (Bedaux 2003).

Nigel Thrift is head of the Division of Life and Environmental Sciences at the University of Oxford. His main research interests are in nonrepresentational theory, international finance, information and communications technology, and the history of time. His recent publications include *Cities* (with Ash Amin; Polity, 2002) and *Knowing Capitalism* (Sage, 2004).

INDEX

Baxandall, M., 217

behavior: cognition and, 218–19; theory of things and, 4–7

Beidelman, Thomas O., 99

belief systems, materiality and, 2–4

Belting, H., 54

Benjamin, Walter, 109, 211, 234

Bergson, Henri, 239–40

Bhabha, Homi, 262

Bible: African Christian healing and, 118–19, 129; Masowe church's dismissal of, 122–24; as material book, 22

Bill, Max, 221–22

biography of things, 188

biological theory, software writing and, 244–46

Bloch, M., 217, 226n.7

body/spirit duality: divine statues of ancient Egypt and, 54–58; Egyptian pyramid culture and, 65–70; mummy culture in ancient Egypt and, 58–62; self-realization and materiality and, 78–80

Bohannan, Paul, 141

Book of the Dead, 60–62

Bourdieu, Pierre, 6–8, 38, 110, 113n.17; cultural theory and work of, 207, 269–70; iconicity of clothing and, 190; representation theory and, 198

Bowker, C. G., 241

Boyer, Dominic C., 176

Bradlow, Frank, 123

Brave New World, 35

Breggin, P., 248

Brenner, Suzanne, 195

Breward, C., 210

Brisson, David, 222

British and Foreign Bible Society, 123

Brown, B., 249

Bruegger, U., 235, 250n.6

Bruno, G., 237–38

Buchli, Victor, 21

Buddhas of Bamiyan, destruction of, 21

Buddhism: critique of materiality in, 1; immateriality in, 21–22, 120–21

Buenza, Daniel, 72

Bulun, Johnny Bulun, 112n.4

bundling of objects: iconicity of clothing and, 194–96; theory of signs and, 187–89

Butterworth, B., 219, 225

Callon, Michel, 165–69, 174–76, 249

Cameroon Grassfields: hierarchies of materiality in, 81–84; self-realization and materiality in, 76–80

Campbell, C., 46n.9

capitalism: commodity money theory and, 156–58, 162n.23; materiality and, 2–4; power and materiality in, 17–20

Capon, Edmund, 101

Caroline Islanders, knotted charts of, 224

Carrier, James, 165–66, 169, 176

Carroll, David, 266

Cassidy, J., 29

casuistry, Islamic banking and, 154–55, 161n.17

Cathcart, Michael, 113n.14

Catholicism: analogical moral reasoning in, 161n.17; hierarchies of materiality and, 82–84; immateriality in, 22; Masowe apostolic church and, 118–19, 131–36

causal relations: bundling of objects and, 188–89; in signs, 185–87

Charmed Technology, 215

Chavanduka, Gordon, 132

Christianity: ancestral spirits and, 198; hierarchies of materiality and, 81–84; iconicity of clothing and, 192–93; Masowe apostolic church and, 118–19, 131–36; materiality and, 28–29, 46n.9; monetary theory and, 145–49, 155–58, 162n.22

Chunuma, Jeff, 101–2

cinema, psychophysics and, 237–40

Clark, A., 240

Clifford, James, 89–90, 98–99

cloth and clothing: cognition theory and, 211–12, 227n.17; historical significance of, 191–93; iconicity of, 189–90; inhabiting of technology through, 212–17; materiality/immateriality pluralism and, 30–35, 193–96; social analysis of, 182–201; subject/object dualism in, 200–201

Clough, P. T., 241

code, in software, 241–46

cognition: animation and emergence of intelligent things and, 210–12; cloth and clothing and role of, 212–17; cognitive anthropology view of, 207–8, 226n.8; ethnomathematics and, 218–19; materiality and, 206–25, 231–49; phenomenology and, 231–33, 249n.2; psychophysics and, 238–40

Cohn, B., 81

Coleman, Elizabeth, 91, 106

Coleman, S., 24, 30, 123

Collins, C., 68

colonialism: end of primitivism and, 211; hierarchies of materiality in, 80–84; iconicity of clothing and, 189–96; materialist approach to, 84–86; self-realization and materiality and, 76–80

Comaroff, Jean, 124, 175, 190–91

Comaroff, John L., 175, 190–91

commodification of Aboriginal art, 88, 91–99, 103–5; scandals involving, 105

commodity materialism, 46n.9; monetary theory and, 156–58

computer modeling, of fourth dimension, 221–23

computer-supported cooperative work (CSCW) studies, 243–46

connectionism, software writing and role of, 245–46

consciousness: cognition theory and role of, 206; psychophysics and, 236–40, 250n.7; self-realization and materiality and, 76–80

consumerism: immateriality and, 20–29; materiality and power and, 15–20

consumption: agency and, 15; Egyptian pyramid culture as catalyst for, 67–70; semiotic ideology and, 191

context, tyranny of subject and, 36–41

contract law, 153–55. *See also* mortgage contract

copyright: identity negotiation and, 106–9; of indigenous art, 91–99, 112n.4, 112n.9; materiality and use, 88, 112n.1; regulation of, 110–11, 114n.24

Corbin, Henry, 147

Coronil, Fernando, 175

cosmology: Masowe spiritual healing and, 125–26; materiality and power and, 15–20; in South Asia, 1–4

cost-plus contract, Islamic model of, 150, 152, 160nn.9–11

Costume Society of America, 227n.15

Costume Society of Great Britain, 227n.15

Cox, John, 170

craft, art distinguished from, 217–19

Crary, J., 235, 237–38, 240

creativity: in cloth and clothing, 212–17; cultural aesthetics and, 97–99

Crump, T., 219

Crystal, D., 243

culture: animation and emergence of intelligent things and, 209–12; appropriation of, 109–10, 114n.23; cognition theory and, 206–8, 226n.1; deterritorializing of, 268–70; ethnomathematics and, 218–19; image and economies of exchange in, 88–111; immateriality in, 20–29; mummy culture in ancient Egypt and, 58–62; objectification and theory of things and, 8–10; property rights issues in, 90–111; purification and role of, 257–60; socialization and, 74–75; tyranny of subject in, 36–41. *See also* material culture; Western art-culture system; *specific cultures*

currency: Aboriginal images on, 112n.4; adequation and abstraction theories concerning, 155–58, 161nn.18–21; monetary theory and, 141–43; nonusurious supplements and, 144–49. *See also* monetary theory

cyborg, mummy as, 59

Dallah al-Baraka (Saudi financial company), 160n.11

Dalton, George, 168

Danandjaja, James, 195

Dasern, P. R., 219

Daston, L., 237

data glove, 213

Davidson, James, 15

death: in Egyptian mummy culture, 58–62; Egyptian pyramids and, 65–70

Debord, Guy, 68

decay, Egyptian mummy culture and ideology of, 60–62

deities: divine statues of ancient Egypt and, 54–58; immateriality and, 21; mummy culture and, 59–62

de la Roche, O., 218

Deleuze, Gilles, 234, 239–40, 268

De Montfort University, 215

De Rerum Natura, 250n.4

derivatives trading: finance theory in Japan and, 169–71, 177n.1; index arbitrage and, 171–72

Derrida, Jacques, 59, 64–65, 241–43

descriptive knowledge, mathematics and, 223–25

Diamond, Sigmund, 264

Dickens, D. R., 68

Dilley, M., 36

Dilley, Roy, 168

Dillon-Mallone, Clive, 125

Docherty, Thomas, 266

Dore, Ronald, 168

Dosse, F., 12

doubling: mummy culture and, 59–62; philosophy of material and, 53–54

Douglas, Mary, 36

"Dreaming, The" (Pintupi ritual), 95–97, 104–5, 113n.18

Durack, Elizabeth, 100–102, 106–8, 111

Durkheim, Émile, 12–13, 36–37, 46n.11, 197, 209, 257–58

Eagleton, Terry, 76

economic theory: anthropology and, 174–77; immateriality and, 25; materiality and, 165–77; pyramid culture and, 62–70; theology and, 1–4, 46n.2

education. entertainment as, 69–70; finance theory and role of, 169–71; objectification in, 9–10

Edwards, Elizabeth, 259

ego, hierarchies of materiality and, 80–81

Egypt: divine statues in ancient Egypt, 54–58; materiality in ancient culture of, 51–70; monumentality and, 15–16; mummy culture in, 58–62; pyramids and cultural materiality in, 62–70

Eisenberg, A., 214

electronic technology: in cloth and clothing, 212–17; memory and, 210, 226n.12; software, 240–46

Electro Textiles, 213

ElekTex, 213–14

Elementary Forms of Religious Life, 36, 46n.11

Elemente der Psychophysik, 236

Elements, 220

El-Gamal, Mahmoud, 150, 152–53

Elias, Norbert, 192

Elliott, C., 248

Elster, John, 72

embalming, mummies of ancient Egypt and practice of, 59–62

embodied mind: cognition theory and concept of, 206, 226nn.2–3; software writing and, 246–49

empty objects, recursive archive theory and, 266–67

Engelke, Matthew, 22, 25, 42

Engels, Friedrich, 72

Enlightenment: cultural theory of, 206, 226n.1; model of memory during, 210

entertainment, as education, 69–70

Epicurean philosophy, 232–33, 250n.4

ethics, humanism and, 37, 47n.13

ethnography: economic theory and, 165–77; indigenous culture and, 89–111; of materiality, 211–12; monetary theory and, 143; on Papua New Guinea, 105; power and materiality and, 18–20, 43–46; religious practices and, 119; on self-realization and materiality, 79–86. *See also* anthropology

ethnomathematics, emergence of, 218–19

Euclidean geometry, 220–21

Evans-Pritchard, E. E., 120–21

evolution, software writing and role of, 245–46

"exotic options" trading, 170–71

Explaining Culture, 207

extension, role of, in finance theory, 172–74

fabric. *See* cloth and clothing

faitich, Latour's concept of, divine statues of ancient Egypt and, 57–58

fashion, electronic technology in, 212–17

Fashion Theory, 227n.15

Faulkner, R. O., 60

Fechner, Gustav Theodor, 236

Feld, Steven, 107

festivals, divine statues of ancient Egypt and, 56–58

fetishism: divine statues of ancient Egypt and, 57–58; Marx's discussion of, 183–84; materiality/immateriality pluralism and, 30, 32; pyramid culture of Egypt and, 65–70

fiber-optic animated motion technology, 215

figure, Lyotard's discussion of, 266

finance theory: abstraction and substitution in, 140–59; anthropology of, 174–77; extension of, 172–74; Islamic institutions and, 147–49; learning and, 169–71; materiality and, 26–29, 165–77; objectification of, 169; performativity of, 167; role of justification in, 171–72. *See also* monetary theory

First Report on the EDVAC, 244

Focillon, Henri, 264

Fon (Cameronian chief), 17; hierarchies of materiality and, 81–84; self-realization and materiality and symbol of, 78–80

forgery, in Aboriginal art, 100–102

Forman, W., 57

Forshee, Jill, 197

Forty, A., 210

Foster, Robert, 30, 142

Foucault, Michel, 198; materiality and power and work of, 19–20; technologies of self and, 74–75, 78

Fourcade-Gournichas, Marion, 166

fourth dimension, visualization of, 221–23

Frame Analysis, 4

Fraser, M., 248

French, S., 240

Frodon, Jean-Michel, 21

funerary ideology: Egyptian mummy culture and, 60–62; Egyptian pyramid culture and, 65–70

futures contracts, 177n.1

Garcia, Marie-France, 166–67

Garsten, C., 25

Geertz, Clifford, 143

Gelfand, Michael, 133

Gell, Alfred, 11–15, 35–36, 40; animation and emergence of intelligent things and, 226n.11; on art and agency, 30, 109, 210; causal relations in signs and, 185–87; cognition theory and, 208, 215; divine statues of ancient Egypt and, 57–58; Egyptian mummy culture and, 61; morality of materiality and, 184; on personlike power of objects, 257; semiotic ideology and, 190–91 gender issues, in cloth and clothing, 212–17

genetic algorithms, 245–46

George, Kenneth, 99

Germany, colonization of Cameroon by, 76–77, 81–84

gharar, Islamic principle of, 152

ghost quality of software, 241–46

Ginzburg, Carlo, 223, 260–61, 263–65

Giza. *See* Great Pyramid of Khufu

global economy, South Asian politics and, 1–4

Goethe, J. W., 262–63, 270n.2

Goffman, Erving, 4, 38

Gombrich, E. H., 5, 219, 260

Gospel of God, 137n.2

Gothic: Art for England, 118–19, 123

Gottdiener, M. C., 68

Granovetter, Mark, 168

Great Pyramid of Khufu, 62–70

Greek culture, monetary theory and, 144–49, 155–58

Green, Maia, 127

Greenberg, Clement, 113n.17

Greer, Germaine, 113n.18

Grierson, Philip, 44

Guattari, Félix, 234

Guidance Residential, 151–52, 154

gun production, materiality of, 74–75

Habermas, Jürgen, 15, 232

"habitus" theory, cognitive anthropology and, 207–8

Hacking, Ian, 36

Hallpike, C. R., 219

Hanbal, Ibn, monetary theory of, 147–48, 151–53

Hanks, W. E., 190

Hansen, Karen Tranberg, 191

Hansen, N., 241–42, 244

Harris, Marvin, 207

Harry, Prince, 113n.12, 113n.20

Hart, Keith, 140

Harvey, David, 10

Haskell, Francis, 263

Hasselström, A., 25

Hayles, K., 240, 242

healing. *See* spiritual healing

Healy, D., 248

Hegel, G. F. W.: on history and culture, 263–65; Latour's comments on, 12; materiality and work of, 8–10, 40, 73–75; Peirce's discussion of, 186

Heidegger, Martin, 155–56, 158, 161n.21, 182, 187, 248, 258–59, 270n.5

Heimat concept, 35

Helmholtz, Hermann von, 236

Henry VIII, 118–19, 136n.1

Herder, Johann Gottfried von, 67, 262–63, 270n.3

hierarchies of materiality, 80–84; clothing and, 193–96

Hijira calendar, 144, 159n.1

Hinduism: critique of materiality in, 1; immateriality in, 21

hippie movement, 46n.9

history: culture and, 256–70; Ginzburg's theory of, 260–61; national time-space theory and, 262–63; of objects, 257–58; recursive archive concept and, 265–68; of theory, economic anthropology and, 176–77

History: The Last Things before the Last, 263–65

History of My Pipe, The, 267

Hitti, Philip, 146

hiyal (Islamic legal strategy), 152–54

Hoban, Caroline Holdstrom, 110–11

Hodgson, Marshall, 144–45

Holland, John, 245

Hollander, Anne, 211

Hollows, Michael, 104

Holmes, Douglas, 177

honey, Masowe rituals and use of, 120–22, 134–36

Hornung, E., 56

Hoskins, Janet, 196

Howsam, Leslie, 123

Hull, John, 167

human-computer interaction (HCI) studies, 243–46

human experience: agency and, 11–15; ancient Egyptian materiality and, 51–70; financial theory and, 28–29; indigenous art and, 95–99; materiality and, 3–4, 8–10, 19–20; software in context of, 241–49; things as source of, 256–70; tyranny of the subject and, 36–41

humanism: animation and emergence of intelligent things and, 209–12; materiality and, 33–35; tyranny of subject and, 37–41

"humility of things," materiality and, 5–7

Husserl, Edmund, 248

Hyperanaglyph, 222

hypergraphics, 222

hypersolids concept, 222

iconicity: of clothing, 189–90; indexicality and, 201; Munn's analysis of, 188–89; semiotic ideology and, 190–91; theory of things and, 217–19

Iconoclash theory, 21

identity: clothing and, 192–93; fraud involving Aboriginal art and, 102–5; negotiations concerning, 105–9

ideology: iconicity of clothing and, 193–96; materiality and, 88–89; monetary theory and, 144–49; of semiotics, 190–91, 203n.6; semiotics of materiality and, 182–83

ijara contract, Islamic monetary theory and, 150–52, 154

ijtihad (interpretation), Islamic banking theory and, 153–54

images: in Aboriginal art, 99, 142n.11; cognition theory and, 207, 226n.7; in Hindu culture, 265–68; in Indian culture, 260–61; memory models and, 210–11; time and context of, 263–65

imaginings framework, for Aboriginal art, 99

immateriality: Masowe apostolic church and, 121–26, 129–36; pluralism with materiality and, 29–35; pyramid culture and, 64–70; religion and, 46n.9; theory of, 20–29. *See also* materiality

inanimate, cognition and role of, 208

index arbitrage, 171–74. *See also* arbitrage

indexicality: iconicity and, 201; materiality and, 185–87; semiotic ideology and, 190–91

indigenous culture: commodification of, 88, 91–99; fraud and forgeries from, 90–111; identity negotiation in, 105–9

Indonesia: iconicity of clothing in, 189–90, 192–96; pebble rituals in cultures of, 137n.9; securitization of Islam in, 149; textuality of clothing in, 196–97; words and objectualization of things and, 197–200

Infineon Technologies, 214–15

Ingold, Tim, 35, 74

intellectual copyright, indigenous art and, 91–99

intelligent things: animation and emergence of, 209–12; cloth and clothing as, 212–17

International Fashion Machines, 215

International Robotics Jackets, 215

International Textile and Apparel Association, 227n.15

Invention of Culture, The, 158

Irvine, J. T., 183

Isaacs, Jennifer, 108

Ishii, Itaru, 175

Islamic Circle of North America, 160n.11

Islamic culture: commodity money theory and banking practices in, 157–58, 162n.24; iconicity of clothing and, 192, 195–96; immateriality and, 28–29, 46n.9; materiality in, 23–24; monetary theory and, 31, 144–49; securitization of banking instruments and religion in, 24–25, 149–55, 161n.16

Italian Journey, 262
I-wear, emergence of, 212

James, 251n.10
Janzen, John, 124
Japan, materiality of finance theory in, 165–77
Jeffreys, M. D., 82–83
Johan Masowe Church, 137n.2
John Maranke Church, 128
Johnson, C., 242
Johnson, J., 242
Johnson, Tim, 107
Johnson, Vivien, 108
Jordan, D., 207
journalism, agency and, 13
Joyce, R. A., 60
Judaism: immateriality and, 28–29, 46n.9; materiality in, 23
Jules-Rosette, Bennetta, 128
jurisprudence, Islamic banking theory and, 153–55
justification, finance theory and role of, 171–72

Kabyle house, Bourdieu's discussion of, 8
Kabyle slipper, 74
Kant, Immanuel: aesthetic indifference concept of, 68; cognition and philosophy of, 208; mathematics and philosophy of, 227n.19; specificity and philosophy of, 157–58; theory of things and, 7; truth defined by, 155, 161nn.18–19
Kapur, Anuradha, 260–61
Kariya, Takeaki, 175
Karnak temple, divine statues in, 56
Kay, C., 242
Keane, Webb, 13, 119; cultural theory and work of, 207; on fetishism, 30; Masowe rituals and work of, 129, 134; on materiality, 24–25, 31–35, 42; on semiotics, 40, 182–83; tyranny of subject and, 36–37

Keenan, James, 154
Keller, Edgar, 192
Keynes, John Maynard, 29
Khalidi, Tarif, 144
khalifa principle, monetary theory and, 145–49
khipu structures, as art, 218–19
kinship obligations, Aboriginal art and, 96–99
Klein, Naomi, 2
Klein bottle, 220
Knorr Cetina, K., 234–35, 250n.6
knowledge: cognition theory and, 211–12; descriptive knowledge, 223–25; monetary theory and role of, 155–58; self-realization and materiality and, 75–80, 86
Knowledge and Human Interests, 15
Konno, Hiroshi, 175
Kopytoff, Igor, 7, 188
Kracauer, S., 235, 256, 262–65
Kraeplin, Emil, 236
Kristeva, J., 61
Kubler, George, 264
Küchler, Susanne, 31, 33–36, 42
Kuper, Adam, 36–37
Kwint, M., 210

Lacan, Jacques, 80
Laclau, Ernesto, 196
Lacovara, P., 66
Lan, David, 132–33
Lancy, D. F., 218
land rights, cultural property and, 93–94
language: architecture and, 198–200; causal relations in signs and, 185–87; iconicity and, 217–19; objectualization of things and, 197–200, 259–60; textuality of clothing and, 196–97
Lapidus, Ira, 144
late purification theory, objects and materiality in, 258–60

Latour, Bruno, 11–15, 30, 38, 40; cognition theory and, 208; divine statues of ancient Egypt and, 57; finance theory and work of, 167–68; hybrid objects concept of, 189; Iconoclash theory of, 21; on materialization, 73–75; on Pasteur, 85; purification discussed by, 257–60; on science, 210; software and work of, 243–46; subject-object purification concept of, 89, 110, 112n.2

Lave, J., 218

Law, John, 167–68

Layard, J., 217

learning, finance theory and, 169–71. *See also* education

Lee, Benjamin, 140, 175

Lehner, M., 62, 64

Leland, Hayne E., 170

Lemonnier, Pierre, 74

Leroi-Gourhan, André, 74

Lévi-Strauss, Claude, 6–7, 43, 211, 217, 221, 264

LiPuma, Edward, 140, 175

Lohr, J., 243

Lomnitz, Claudio, 107

Loos, Adolf, 184, 191

Lucas, Gavin, 21

Lucretius, 232, 250n.4

Lukács, Georg, 157, 162n.23, 182, 202n.4

Luminex clothing, 215

Lupton, E., 250n.5

Luxor Casino and Hotel (Las Vegas), Egyptian pyramid culture and, 67–70

Lyotard, Jean-François, 40–41, 266–68

machines: human life in context of, 231–33, 249n.3; psychophysics theory and, 238–40; software writing and, 241–46

MacKenzie, Donald, 26–27, 167–69, 172–74, 176

malaggan material, 227n.14

Malaysia: iconicity of clothing in, 192; securitization of Islam in, 149

Mankiewicz, R., 220

Mann, 217

Mann, Thomas, 58

Manning, 89

Marcus, George, 110, 177

Marika, Wandjuk, 88, 91–99, 105, 108–9

market forces, economic theory and, 166–67, 175–77

Market Wizards, 170

marriage: hierarchies of materialism and, 82–84; self-realization and materiality in, 77–80

Marshall Islanders, stick charts of, 223–25

Martin, Luther, 78

Marx, Karl: alienated and nonalienated labor discussed by, 187; on capitalism and exploitation, 85–86; doctoral thesis of, 250n.4; fetishism discussed by, 183–84; hierarchies of materiality and work of, 80–84; on materialism, 72–75; self-realization and materiality in work of, 75–76, 78

Marxism: commodity money theory and, 156–58; materiality and work of, 17–20; objectification theory and, 10; philosophy of finance and, 29; praxis and, 2–4; theory of things and, 6–7

Masedza, Shoniwa. *See* Masowe, Johane

Masowe, Johane, 122–26, 134–36, 137n.6

Masowe weChishanu Church, 22, 119–20; evolution of, 122–26, 136n.2; honey rituals of, 120–22, 134–36; immateriality in, 129–36; pebble and prayer rituals in, 129–31, 137nn.8–9; spiritual healing practices of, 126–29; view of materiality in, 121–22; water in rituals of, 133–36; white robes of, 126–27

material culture: apostolic view of, 121–22; architecture and, 198–200; causal relations in signs and, 185–87; characteristics of, 5–7; clothing and, 193–96; philosophy of, 53–54; religion and, 119; social analysis, 182–201 materialism: materiality and, 72–86; psycho-physics and, 237–40, 251n.9, 251n.11; of software, 240–46, 251n.11

materiality: in Aboriginal indigenous culture, 91–99; in African Christian healing, 118–36; agency and, 11–15; animation and emergence of intelligent things and, 209–12; of artifacts, 109–11; cognition and, 206–25, 231–49; colonialism and, 84–86; defined, 4; Egyptian pyramid culture and, 52–70; figural theory and, 266–67; of finance theory, 26–29, 165–77; hierarchies of, 80–84; inside/outside concepts and, 231–33; materialism and, 72–86; mathematics and, 219–23; money and, 140–59; morality and, 183–85; objectification and, 7–10, 257–60; pluralism with immateriality and, 29–35; poetic dimension of, 251n.12; power and, 15–20; religion and, 1–4; semiotics of, 30–32, 40, 42–43, 182–83; software writing and, 241–49; theory of things and, 4–7; tyranny of subject and, 36–41. *See also* immateriality

mathematics: art and, 33–35; properties of, 219–25

Mathematics Elsewhere, 224–25

mattang charts, 223–24

Maurer, Bill, 23–31, 42–43, 119, 177, 197

"mausoleum culture," Egyptian pyramids and, 66

Mauss, Marcel, 13, 34, 39, 47n.14, 74; iconicity of clothing and work of, 192; "total social fact" concept of, 97

Maxwell, David, 127, 132

maya (Hindu concept of), materiality and, 1

Mayan pyramids, Luxor Hotel reproductions of, 68

McCarthy, Anna, 234

McCulloch, M., 243

McCulloch, S., 100–102

McCulloch-Uehlin, S., 104

McDannell, Colleen, 118, 119, 123, 127

McDonald, John, 100

Mead, George Herbert, 193–94

Méadel, C., 249

meddo charts, 223

medical science, spiritual healing in relation to, 126–29

medicine, electronic clothing applications in, 215

mediums, Masowe use of, 133–36. *See also* witchcraft, Masowe belief in

Melanesia: materiality/immateriality pluralism in, 29–30; monetary theory and, 141–43

Memoirs of an Armchair, 267

memory: animation and emergence of intelligent things and, 210–12; Egyptian pyramid culture and, 65–70; materialization of, in Egyptian divine statues, 56–58

Memphite theology, divine images in, 55–58

Merlan, Francesca, 110

Merleau-Ponty, Maurice, 6, 234, 248, 249n.1

Mertzl, J. M., 248

Meskell, Lynn, 15–17, 22–23, 24, 41–42, 119

metaphor, social context for, 217

Meyer, Birgit, 124, 127

micro-encapsulation technology, in clothing, 215

Mikami, Yoshihiro, 175

Miller, Daniel, 20, 26, 29, 32, 39, 46n.10, 110, 119, 160n.5, 165–66, 168–69, 175–76, 192, 194

Millo, Y., 27, 167

Milpurrurru, George, 112n.4

Milpurrurru v. Indofurn Pty. Ltd., 112n.4

mimesis, mummy culture and, 59–62

Mimica, J., 219

Minima Moralia, 269

missionaries, hierarchies of materiality and work of, 82–84

Mitchell, M., 245–46

MIT Media Lab, 215

Miyazaki, Hirokazu, 25–29, 42–43

mnemic image, 210–11; art *vs.* utilitarianism in, 218–19

Mnemosyne Atlas, 210

Moctezume, E. M., 33

modernism: Aboriginal art and, 107–9, 113n.17; mathematics and, 221–23; pyramids in comparison to, 62–70

Mol, Annemarie, 168

monetary theory: anthropological research and, 158–59; Kant's philosophy and, 155, 161nn.18–19; materiality and, 23–26, 30–31, 140–59; nonusorious supplements, 144–49; semiotic ideology and, 199–200, 202n.8. *See also* currency; finance theory

monumentality of ancient Egypt: materiality and power and, 15–20; pyramid culture and, 64–70

Moore, R. D., 232

morality: iconicity of clothing and, 191–93; materiality and, 183–85

Morenz, S., 55

Morphy, Howard, 93, 142n.11

mortgage contracts, Islamic financial theory and, 150–55, 160nn.9–11

mortuary practices, Egyptian pyramid culture and, 66–70

Mouffe, Chantal, 196

mp3 players, in clothing, 214–15

Mtanti, John, 137n.9

Mukonyora, Isabel, 126

mummies: cultural materiality concerning, 58–62; Egyptian materiality concerning, 51–70; Egyptian pyramid culture and, 66–70; philosophy of material and, 53–54

Mundine, Djon, 100–102

Munn, Nancy, 27, 187–89, 202n.5

Münsterberg, Hugo, 236–38, 250n.8

Munungmurra, Yangarininy, 112n.4

murabaha (Islamic cost-plus contracts), 150, 152, 154

Murphy, John, 170

Murtaugh, M., 218

"muscular Ram" phenomenon (India), 260–61

Museum of Modern Art, 213

Musonza, Pauros Mugwagwa, 137n.6

Mu'tazilite doctrine, monetary theory and, 146–48, 151–52, 154

mutuero (Masowe ritual), 129–31

Myers, Fred, 18–20, 25, 42, 197

Nardi, B. A., 245

National Aboriginal Art Prize, 102

national time-space, object contextualization in, 262–63

naturalism, machinery and materiality *vs.,* 232–33, 250n.4

natural society concept, Islamic banking practices and, 157–58

Neftci, Salih N., 167

neoclassical economics, anthropology and sociology and, 168

neural networks, 245–46

neurological consciousness: cognition theory and, 206–8, 226n.3; numerosity and, 225

New Kingdom (Egypt, 1539–1070 B.C.), tombs of, 53–55

New York Times, 214

Nicklin, Lenore, 100–101

Nietzsche, Friedrich, 155, 269

No Logo, 2

numerosity, mathematics and, 225

objectification: in African Christian healing, 118–36; agency and, 13–15; ancient Egyptian materiality and, 51–70; cultural property rights and, 88–111; divine statues of ancient Egypt and, 54–58; Egyptian pyramid culture and, 65–70; finance theory and, 169, 174–77; immateriality and, 21; indigenous art and, 95–99; materiality and, 7–10; tyranny of subject and, 37–41 objects, theory of: animation and emergence of intelligent things and, 209–12; artifacts and, 5–7; bundling and openness in, 187–89; causal relations in signs and, 185–87; commodification of Aboriginal art and, 95–99, 109–10, 112n.7; iconicity and, 217–19; national time-space and, 262–63; subject possibilities and, 200–201; words and objectualization of things and, 197–200. *See also* subject/object dualism

obviation, Islamic banking institutions and, 153

O'Connor, Kaori, 20–21

O'Day, V. L., 245

Office of the Comptroller of the Currency, 160n.11

O'Hanlon, M., 32

Olguin, F. S., 33

Ollman, Bertrell, 187

O'Neil, Robert, 83

On Growth and Form, 221

options, derivatives and, 177n.1

Options Markets, 170

Order of Things, The, 19

"Original Affluent Society, The," 19–20

originary crafting, ancient Egyptian materiality and, 51–70

Outline of a Theory of Practice, 6

ownership, identity negotiation and, 105–9

painting: of Aboriginal indigenous peoples, 89, 95–99, 107–9; materiality of, 90–91

pairing, philosophy of material and, 53–54

Papunya culture, 89–93

Papunya Tula Artists, 93, 113n.14

Parker, R., 212

Pasteur, Louis, 73–74, 85

pebble ritual, Masowe use of, 129–31, 137nn.8–9

Peirce, Charles Sanders, 31, 185–87, 190, 201nn.1–3

Pentecostalism: Masowe weChishanu Church and, 129–36; materiality/immateriality pluralism and, 30

perception, psychophysics and, 236–40, 250n.7

perception and aperception, 250n.6

"performativity of finance theory," concept of, 167, 172

personification, agency and, 14

Peter Stripes Fabrics, 112n.4

Petyarre, Kathleen, 102

phenomenology: cognitive science and, 231–33, 249n.2; materialization of materiality and, 74–75

Phenomenology of Spirit, 8

"phi effect," 236, 250n.7

Phillips, John, 118–19

philosophy: anthropology and, 15, 46n.6; of material, 53–54

Philosophy of Money, 27

Philosophy of Right, The, 9

physiogonomic circularity, 260–61, 265

Piaget, Jean, 219

Pickering, Andrew, 168

Pinney, Christopher, 40–41, 189

Pintupi culture: art created in, 99, 142n.11; art forgeries in, 102–5; ethnographic research on, 112n.3; *yurti* concept of, 95–99, 112n.8

Piranesi, Giambattista, 67

Plato, monetary theory and philosophy of, 156, 158, 161n.20

poetry, in materiality, 251n.12

Polanyi, Karl, 166, 168

politics, global economy in South Asia and, 1–4

Postone, Moishe, 156–57, 162n.23

postsocial theory, materiality and, 234–35

poverty, materiality and, 2–4

power: ancient Egyptian materiality and, 51–70; in Egyptian pyramid culture, 68–70; materiality and, 15–20; self-realization and materiality and, 75–80

practice, agency and, 11–15

praxis: Marxism and, 2–4; self-realization and materiality in work of, 75–76, 78–80

prayers, Masowe rituals for, 129–31

Price, Sally, 89

price adjustments, role of arbitrage in, 172

Pricing the Priceless Child, 46n.9

primitivism: colonialism and end of, 211; ethnographic debates concerning, 89

production, social analysis of materiality and, 186–87

projectionist fallacy, culture and, 209

property rights: commodification of Aboriginal art and, 95–99, 101–2, 112n.9; culture and, 88–111; power and materiality and, 17–20

Protestantism: African Christian healing and, 118–36; immateriality in, 22; Masowe weChishanu Church and, 123–24; materialism and, 200; money in, 24; morality of materiality and, 184–85; Reformation and, 28

Protevi, J., 231

Pryke, M., 27

psychoanalysis: cognition theory and, 211–12; materiality/immateriality pluralism and, 29–30

psychophysics, theories of, 235–40, 250n.7, 251n.9

Ptah (Egyptian creator god), 55

purification (subject/object): Aboriginal art and, 110–11; agency theory and, 11–15; cultural property and, 89; culture and, 257–60; late purification, 258–60; materiality and, 40–41

Puritan ethos, 46n.9

pyramids, Egyptian materiality and, 51–70

Quaestiones Disputatae de Veritate, 161n.18

"qualisigns," Munn's concept of, 187, 202n.5

Quilter, J., 218

Quinet, Edgar, 263

Quinn, Bradley, 212–14

Quirke, S., 57

Qur'an: Islamic banking institutions and, 152–55; monetary theory and role of, 144–49, 159n.2; *riba* prohibition in, 149–50, 160n.8

Rabehoraisoa, V., 249

race, Aboriginal art and issues of, 111

Ranger, Terence, 132–33, 137n.9

recontextualization of indigenous culture, 92, 99

recursive archive, theory of, 265–68

Reflections on the Philosophy of History of Mankind, 262–63

Reformation: African Christian healing and, 118–36; violence during, 28

regime of value, Aboriginal culture and, 90, 97–99, 105

religion: apostolic view of, 121–22; divine statues of ancient Egypt and, 54–58; global principles of, 1–4; immateriality in, 22–23; Islamic banking instruments and, 152–55, 161n.16; material culture and, 119; materiality of, 22, 121–31; monetary theory and, 147–49; philosophy of material and, 53–54. See also *specific religions*

representation theory: architecture and, 198–200; divine statues of ancient Egypt and, 57–58; immateriality and, 28–29, 46n.9; indigenous art and, 90–91; materiality/immateriality pluralism and, 29–35; money and failure of, 141–43; philosophy of material and, 53–54; screenness and, 233–40, 250n.6; software in context of, 241–42

Reynolds, Pamela, 132–33

riba prohibition, Islamic monetary theory and, 149, 152–55, 160n.8

Rieman surface, 220

Riles, Annelise, 20, 169, 176–77

rituals: Aboriginal cultural property and, 93–

99; architecture and, 198–200; divine statues of ancient Egypt and, 55–58; in Egyptian mummy culture, 58–62; pebble and prayer rituals in Masowe Church, 129–31; Pintupi *tjukurrpa,* 95; spiritual healing in Masowe Apostolic Church, 126–29

Robbins, Joel, 124–25

robotics, cloth and clothing production and, 212–17

Rogan, M. (Father), 82

Rohlen, Thomas, 169

Rose, N., 20, 248

Rowlands, Michael, 9, 16–17, 19–20, 24, 42

R&T Textiles Pty. Ltd., 112n.4

Rubin, William, 89

Rubinstein, Mark, 170

Sahlins, Marshall, 19–20, 22, 168

Saleh, Nabil A., 150, 152

Santos, B., 249

Sartre, Jean-Paul, 10, 12

Saussure, Ferdinand de, 147, 183, 185

Savage Mind, The, 264

Sax, Joseph, 112n.9

Schluchter, W., 236

Schoffeleers, Matthew van, 124

Schull, N. D., 68

Schulte Nordholt, Henk, 192–93

Schutz, 235

Schwager, Jack, 170

science: agency theory and, 11–15; human life in context of, 231–33; materialization of materiality in, 73–75; mathematics and, 221–23

screenness: psychophysics and theories of, 236–40; role of, in Western culture, 233–40; of software, 240–46

sculpture, divine statues of ancient Egypt as, 54–58

Second Council of Constantinople, Anathemas of, 146

second nature, mummy culture as creation of, 59–62

securitization: extension of finance theory in, 173–74; financial theory and, 27–29; in Islam, 24–25, 149–55

Sedgwick, E. K., 244

Sekai securities firm, 169–77

self-realization: finance theory and, 174; forgery as tool for, 101–2; hierarchies of materiality and, 80–84; iconicity of clothing and, 195–96; materialism and, 72–73; materiality and, 75–80

Sellars, W., 232

"Selling off the Dreaming," 113n.18

semiology, Saussure's concept of, 185–86

semiotics: architecture and, 197–200; causal relations in signs and, 185–87; of clothing, 193–96; ideology of, 190–91, 203n.6; materiality and, 30–32, 40, 42–43, 182–83; textuality of clothing and, 196–97; words and objectualization of things and, 197–200

Sense of Order, The, 5

"sensory presence," indigenous culture and, 95

sexuality, self-realization and materiality in Africa and, 79–80

shari'a scholarship, monetary theory and, 152–55

Shell, Marc, 140–41, 144–45, 147, 155–58, 161n.18, 162n.22

Shipwrecked Sailor, The, 56

signs: causal relations in, 185–87; semiotics of materiality and, 182–83; subject/object dualism and, 183–85, 200–201

Silverstein, Michael, 196, 199–200

Simmel, Georg, 4, 10, 27, 52, 62, 65, 195–96

situated experience: ancient Egyptian materiality and, 51–70; mathematics and, 223–25

Smith, Adam, 157, 162n.24

Sobchack, V., 249n.2

social anthropology: Aboriginal indigenous culture and, 95–99; ancient Egyptian materiality and, 52–70; architecture and, 198–200; finance theory and, 175–77; Latour's critique of, 12; of material culture, 182–201; monetary theory and, 140–43; object theory and, 257–60; software writing and, 246–49. *See also* anthropology

Social Construction of What?, The, 37

Social Life of Things, The, 7

social relations: clothing and hierarchies in, 193–96; cultural products of, 74–75; economic theory and, 168; hierarchies of value and, 109–10; Masowe spiritual healing and, 124–26; materiality and, 3–4; social fields model, identity negotiation and, 106–9; tyranny of subject in, 36–41, 46n.12

Socrates, 161n.20

software, materiality of, 240–46

Sohn-Rethel, Alfred, 156–57

South Asia, history of materiality in, 1–4

"space of calculability" concept, economics and, 166–67

spatial relations: mathematics and, 223–25; software and, 240–46

spectacle, Egyptian pyramid culture and concept of, 68

spells, mummy culture and casting of, 60–62

Sperber, Daniel, 207, 217

spiritual healing, Masowe practice of, 124–29; social structure and, 132–36; water rituals and, 133–36

Spyer, Patricia, 191

Stafford, Barbara Maria, 208, 210, 215, 217, 221, 226n.1

Stallybrass, Peter, 183

Standard Federal Bank, 151

Star, S. L., 241

Stark, David, 172

Starlab, 215

statues: divine statues of ancient Egypt, 54–58; Egyptian materiality concerning, 51–70

Story of the Eye, 267–68

storytelling, print and photography and demise of, 211

Straightening Spears (painting), 96

Strathern, Marilyn, 29, 32, 36, 38, 88; agency theory and, 13–14; on demise of objects, 258; iconicity of clothing and work of, 193; on identity negotiation, 105; on materiality, 260; monetary theory and, 142–43; recursive archive theory and, 266–68; on software, 241

Strohecker, C., 224

structuralism: agency and, 11–15; materiality and, 6–7; mathematics and, 221–23

style, iconicity of clothing and, 195–96

subjectivity: finance theory and, 174, 177n.2; hierarchies of materiality and, 80–81

subject/object dualism: African Christian healing and, 118–36; agency and, 14–15; ancient Egyptian materiality and, 51–70; cultural property rights and, 88–111; materiality and, 3–4, 43–46; materialization of materiality and, 73–86; social analysis of materiality and, 183–85; tyranny of subject, 36–41

substitution, monetary theory and, 141–43

Sumbanese culture. *See* Indonesia

Summa Theologica, 161nn.18–19

Sundkler, Bengt, 137n.9

Sunni Islam, Islamic banking theory and, 153–54

superficiality, materiality and, 32–33

surface aesthetics: electronic textiles and, 216–17; topology and, 220–23, 225

Swartz, M., 207

symbolism: causal relations in signs and, 186–87, 201n.3, 202n.7; monetary theory and, 144–49

symmetry, iconicity and, 217–19

Tada conglomerate, 172–76

Tambiah, Stanley, 22, 119–21

taqlid, Islamic banking theory and, 153

Tarde, Gabriel, 235

Taussig, M., 59

tawhid, Islamic principle of, 158–59

Taylor, Christopher, 133

Taylor, Jean Gelman, 192

Taylor, M. C., 59, 64, 68–69

Taylorism, finance theory and, 176

Taymiyya, Ibn, 147

Technical Analysis of Futures Markets, 170

technology: animation and emergence of intelligent things and, 209–12; cloth and clothing and inhabiting of, 212–17; cognition and, 208; immateriality and, 25, 35; materialization of materiality and, 74–75; semiotic ideology and, 199–200; software writing and, 247–49

Textile: The Journal of Cloth and Culture, 227n.15

Textile History, 227n.15

textiles. *See* cloth and clothing

Textile Society of America, 227n.15

textual authority: in clothing, 196–97; Masowe church's dismissal of, 122–23; of software, 243–46

Thailand, Buddhism in, 22

theology, critique of materiality and, 1–4

theory, material effects of, 25–26

"Theses on Feuerbach," 72

things, theory of: animation and emergence of intelligent things, 209–12; basic principles of, 4–7; causal relations in signs and, 185–87; cognition and, 217–19; culture and role of, 207–8; historicity of, 191–93; human experience in context of, 256–70; materiality and, 3–4; objectification and, 7–10; philosophy of material and, 53–54; self-realization and materiality and, 75–80; semiotics of materiality and, 182–83; words and objectualization of, 197–200

Thomas, Nicholas, 92, 168, 193, 259

Thomas Aquinas (St.), 161nn.18–19

Thompson, D'Arcy Wentworth, 221

Thoreau, Henry David, 183–84, 191

Thrift, Nigel, 34–36, 38, 42, 178

Tilley, C., 217

Timberland Company, 214

time, history and, 263–65

Time and Free Will, 239–40

Tiv society, abstract value in, 141

Tolson, Turkey, 96, 102–5, 108–9

tombs: Egyptian pyramid culture and, 65–70; philosophy of material in ancient Egypt and, 53–54

topology, material culture and study of, 220–23, 225

"total social fact" concept, Aboriginal culture and, 97

Trinidad, materiality in, 32, 39, 44

Trouillot, M.-R., 66–67

truth, monetary theory and role of, 155–58, 161nn.18–21

Tschumi, Bernard, 68–69

T-shirts, indigenous art used on, 91–99

Turner, Victor, 106, 109–10, 124

Tutankhamun, tomb of, 69

Tylor, Edward, 207

"tyranny of the subject," materiality and, 3–4

Ulmer, G., 242

unconscious, software and role of, 241–46

Ungeistige theory, cognition and, 208

United Bank of Kuwait (UBK), 160n.11

United Mortgage of America, 151

Urban, Greg, 196

Urton, G., 218

U.S. Federal Home Loan Mortgage Corporation (Freddie Mac), 150–51, 160n.13, 161n.14

utilitarianism, art and, 217–19

utopianism, materiality and, 26–29

value, theory of: Aboriginal art and, 90, 97–99, 105; identity negotiation and, 106–9; monetary theory and, 141–43, 155–58, 161n.18; morality of materiality and, 184–85; role of objects in, 187–89; in social dramas, 109–10

van Dijk, Kees, 195

Varela, Francisco, 249n.2

Veblen, Thorstein, 191

Venn Diagram, 221

Verran, H., 232

Vidler, A., 241

Virilio, P., 247

virtualism: finance theory and, 165; immateriality and, 29, 46n.10

von Neumann, John, 244

Wagner, Roy, 153, 158–59

Warburg, Aby, 210

Warburg Institute, 260

Warhol, Andy, 59

Warnier, Jean-Pierre, 74, 76, 78, 226n.7

Wassmann, J., 219

water, Masowe rituals and, 133–36

Watt, W. Montgomery, 145

Weber, John, 113n.15, 113n.18

Weber, Max, 110, 113n.17, 183

Webster, A., 248

Wells, Edgar, 93

Werbner, Richard, 126

West, G., 129

Western art-culture system: Aboriginal art in

context of, 90, 97–99, 112n.10; forgeries of Aboriginal art and, 101–2, 113nn.13–14; modern art aesthetics and, 113n.17; screenness in, 233–40; software in, 240–46

Western Desert painting movement, 90

Whitlam, Gough, 95

Williams, Raymond, 10–11

Willis, Anne-Marie, 113n.18

Wilson, D., 217

witchcraft, Masowe belief in, 124–26, 132–36, 137n.6

Wordsworth, William, 233

"Work of Art in the Age of Mechanical Reproduction, The," 109

Wulff, F., 25

Wundt, Wilhelm, 236, 250n.6

Yarnangu people, 95

Yolngu culture: commodification of, 88, 91–99; forgeries of, 100–102

Yoshimoto, Yoshio, 175

Yotsuzuka, Toshiki, 175

Young, J. E., 210

Zaloom, Caitlin, 25, 34–35

Zammito, John H., 262

Zandee, J., 60–62

Zaslavsky, C., 219

Zelizer, Vivianna, 46n.9, 141

Žižek, Slavoj, 75, 143

Zolotow, Charlotte, 187

Library of Congress Cataloging-in-Publication Data
Materiality / edited by Daniel Miller.
p. cm.
Includes bibliographical references and index.
ISBN 0-8223-3530-1 (cloth : alk. paper)
ISBN 0-8223-3542-5 (pbk. : alk. paper)
1. Material culture. 2. Materialism. I. Miller, Daniel, 1954–
GN406.M38 2005
306.4′6—dc22   2005005701